Ho Math Chess 何数棋谜 益智健脑非药物良方
Frankho Puzzle for KIDS – Brain Fitness Workbook
© 2007 – 2016 Frank Ho, Amanda Ho all rights reserved www.mathandchess.com

Mailing address:

Ho Math Chess Learning Centre
2586 Waterloo Street
Vancouver, BC
V6R 3H5
Canada

Telephone 604－263－4321
mathandchess@telus.net
www.mathandchess.com

Copyright © 2016 by Frank Ho, Amanda Ho

All rights reserved. No part of this book may be reproduced in any form or by any means whatsoever without written permission from the Publisher.

一个做数学练头脑的高档培训中心

兒童趣味游戏数学專科培训中心

(專教资优兒童 4 歲或以上)

全球唯一独特发明,兒童智能数学＋

国际象棋＋谜题＋奥数融合教材

资优数学　SSAT　儿童趣味数学

数学 IQ 智能健脑思维　奥数加强

| Ho Math Chess　何数棋谜 益智健脑非药物良方 |
| Frankho Puzzle for KIDS – Brain Fitness Workbook |
| © 2007 – 2016 Frank Ho, Amanda Ho all rights reserved www.mathandchess.com |

何数棋谜 - 何数学棋艺学习中心

只见棋谜不见题　劝君迷路不哭涕

数学象棋加谜题　健脑思维眞神奇

Preface

Frankho Puzzles™ were invented by Mr. Frank Ho, a Canadian math teacher and founder of Ho Math and Chess. The puzzles included in this workbook were jointly created by Frank Ho and Amanda Ho.

Game play is a good way to inspire children's interest in learning math and chess has proven to be effective. Frankho Puzzles™ are a special kind of math puzzles that are solved by using addition, subtraction, multiplication, division, or factoring and by following chess moves and logic. Frankho Puzzles™ are one-of-a-kind puzzles that help children improve their computing, logic, and chess abilities all in one workbook and at the same time.

Since most children like puzzles and games, Frankho Puzzles™ are a good approach for children to master math computation skills whether they are interested in playing chess or not since most children like puzzles and there are no chess strategies or tactics required when working on Frankho Puzzles™ other than the knowledge of basic chess moves. Frankho Puzzles™ were created use Frank's trademarked Geometric Chess Symbols

(Trademarked 1069744). Children explore the calculation pathways by using clues such as common squares intersected by chess moves. This logical thinking process adds a fun element to the learning of basic arithmetic computation.

What makes Frankho Puzzles™ intriguing is that even though there is only one final answer; the immediate answers in the process of calculating may be different due to the reason that a chess move has many possibilities. Many math concepts such as operations of intersections and order of operations are included in the puzzles. Children also are taught the concepts of line interactions, tree structures, and logic while having fun working on math-oriented puzzles.

Frankho Puzzles™ are educational, fun and, addictive.
For more details, please contact Ho Math and Chess at mathandchess@telus.net.

Frank Ho, Amanda Ho
October, 2016

Ho Math and Chess = *A Cool and Fun Way to Learn Math!* ™

Ho Math Chess　　　何数棋谜　益智健脑非药物良方
Frankho Puzzle for KIDS - Brain Fitness Workbook
© 2007 — 2016 Frank Ho, Amanda Ho all rights reserved www.mathandchess.com

What special is about Frankho Puzzles™?

- They are unique math puzzles (over 200) combining with math, chess, Sudoku and logic.

- They do not require any high-level math skills other than addition, subtraction, multiplication, division, factoring, comparisons, pattern recognition and visualization.

- The chess skills required are very elementary. Students are only required to know how each chess piece moves and how it is represented by a corresponding Geometric Chess Symbol – invented and trademarked by Frank Ho.

- All the puzzles can be solved by students with minimum teacher's guidance.

- The puzzles train students to be patient and use their problem-solving ability. They can be addictive when students want to solve them by themselves.

- The abilities learned by doing the puzzles can be applied to help students succeed in the school math curriculum.

Ho Math Chess 何数棋谜 益智健脑非药物良方
Frankho Puzzle for KIDS – Brain Fitness Workbook
© 2007 — 2016 Frank Ho, Amanda Ho all rights reserved www.mathandchess.com

How to solve Frankho Puzzles™

Rule: The numbers 1, 2, 3, 4, and 5 must appear only once in every row or column.

Step 1: The squares with numbers in them shall be the ones we pay attention first. These numbers are results of calculations according to some arithmetic operator(s) and chess moves(s) as indicated by darker arrow(s).

Step 2: Look at the number 4 at $e2$: $d1 + e1 + e2 = 4$, and we know that only $1 + 2 + 1 = 4$, which means $d1 = e2 = 1, e1 = 2$.

Step 3: The number 8 at $c5$: $b5 + c5 = 8$, $3 + 5 = 8$. This means $e5$ is not 3, nor 5; $e1 = 2$ and $e2 = 1$, so $e5$ cannot be 1, nor 2 either; so $e5 = 4$.

Step 4: Look at $b4$ and $a3$: $4 + 5 = 9$, $4 + 1 = 5$, which means $a4 = 4, a3 = 5, b4 = 1$. $e3$ is not $1(e2), 1(e2), 4(e5)$, nor $5(a3)$, so $e3 = 3$, and $e4 = 5$.

Step 5: $d5$ is not $1(d1), 4(e5), 3$ or 5 ($b5$ or $c5$), so $d5 = 2$, and $a5 = 1$.

Step 6: $a1$ is not $1(d1), 2(e1), 4$ or $5(a3$ or $a4)$, so $a1 = 3$. And $a2 = 2$.

Step 7: Look at 7 at $c2$. $b2 + c2 = 7$, $2 + 5 = 7, 3 + 4 = 7$, since $a2 = 2$, so $b2 + c2 = 3 + 4$. We can conclude $d2 = 5$. And $a1 = 3$, $b1$ is not 3, $b1 = 4, b2 = 3$

Step 8: $d4$ is not 1, 5, 2, nor 4, so $d4 = 3$, and $d3 = 4$.

Step 9: Now we can fill in the rest blanks. $b5 = 5, c5 = 3, b3 = 2, and\ c3 = 1$.

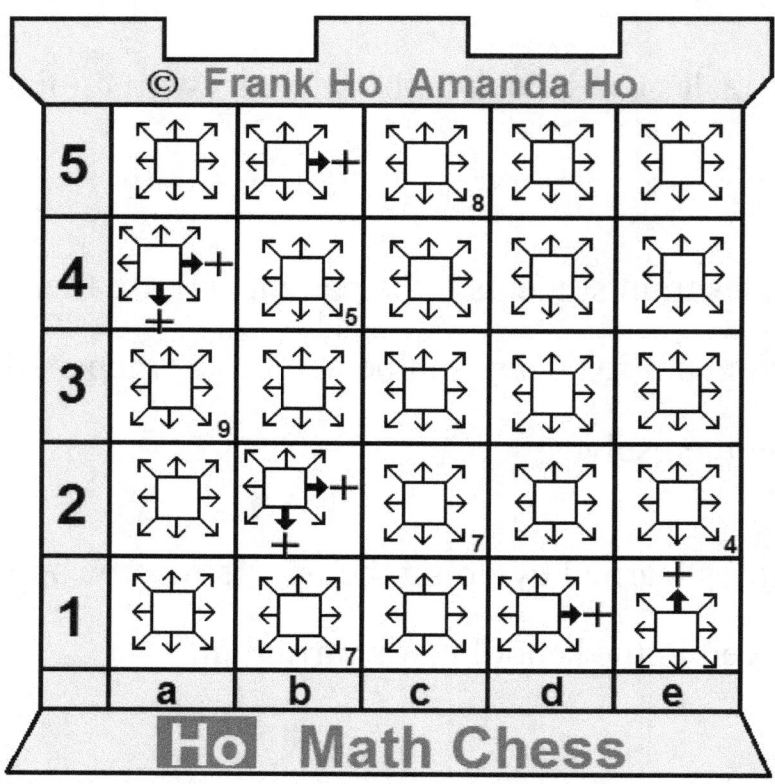

Ho Math Chess 何数棋谜 益智健脑非药物良方
Frankho Puzzle for KIDS – Brain Fitness Workbook
© 2007 — 2016 Frank Ho, Amanda Ho all rights reserved www.mathandchess.com

Frankho Puzzle™ # 1

Rule All the digits 1 to 5 must appear exactly once in every row and column. The number appears in the bottom right-hand corner is the end result calculated according to arithmetic operator(s) and chess move(s) as indicated by darker arrow(s).

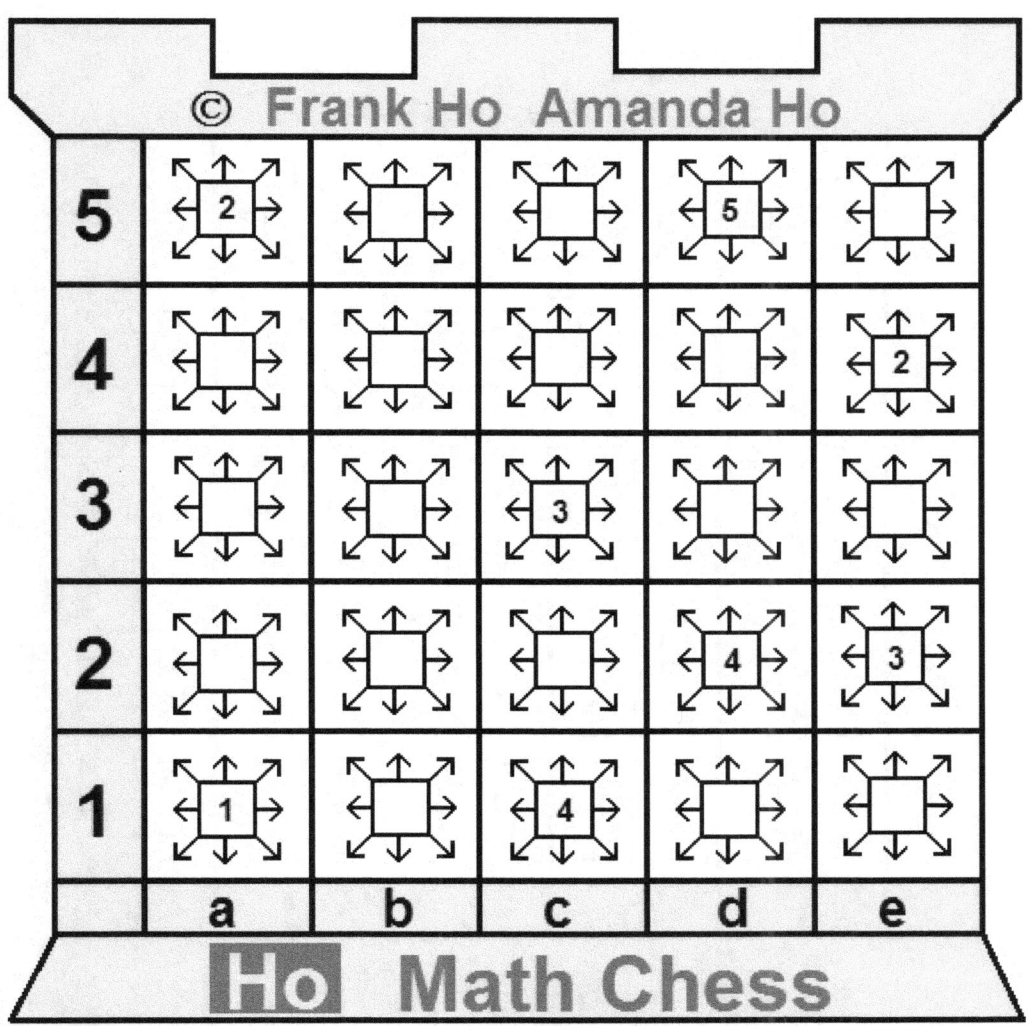

Frankho Puzzle™ # 2

Rule All the digits 1 to 5 must appear exactly once in every row and column. The number appears in the bottom right-hand corner is the end result calculated according to arithmetic operator(s) and chess move(s) as indicated by darker arrow(s).

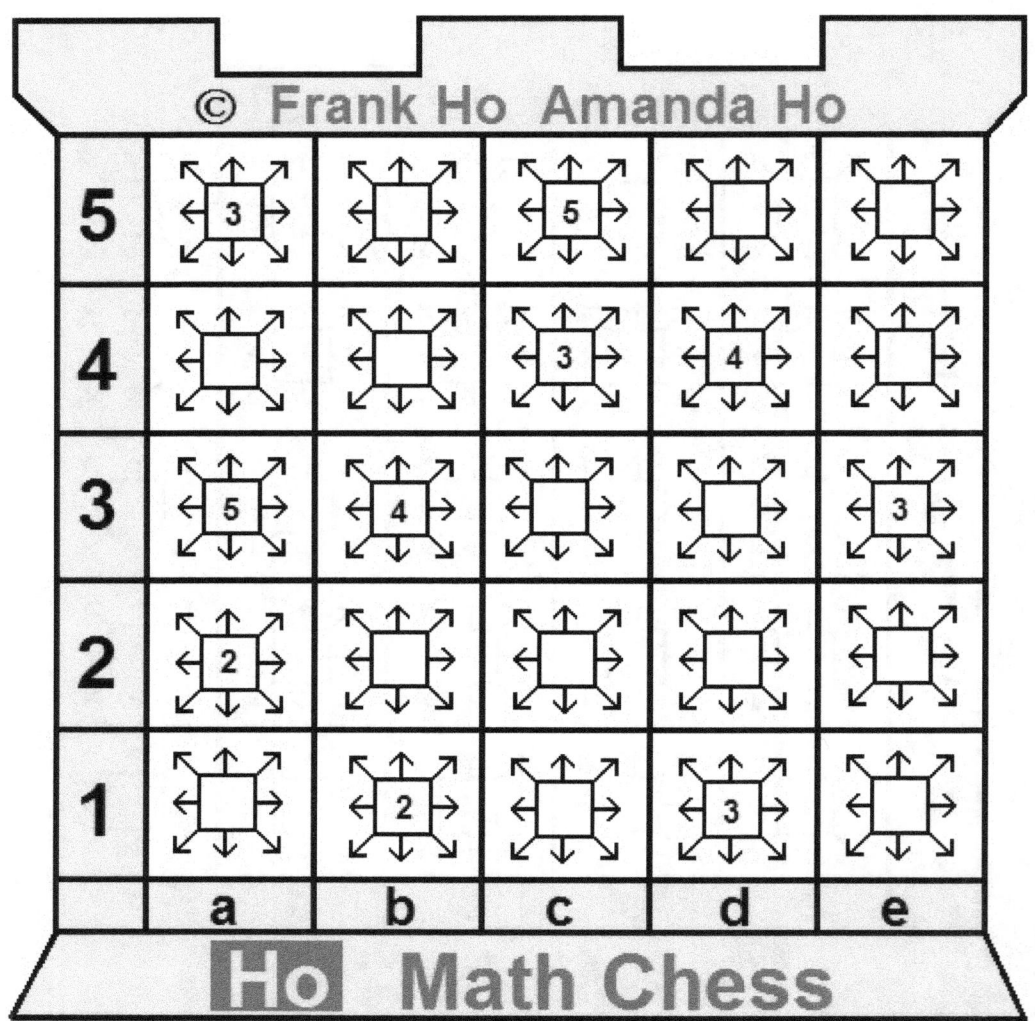

Ho Math Chess 何数棋谜 益智健脑非药物良方
Frankho Puzzle for KIDS – Brain Fitness Workbook

© 2007 — 2016 Frank Ho, Amanda Ho all rights reserved www.mathandchess.com

Frankho Puzzle™ # 3

Rule All the digits 1 to 5 must appear exactly once in every row and column. The number appears in the bottom right-hand corner is the end result calculated according to arithmetic operator(s) and chess move(s) as indicated by darker arrow(s).

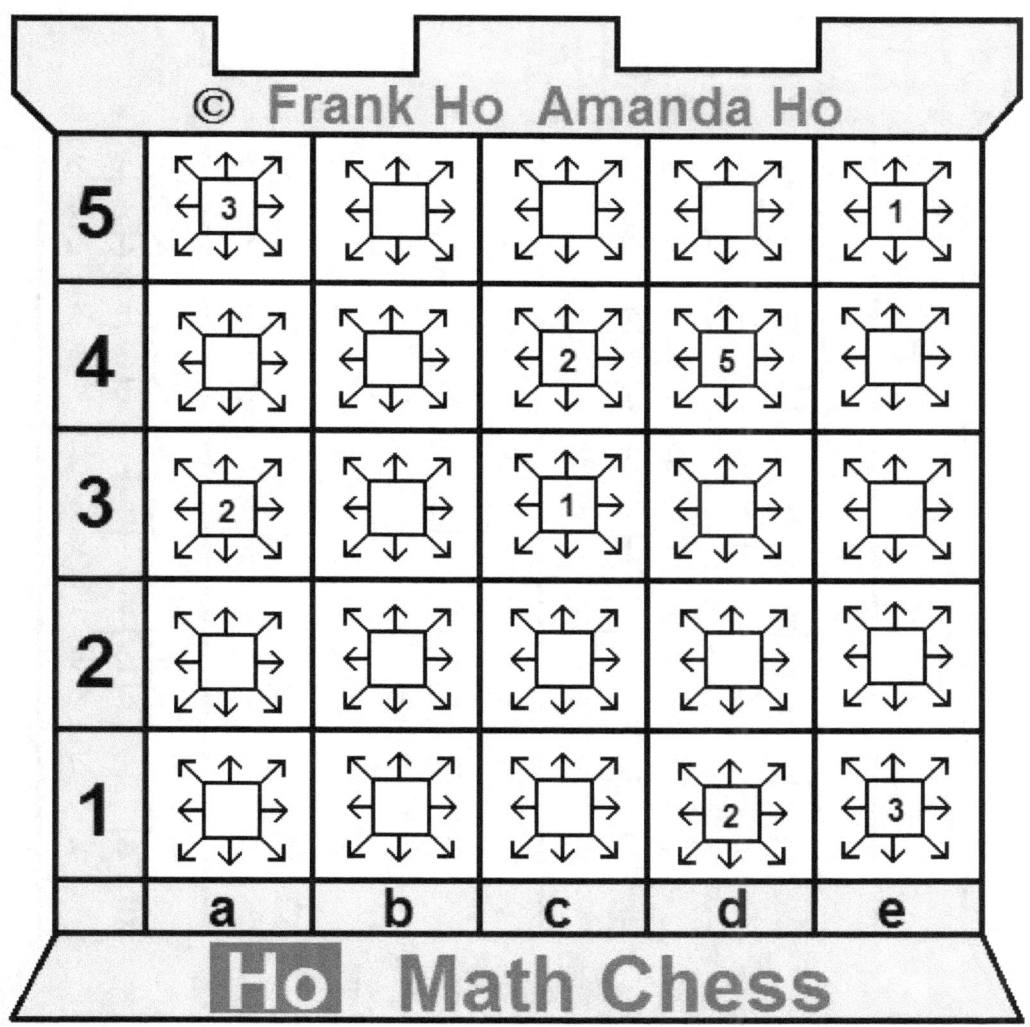

Ho Math Chess 何数棋谜 益智健脑非药物良方
Frankho Puzzle for KIDS – Brain Fitness Workbook

© 2007 — 2016 Frank Ho, Amanda Ho all rights reserved www.mathandchess.com

Frankho Puzzle™ # 4

Rule All the digits 1 to 5 must appear exactly once in every row and column. The number appears in the bottom right-hand corner is the end result calculated according to arithmetic operator(s) and chess move(s) as indicated by darker arrow(s).

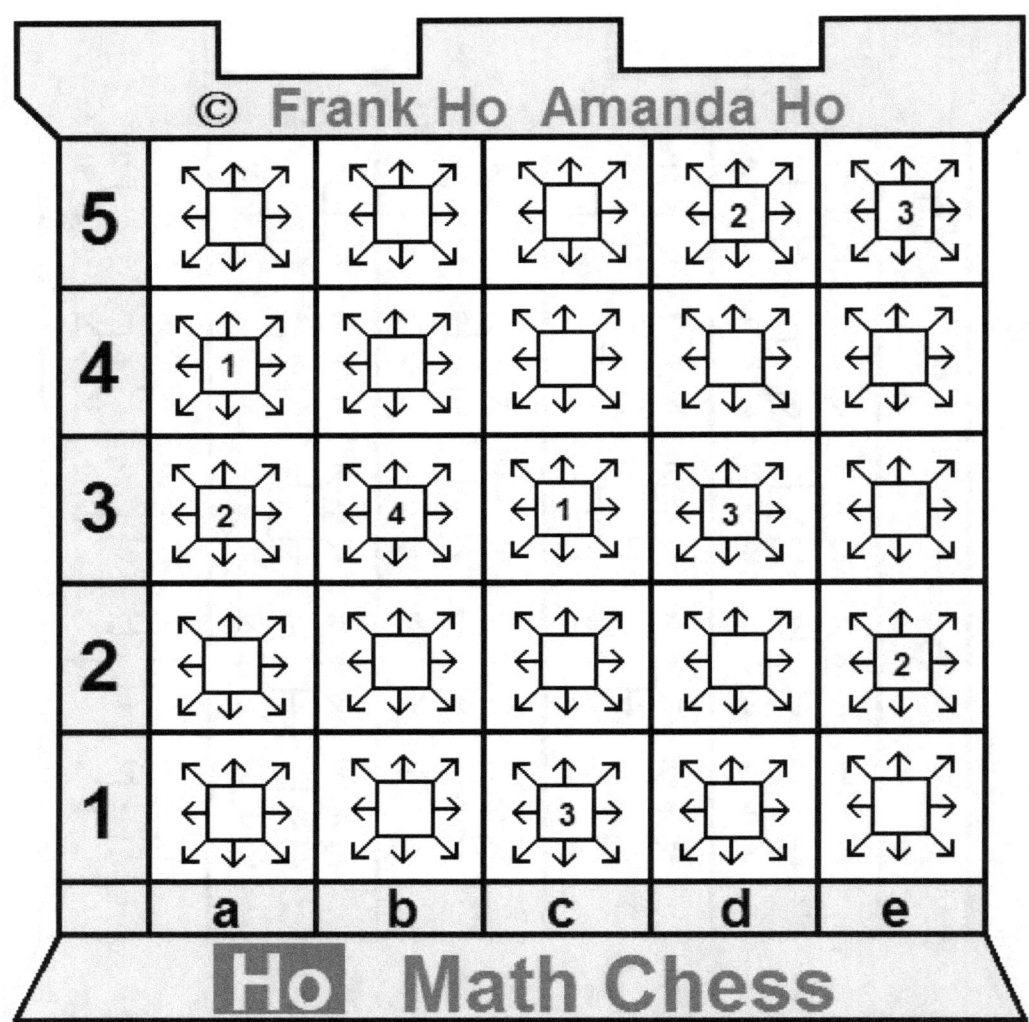

Ho Math Chess 何数棋谜 益智健脑非药物良方
Frankho Puzzle for KIDS – Brain Fitness Workbook
© 2007 — 2016 Frank Ho, Amanda Ho all rights reserved www.mathandchess.com

Frankho Puzzle™ # 5

Rule All the digits 1 to 5 must appear exactly once in every row and column. The number appears in the bottom right-hand corner is the end result calculated according to arithmetic operator(s) and chess move(s) as indicated by darker arrow(s).

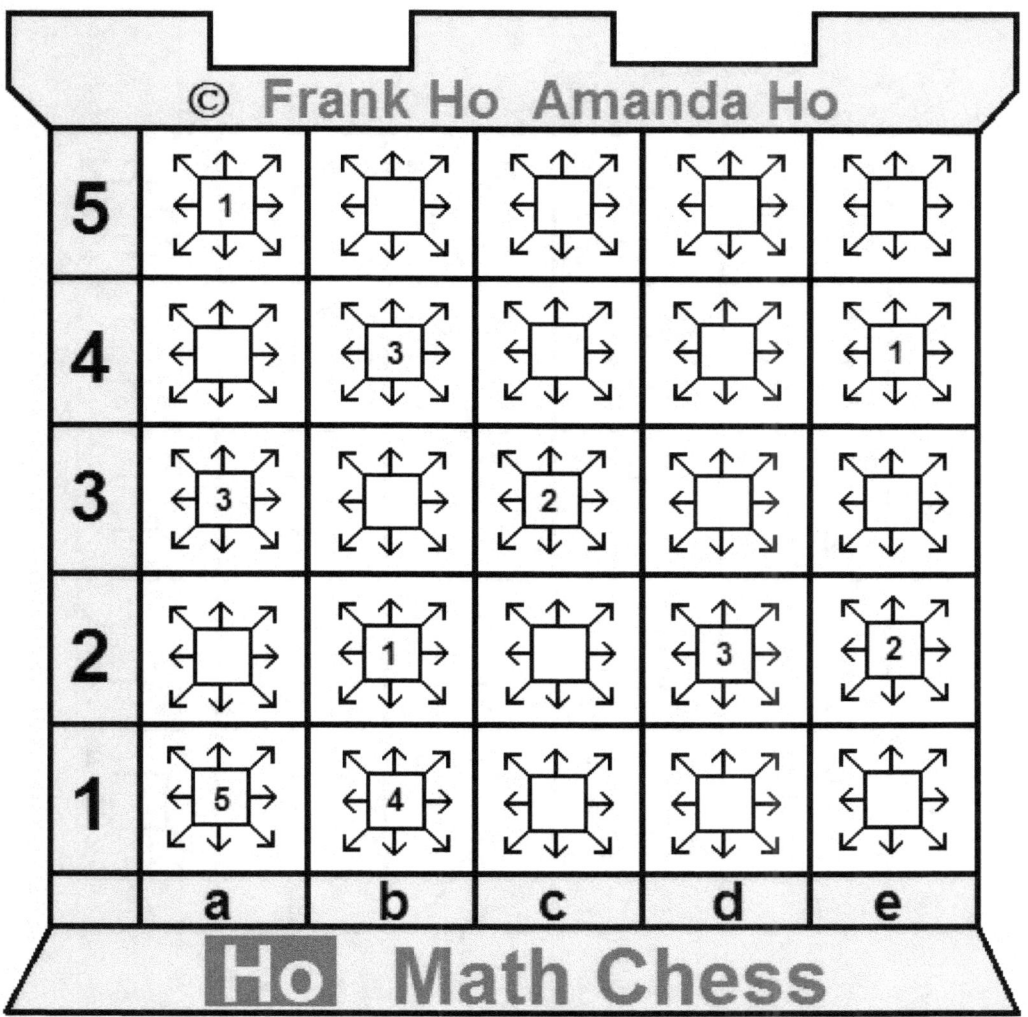

Ho Math Chess 何数棋谜 益智健脑非药物良方
Frankho Puzzle for KIDS – Brain Fitness Workbook
© 2007 — 2016 Frank Ho, Amanda Ho all rights reserved www.mathandchess.com

Frankho Puzzle™ # 6

Rule All the digits 1 to 5 must appear exactly once in every row and column. The number appears in the bottom right-hand corner is the end result calculated according to arithmetic operator(s) and chess move(s) as indicated by darker arrow(s).

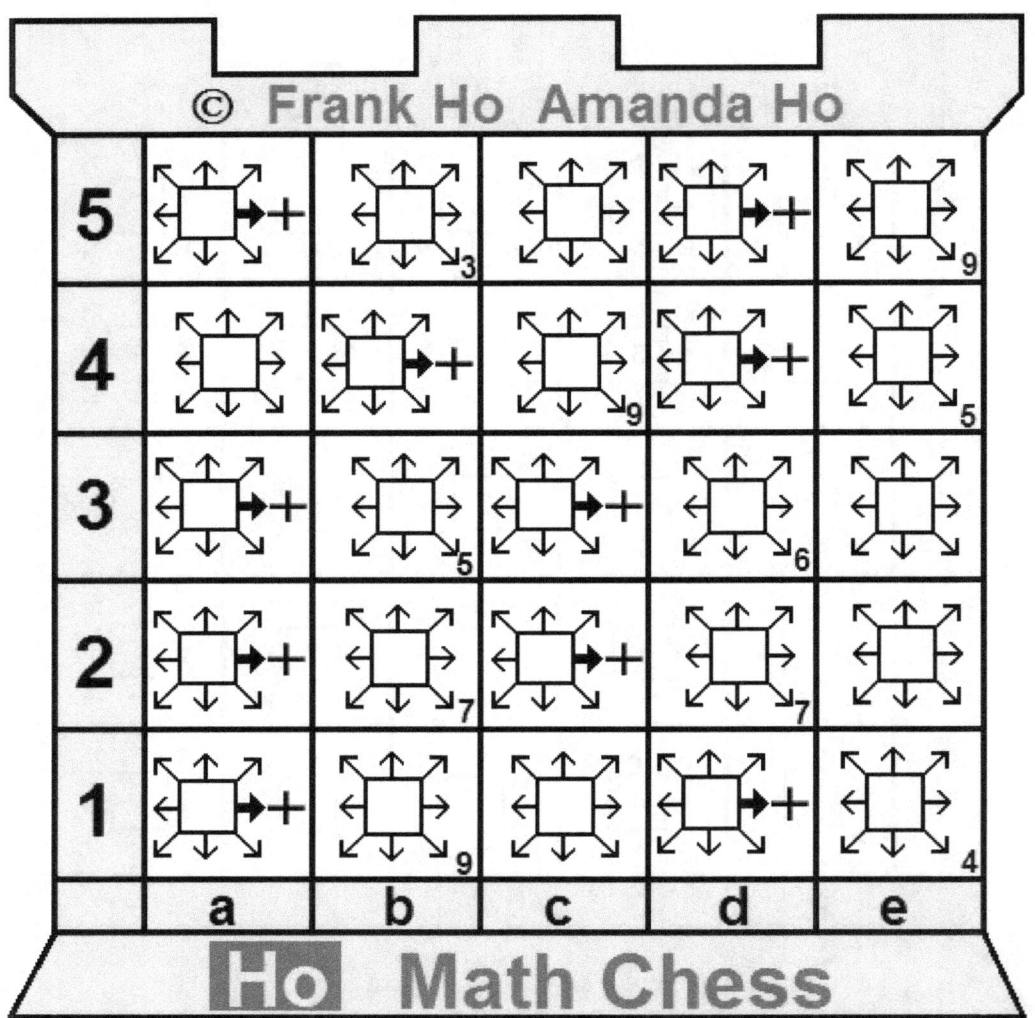

Ho Math Chess 何数棋谜 益智健脑非药物良方
Frankho Puzzle for KIDS – Brain Fitness Workbook
© 2007 – 2016 Frank Ho, Amanda Ho all rights reserved www.mathandchess.com

Frankho Puzzle™ # 7

Rule All the digits 1 to 5 must appear exactly once in every row and column. The number appears in the bottom right-hand corner is the end result calculated according to arithmetic operator(s) and chess move(s) as indicated by darker arrow(s).

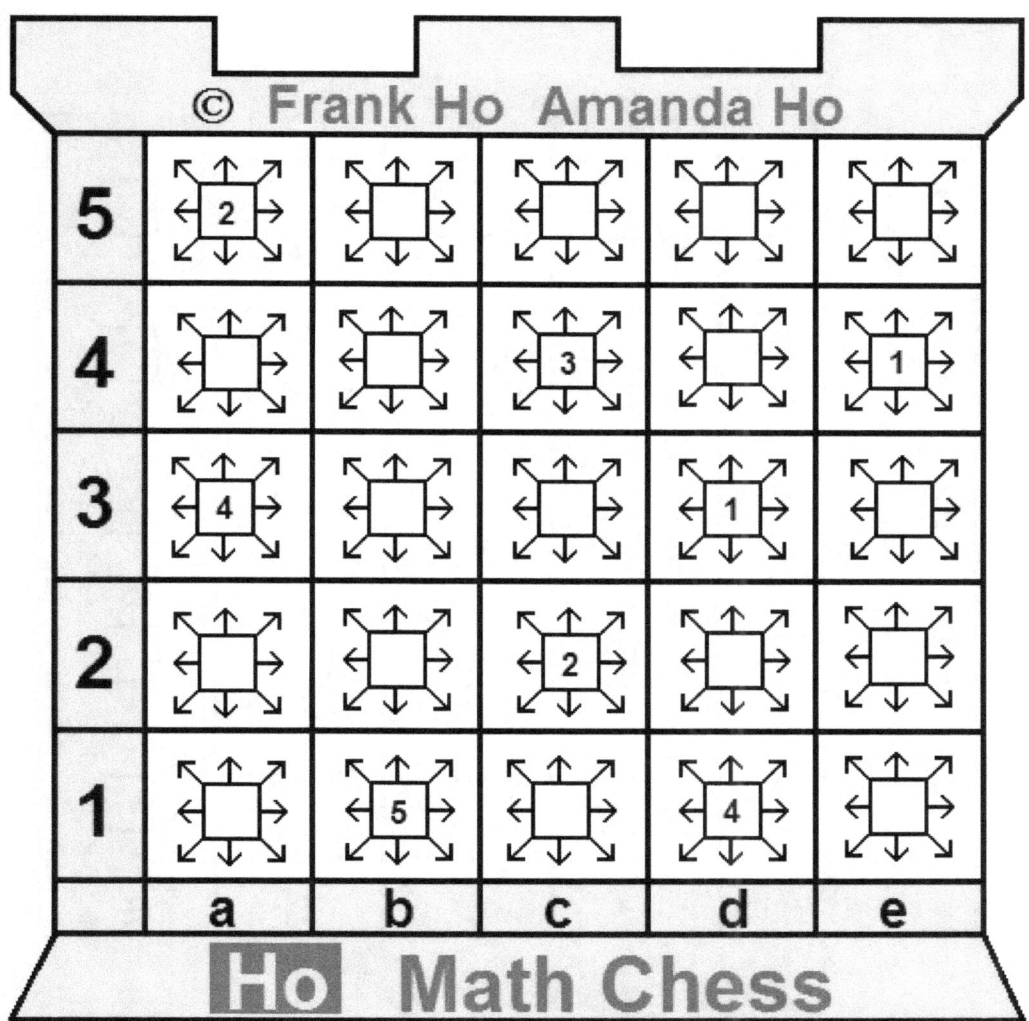

Frankho Puzzle™ # 8

Rule All the digits 1 to 5 must appear exactly once in every row and column. The number appears in the bottom right-hand corner is the end result calculated according to arithmetic operator(s) and chess move(s) as indicated by darker arrow(s).

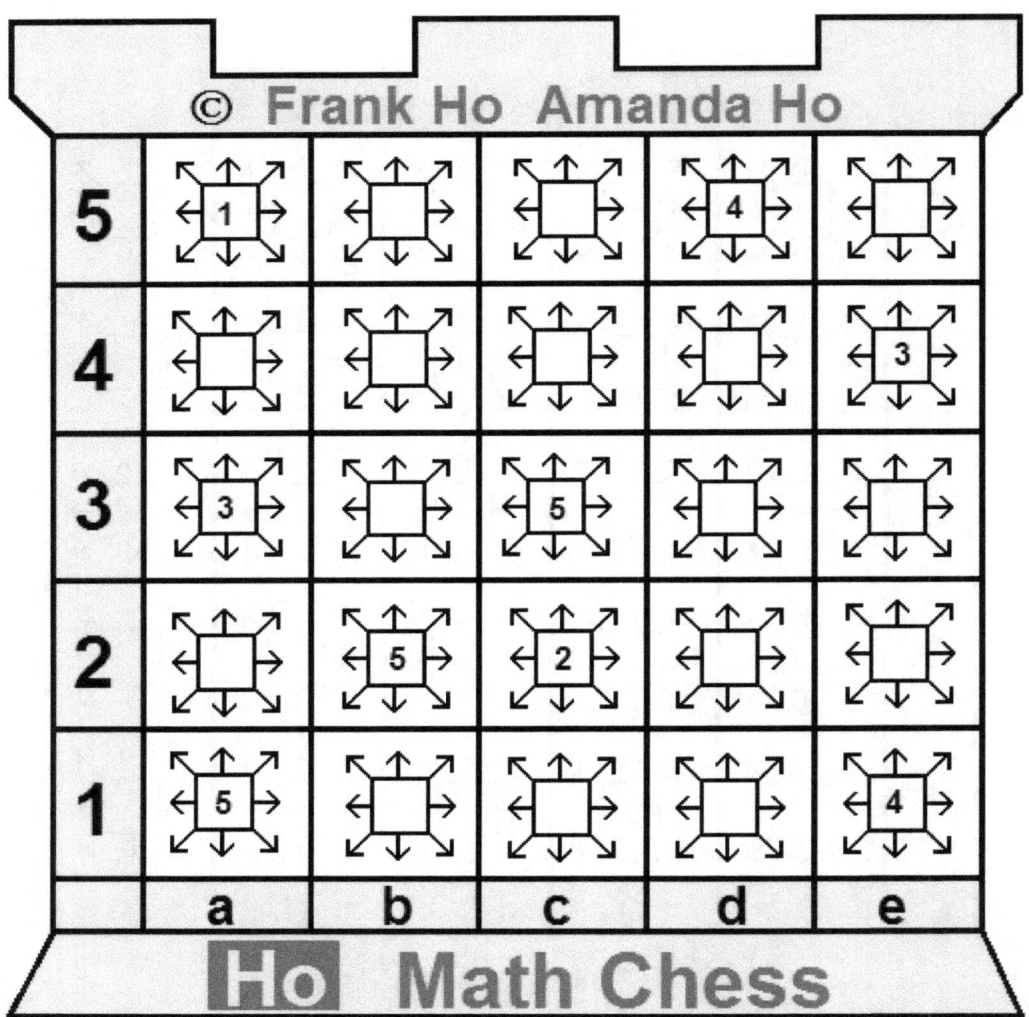

Ho Math Chess 何数棋谜 益智健脑非药物良方
Frankho Puzzle for KIDS – Brain Fitness Workbook
© 2007 — 2016 Frank Ho, Amanda Ho all rights reserved www.mathandchess.com

Frankho Puzzle™ # 9

Rule All the digits 1 to 5 must appear exactly once in every row and column. The number appears in the bottom right-hand corner is the end result calculated according to arithmetic operator(s) and chess move(s) as indicated by darker arrow(s).

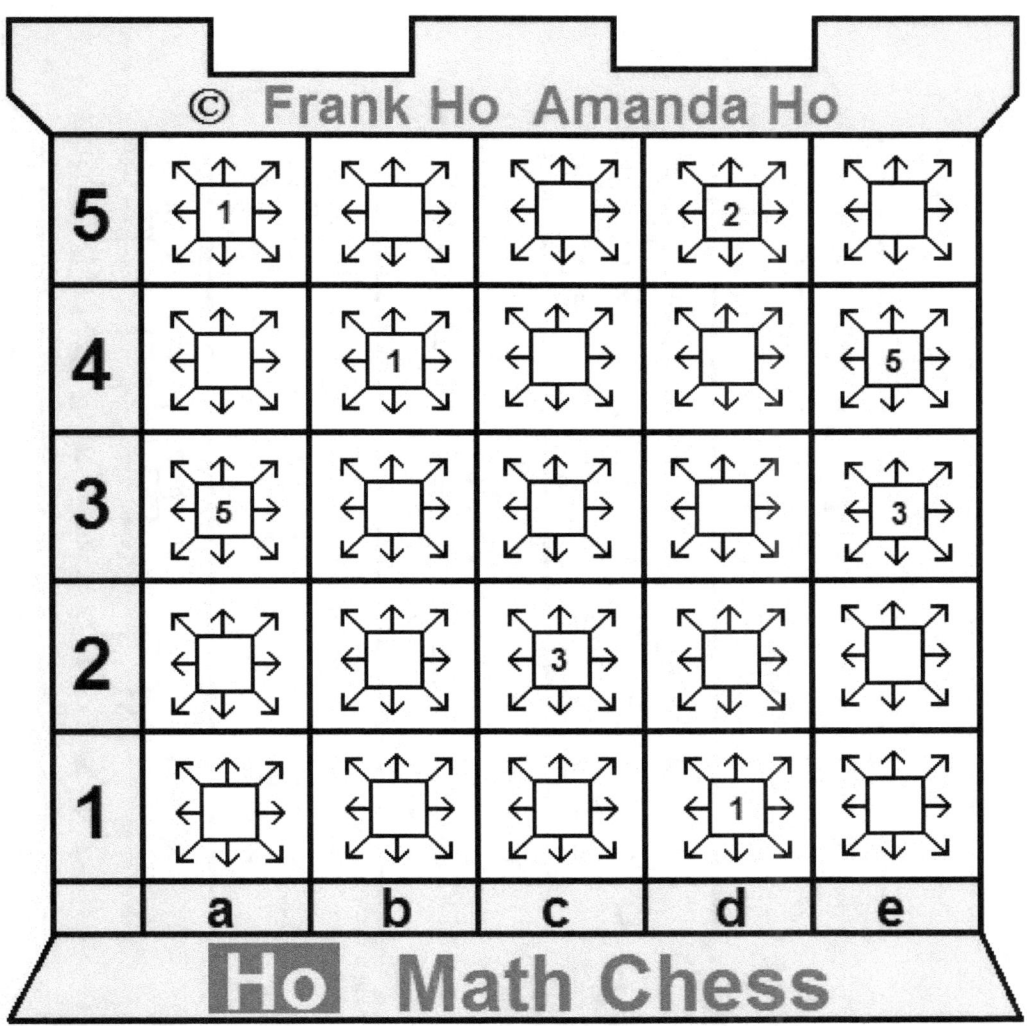

Frankho Puzzle™ # 10

Rule All the digits 1 to 5 must appear exactly once in every row and column. The number appears in the bottom right-hand corner is the end result calculated according to arithmetic operator(s) and chess move(s) as indicated by darker arrow(s).

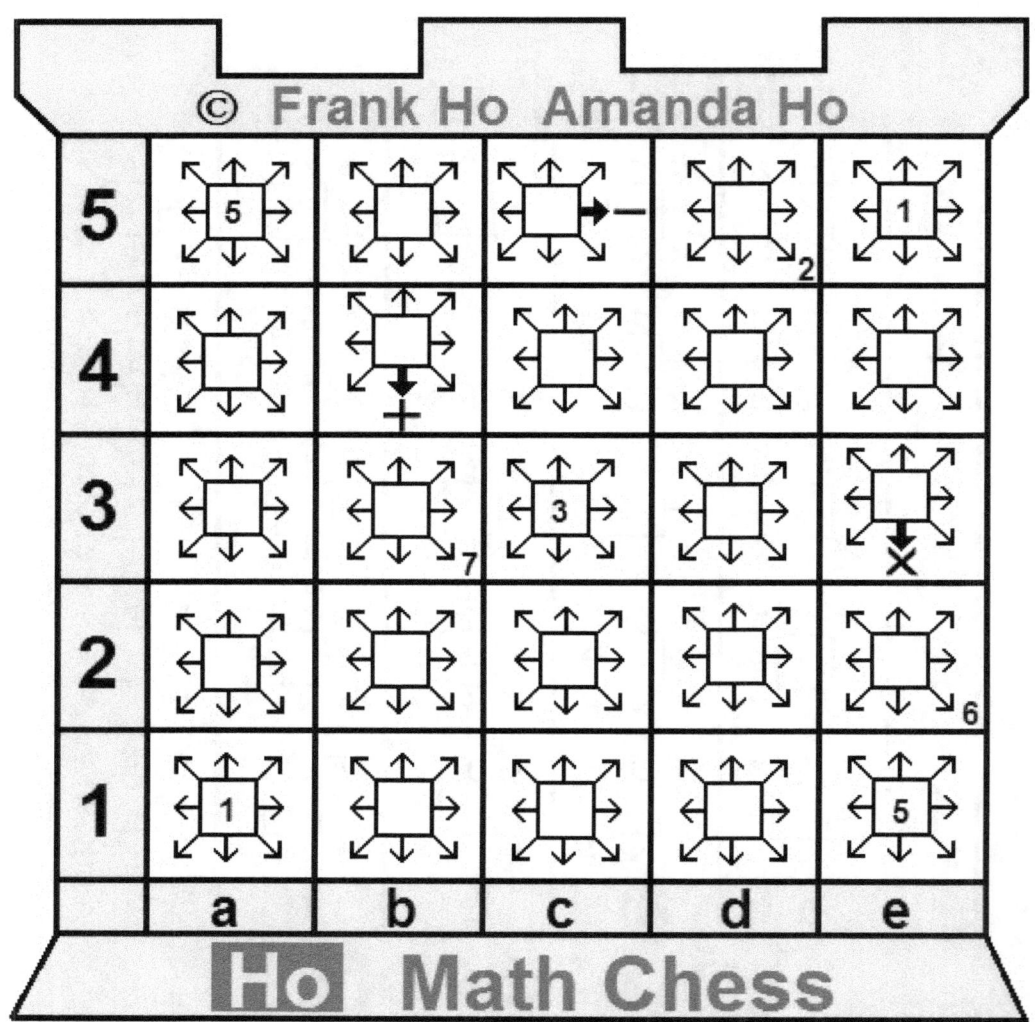

Ho Math Chess 何数棋谜 益智健脑非药物良方
Frankho Puzzle for KIDS – Brain Fitness Workbook
© 2007 — 2016 Frank Ho, Amanda Ho all rights reserved www.mathandchess.com

Frankho Puzzle™ # 11

Rule All the digits 1 to 5 must appear exactly once in every row and column. The number appears in the bottom right-hand corner is the end result calculated according to arithmetic operator(s) and chess move(s) as indicated by darker arrow(s).

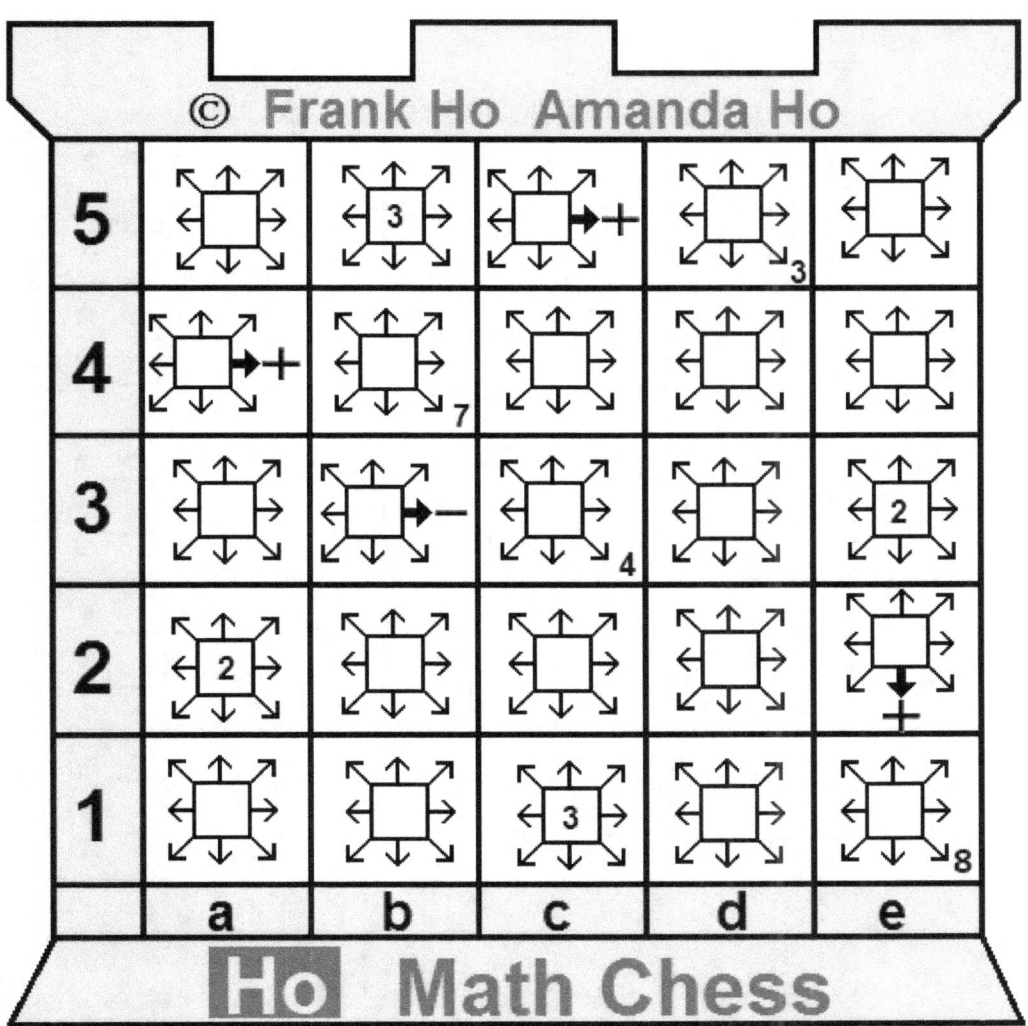

Frankho Puzzle™ # 12

Rule All the digits 1 to 5 must appear exactly once in every row and column. The number appears in the bottom right-hand corner is the end result calculated according to arithmetic operator(s) and chess move(s) as indicated by darker arrow(s).

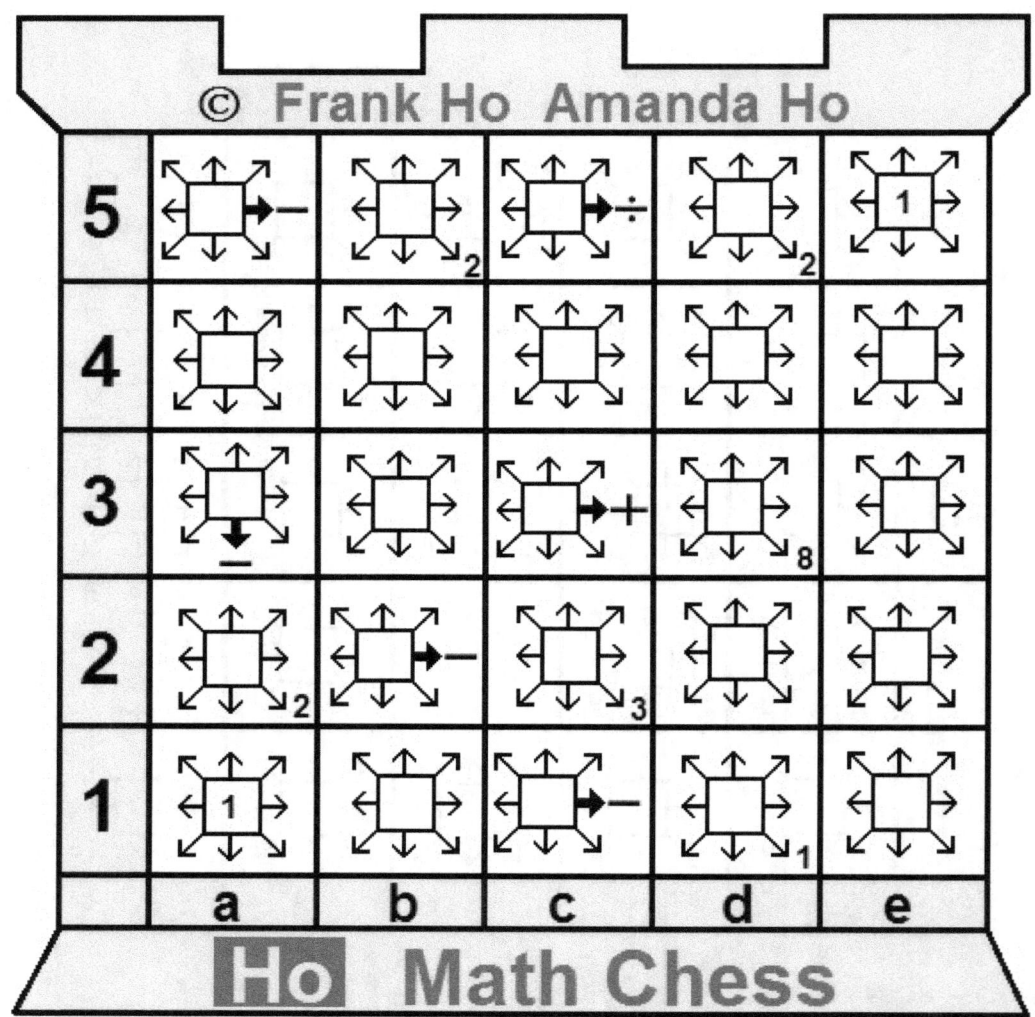

Ho Math Chess 何数棋谜 益智健脑非药物良方
Frankho Puzzle for KIDS – Brain Fitness Workbook
© 2007 — 2016 Frank Ho, Amanda Ho all rights reserved www.mathandchess.com

Frankho Puzzle™ # 13

Rule All the digits 1 to 5 must appear exactly once in every row and column. The number appears in the bottom right-hand corner is the end result calculated according to arithmetic operator(s) and chess move(s) as indicated by darker arrow(s).

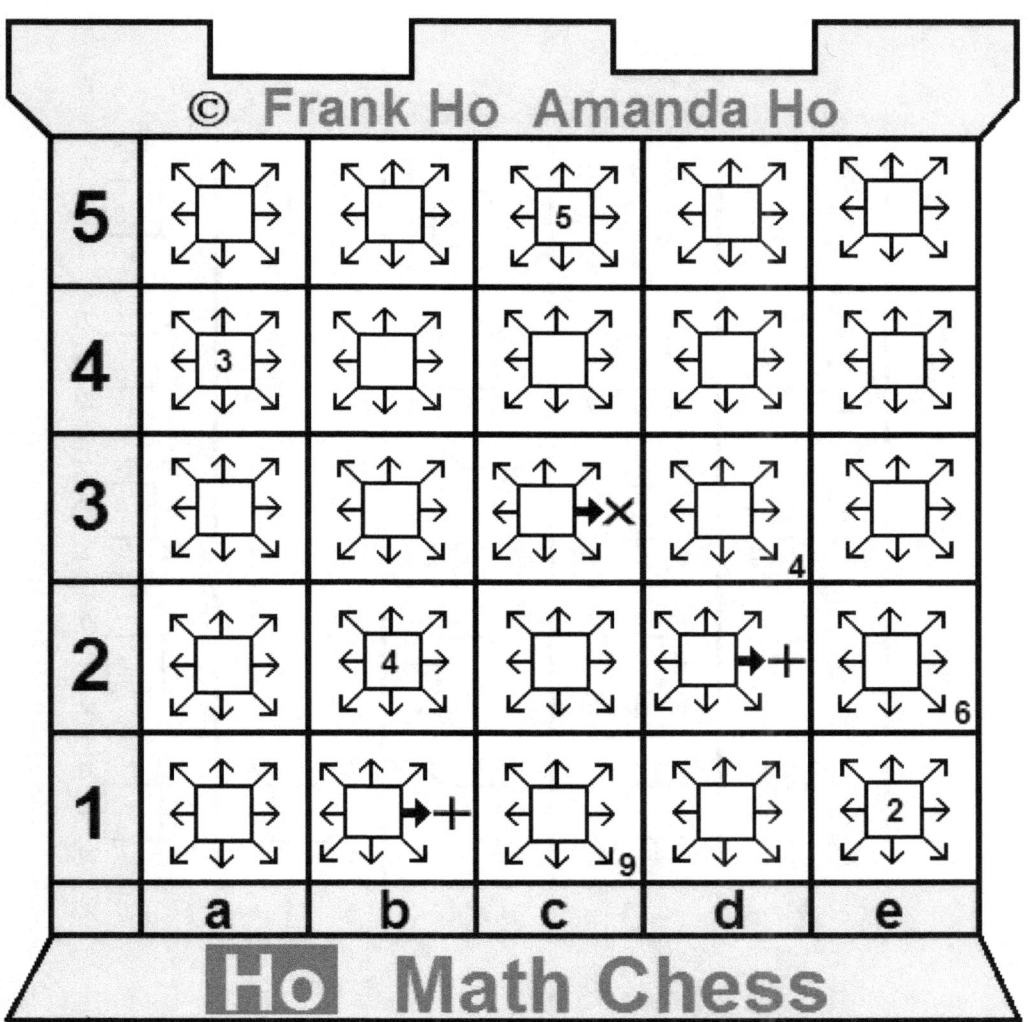

Frankho Puzzle™ # 14

Rule All the digits 1 to 5 must appear exactly once in every row and column. The number appears in the bottom right-hand corner is the end result calculated according to arithmetic operator(s) and chess move(s) as indicated by darker arrow(s).

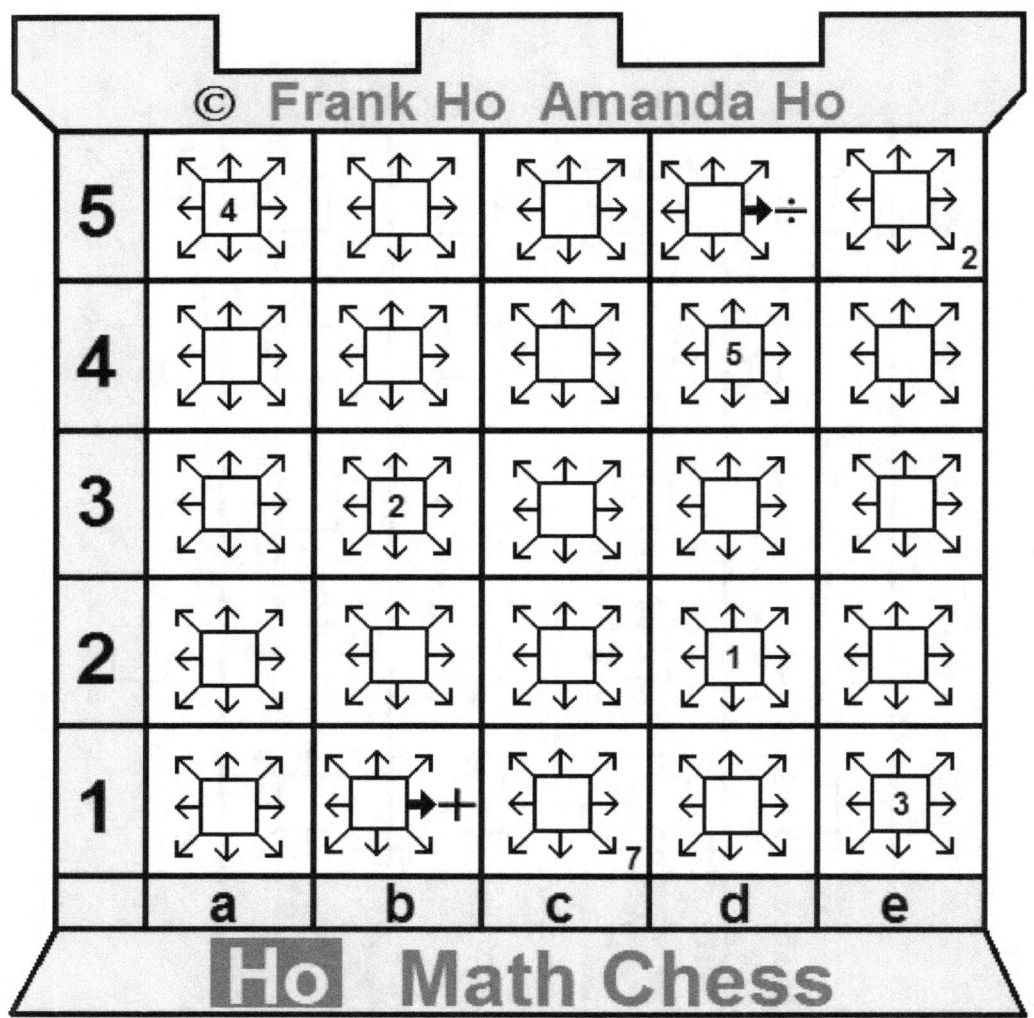

Ho Math Chess 何数棋谜 益智健脑非药物良方
Frankho Puzzle for KIDS – Brain Fitness Workbook
© 2007 – 2016 Frank Ho, Amanda Ho all rights reserved www.mathandchess.com

Frankho Puzzle™ # 15

Rule All the digits 1 to 5 must appear exactly once in every row and column. The number appears in the bottom right-hand corner is the end result calculated according to arithmetic operator(s) and chess move(s) as indicated by darker arrow(s).

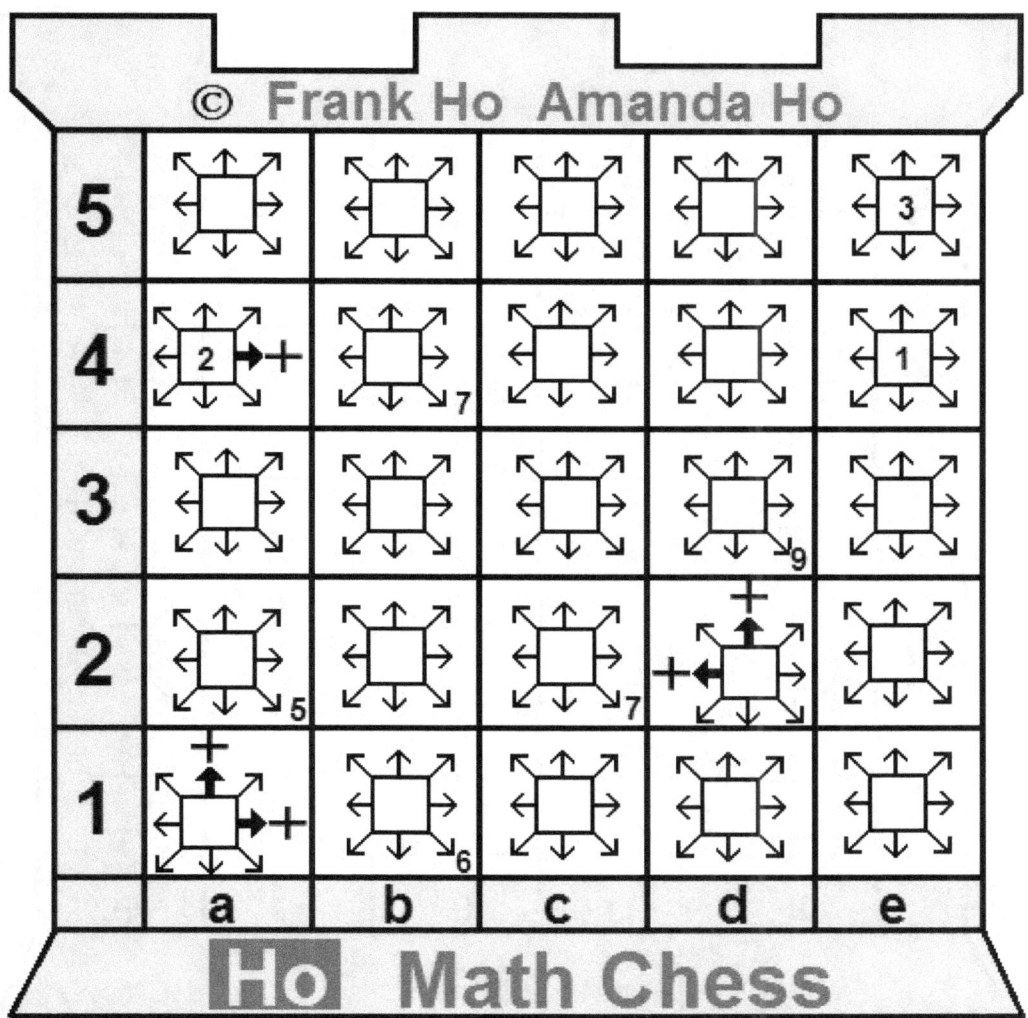

Frankho Puzzle™ # 16

Rule All the digits 1 to 5 must appear exactly once in every row and column. The number appears in the bottom right-hand corner is the end result calculated according to arithmetic operator(s) and chess move(s) as indicated by darker arrow(s).

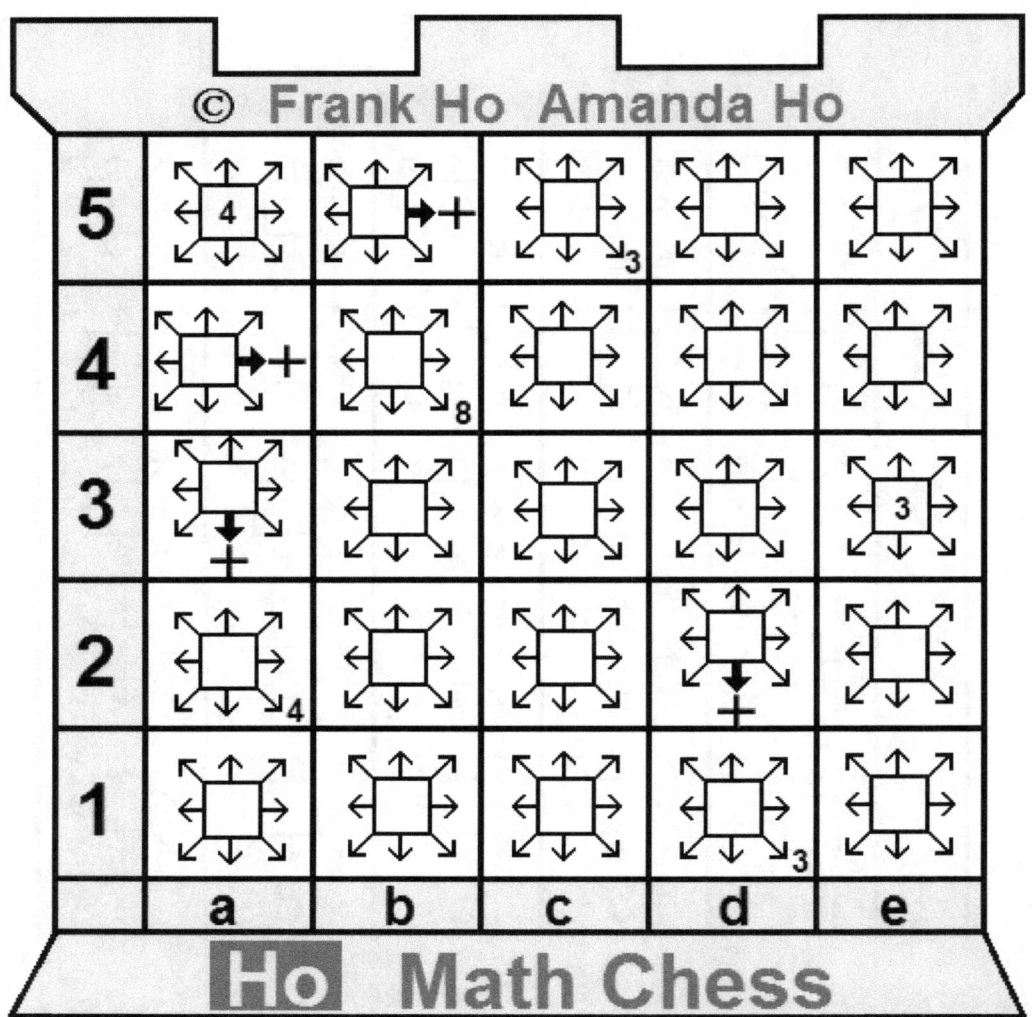

Frankho Puzzle™ # 17

Rule All the digits 1 to 5 must appear exactly once in every row and column. The number appears in the bottom right-hand corner is the end result calculated according to arithmetic operator(s) and chess move(s) as indicated by darker arrow(s).

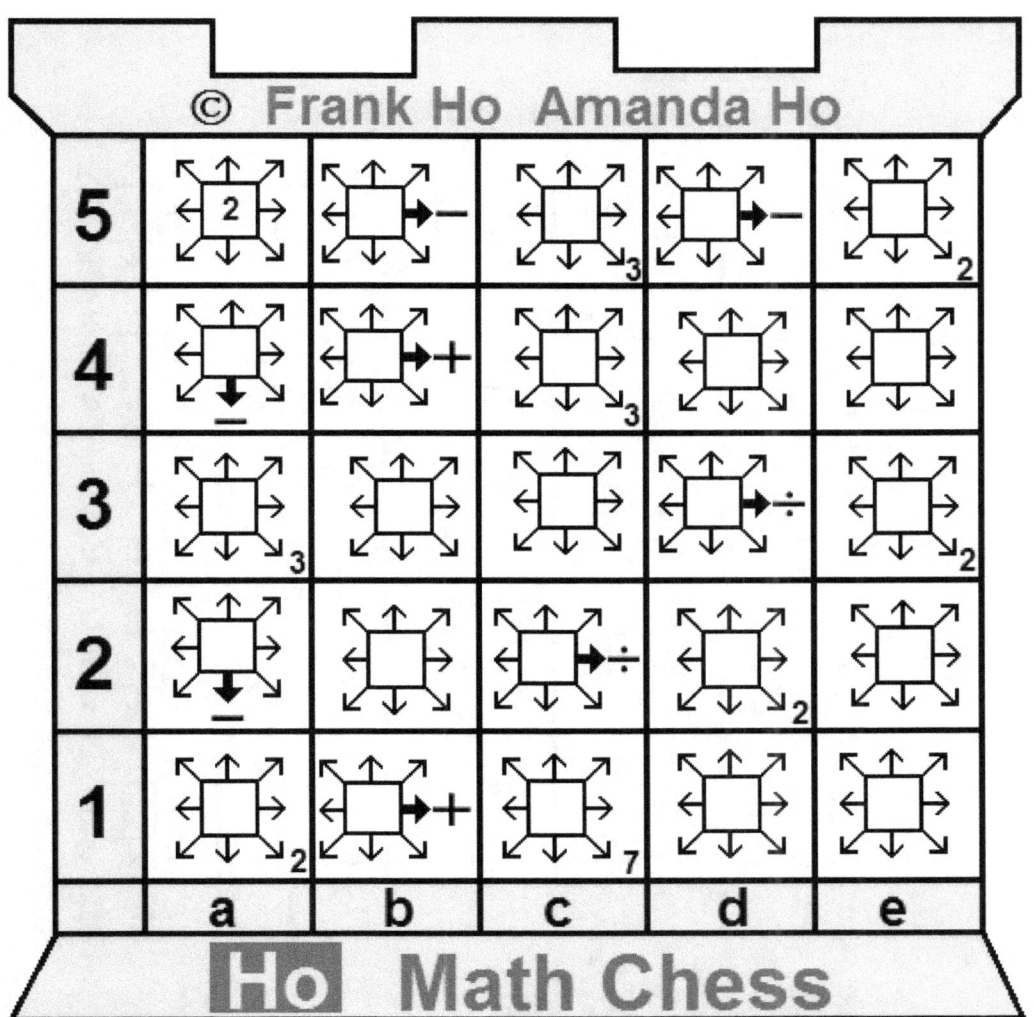

Frankho Puzzle™ # 18

Rule All the digits 1 to 5 must appear exactly once in every row and column. The number appears in the bottom right-hand corner is the end result calculated according to arithmetic operator(s) and chess move(s) as indicated by darker arrow(s).

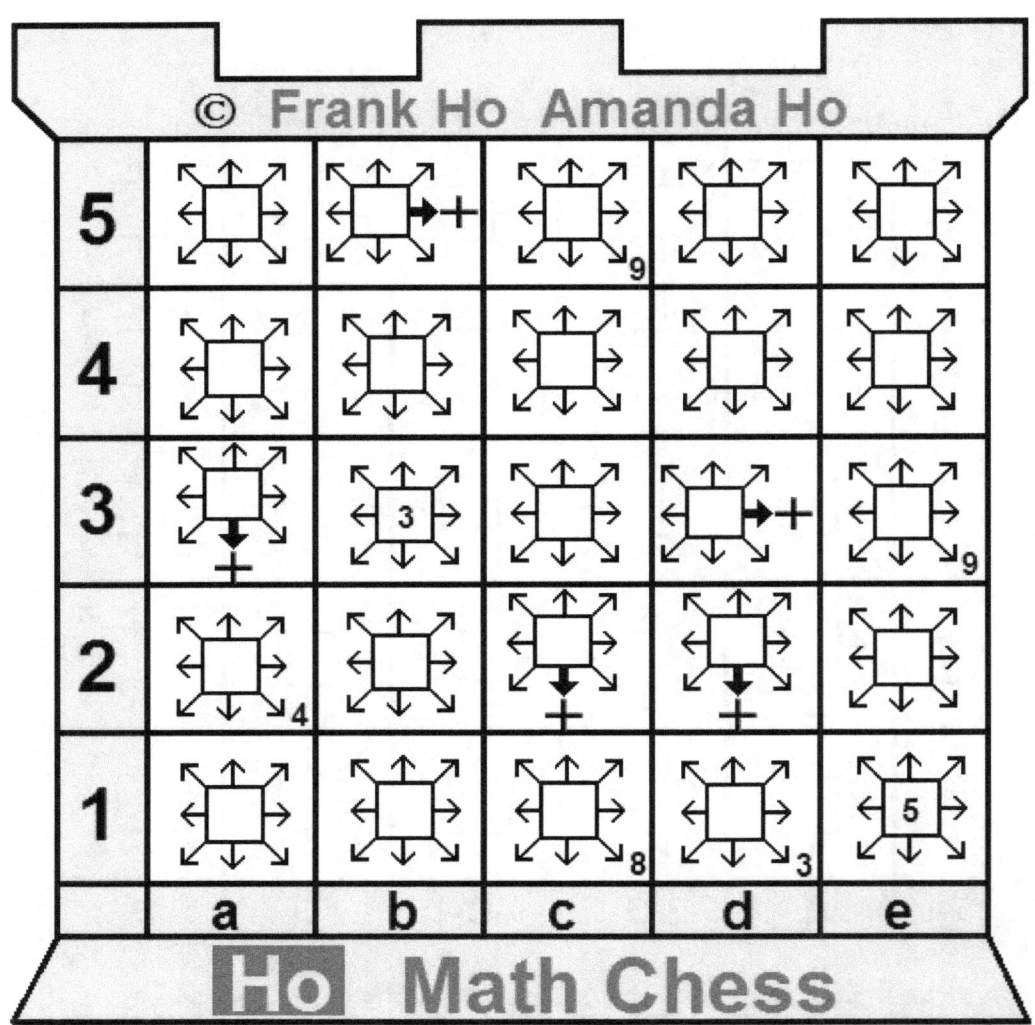

Ho Math Chess 何数棋谜 益智健脑非药物良方
Frankho Puzzle for KIDS – Brain Fitness Workbook
© 2007 — 2016 Frank Ho, Amanda Ho all rights reserved www.mathandchess.com

Frankho Puzzle™ # 19

Rule All the digits 1 to 5 must appear exactly once in every row and column. The number appears in the bottom right-hand corner is the end result calculated according to arithmetic operator(s) and chess move(s) as indicated by darker arrow(s).

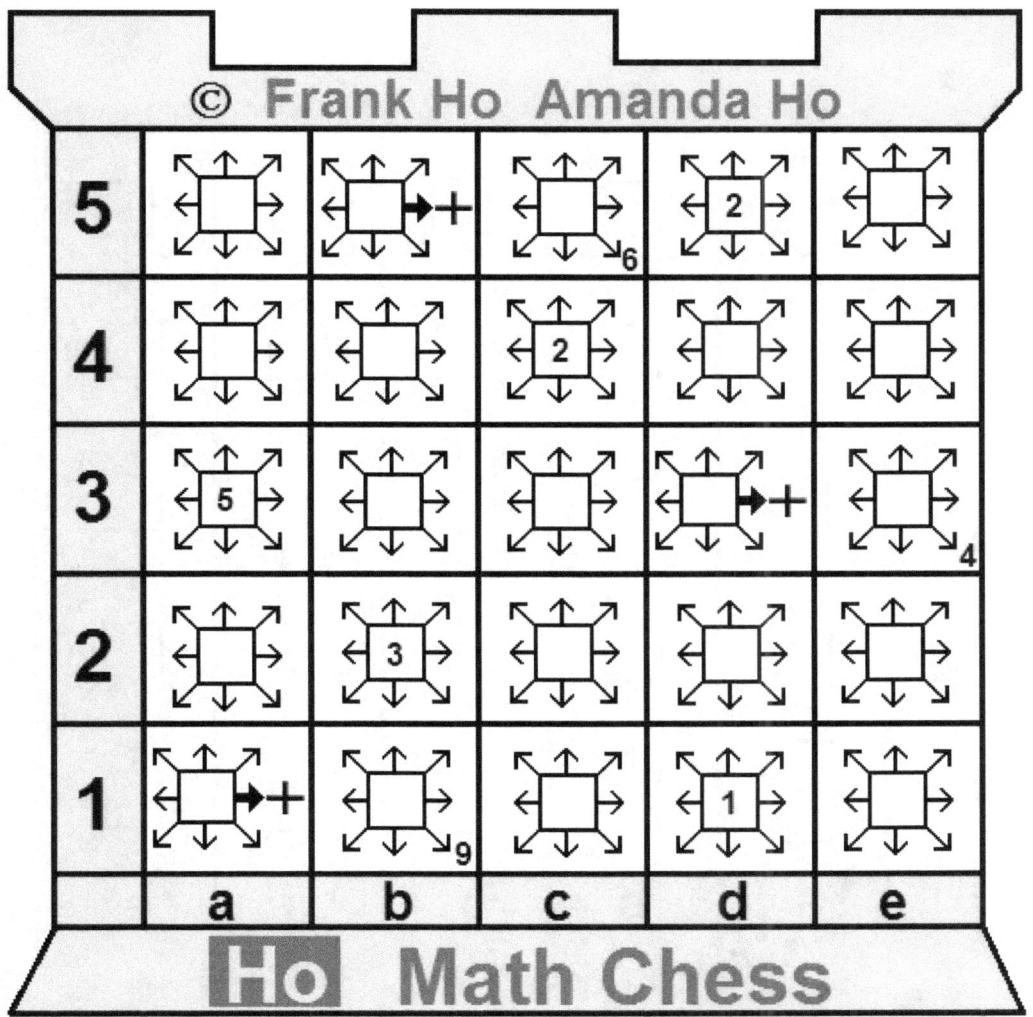

Frankho Puzzle™ # 20

Rule All the digits 1 to 5 must appear exactly once in every row and column. The number appears in the bottom right-hand corner is the end result calculated according to arithmetic operator(s) and chess move(s) as indicated by darker arrow(s).

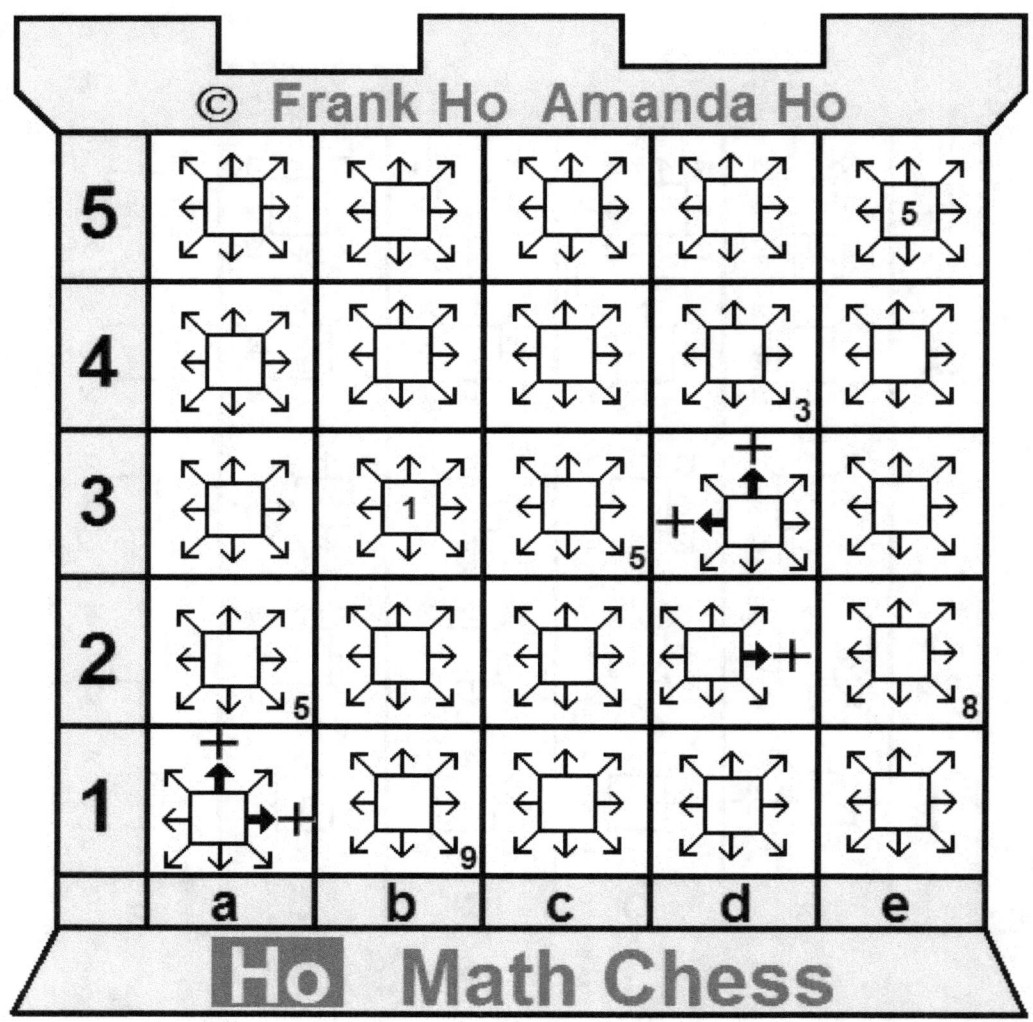

Ho Math Chess 何数棋谜 益智健脑非药物良方
Frankho Puzzle for KIDS – Brain Fitness Workbook

© 2007 — 2016 Frank Ho, Amanda Ho all rights reserved www.mathandchess.com

Frankho Puzzle™ # 21

Rule All the digits 1 to 5 must appear exactly once in every row and column. The number appears in the bottom right-hand corner is the end result calculated according to arithmetic operator(s) and chess move(s) as indicated by darker arrow(s).

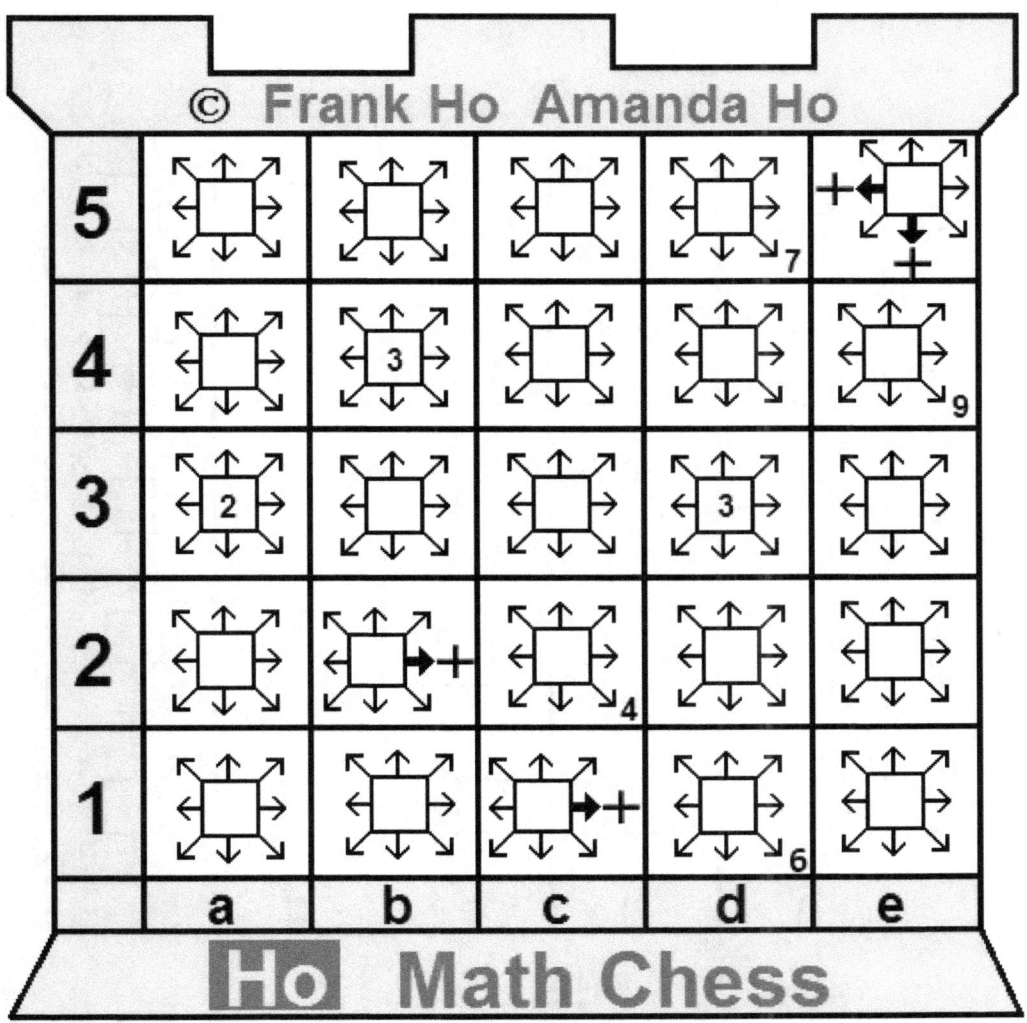

Frankho Puzzle™ # 22

Rule All the digits 1 to 5 must appear exactly once in every row and column. The number appears in the bottom right-hand corner is the end result calculated according to arithmetic operator(s) and chess move(s) as indicated by darker arrow(s).

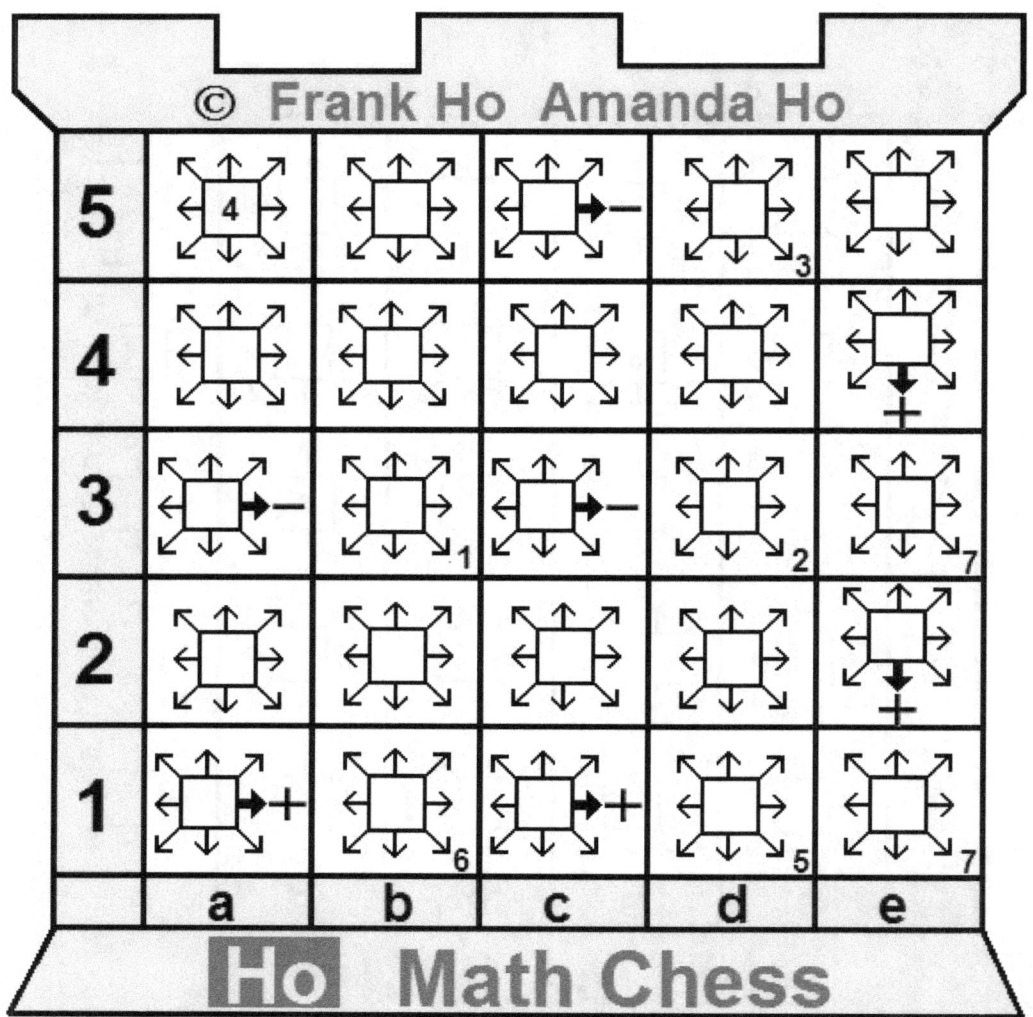

Ho Math Chess 何数棋谜 益智健脑非药物良方
Frankho Puzzle for KIDS – Brain Fitness Workbook
© 2007 — 2016 Frank Ho, Amanda Ho all rights reserved www.mathandchess.com

Frankho Puzzle™ # 23

Rule All the digits 1 to 5 must appear exactly once in every row and column. The number appears in the bottom right-hand corner is the end result calculated according to arithmetic operator(s) and chess move(s) as indicated by darker arrow(s).

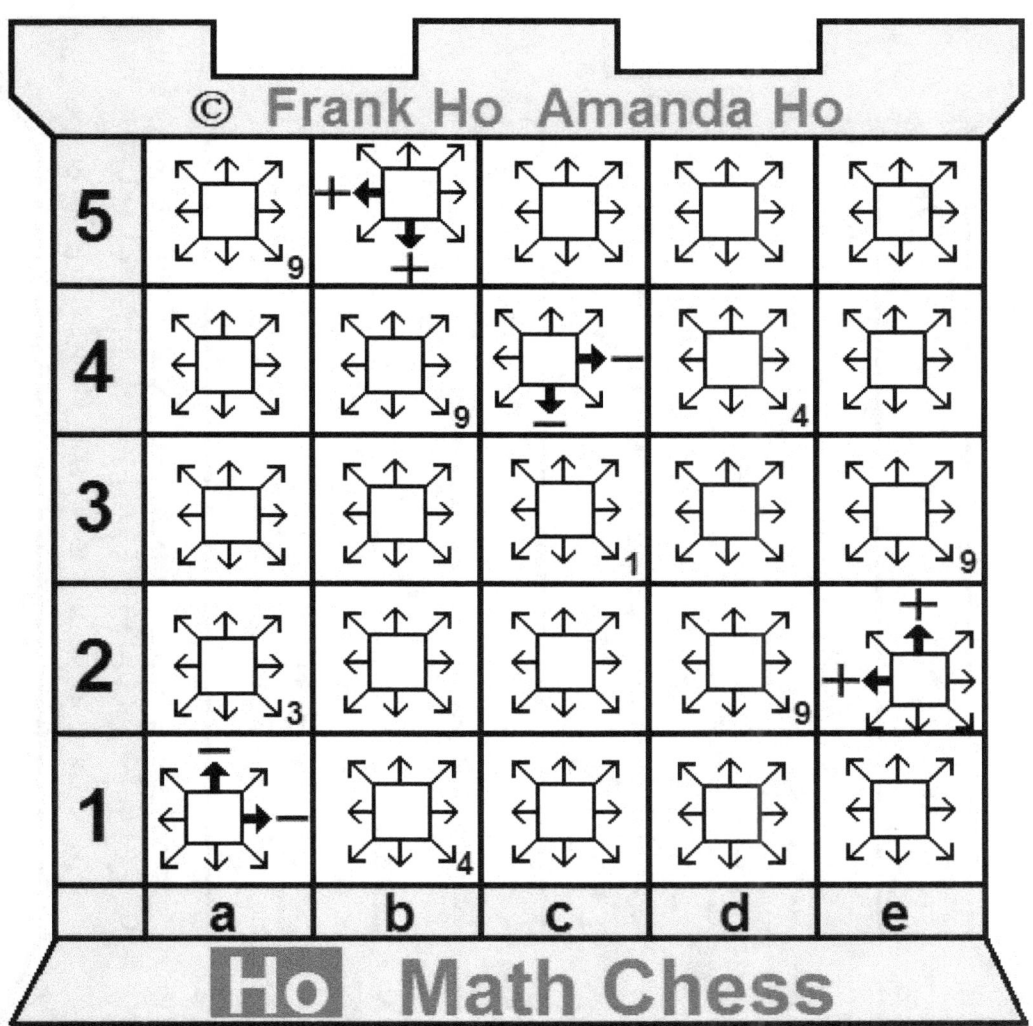

Ho Math Chess 何数棋谜 益智健脑非药物良方
Frankho Puzzle for KIDS – Brain Fitness Workbook
© 2007 — 2016 Frank Ho, Amanda Ho all rights reserved www.mathandchess.com

Frankho Puzzle™ # 24

Rule All the digits 1 to 5 must appear exactly once in every row and column. The number appears in the bottom right-hand corner is the end result calculated according to arithmetic operator(s) and chess move(s) as indicated by darker arrow(s).

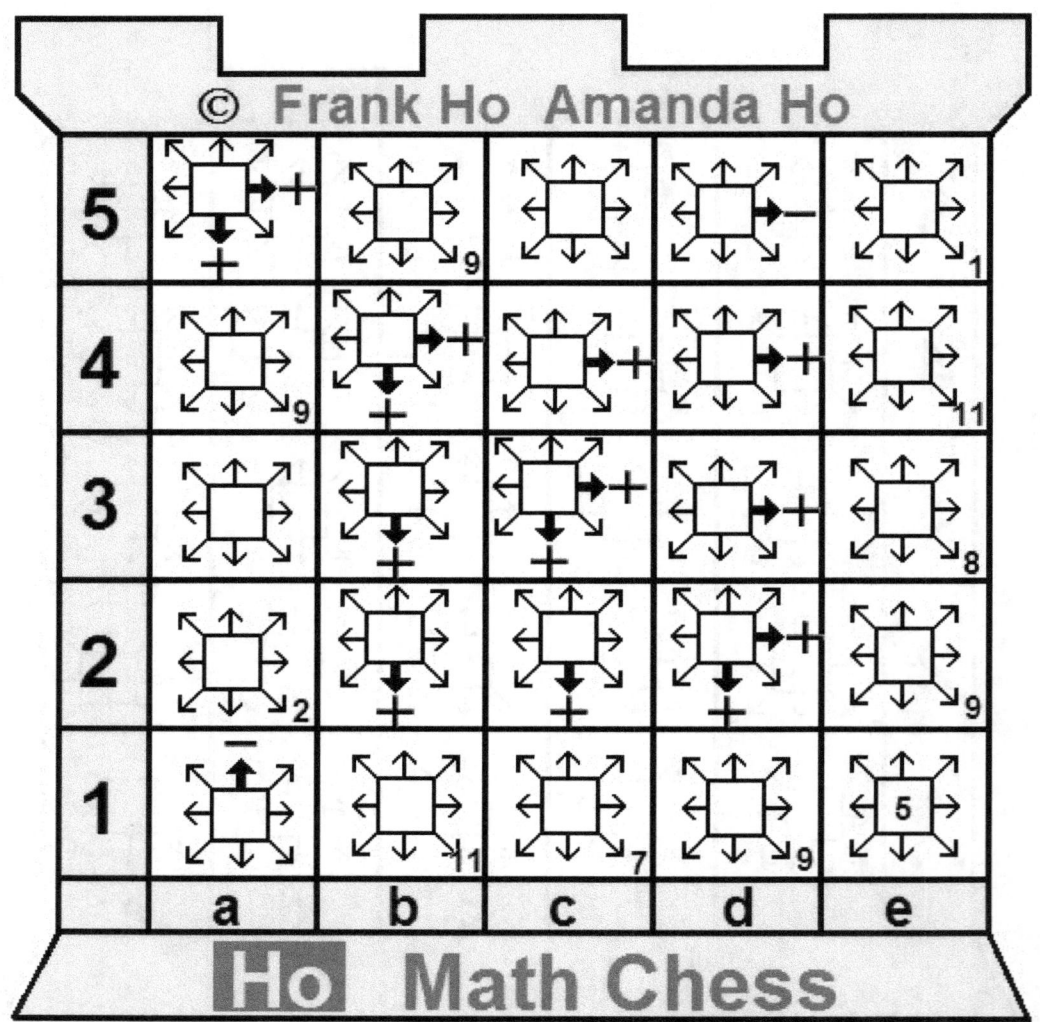

Ho Math Chess 何数棋谜 益智健脑非药物良方
Frankho Puzzle for KIDS – Brain Fitness Workbook
© 2007 — 2016 Frank Ho, Amanda Ho all rights reserved www.mathandchess.com

Frankho Puzzle™ # 25

Rule All the digits 1 to 5 must appear exactly once in every row and column. The number appears in the bottom right-hand corner is the end result calculated according to arithmetic operator(s) and chess move(s) as indicated by darker arrow(s).

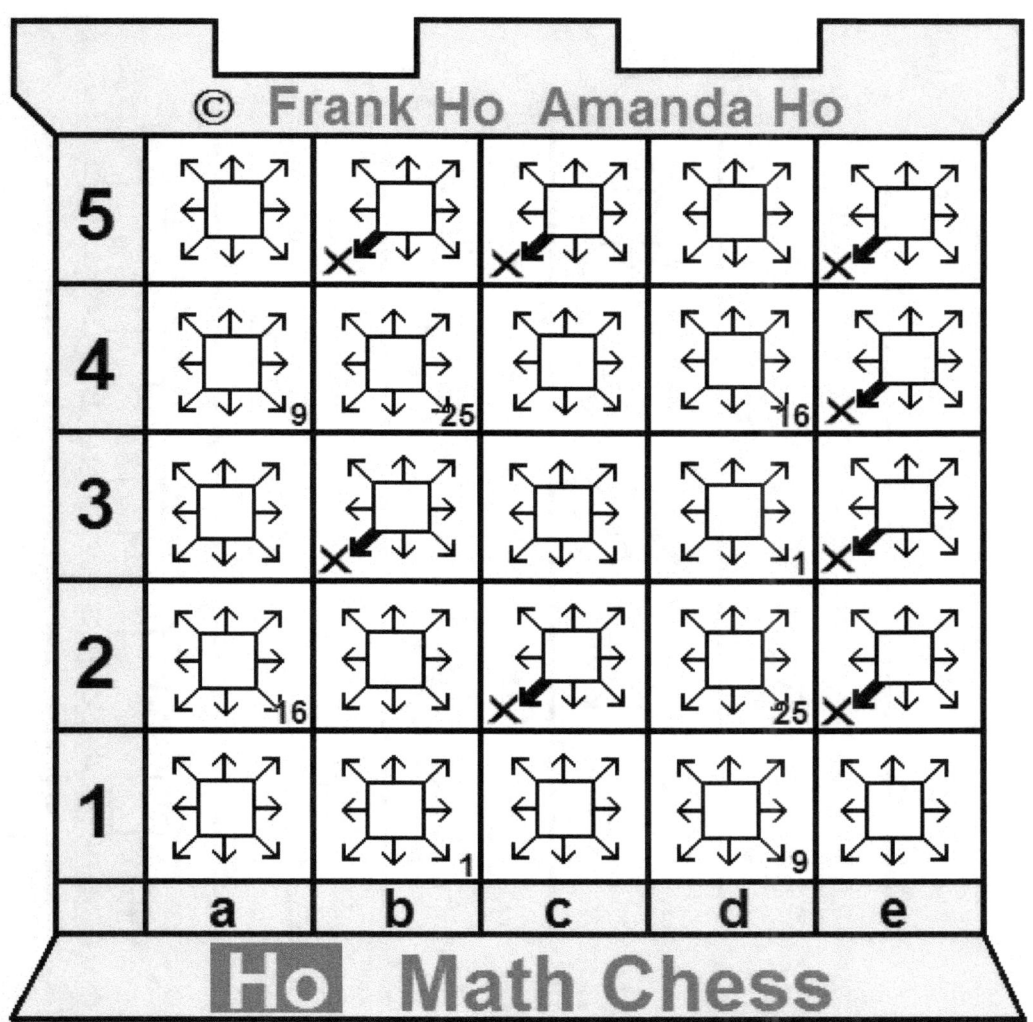

Frankho Puzzle™ # 26

Rule All the digits 1 to 5 must appear exactly once in every row and column. The number appears in the bottom right-hand corner is the end result calculated according to arithmetic operator(s) and chess move(s) as indicated by darker arrow(s).

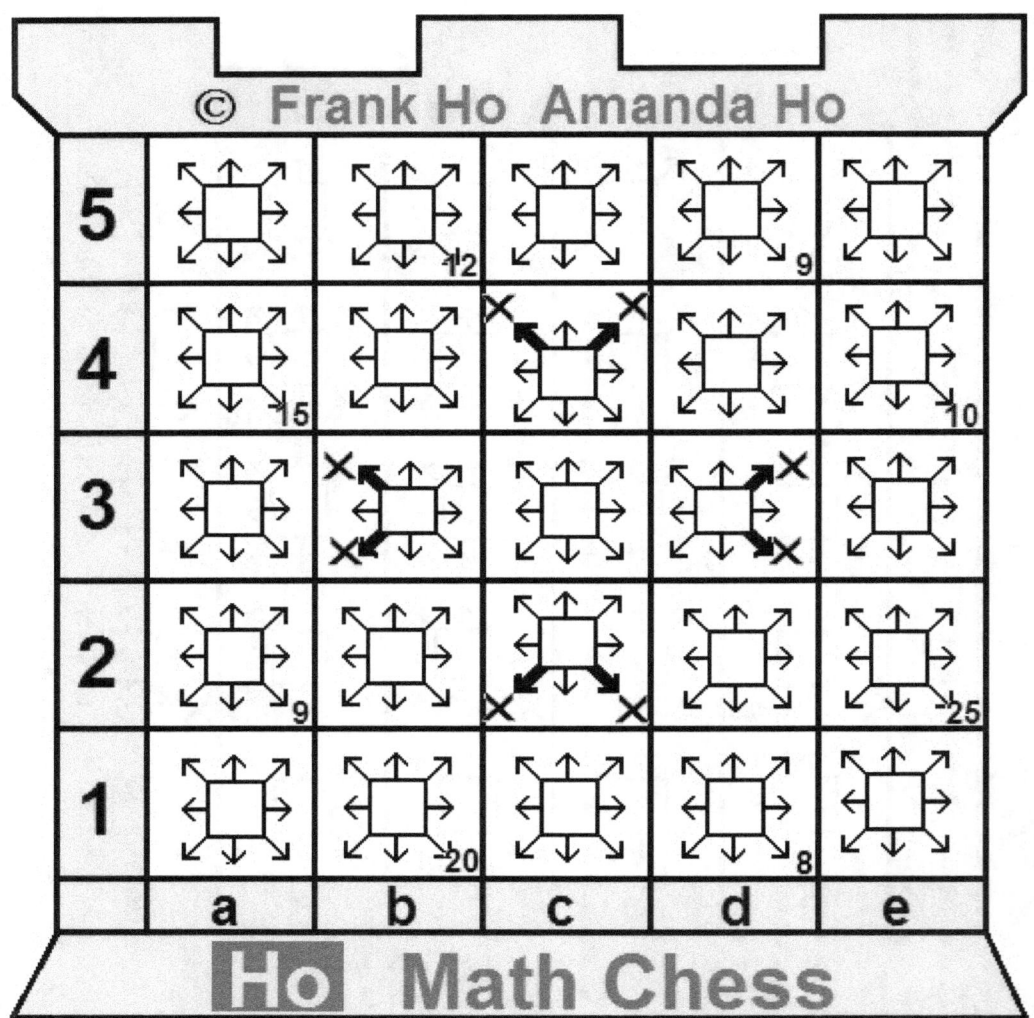

Frankho Puzzle™ # 27

Rule All the digits 1 to 5 must appear exactly once in every row and column. The number appears in the bottom right-hand corner is the end result calculated according to arithmetic operator(s) and chess move(s) as indicated by darker arrow(s).

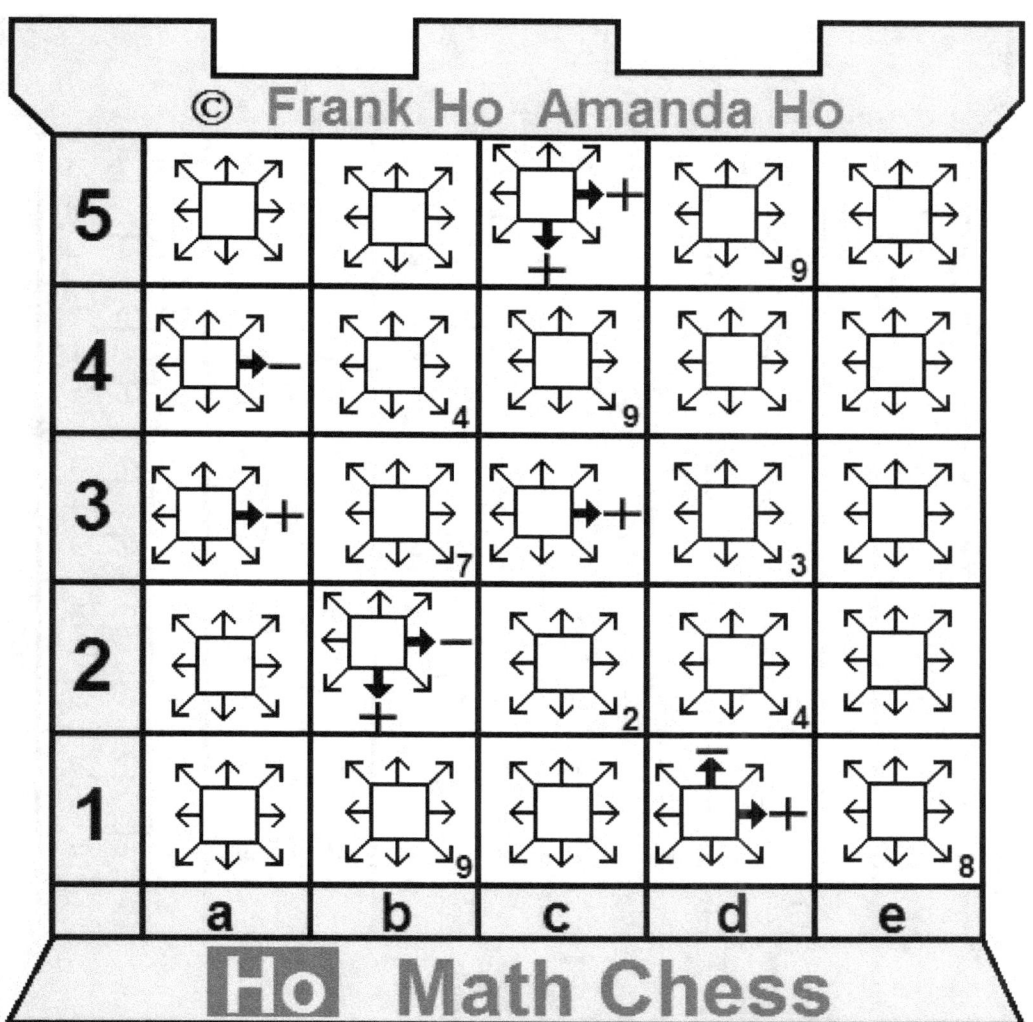

Ho Math Chess
何数棋谜 益智健脑非药物良方
Frankho Puzzle for KIDS – Brain Fitness Workbook
© 2007 — 2016 Frank Ho, Amanda Ho all rights reserved www.mathandchess.com

Frankho Puzzle™ # 28

Rule All the digits 1 to 5 must appear exactly once in every row and column. The number appears in the bottom right-hand corner is the end result calculated according to arithmetic operator(s) and chess move(s) as indicated by darker arrow(s).

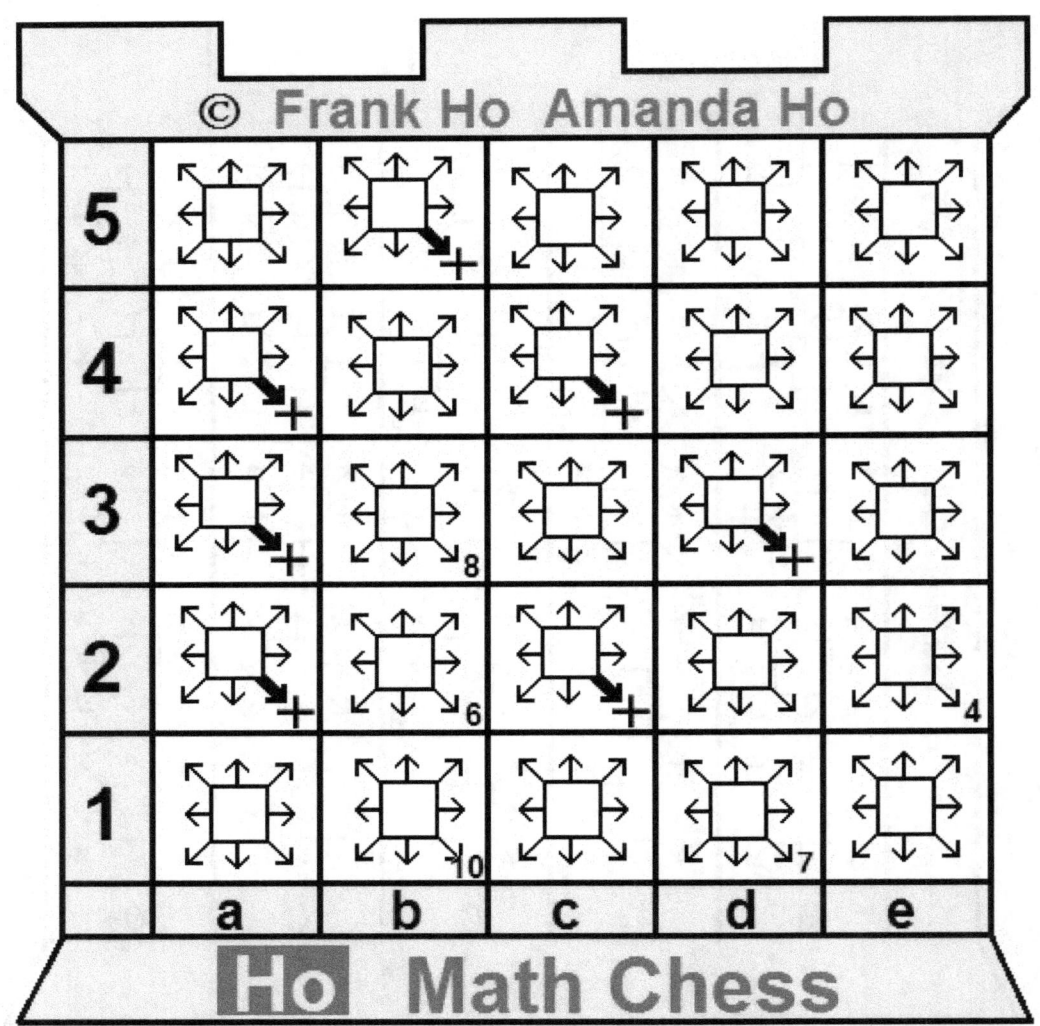

Ho Math Chess 何数棋谜 益智健脑非药物良方
Frankho Puzzle for KIDS – Brain Fitness Workbook
© 2007 — 2016 Frank Ho, Amanda Ho all rights reserved www.mathandchess.com

Frankho Puzzle™ # 29

Rule All the digits 1 to 5 must appear exactly once in every row and column. The number appears in the bottom right-hand corner is the end result calculated according to arithmetic operator(s) and chess move(s) as indicated by darker arrow(s).

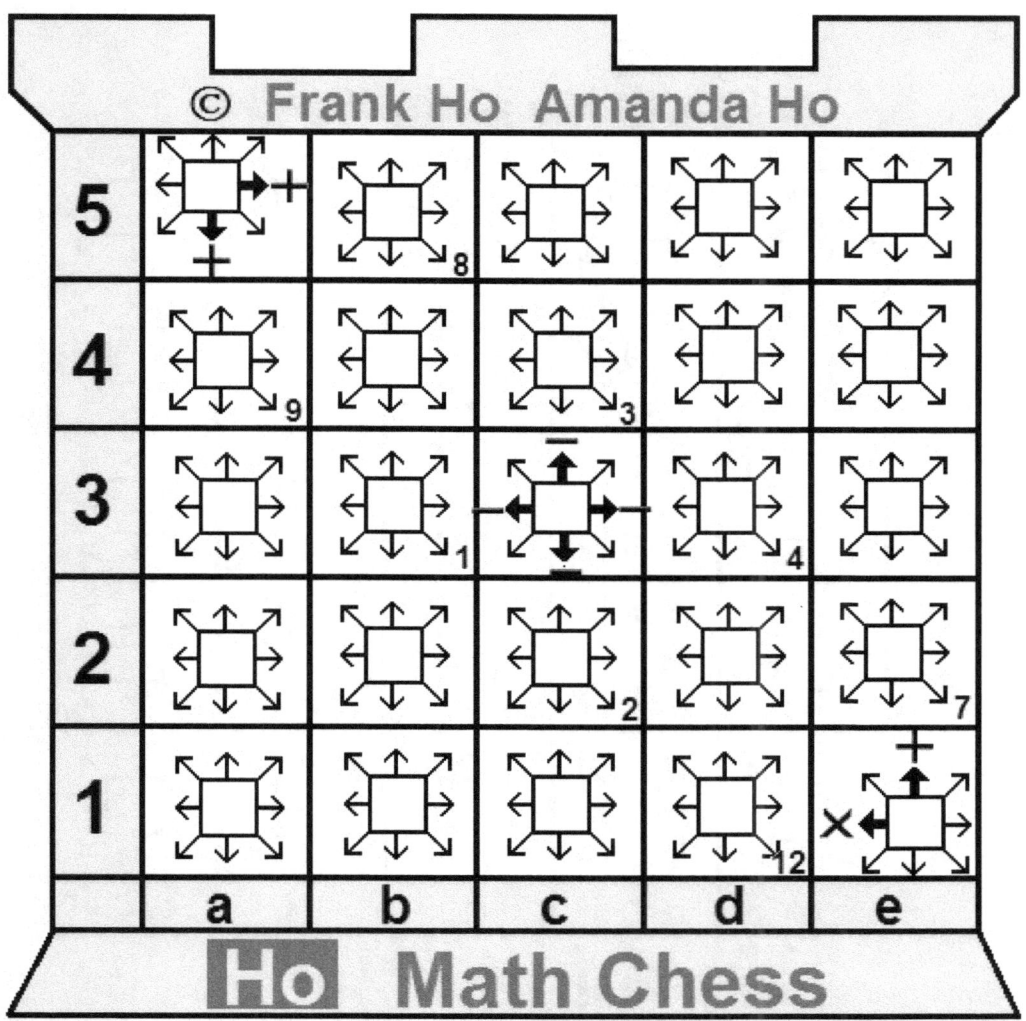

Ho Math Chess 何数棋谜 益智健脑非药物良方
Frankho Puzzle for KIDS – Brain Fitness Workbook

© 2007 — 2016 Frank Ho, Amanda Ho all rights reserved www.mathandchess.com

Frankho Puzzle™ # 30

Rule All the digits 1 to 5 must appear exactly once in every row and column. The number appears in the bottom right-hand corner is the end result calculated according to arithmetic operator(s) and chess move(s) as indicated by darker arrow(s).

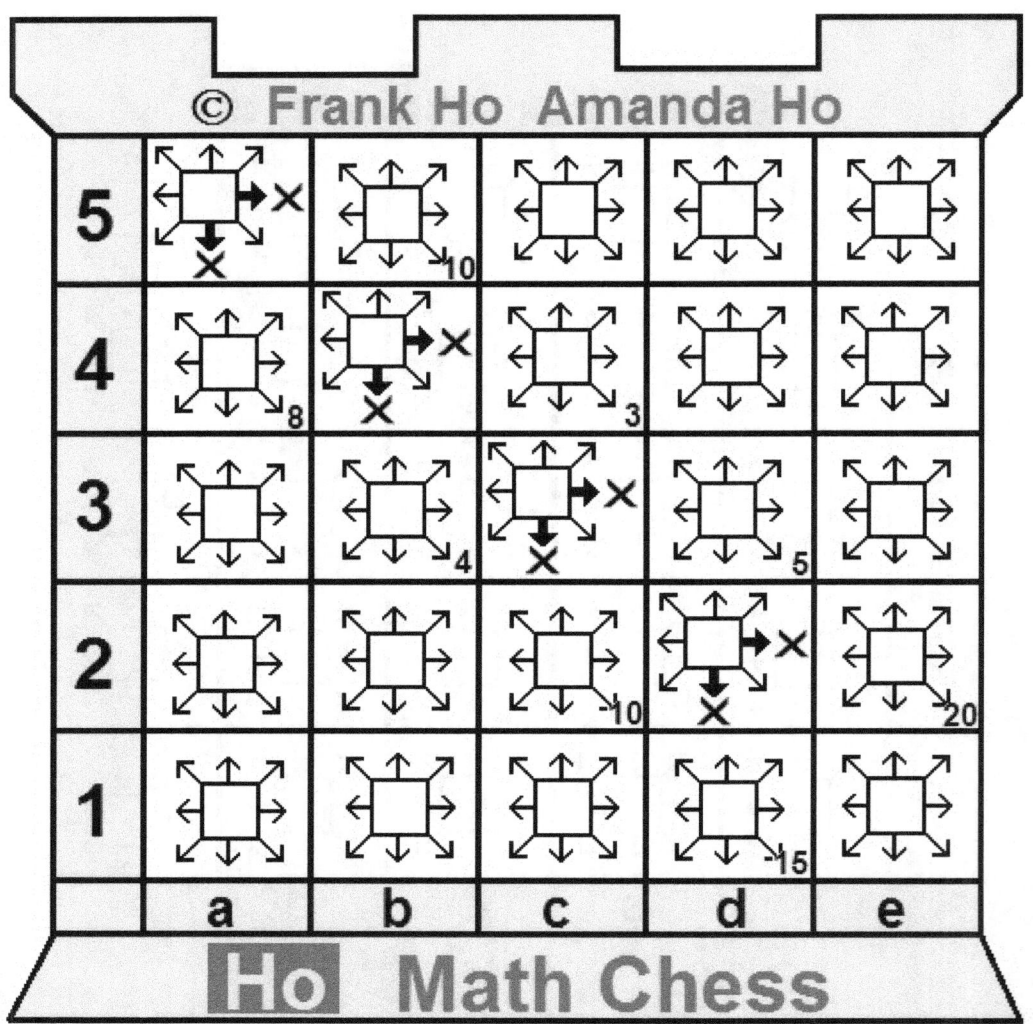

Ho Math Chess 何数棋谜 益智健脑非药物良方
Frankho Puzzle for KIDS – Brain Fitness Workbook

© 2007 — 2016 Frank Ho, Amanda Ho all rights reserved www.mathandchess.com

Frankho Puzzle™ # 31

Rule All the digits 1 to 5 must appear exactly once in every row and column. The number appears in the bottom right-hand corner is the end result calculated according to arithmetic operator(s) and chess move(s) as indicated by darker arrow(s).

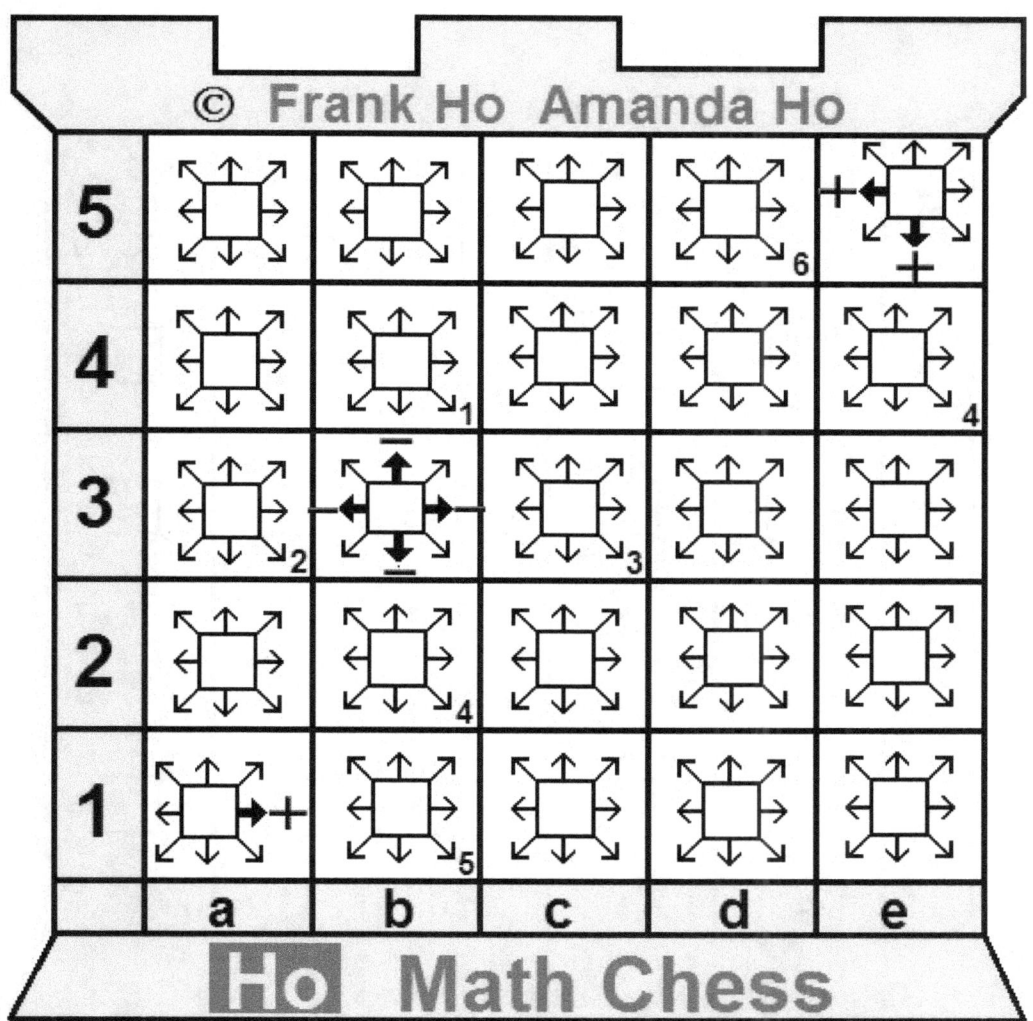

Ho Math Chess 何数棋谜 益智健脑非药物良方
Frankho Puzzle for KIDS – Brain Fitness Workbook
© 2007 — 2016 Frank Ho, Amanda Ho all rights reserved www.mathandchess.com

Frankho Puzzle™ # 32

Rule All the digits 1 to 5 must appear exactly once in every row and column. The number appears in the bottom right-hand corner is the end result calculated according to arithmetic operator(s) and chess move(s) as indicated by darker arrow(s).

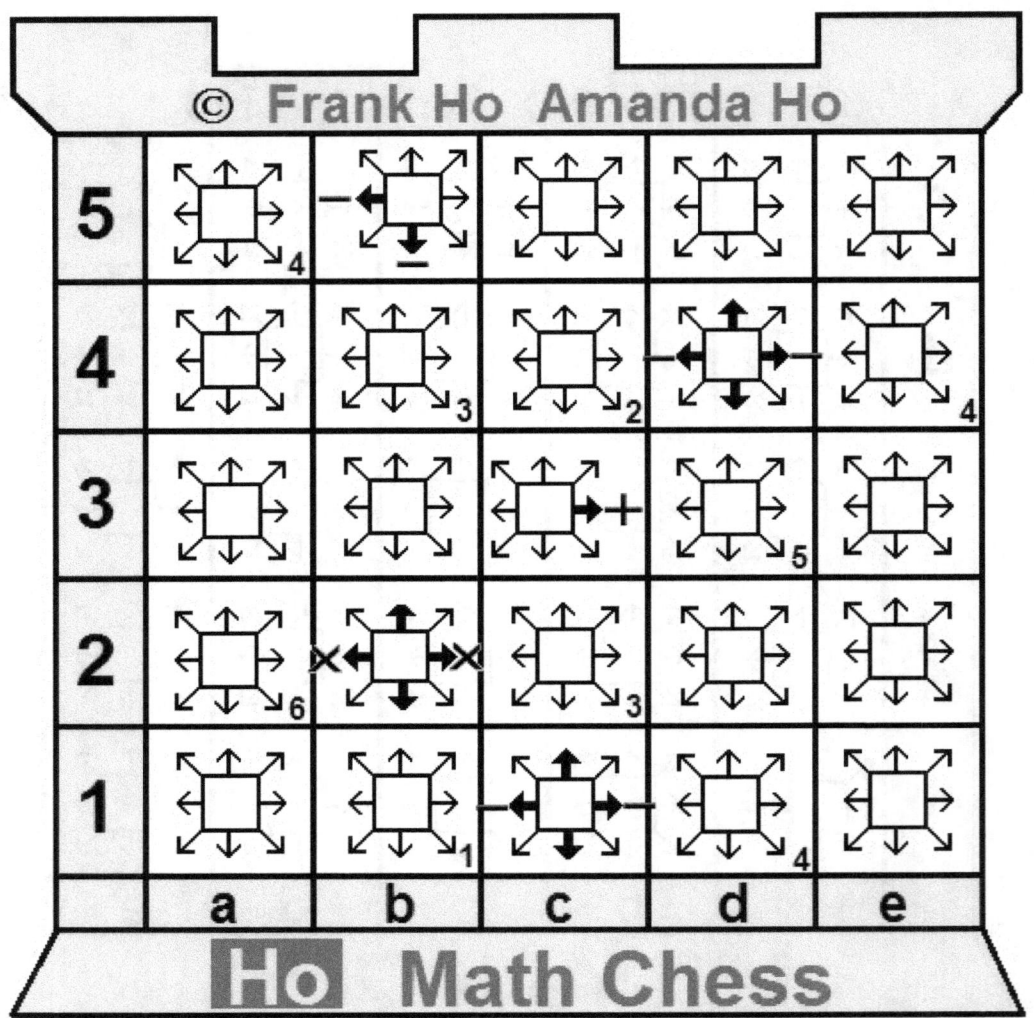

36

Ho Math Chess 何数棋谜 益智健脑非药物良方
Frankho Puzzle for KIDS – Brain Fitness Workbook
© 2007 — 2016 Frank Ho, Amanda Ho all rights reserved www.mathandchess.com

Frankho Puzzle™ # 33

Rule All the digits 1 to 5 must appear exactly once in every row and column. The number appears in the bottom right-hand corner is the end result calculated according to arithmetic operator(s) and chess move(s) as indicated by darker arrow(s).

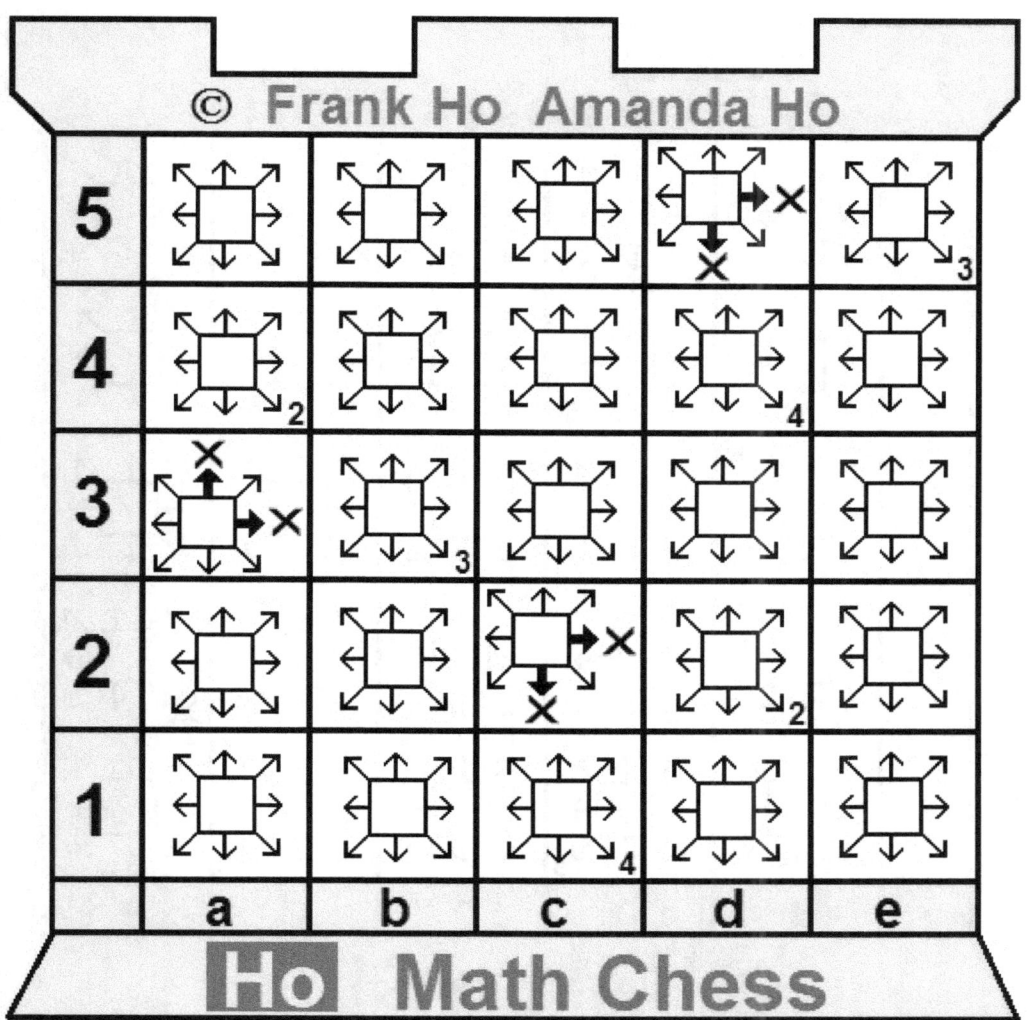

Ho Math Chess 何数棋谜 益智健脑非药物良方
Frankho Puzzle for KIDS – Brain Fitness Workbook
© 2007 – 2016 Frank Ho, Amanda Ho all rights reserved www.mathandchess.com

Frankho Puzzle™ # 34

Rule All the digits 1 to 5 must appear exactly once in every row and column. The number appears in the bottom right-hand corner is the end result calculated according to arithmetic operator(s) and chess move(s) as indicated by darker arrow(s).

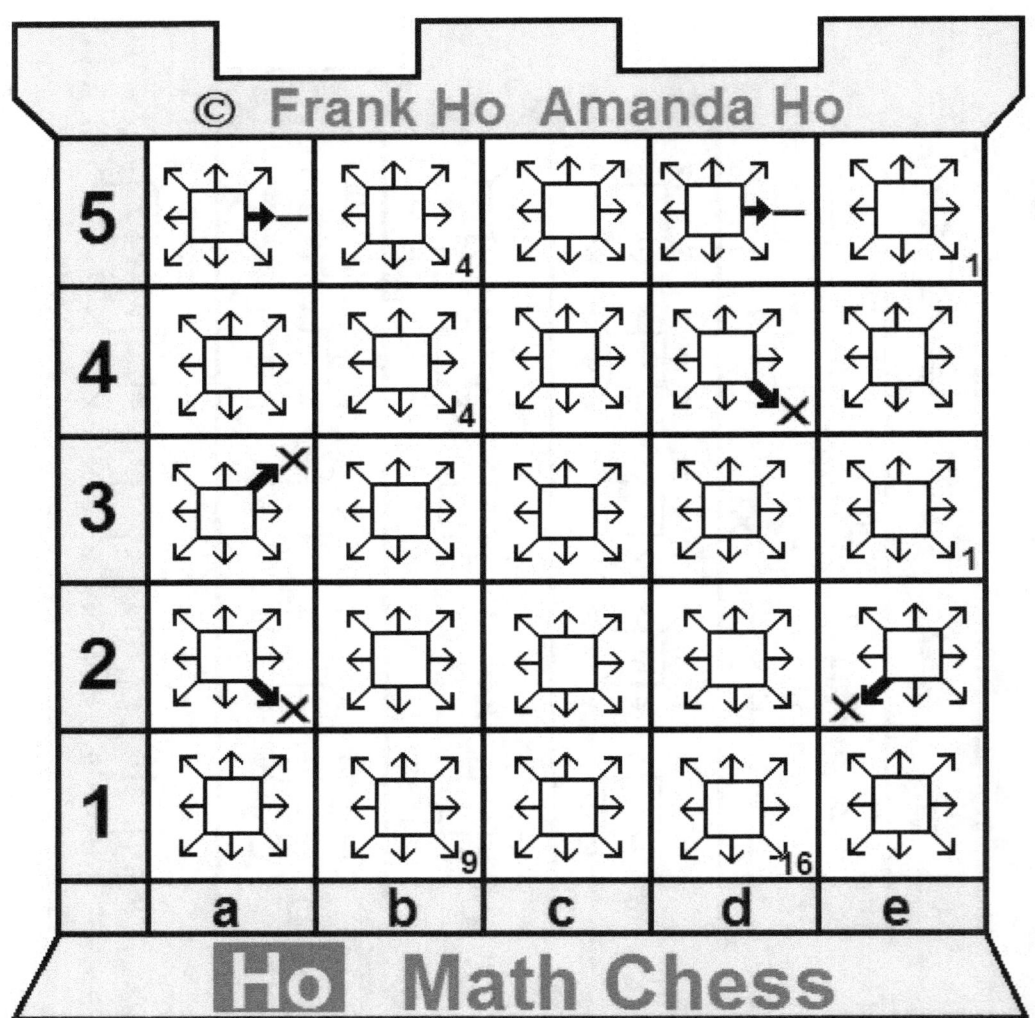

Ho Math Chess 何数棋谜 益智健脑非药物良方
Frankho Puzzle for KIDS – Brain Fitness Workbook
© 2007 — 2016 Frank Ho, Amanda Ho all rights reserved www.mathandchess.com

Frankho Puzzle™ # 35

Rule All the digits 1 to 5 must appear exactly once in every row and column. The number appears in the bottom right-hand corner is the end result calculated according to arithmetic operator(s) and chess move(s) as indicated by darker arrow(s).

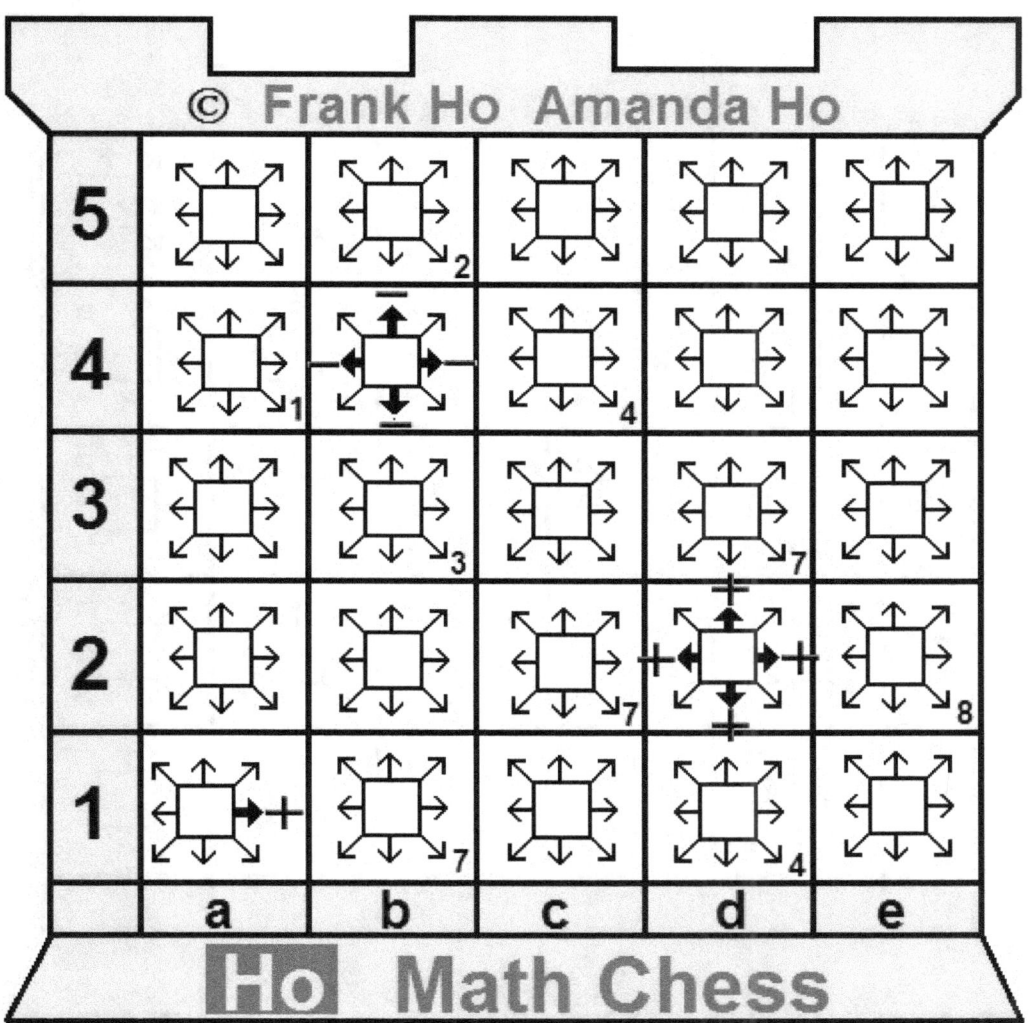

Ho Math Chess 何数棋谜 益智健脑非药物良方
Frankho Puzzle for KIDS – Brain Fitness Workbook
© 2007 — 2016 Frank Ho, Amanda Ho all rights reserved www.mathandchess.com

Frankho Puzzle™ # 36

Rule All the digits 1 to 5 must appear exactly once in every row and column. The number appears in the bottom right-hand corner is the end result calculated according to arithmetic operator(s) and chess move(s) as indicated by darker arrow(s).

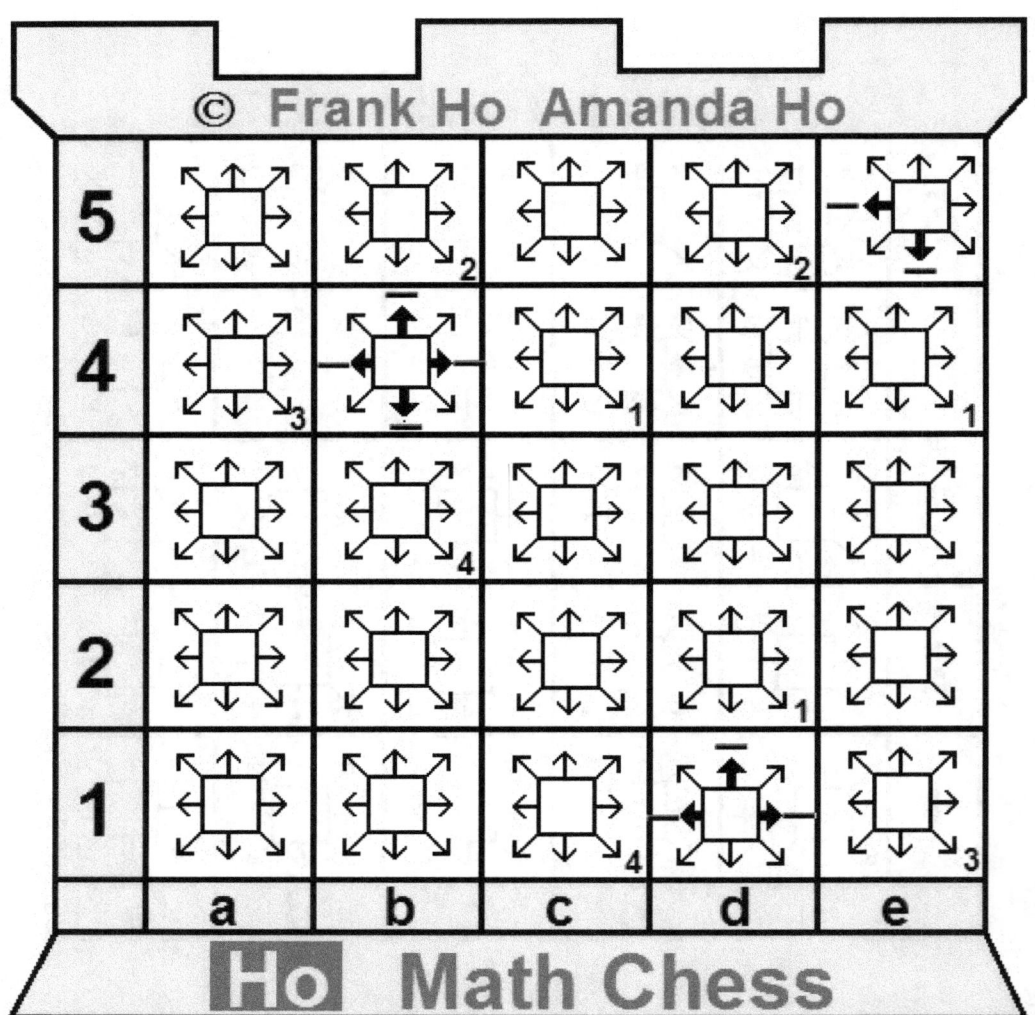

40

Ho Math Chess 何数棋谜 益智健脑非药物良方
Frankho Puzzle for KIDS – Brain Fitness Workbook
© 2007 — 2016 Frank Ho, Amanda Ho all rights reserved www.mathandchess.com

Frankho Puzzle™ # 37

Rule All the digits 1 to 5 must appear exactly once in every row and column. The number appears in the bottom right-hand corner is the end result calculated according to arithmetic operator(s) and chess move(s) as indicated by darker arrow(s).

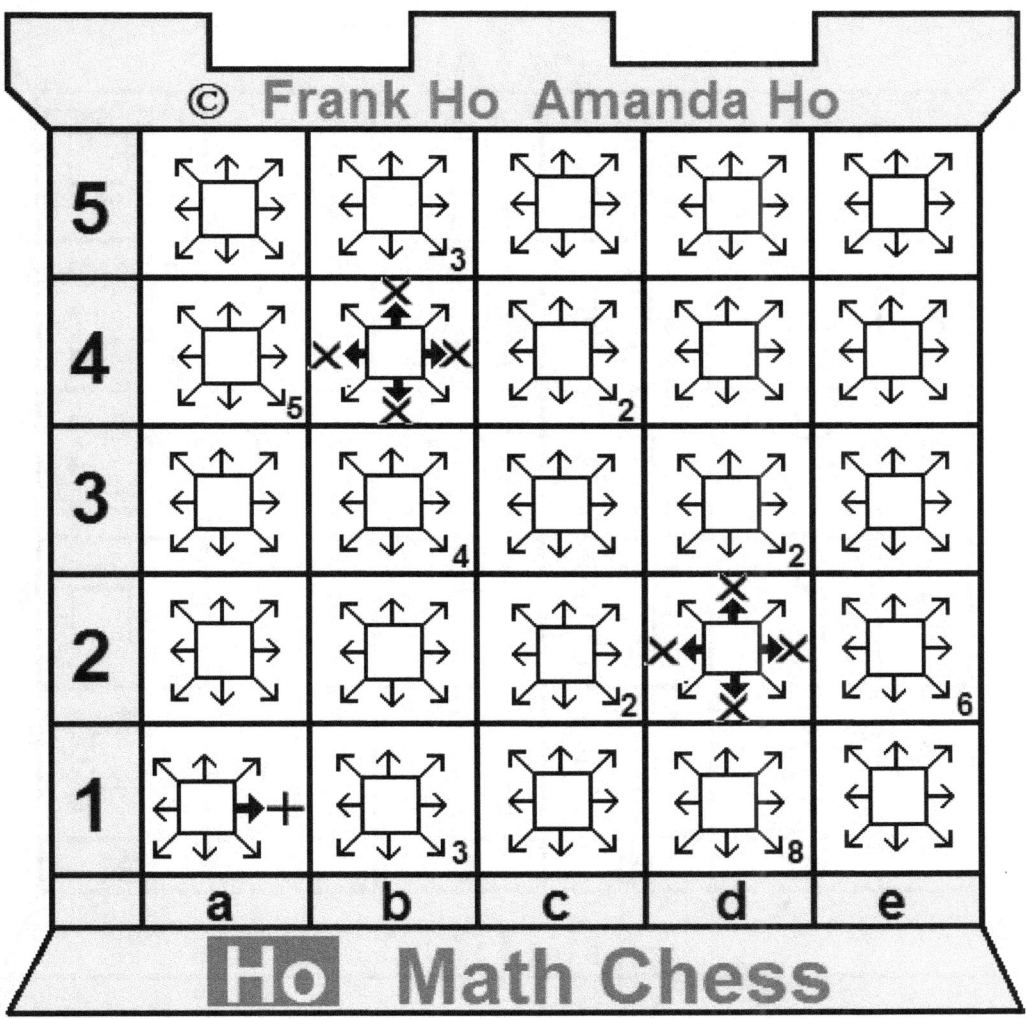

Ho Math Chess 何数棋谜 益智健脑非药物良方
Frankho Puzzle for KIDS – Brain Fitness Workbook

© 2007 — 2016 Frank Ho, Amanda Ho all rights reserved www.mathandchess.com

Frankho Puzzle™ # 38

Rule All the digits 1 to 5 must appear exactly once in every row and column. The number appears in the bottom right-hand corner is the end result calculated according to arithmetic operator(s) and chess move(s) as indicated by darker arrow(s).

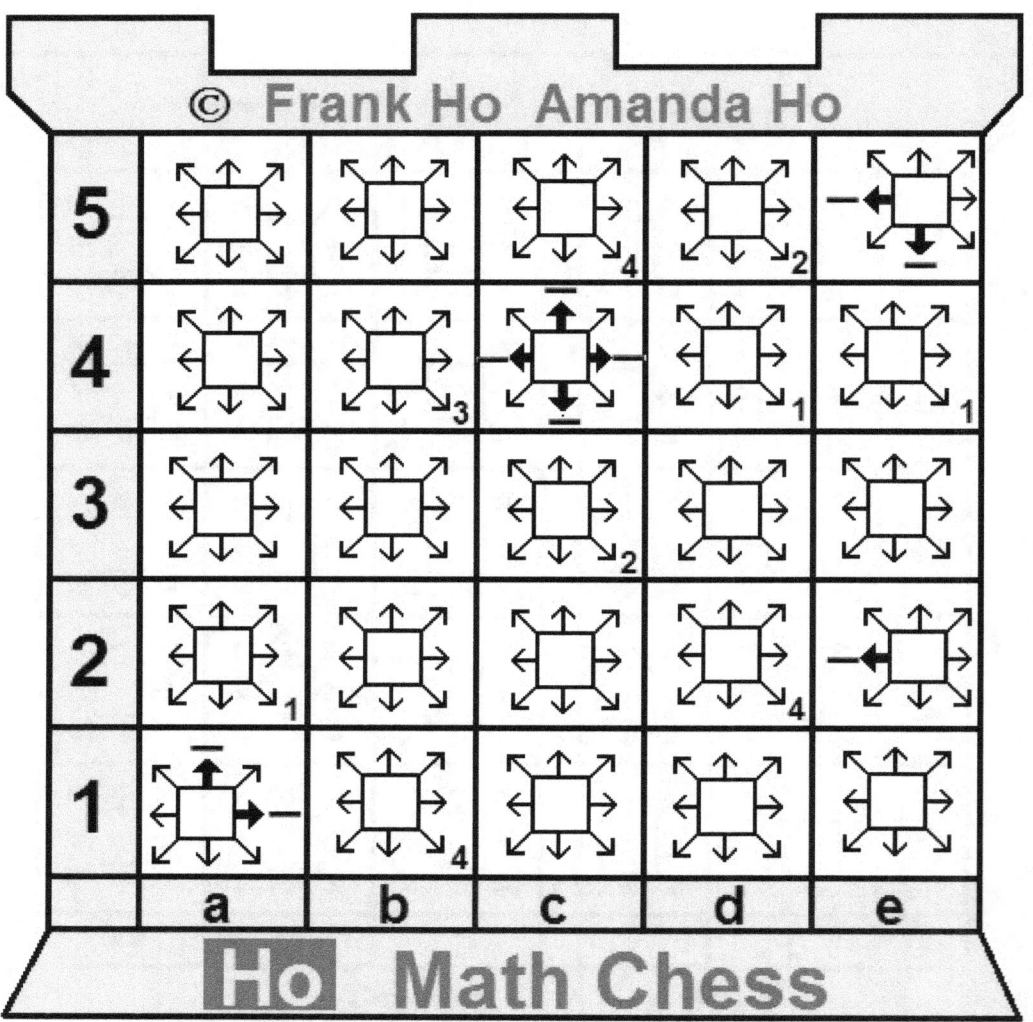

Ho Math Chess 何数棋谜 益智健脑非药物良方
Frankho Puzzle for KIDS – Brain Fitness Workbook
© 2007 – 2016 Frank Ho, Amanda Ho all rights reserved www.mathandchess.com

Frankho Puzzle™ # 39

Rule All the digits 1 to 5 must appear exactly once in every row and column. The number appears in the bottom right-hand corner is the end result calculated according to arithmetic operator(s) and chess move(s) as indicated by darker arrow(s).

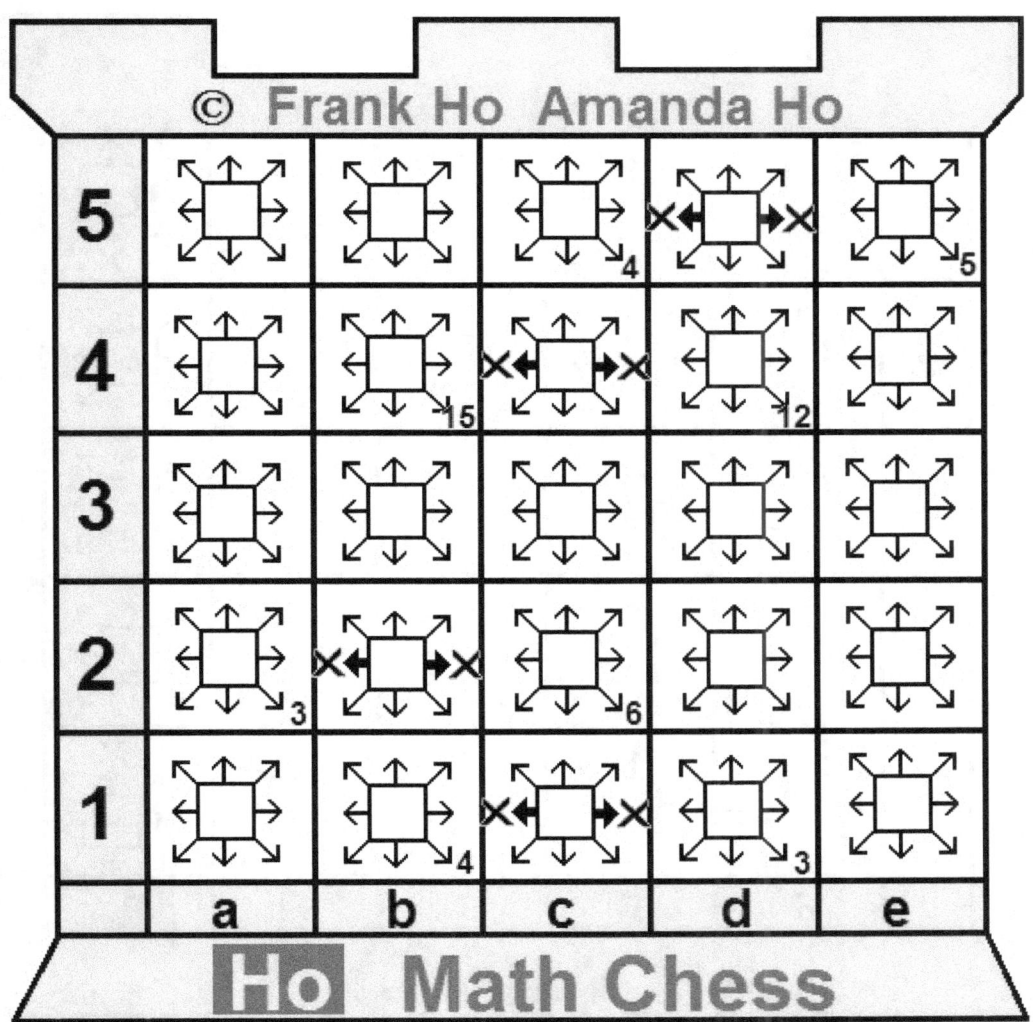

Frankho Puzzle™ # 40

Rule All the digits 1 to 5 must appear exactly once in every row and column. The number appears in the bottom right-hand corner is the end result calculated according to arithmetic operator(s) and chess move(s) as indicated by darker arrow(s).

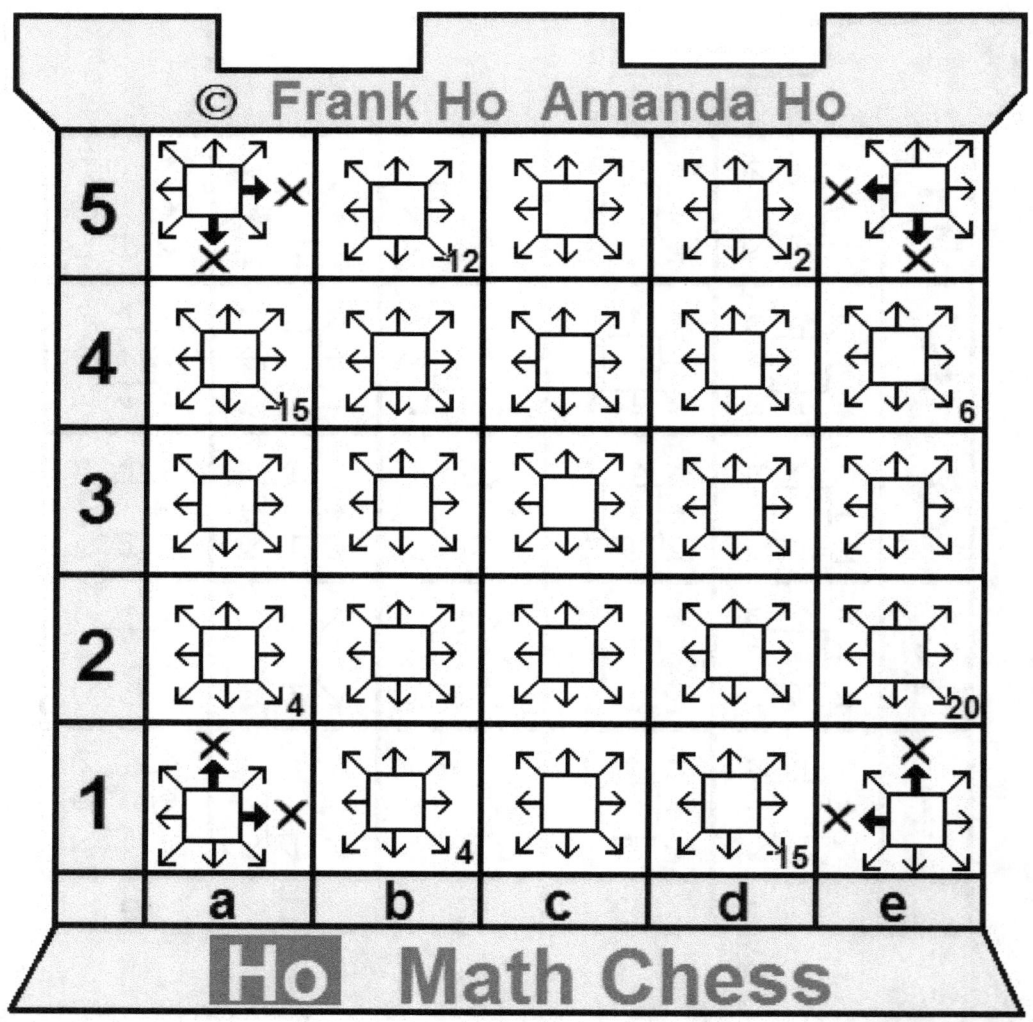

Ho Math Chess 何数棋谜 益智健脑非药物良方
Frankho Puzzle for KIDS – Brain Fitness Workbook
© 2007 — 2016 Frank Ho, Amanda Ho all rights reserved www.mathandchess.com

Frankho Puzzle™ # 41

Rule All the digits 1 to 5 must appear exactly once in every row and column. The number appears in the bottom right-hand corner is the end result calculated according to arithmetic operator(s) and chess move(s) as indicated by darker arrow(s).

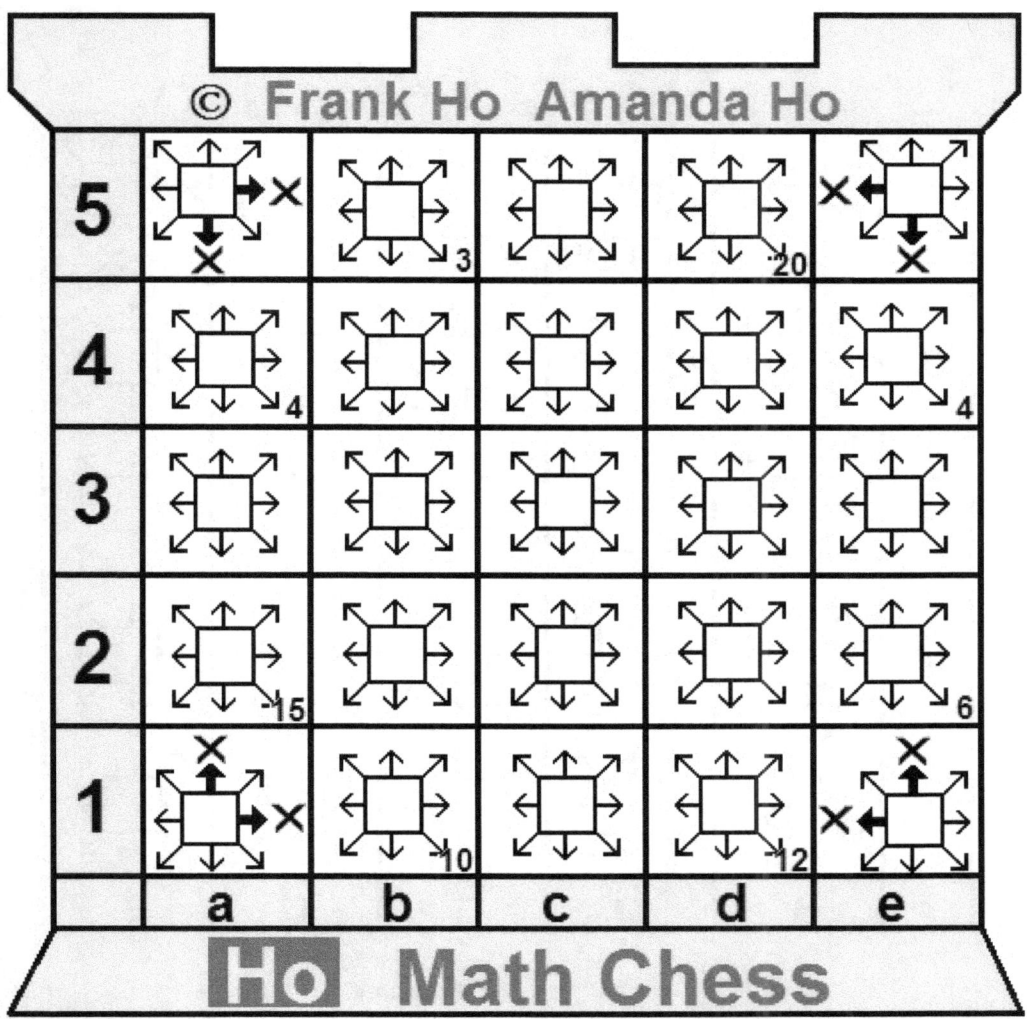

Frankho Puzzle™ # 42

Rule All the digits 1 to 5 must appear exactly once in every row and column. The number appears in the bottom right-hand corner is the end result calculated according to arithmetic operator(s) and chess move(s) as indicated by darker arrow(s).

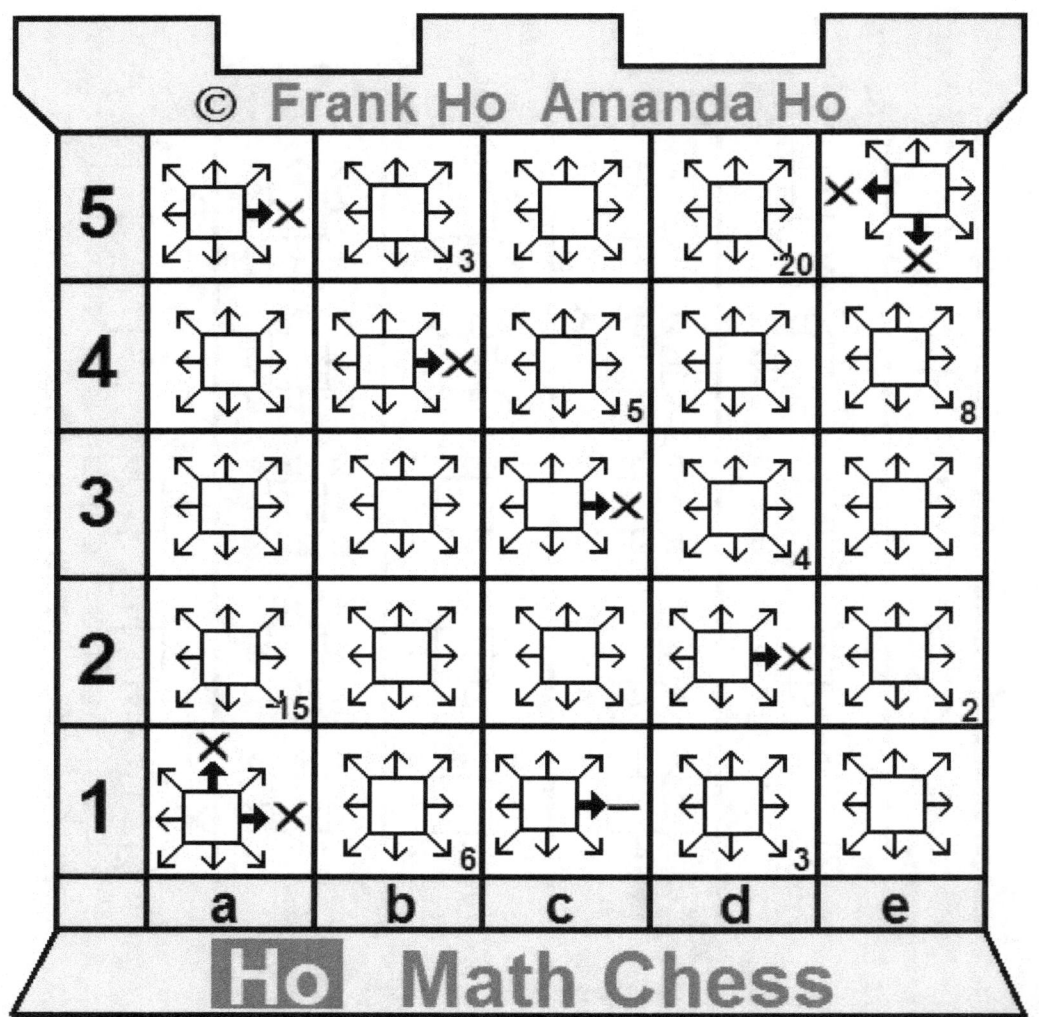

Ho Math Chess 何数棋谜 益智健脑非药物良方
Frankho Puzzle for KIDS – Brain Fitness Workbook
© 2007 — 2016 Frank Ho, Amanda Ho all rights reserved www.mathandchess.com

Frankho Puzzle™ # 43

Rule All the digits 1 to 5 must appear exactly once in every row and column. The number appears in the bottom right-hand corner is the end result calculated according to arithmetic operator(s) and chess move(s) as indicated by darker arrow(s).

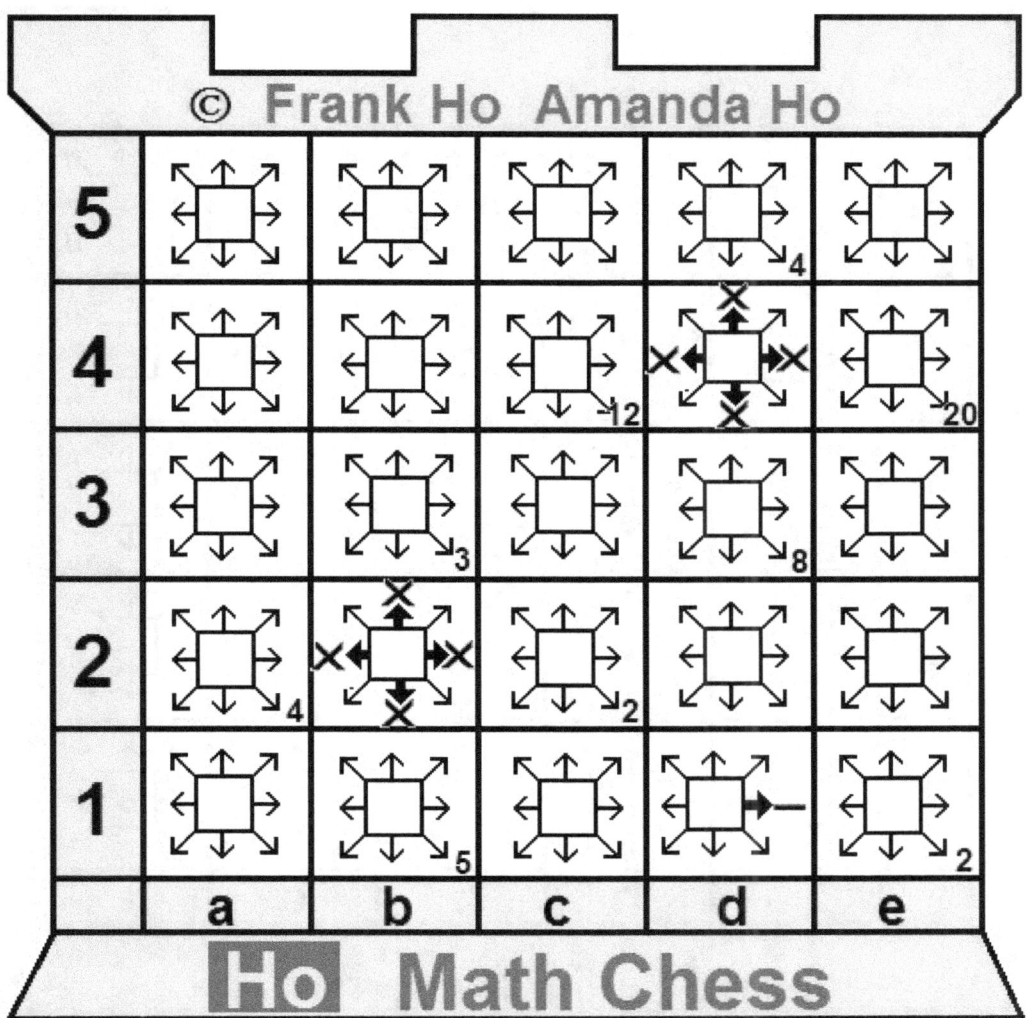

Ho Math Chess 何数棋谜 益智健脑非药物良方
Frankho Puzzle for KIDS – Brain Fitness Workbook
© 2007 — 2016 Frank Ho, Amanda Ho all rights reserved www.mathandchess.com

Frankho Puzzle™ # 44

Rule All the digits 1 to 5 must appear exactly once in every row and column. The number appears in the bottom right-hand corner is the end result calculated according to arithmetic operator(s) and chess move(s) as indicated by darker arrow(s).

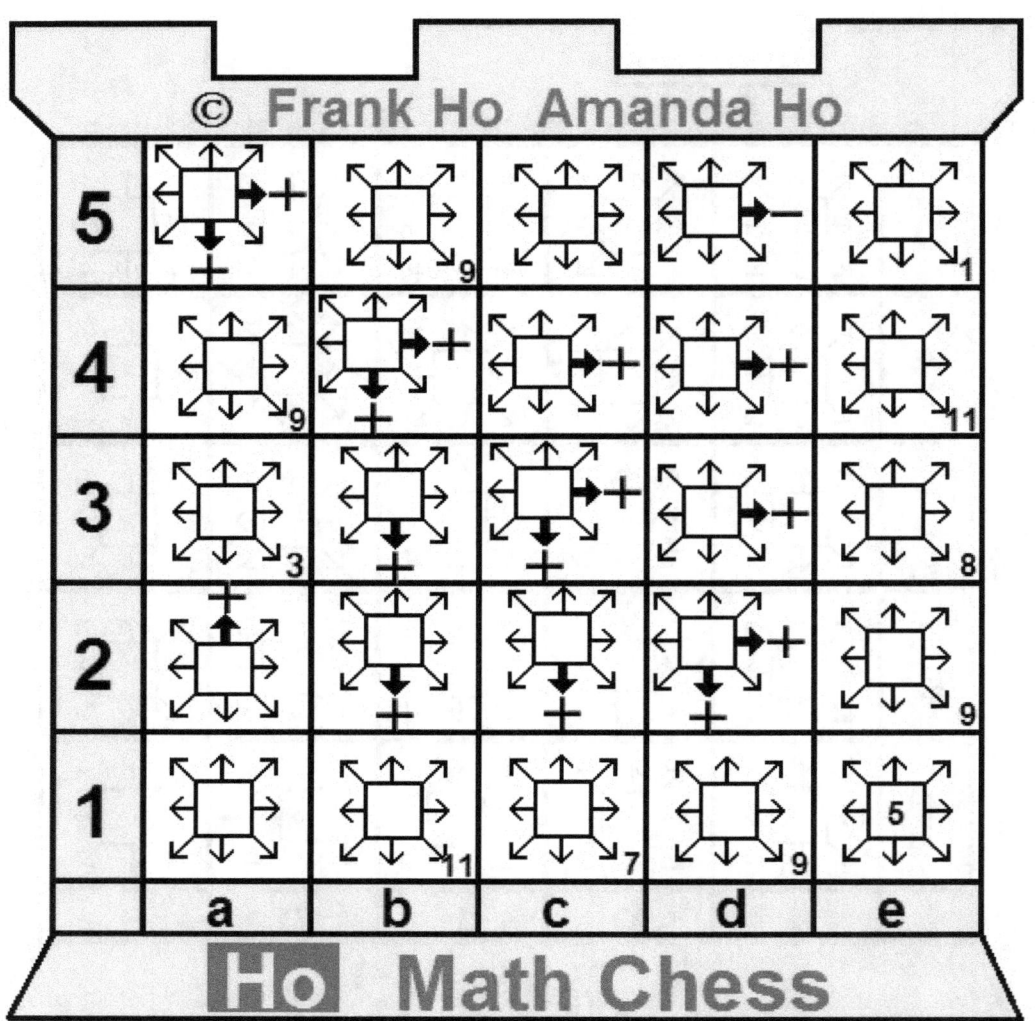

48

Frankho Puzzle™ # 45

Rule All the digits 1 to 5 must appear exactly once in every row and column. The number appears in the bottom right-hand corner is the end result calculated according to arithmetic operator(s) and chess move(s) as indicated by darker arrow(s).

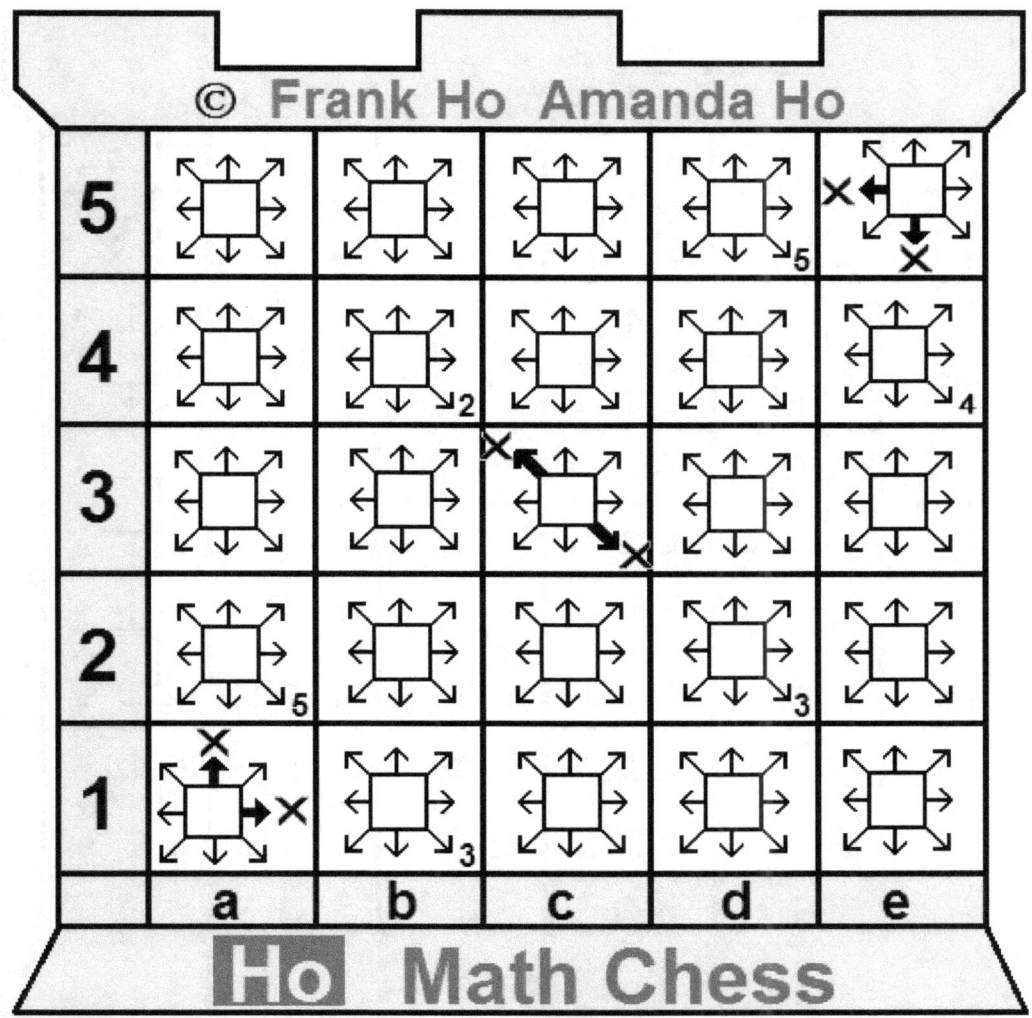

Frankho Puzzle™ # 46

Rule All the digits 1 to 5 must appear exactly once in every row and column. The number appears in the bottom right-hand corner is the end result calculated according to arithmetic operator(s) and chess move(s) as indicated by darker arrow(s).

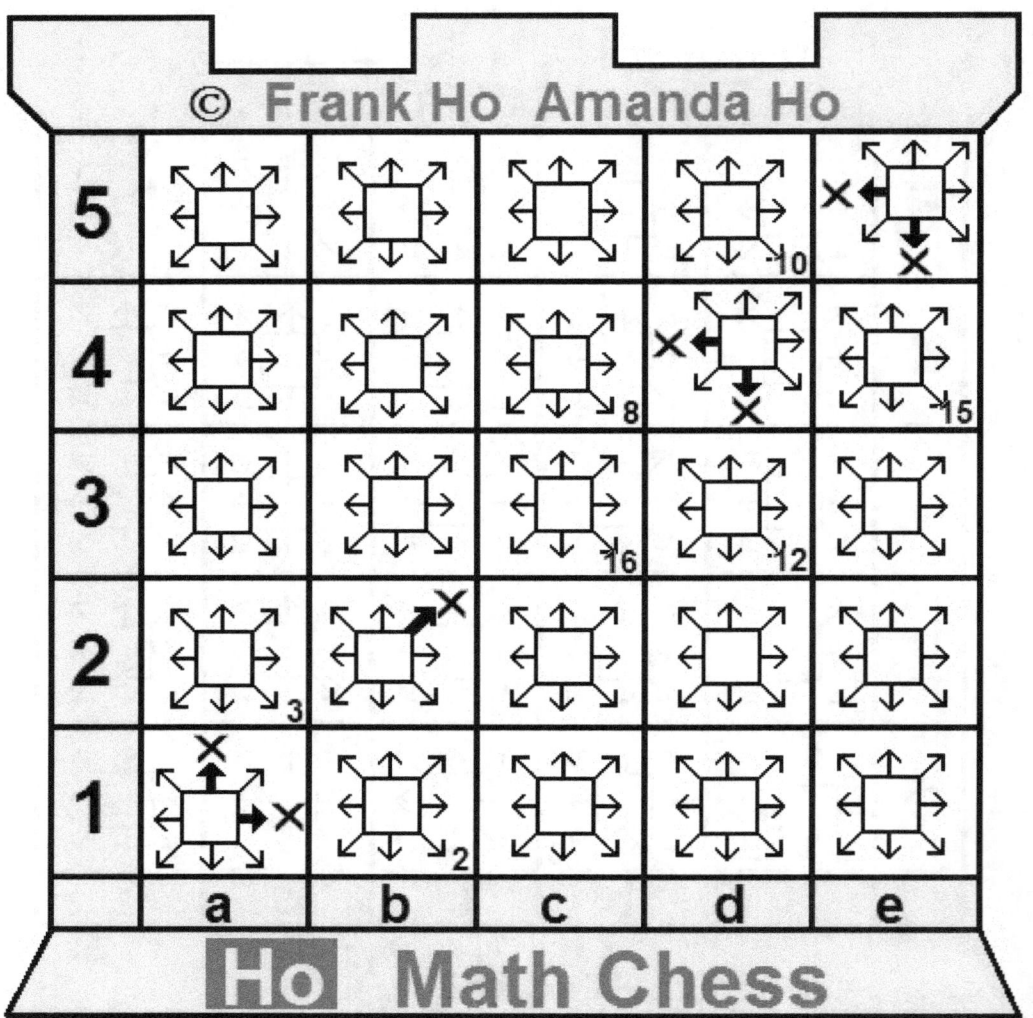

Ho Math Chess 何数棋谜 益智健脑非药物良方
Frankho Puzzle for KIDS – Brain Fitness Workbook
© 2007 — 2016 Frank Ho, Amanda Ho all rights reserved www.mathandchess.com

Frankho Puzzle™ # 47

Rule All the digits 1 to 5 must appear exactly once in every row and column. The number appears in the bottom right-hand corner is the end result calculated according to arithmetic operator(s) and chess move(s) as indicated by darker arrow(s).

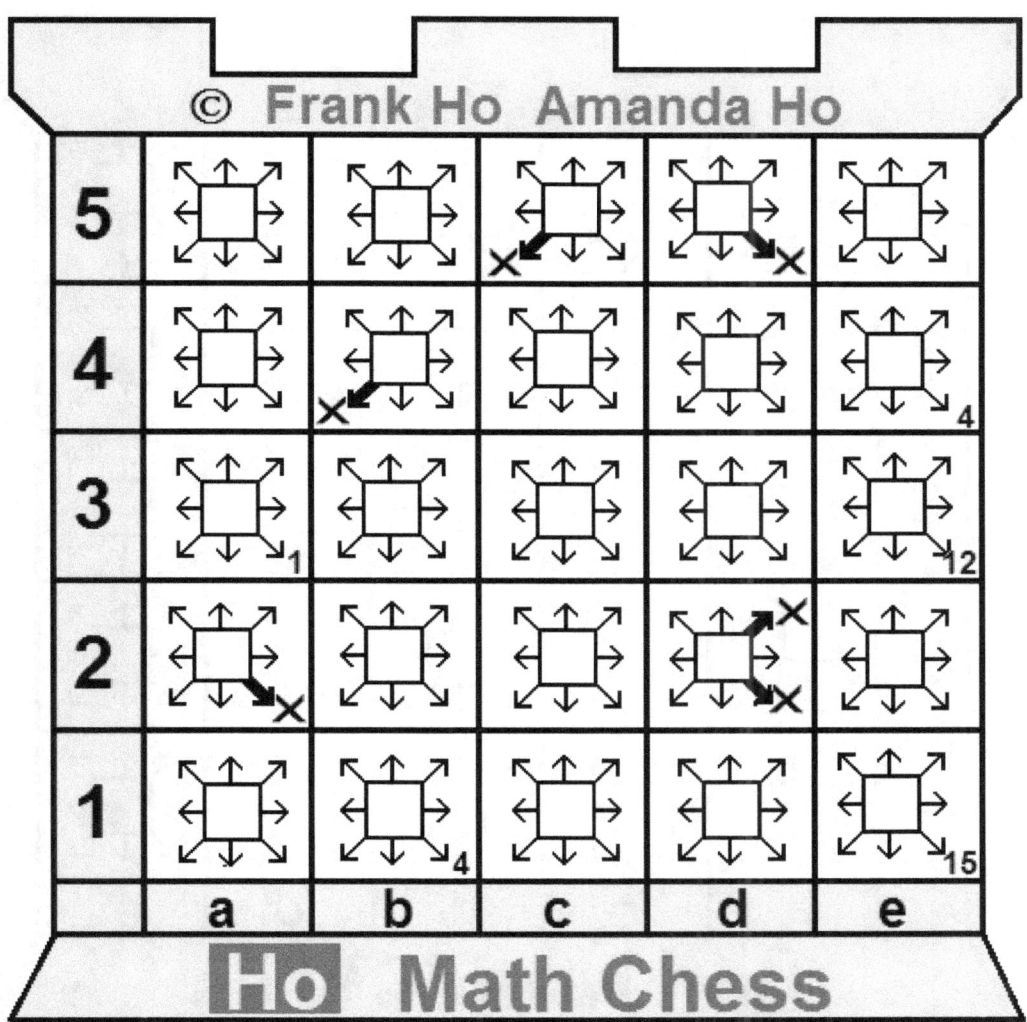

Ho Math Chess 何数棋谜 益智健脑非药物良方
Frankho Puzzle for KIDS – Brain Fitness Workbook
© 2007 – 2016 Frank Ho, Amanda Ho all rights reserved www.mathandchess.com

Frankho Puzzle™ # 48

Rule All the digits 1 to 5 must appear exactly once in every row and column. The number appears in the bottom right-hand corner is the end result calculated according to arithmetic operator(s) and chess move(s) as indicated by darker arrow(s).

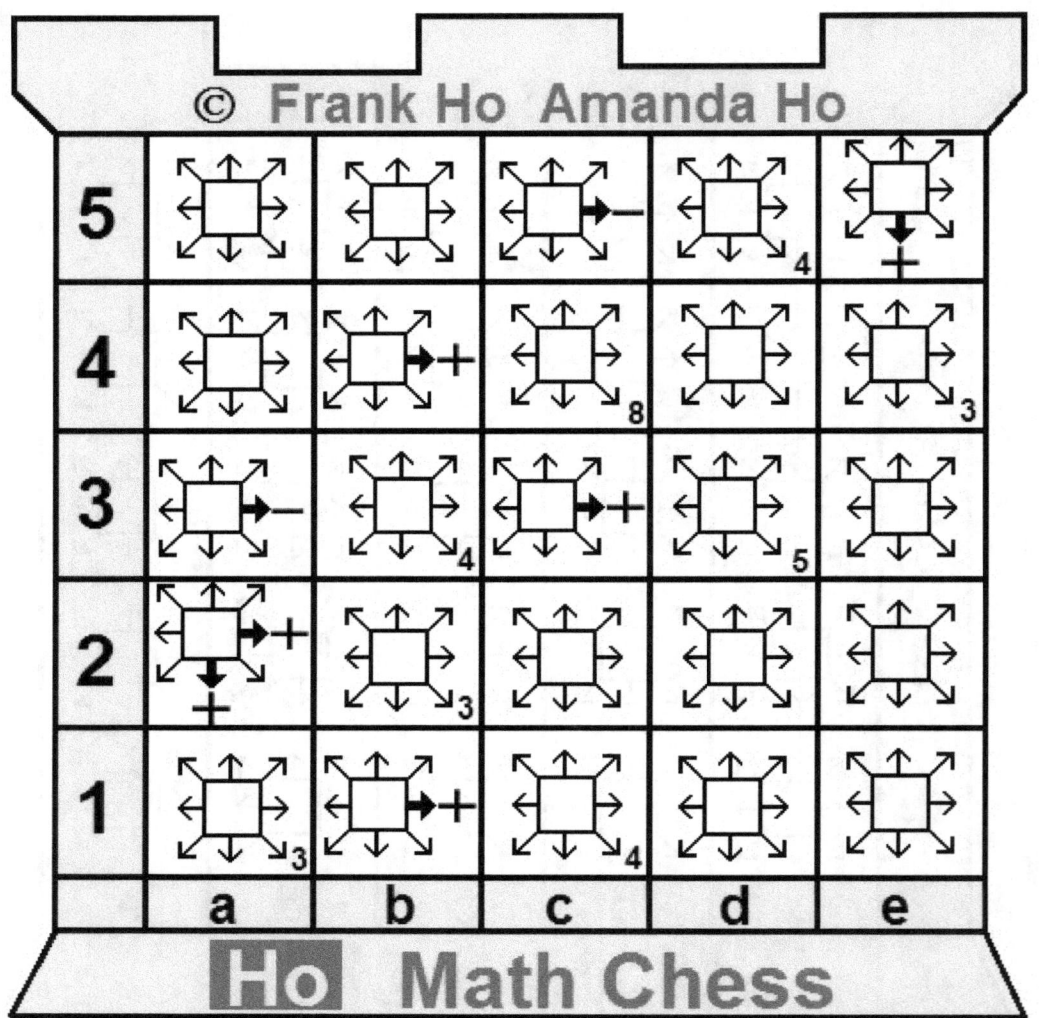

Ho Math Chess 何数棋谜 益智健脑非药物良方
Frankho Puzzle for KIDS – Brain Fitness Workbook
© 2007 – 2016 Frank Ho, Amanda Ho all rights reserved www.mathandchess.com

Frankho Puzzle™ # 49

Rule All the digits 1 to 5 must appear exactly once in every row and column. The number appears in the bottom right-hand corner is the end result calculated according to arithmetic operator(s) and chess move(s) as indicated by darker arrow(s).

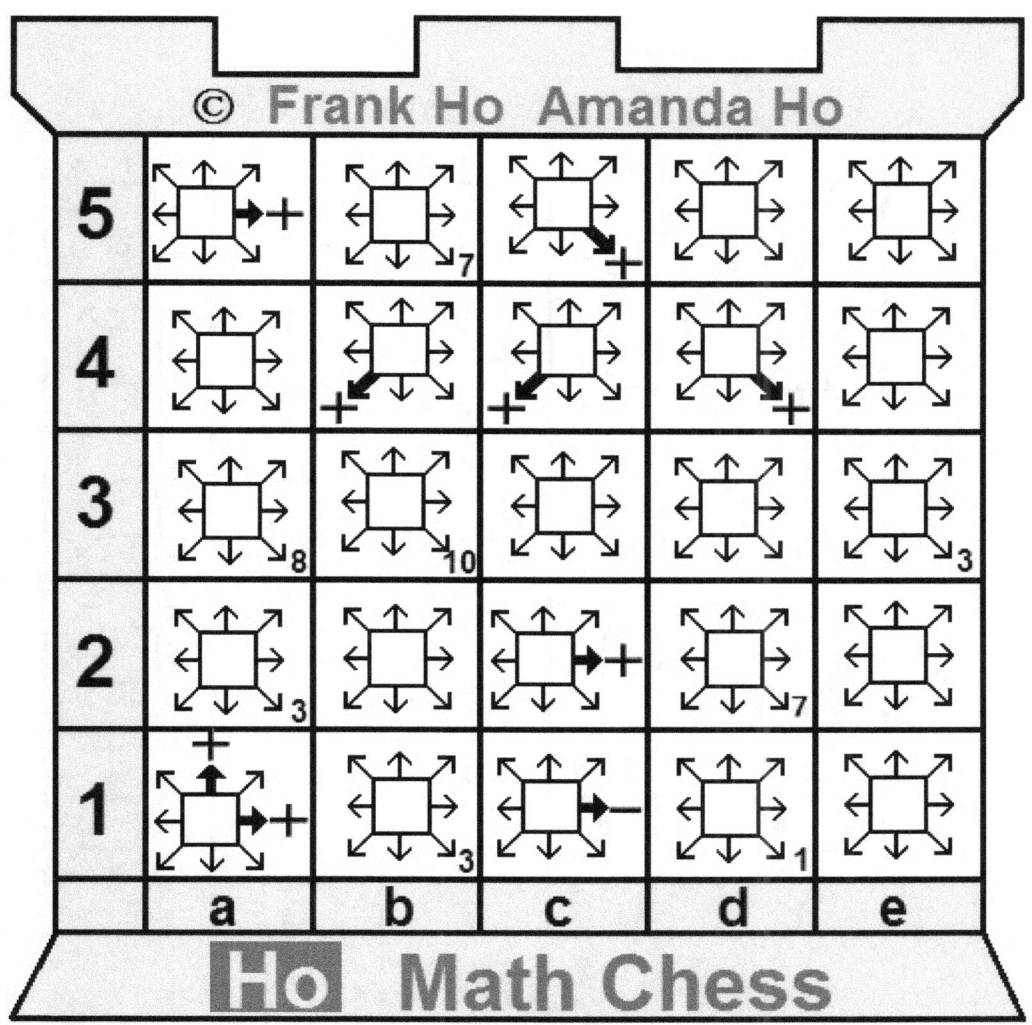

Frankho Puzzle™ # 50

Rule All the digits 1 to 5 must appear exactly once in every row and column. The number appears in the bottom right-hand corner is the end result calculated according to arithmetic operator(s) and chess move(s) as indicated by darker arrow(s).

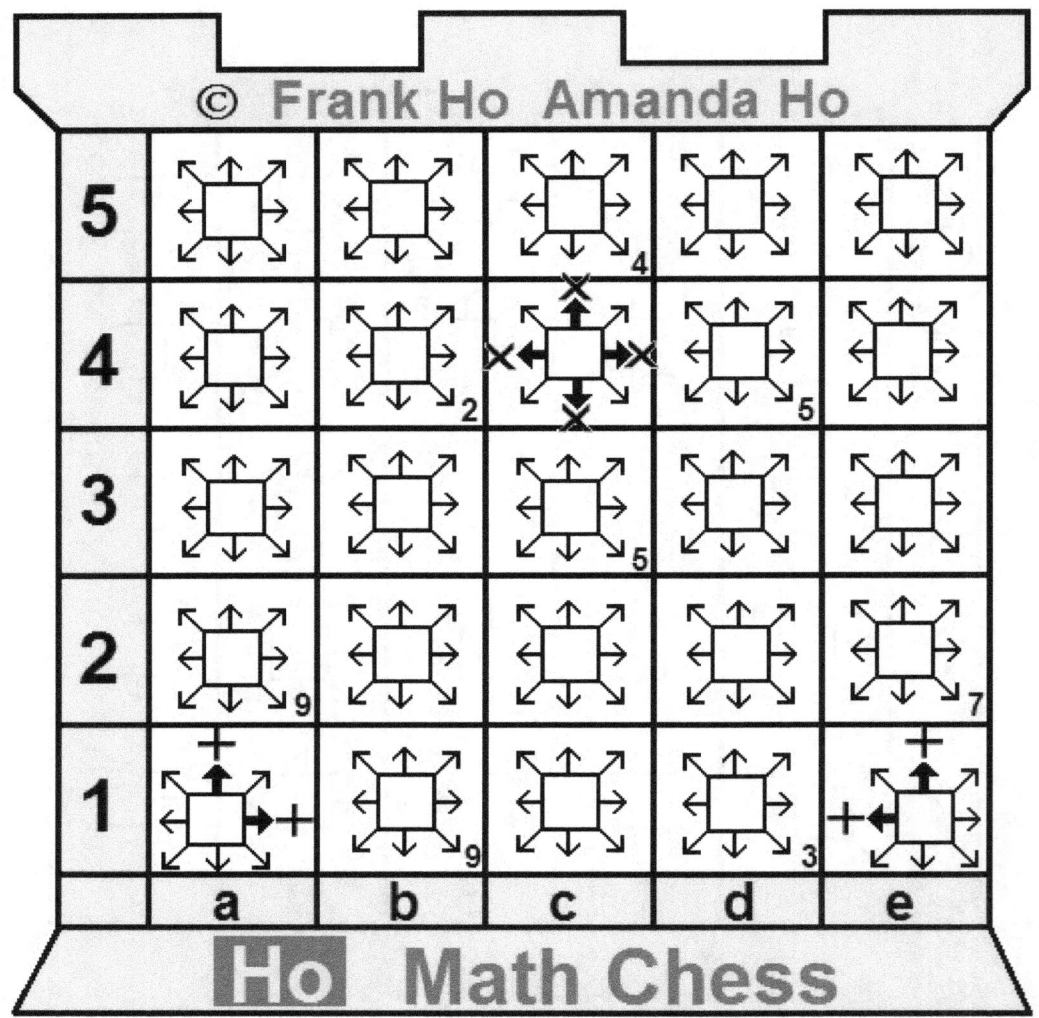

Frankho Puzzle™ # 51

Rule All the digits 1 to 5 must appear exactly once in every row and column. The number appears in the bottom right-hand corner is the end result calculated according to arithmetic operator(s) and chess move(s) as indicated by darker arrow(s).

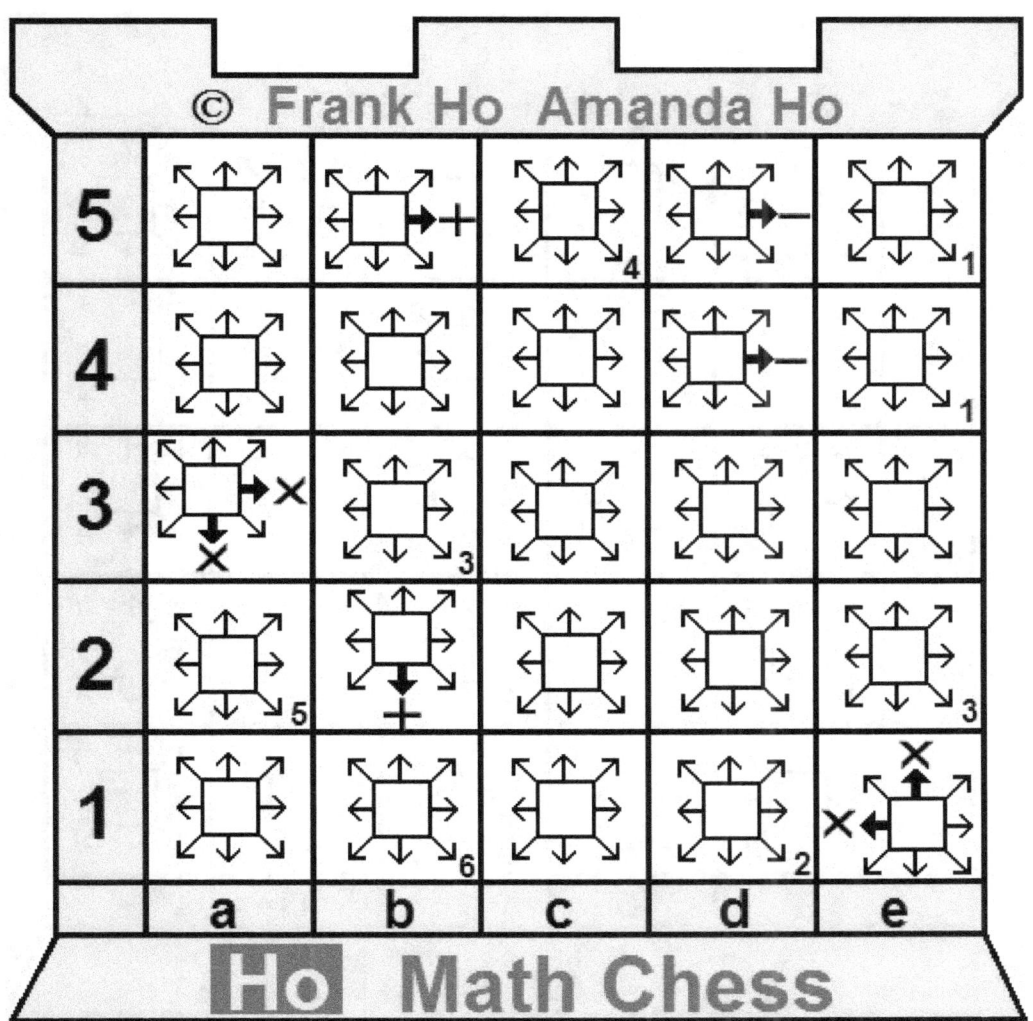

Frankho Puzzle™ # 52

Rule All the digits 1 to 5 must appear exactly once in every row and column. The number appears in the bottom right-hand corner is the end result calculated according to arithmetic operator(s) and chess move(s) as indicated by darker arrow(s).

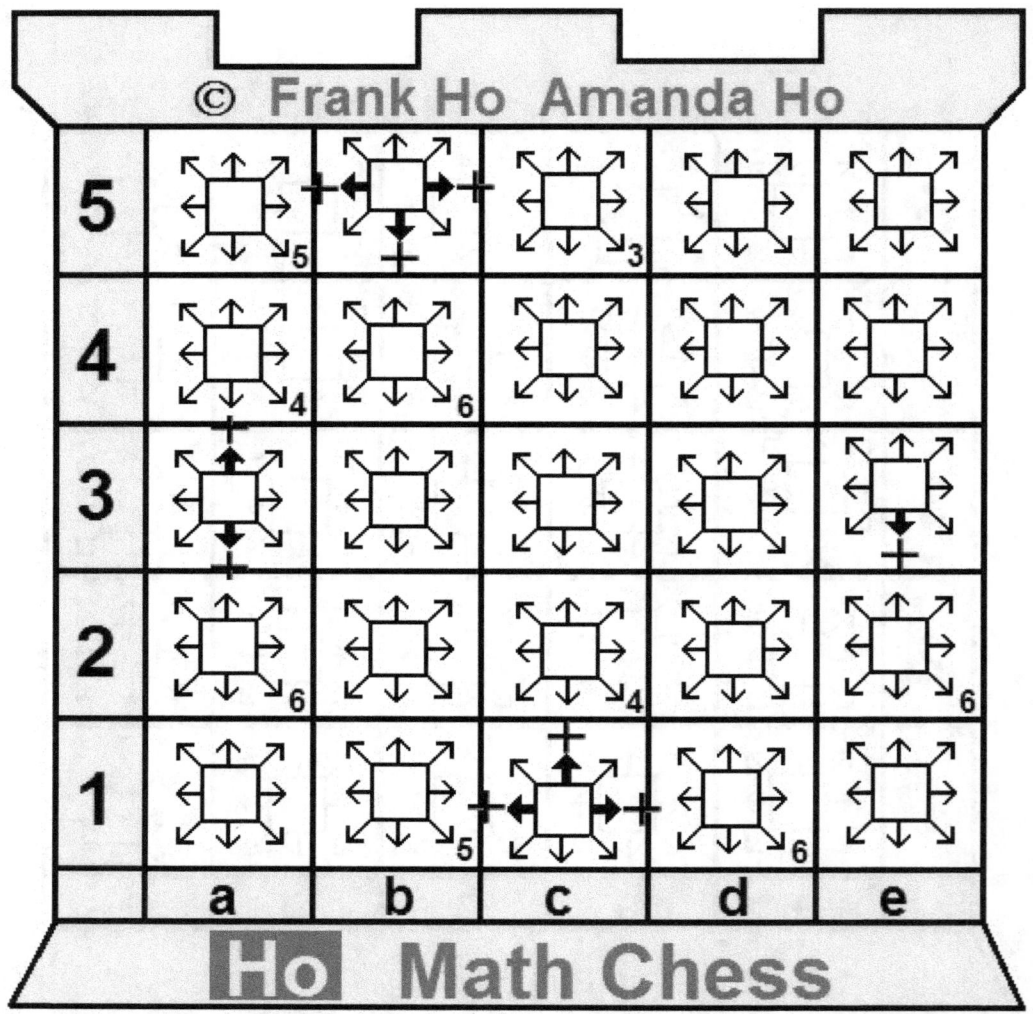

Ho Math Chess 何数棋谜 益智健脑非药物良方
Frankho Puzzle for KIDS – Brain Fitness Workbook
© 2007 — 2016 Frank Ho, Amanda Ho all rights reserved www.mathandchess.com

Frankho Puzzle™ # 53

Rule All the digits 1 to 5 must appear exactly once in every row and column. The number appears in the bottom right-hand corner is the end result calculated according to arithmetic operator(s) and chess move(s) as indicated by darker arrow(s).

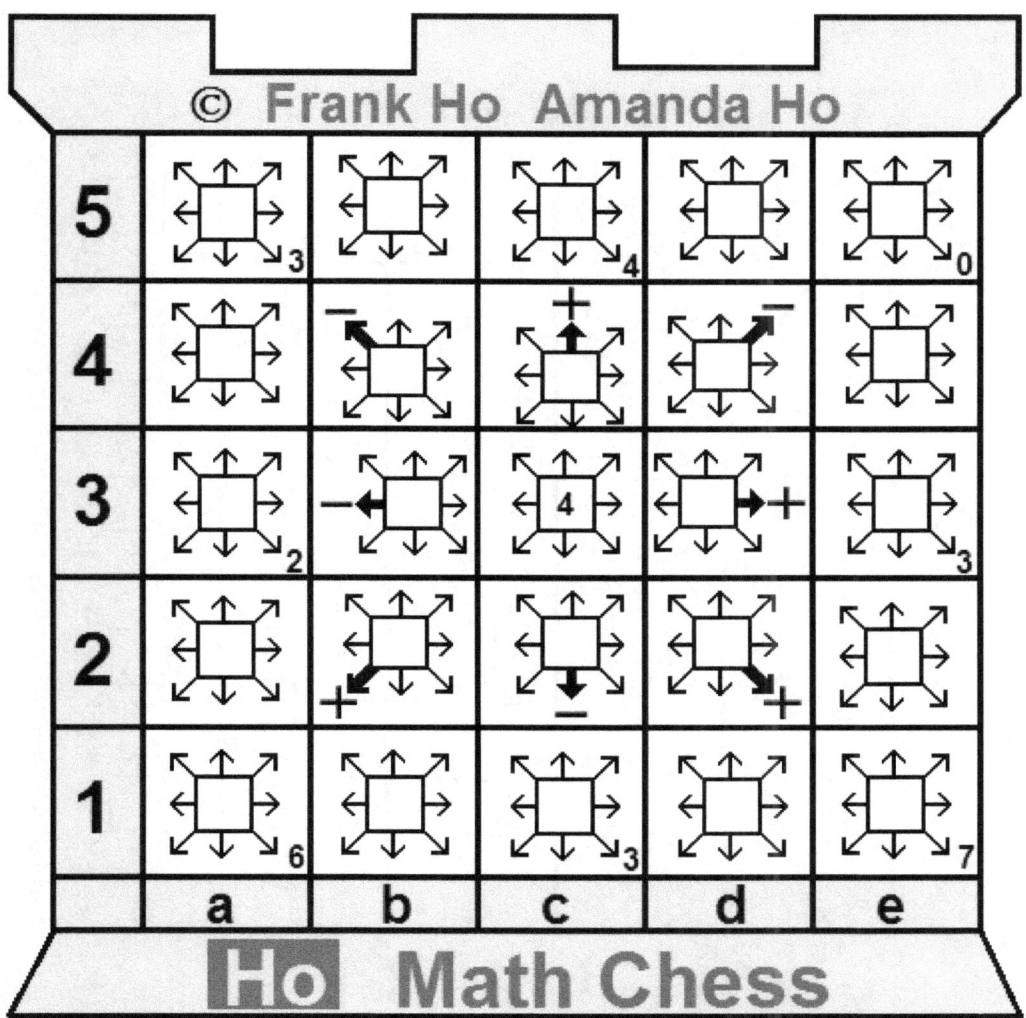

Frankho Puzzle™ # 54

Rule All the digits 1 to 5 must appear exactly once in every row and column. The number appears in the bottom right-hand corner is the end result calculated according to arithmetic operator(s) and chess move(s) as indicated by darker arrow(s).

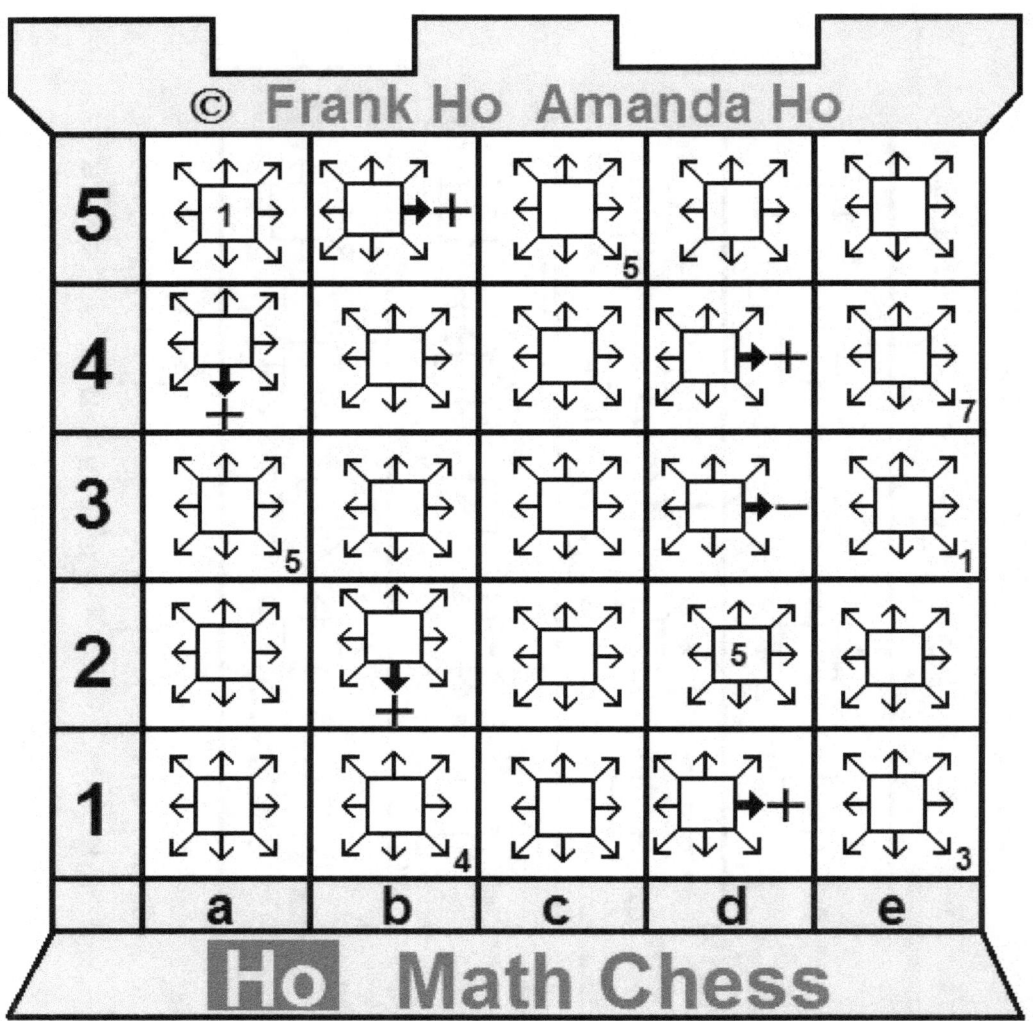

Ho Math Chess 何数棋谜 益智健脑非药物良方
Frankho Puzzle for KIDS – Brain Fitness Workbook
© 2007 – 2016 Frank Ho, Amanda Ho all rights reserved www.mathandchess.com

Frankho Puzzle™ # 55

Rule All the digits 1 to 5 must appear exactly once in every row and column. The number appears in the bottom right-hand corner is the end result calculated according to arithmetic operator(s) and chess move(s) as indicated by darker arrow(s).

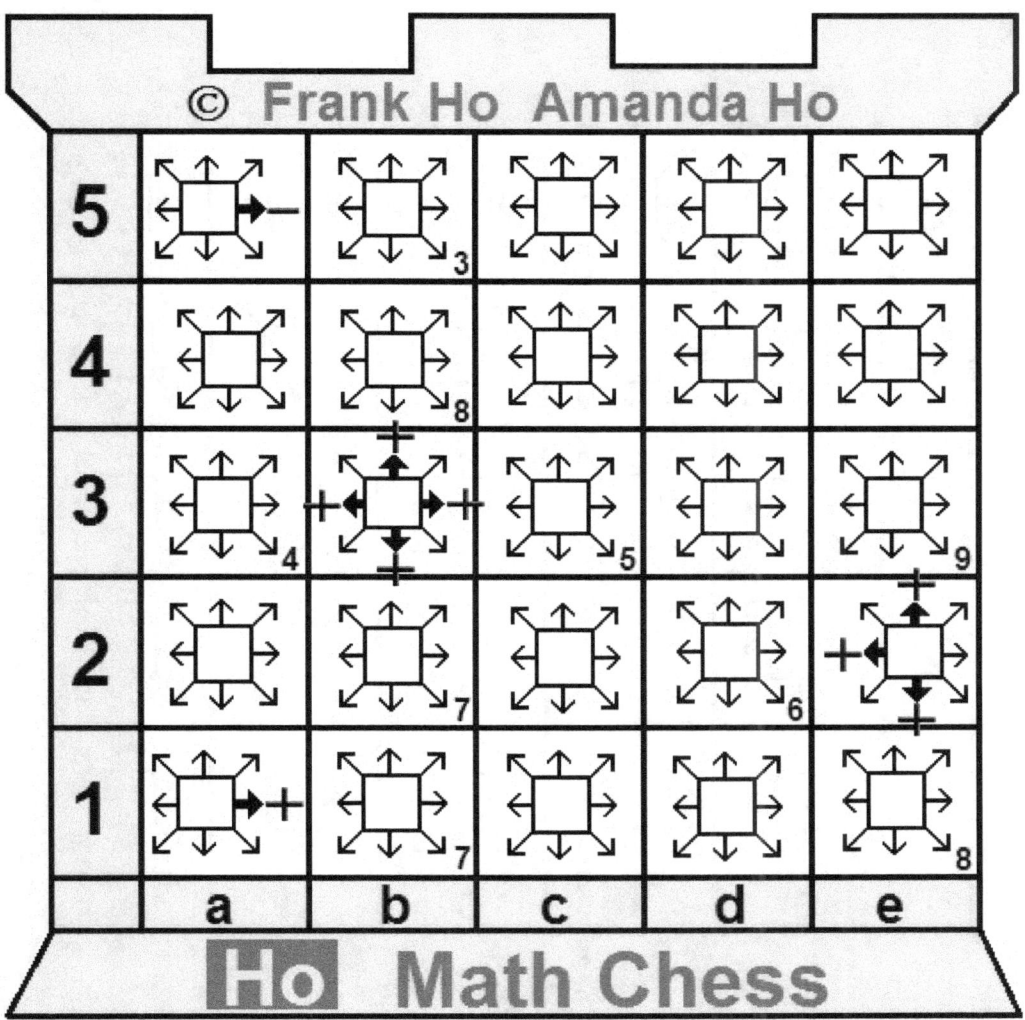

Ho Math Chess 何数棋谜 益智健脑非药物良方
Frankho Puzzle for KIDS – Brain Fitness Workbook
© 2007 — 2016 Frank Ho, Amanda Ho all rights reserved www.mathandchess.com

Frankho Puzzle™ # 56

Rule All the digits 1 to 5 must appear exactly once in every row and column. The number appears in the bottom right-hand corner is the end result calculated according to arithmetic operator(s) and chess move(s) as indicated by darker arrow(s).

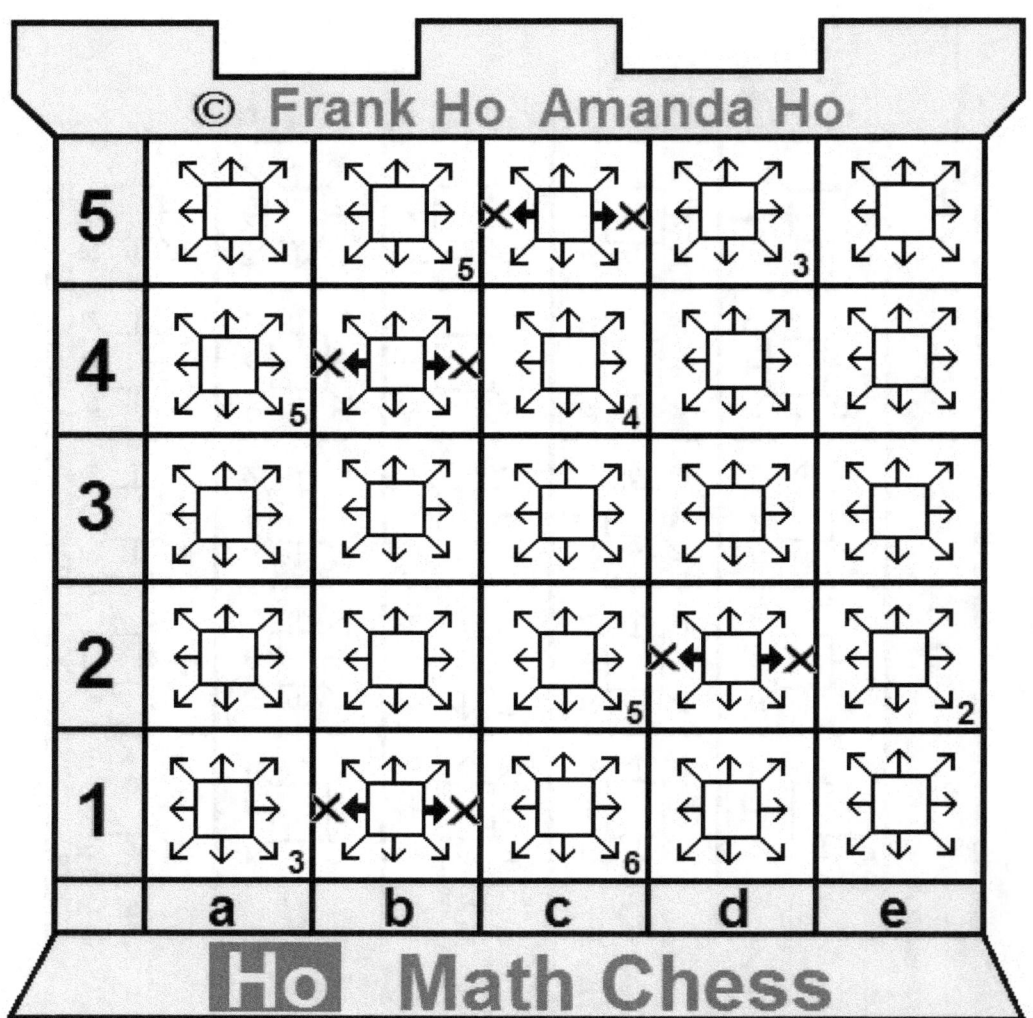

Frankho Puzzle™ # 57

Rule All the digits 1 to 5 must appear exactly once in every row and column. The number appears in the bottom right-hand corner is the end result calculated according to arithmetic operator(s) and chess move(s) as indicated by darker arrow(s).

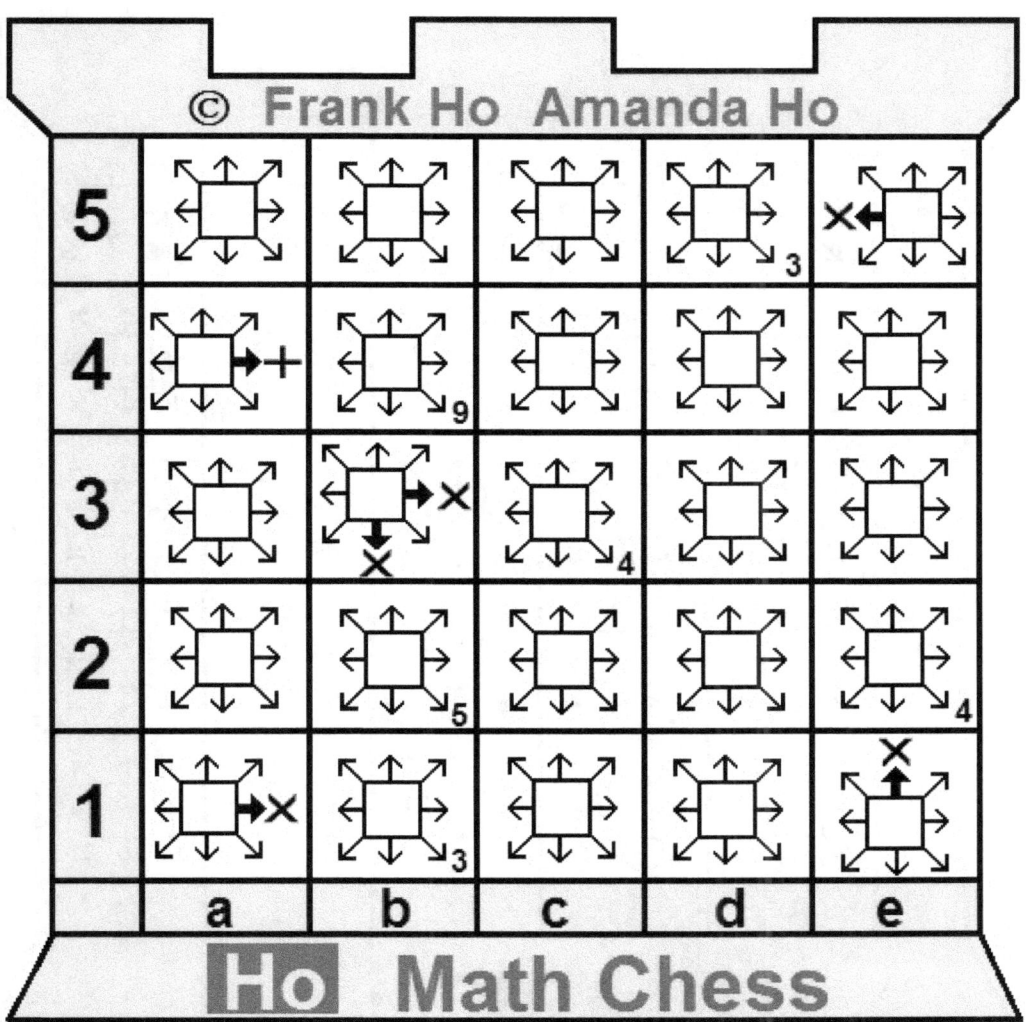

Frankho Puzzle™ # 58

Rule All the digits 1 to 5 must appear exactly once in every row and column. The number appears in the bottom right-hand corner is the end result calculated according to arithmetic operator(s) and chess move(s) as indicated by darker arrow(s).

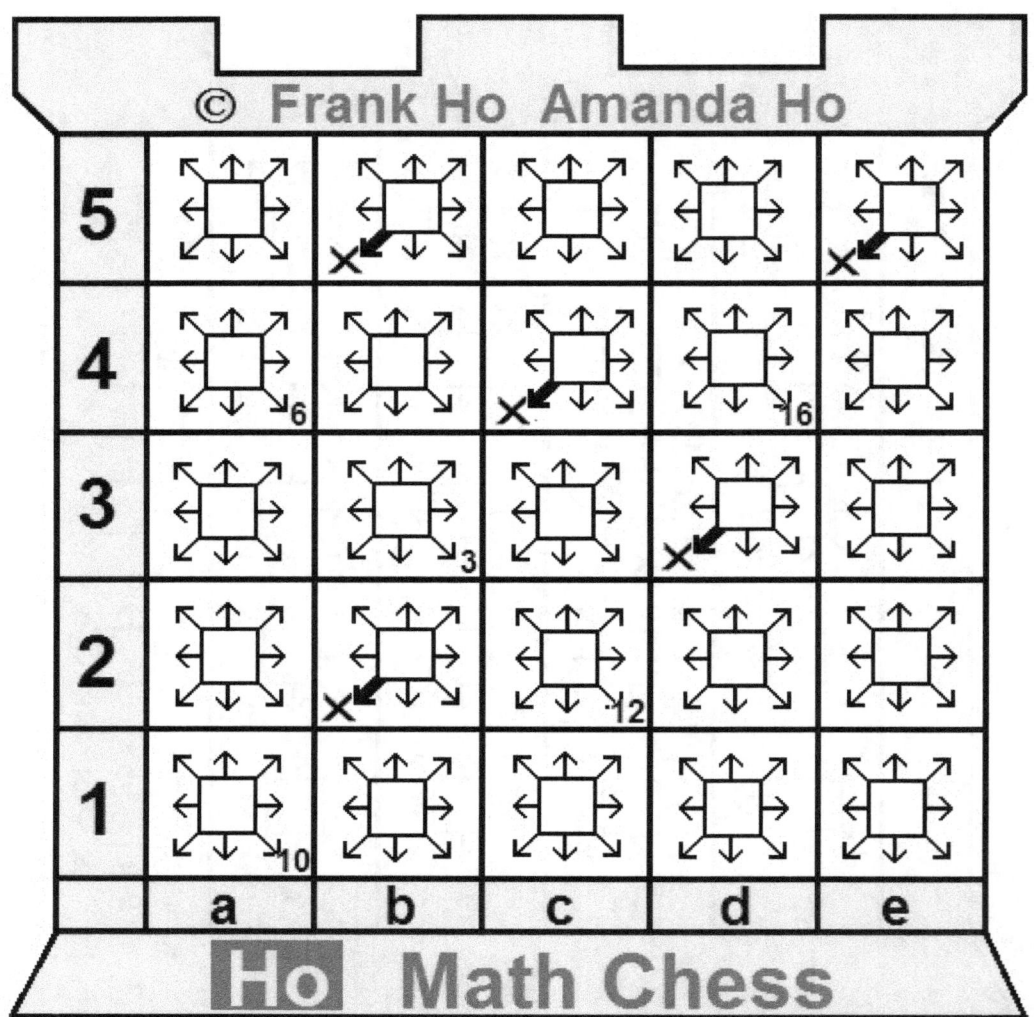

Ho Math Chess 何数棋谜 益智健脑非药物良方
Frankho Puzzle for KIDS – Brain Fitness Workbook
© 2007 – 2016 Frank Ho, Amanda Ho all rights reserved www.mathandchess.com

Frankho Puzzle™ # 59

Rule All the digits 1 to 5 must appear exactly once in every row and column. The number appears in the bottom right-hand corner is the end result calculated according to arithmetic operator(s) and chess move(s) as indicated by darker arrow(s).

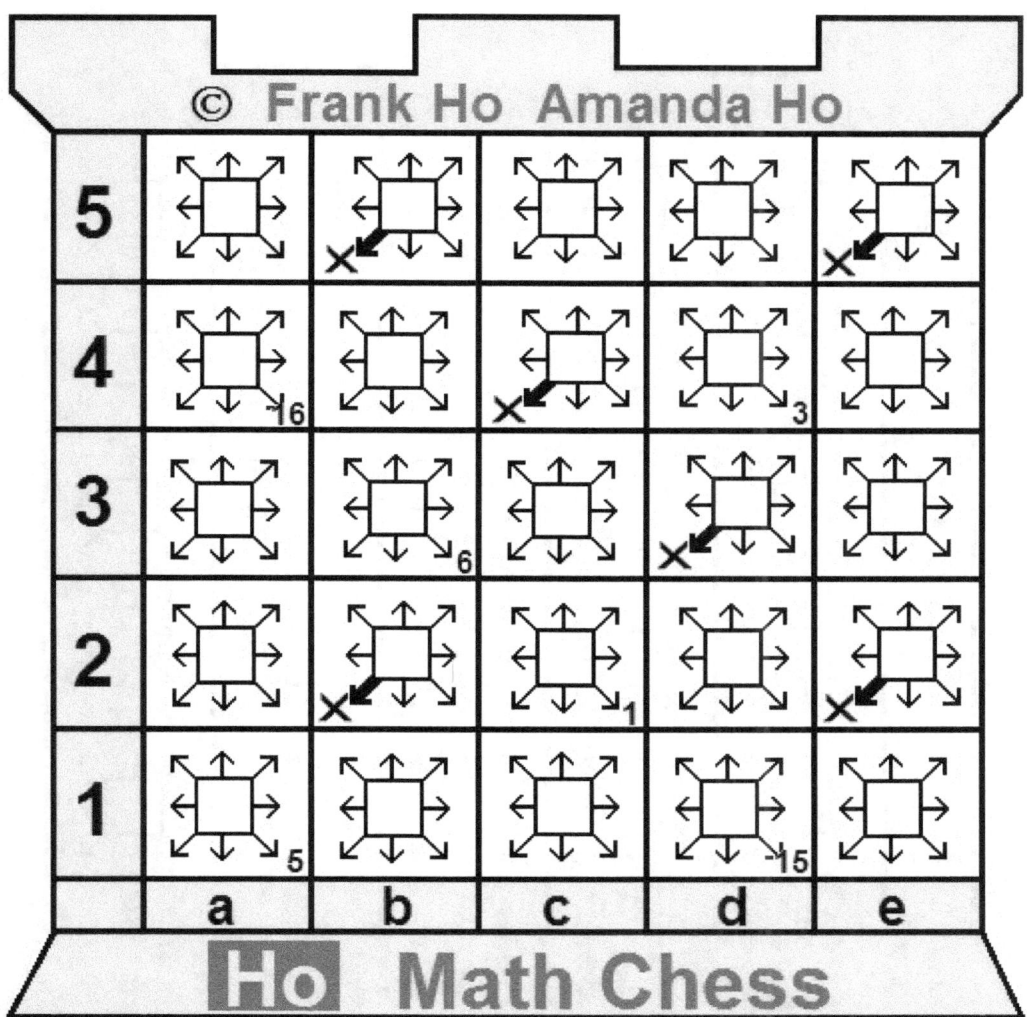

Frankho Puzzle™ # 60

Rule All the digits 1 to 5 must appear exactly once in every row and column. The number appears in the bottom right-hand corner is the end result calculated according to arithmetic operator(s) and chess move(s) as indicated by darker arrow(s).

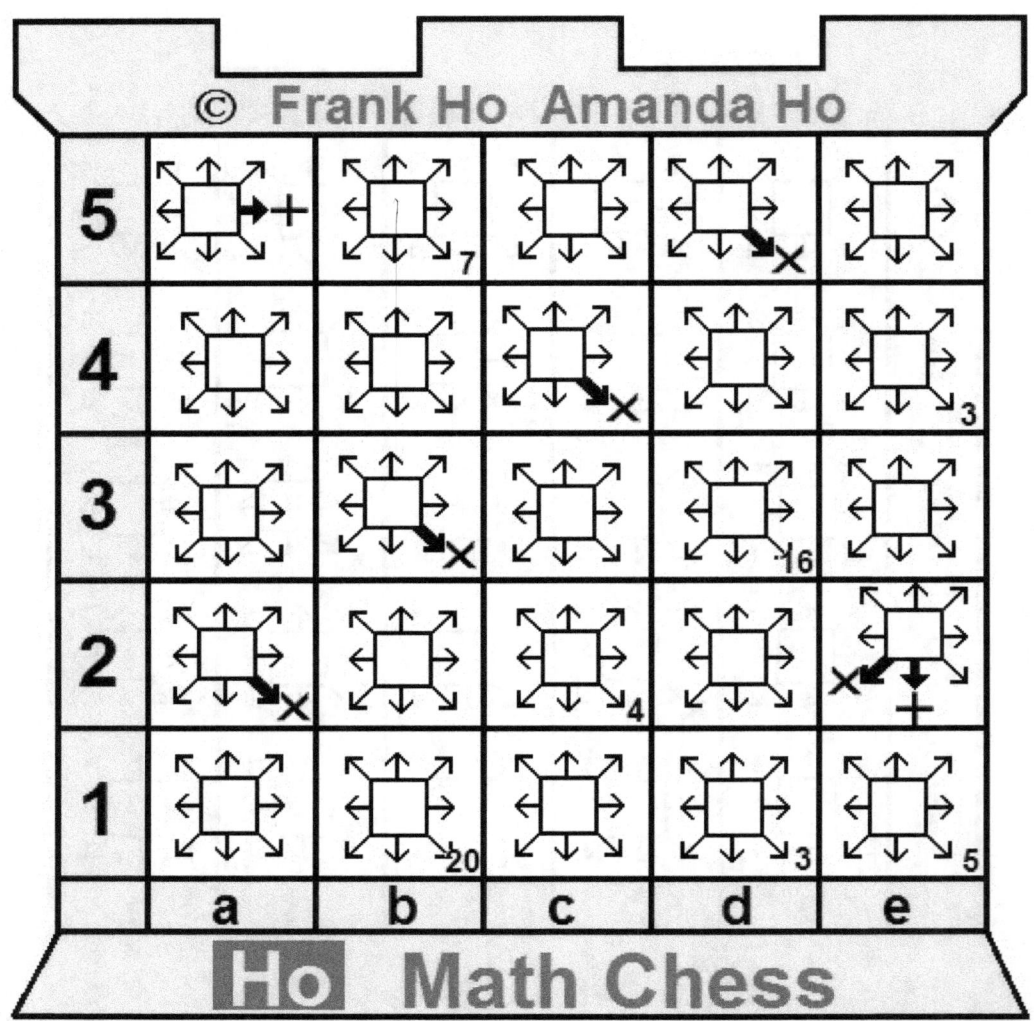

Ho Math Chess 何数棋谜 益智健脑非药物良方
Frankho Puzzle for KIDS – Brain Fitness Workbook
© 2007 — 2016 Frank Ho, Amanda Ho all rights reserved www.mathandchess.com

Frankho Puzzle™ # 61

Rule All the digits 1 to 5 must appear exactly once in every row and column. The number appears in the bottom right-hand corner is the end result calculated according to arithmetic operator(s) and chess move(s) as indicated by darker arrow(s).

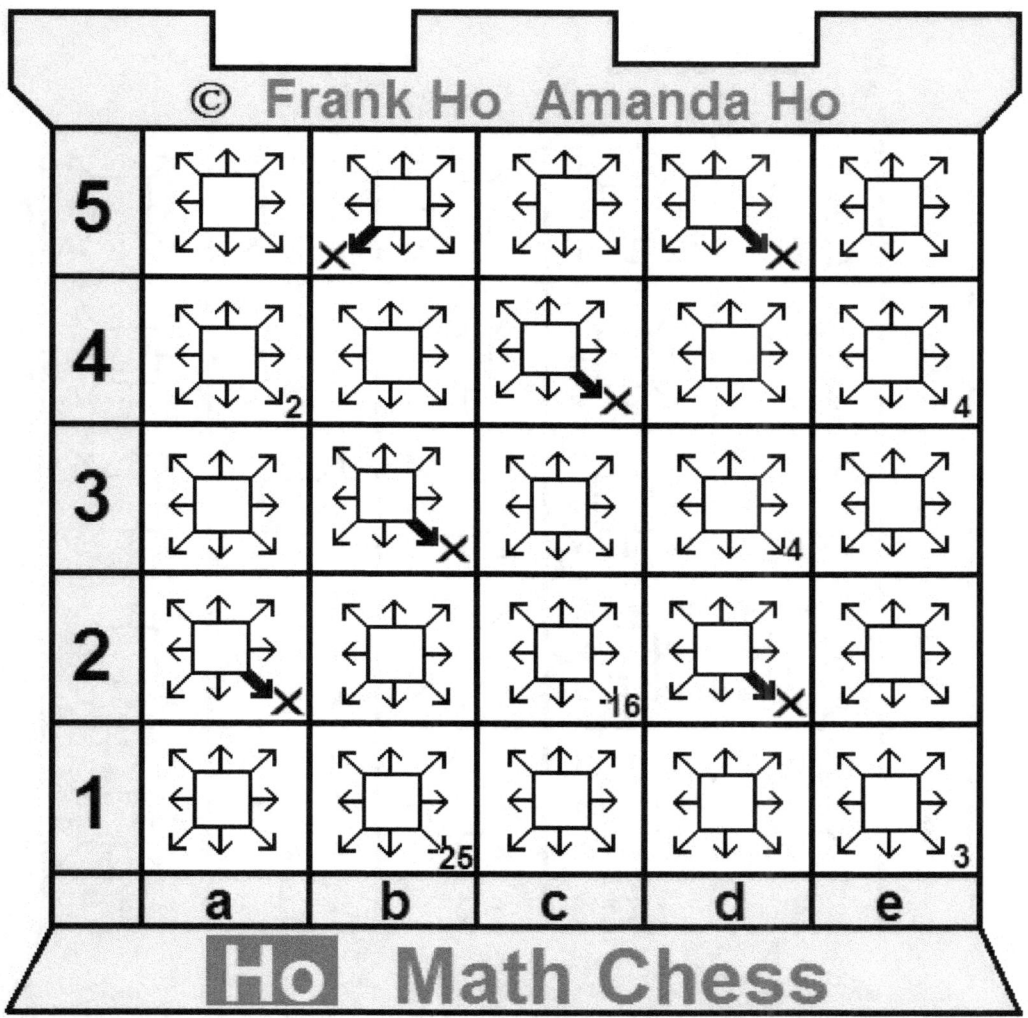

65

Ho Math Chess 何数棋谜 益智健脑非药物良方
Frankho Puzzle for KIDS – Brain Fitness Workbook
© 2007 — 2016 Frank Ho, Amanda Ho all rights reserved www.mathandchess.com

Frankho Puzzle™ # 62

Rule All the digits 1 to 5 must appear exactly once in every row and column. The number appears in the bottom right-hand corner is the end result calculated according to arithmetic operator(s) and chess move(s) as indicated by darker arrow(s).

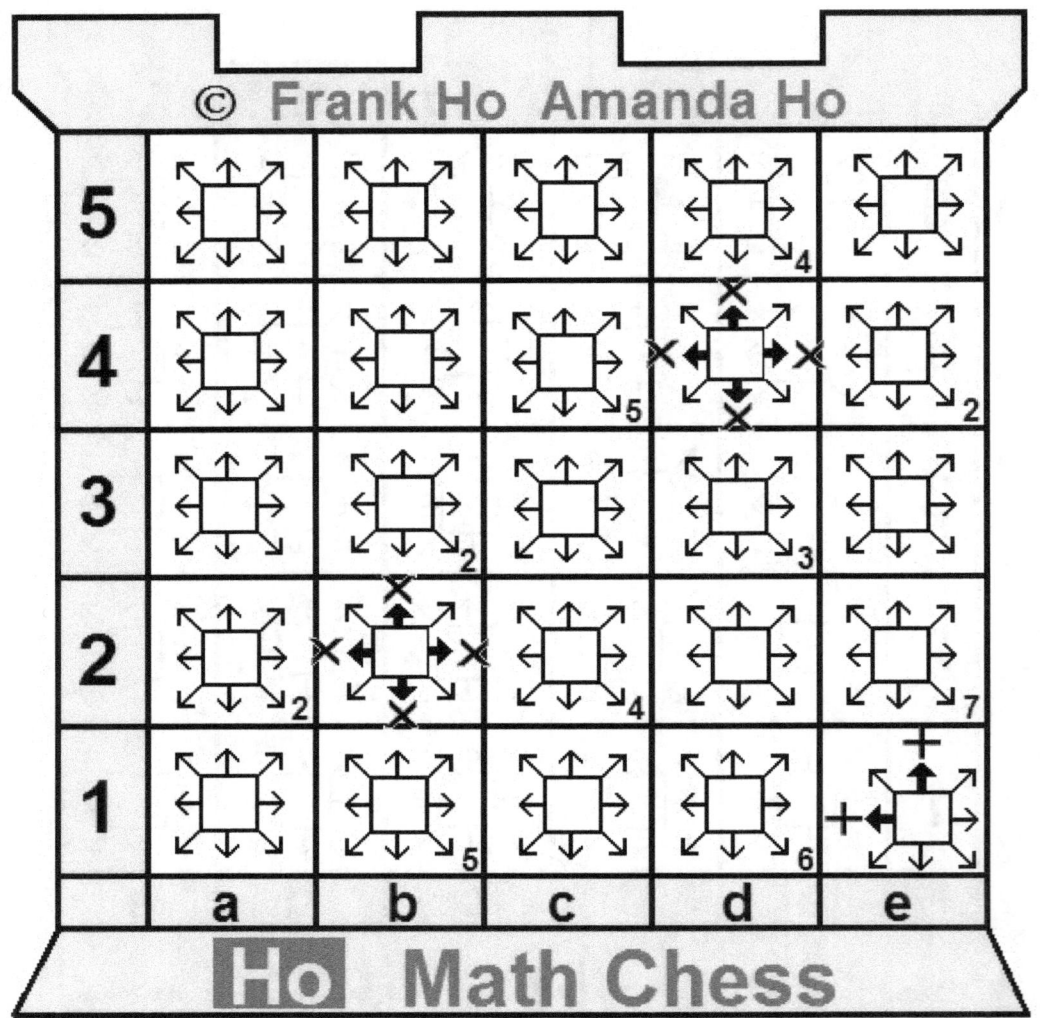

Frankho Puzzle™ # 63

Rule All the digits 1 to 5 must appear exactly once in every row and column. The number appears in the bottom right-hand corner is the end result calculated according to arithmetic operator(s) and chess move(s) as indicated by darker arrow(s).

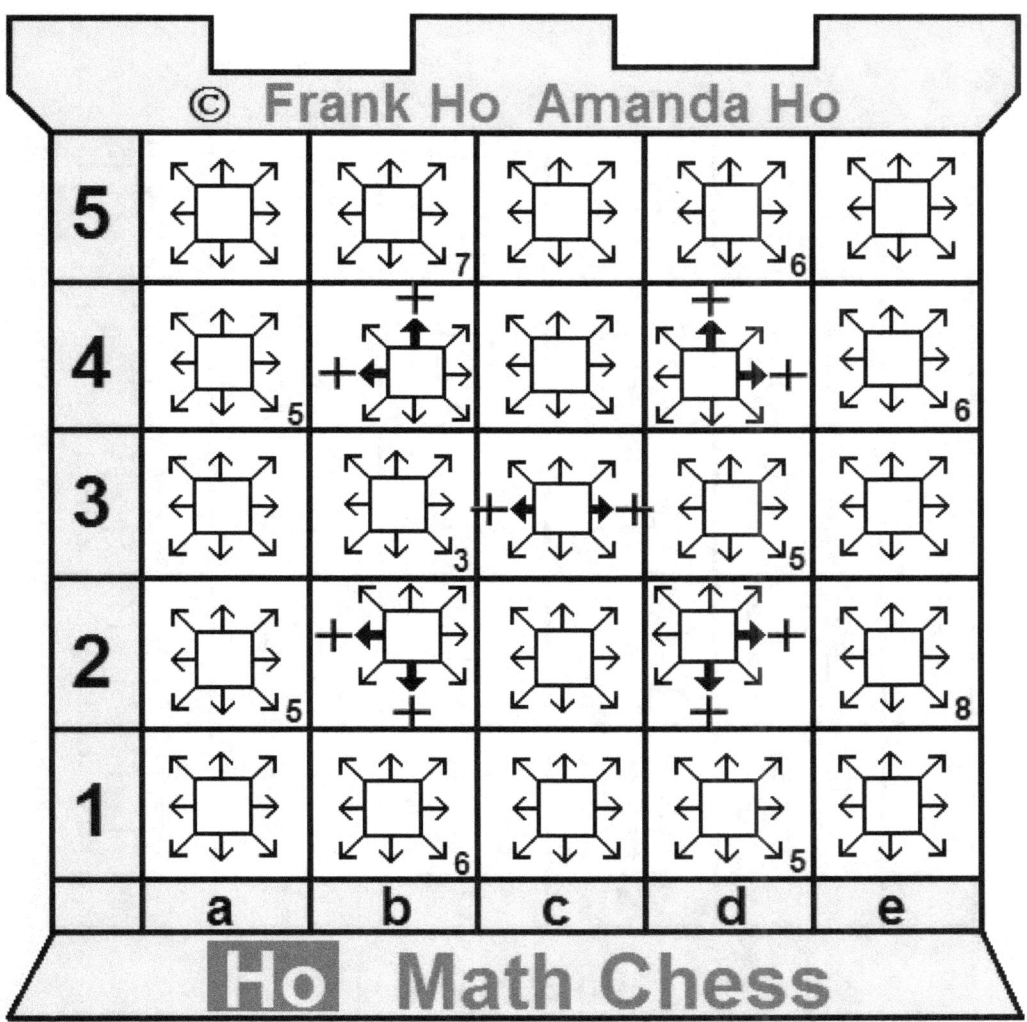

Frankho Puzzle™ # 64

Rule All the digits 1 to 5 must appear exactly once in every row and column. The number appears in the bottom right-hand corner is the end result calculated according to arithmetic operator(s) and chess move(s) as indicated by darker arrow(s).

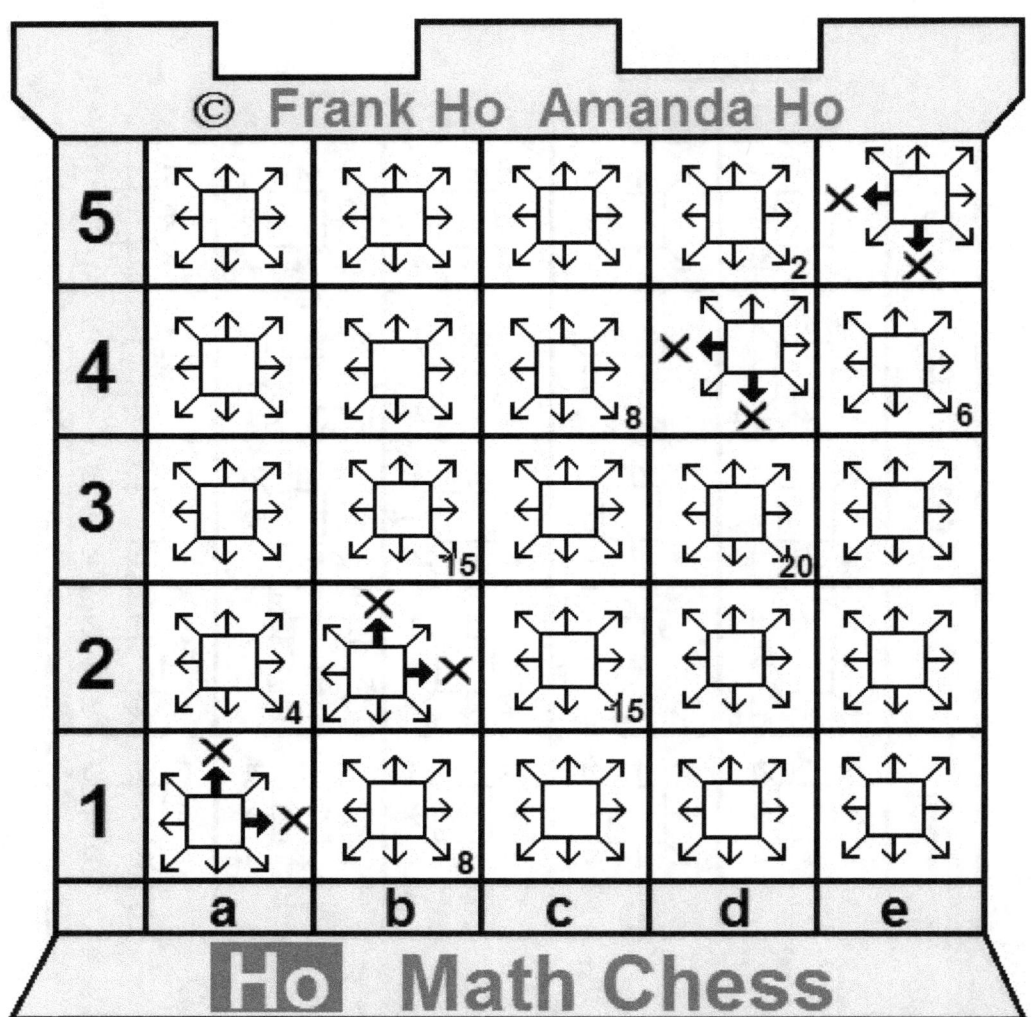

Ho Math Chess 何数棋谜 益智健脑非药物良方
Frankho Puzzle for KIDS – Brain Fitness Workbook
© 2007 — 2016 Frank Ho, Amanda Ho all rights reserved www.mathandchess.com

Frankho Puzzle™ # 65

Rule All the digits 1 to 5 must appear exactly once in every row and column. The number appears in the bottom right-hand corner is the end result calculated according to arithmetic operator(s) and chess move(s) as indicated by darker arrow(s).

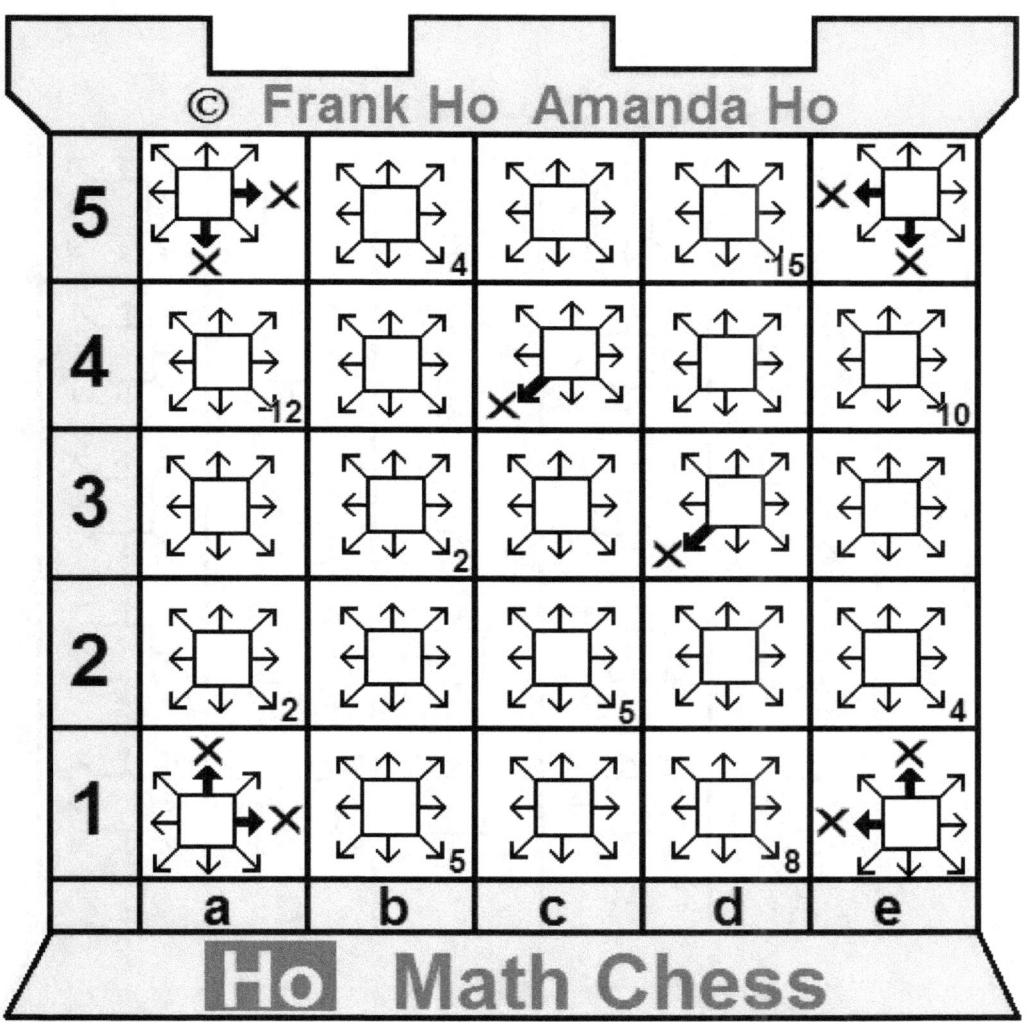

Frankho Puzzle™ # 66

Rule All the digits 1 to 5 must appear exactly once in every row and column. The number appears in the bottom right-hand corner is the end result calculated according to arithmetic operator(s) and chess move(s) as indicated by darker arrow(s).

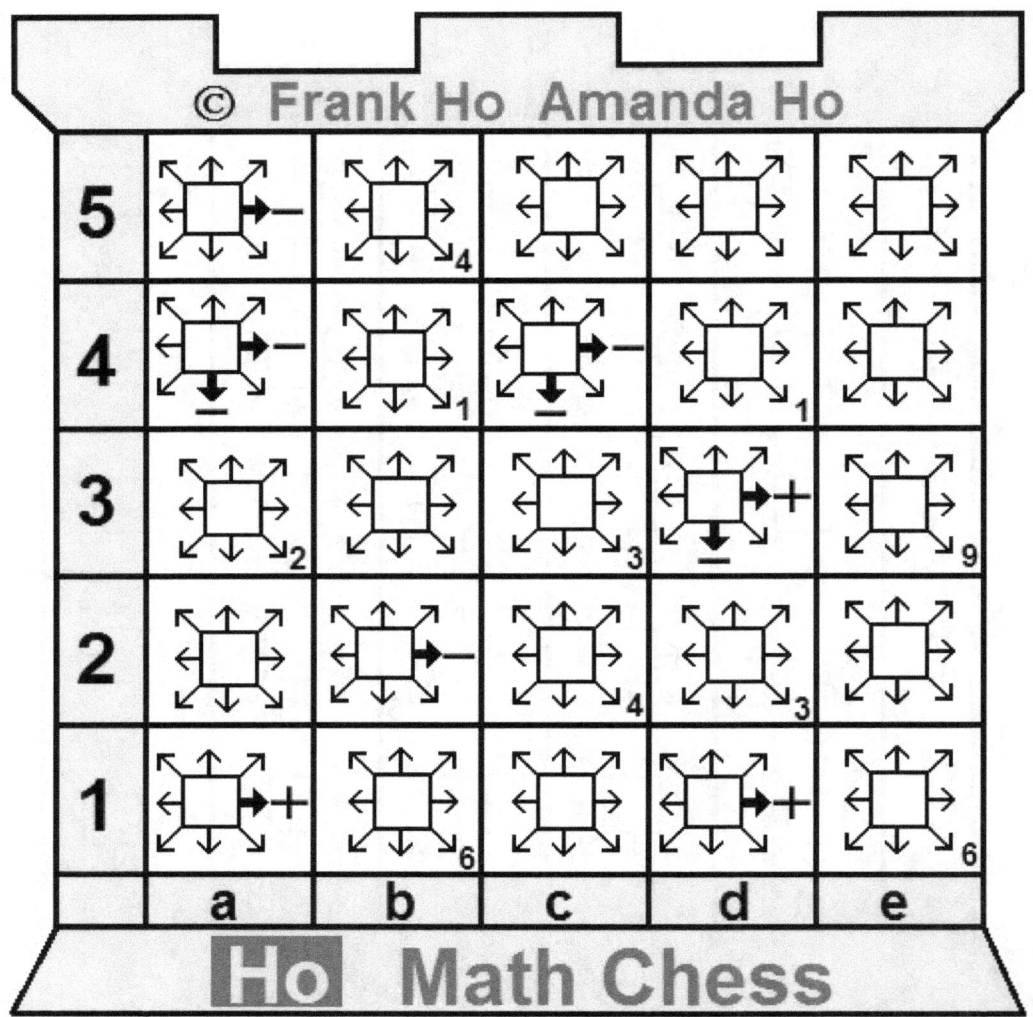

Ho Math Chess 何数棋谜 益智健脑非药物良方
Frankho Puzzle for KIDS – Brain Fitness Workbook
© 2007 — 2016 Frank Ho, Amanda Ho all rights reserved www.mathandchess.com

Frankho Puzzle™ # 67

Rule All the digits 1 to 5 must appear exactly once in every row and column. The number appears in the bottom right-hand corner is the end result calculated according to arithmetic operator(s) and chess move(s) as indicated by darker arrow(s).

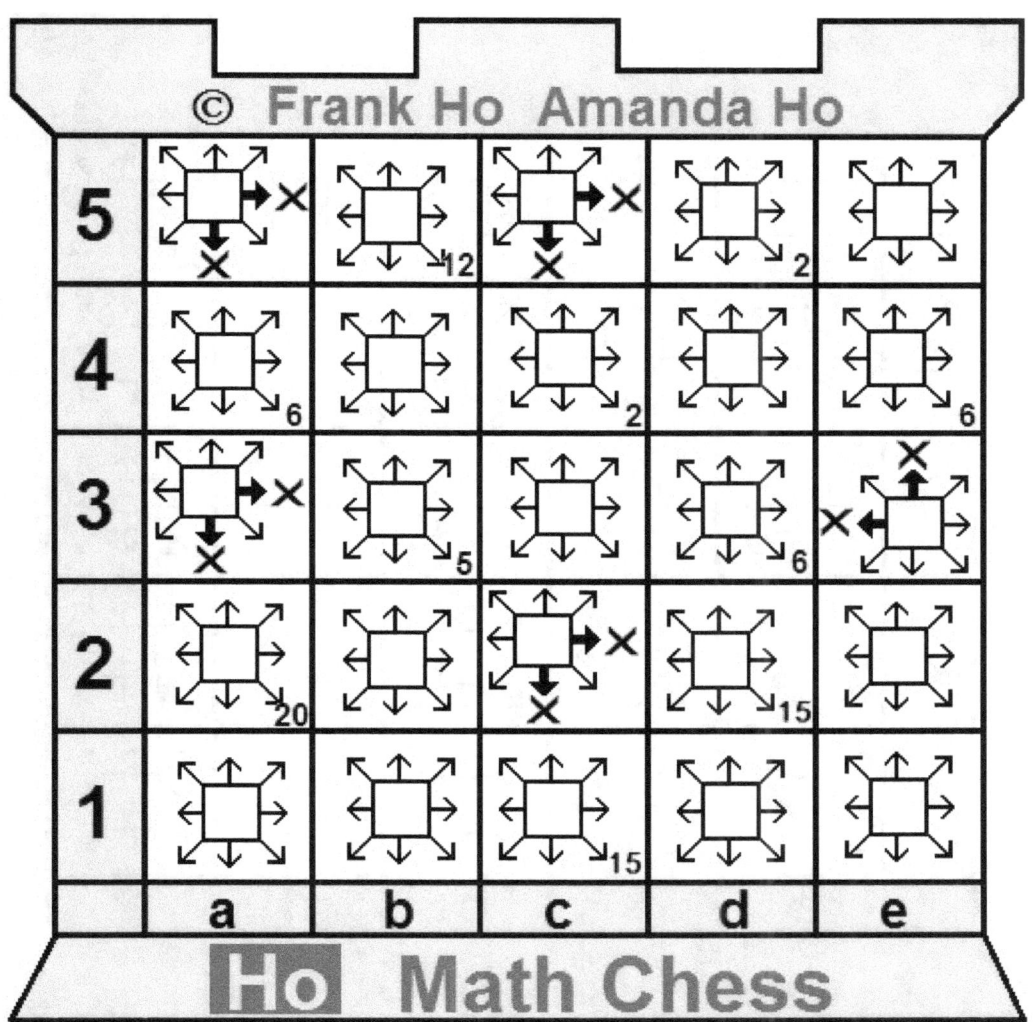

71

Ho Math Chess 何数棋谜 益智健脑非药物良方
Frankho Puzzle for KIDS – Brain Fitness Workbook

© 2007 — 2016 Frank Ho, Amanda Ho all rights reserved www.mathandchess.com

Frankho Puzzle™ # 68

Rule All the digits 1 to 5 must appear exactly once in every row and column. The number appears in the bottom right-hand corner is the end result calculated according to arithmetic operator(s) and chess move(s) as indicated by darker arrow(s).

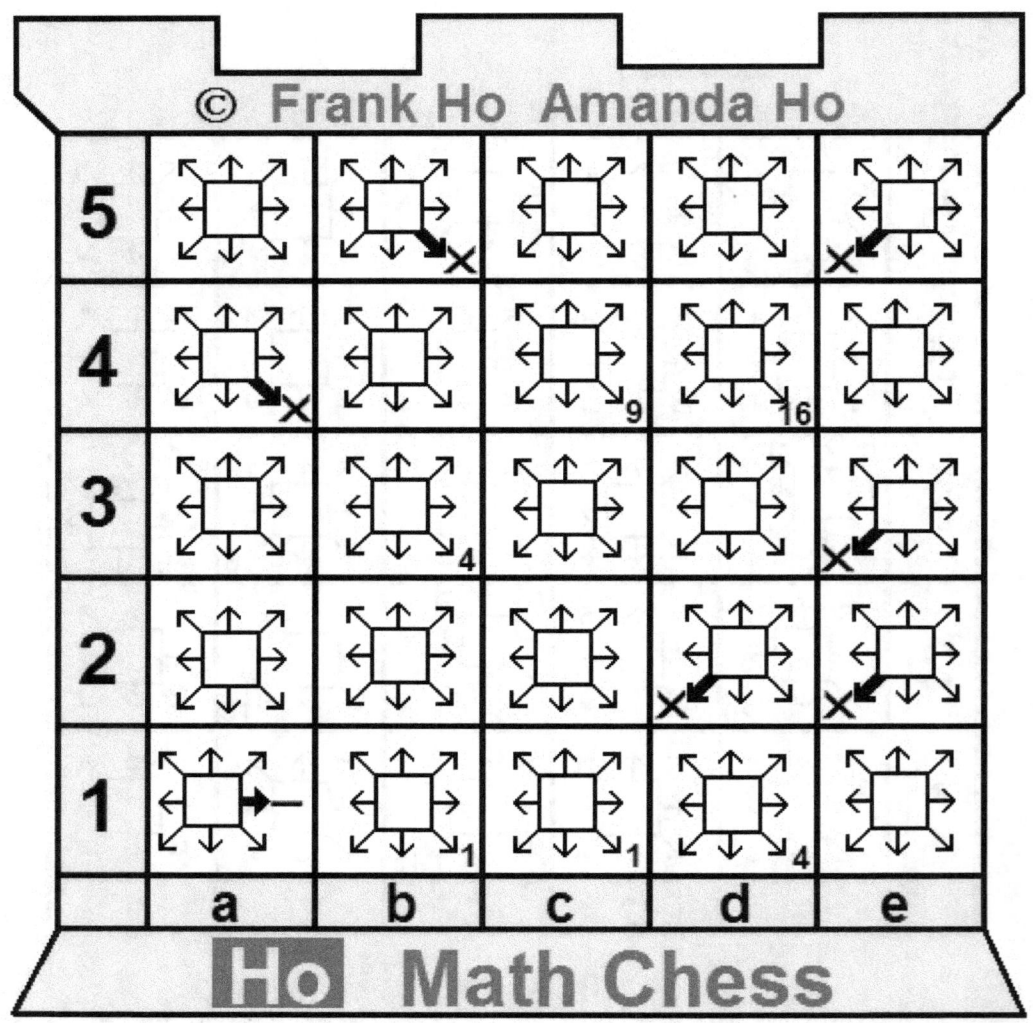

Ho Math Chess 何数棋谜 益智健脑非药物良方
Frankho Puzzle for KIDS – Brain Fitness Workbook
© 2007 — 2016 Frank Ho, Amanda Ho all rights reserved www.mathandchess.com

Frankho Puzzle™ # 69

Rule All the digits 1 to 5 must appear exactly once in every row and column. The number appears in the bottom right-hand corner is the end result calculated according to arithmetic operator(s) and chess move(s) as indicated by darker arrow(s).

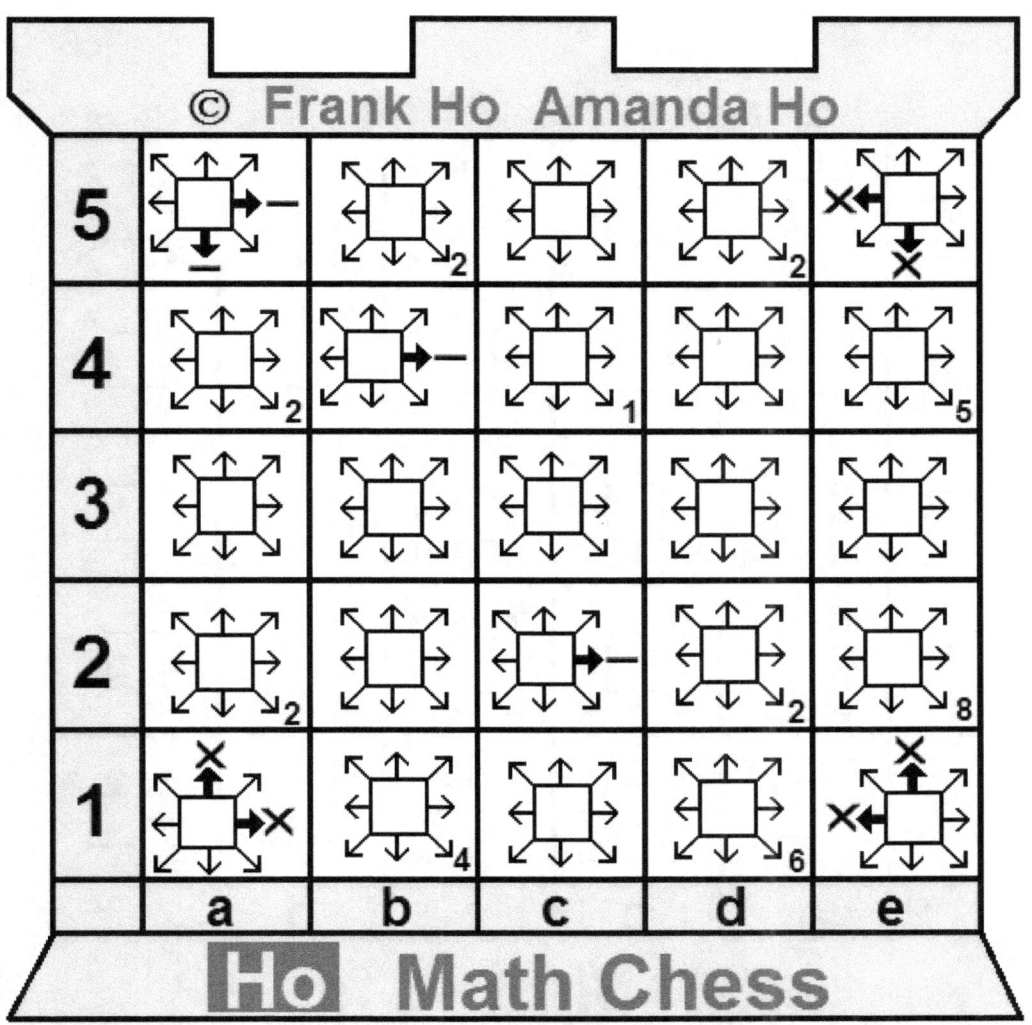

Frankho Puzzle™ # 70

Rule All the digits 1 to 5 must appear exactly once in every row and column. The number appears in the bottom right-hand corner is the end result calculated according to arithmetic operator(s) and chess move(s) as indicated by darker arrow(s).

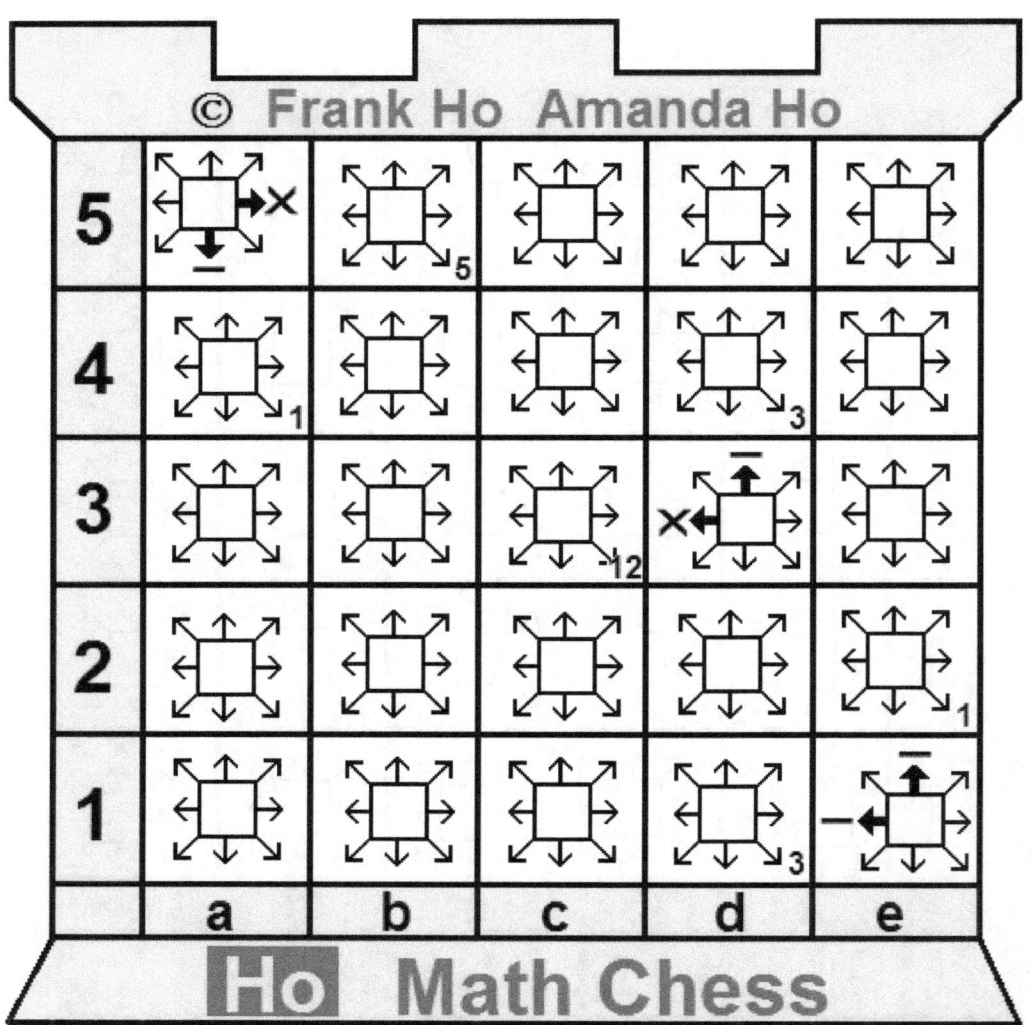

Ho Math Chess 何数棋谜 益智健脑非药物良方
Frankho Puzzle for KIDS – Brain Fitness Workbook
© 2007 — 2016 Frank Ho, Amanda Ho all rights reserved www.mathandchess.com

Frankho Puzzle™ # 71

Rule All the digits 1 to 5 must appear exactly once in every row and column. The number appears in the bottom right-hand corner is the end result calculated according to arithmetic operator(s) and chess move(s) as indicated by darker arrow(s).

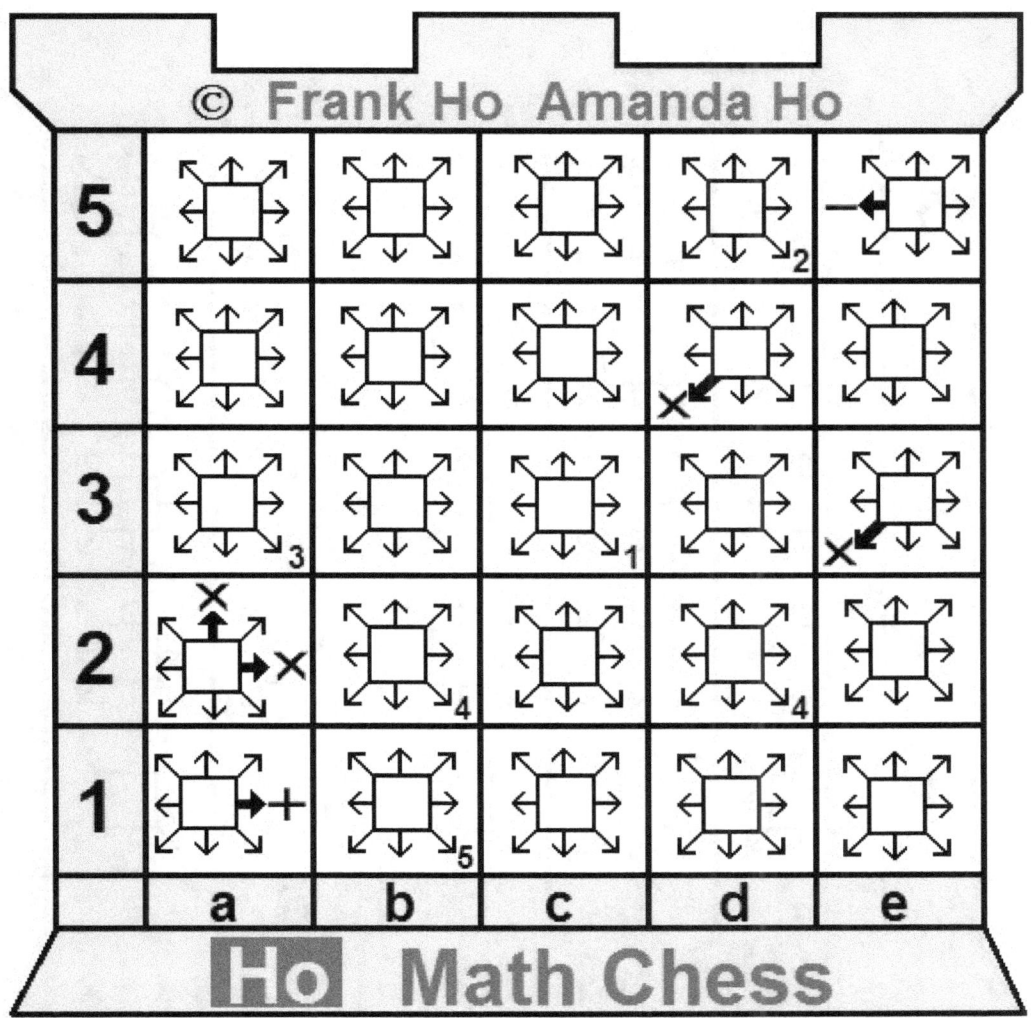

Ho Math Chess 何数棋谜 益智健脑非药物良方
Frankho Puzzle for KIDS – Brain Fitness Workbook
© 2007 — 2016 Frank Ho, Amanda Ho all rights reserved www.mathandchess.com

Frankho Puzzle™ # 72

Rule All the digits 1 to 5 must appear exactly once in every row and column. The number appears in the bottom right-hand corner is the end result calculated according to arithmetic operator(s) and chess move(s) as indicated by darker arrow(s).

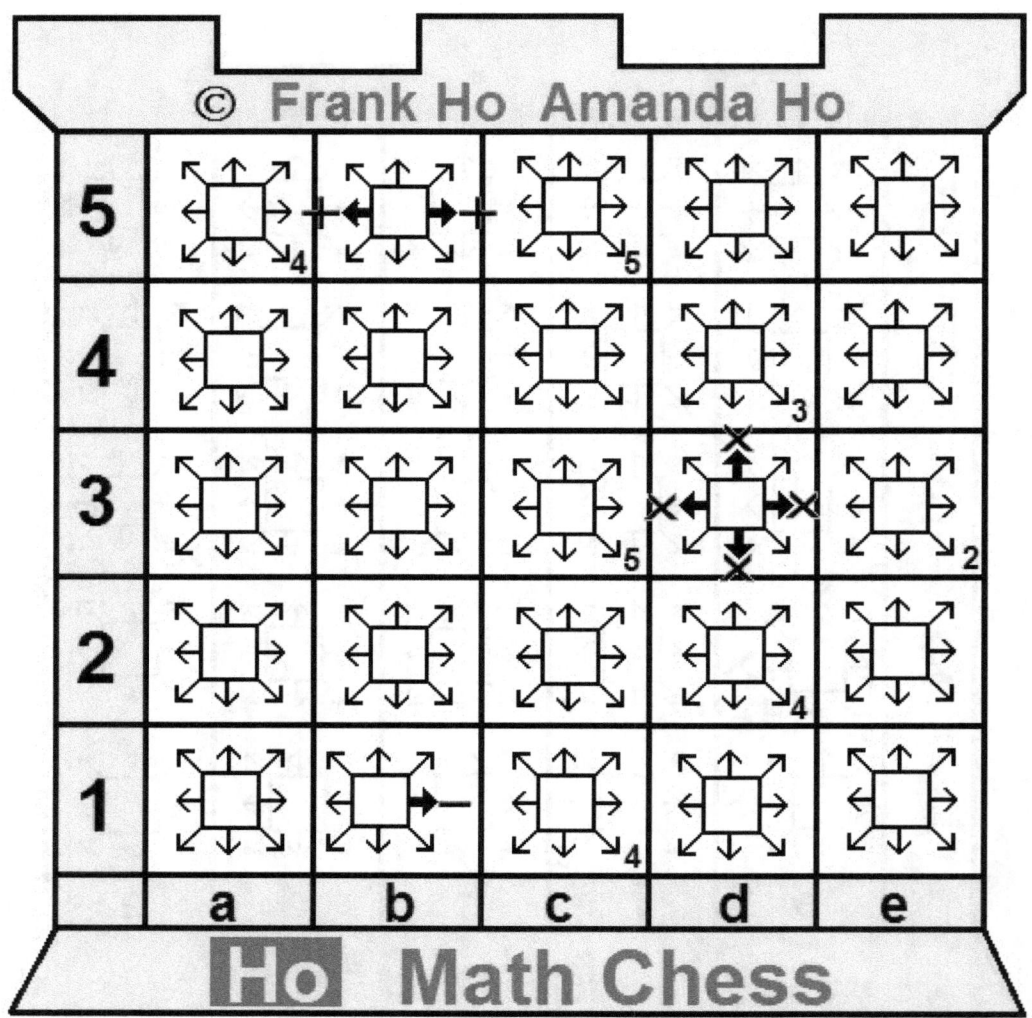

Frankho Puzzle™ # 73

Rule All the digits 1 to 5 must appear exactly once in every row and column. The number appears in the bottom right-hand corner is the end result calculated according to arithmetic operator(s) and chess move(s) as indicated by darker arrow(s).

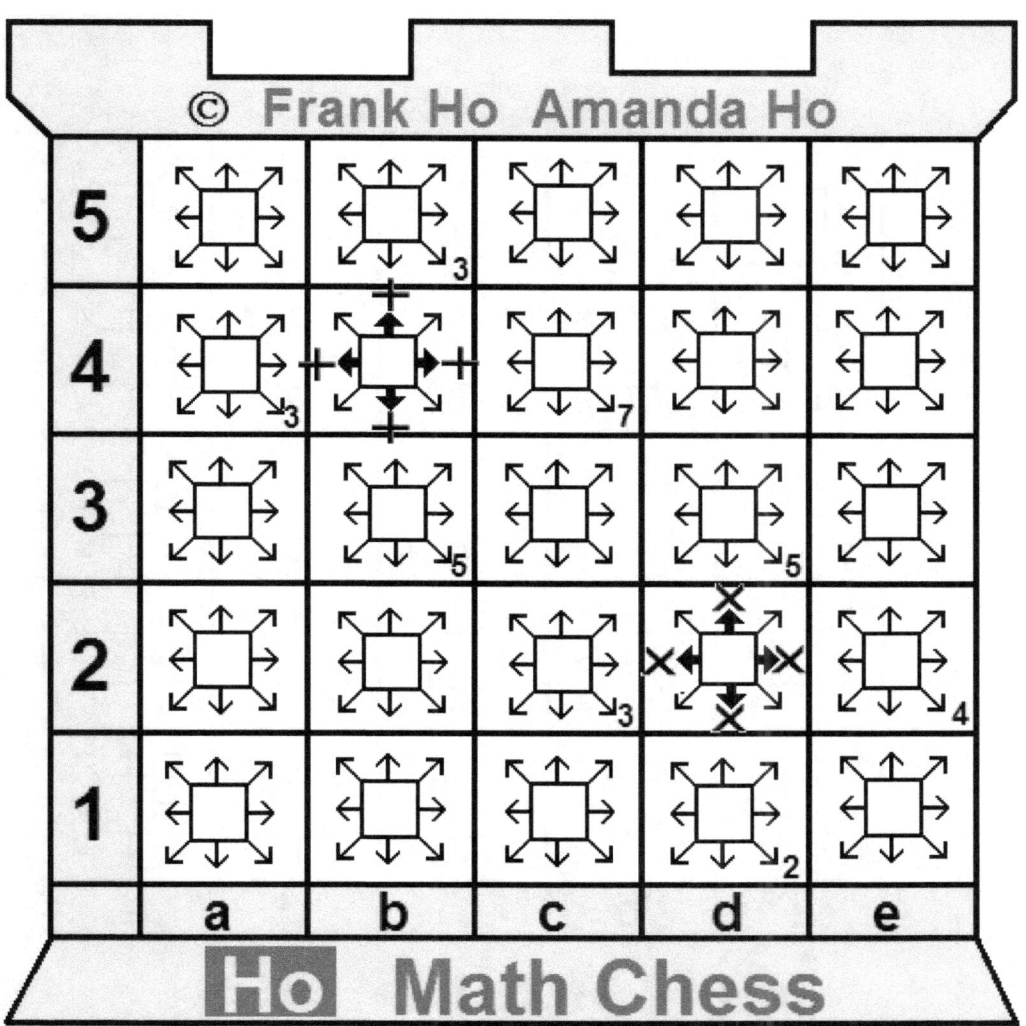

Frankho Puzzle™ # 74

Rule All the digits 1 to 5 must appear exactly once in every row and column. The number appears in the bottom right-hand corner is the end result calculated according to arithmetic operator(s) and chess move(s) as indicated by darker arrow(s).

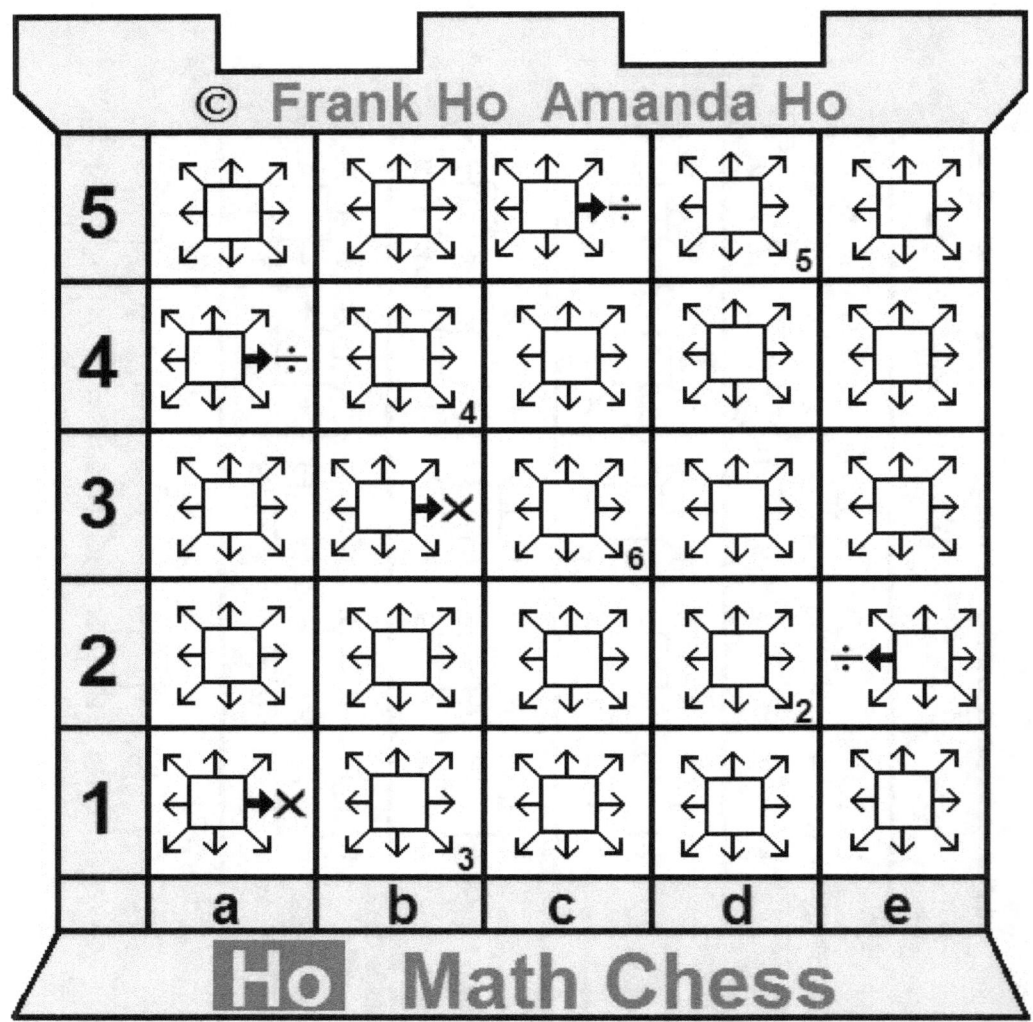

Frankho Puzzle™ # 75

Rule All the digits 1 to 5 must appear exactly once in every row and column. The number appears in the bottom right-hand corner is the end result calculated according to arithmetic operator(s) and chess move(s) as indicated by darker arrow(s).

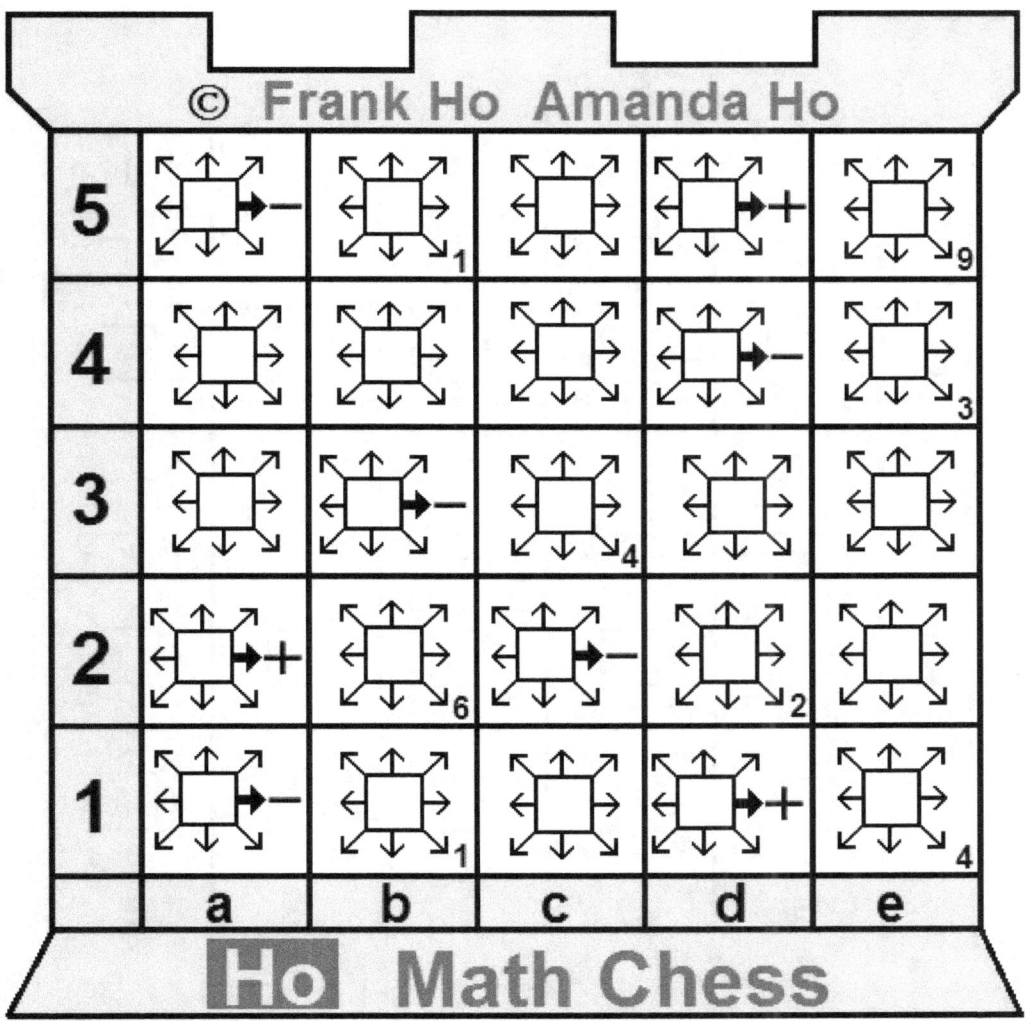

Frankho Puzzle™ # 76

Rule All the digits 1 to 5 must appear exactly once in every row and column. The number appears in the bottom right-hand corner is the end result calculated according to arithmetic operator(s) and chess move(s) as indicated by darker arrow(s).

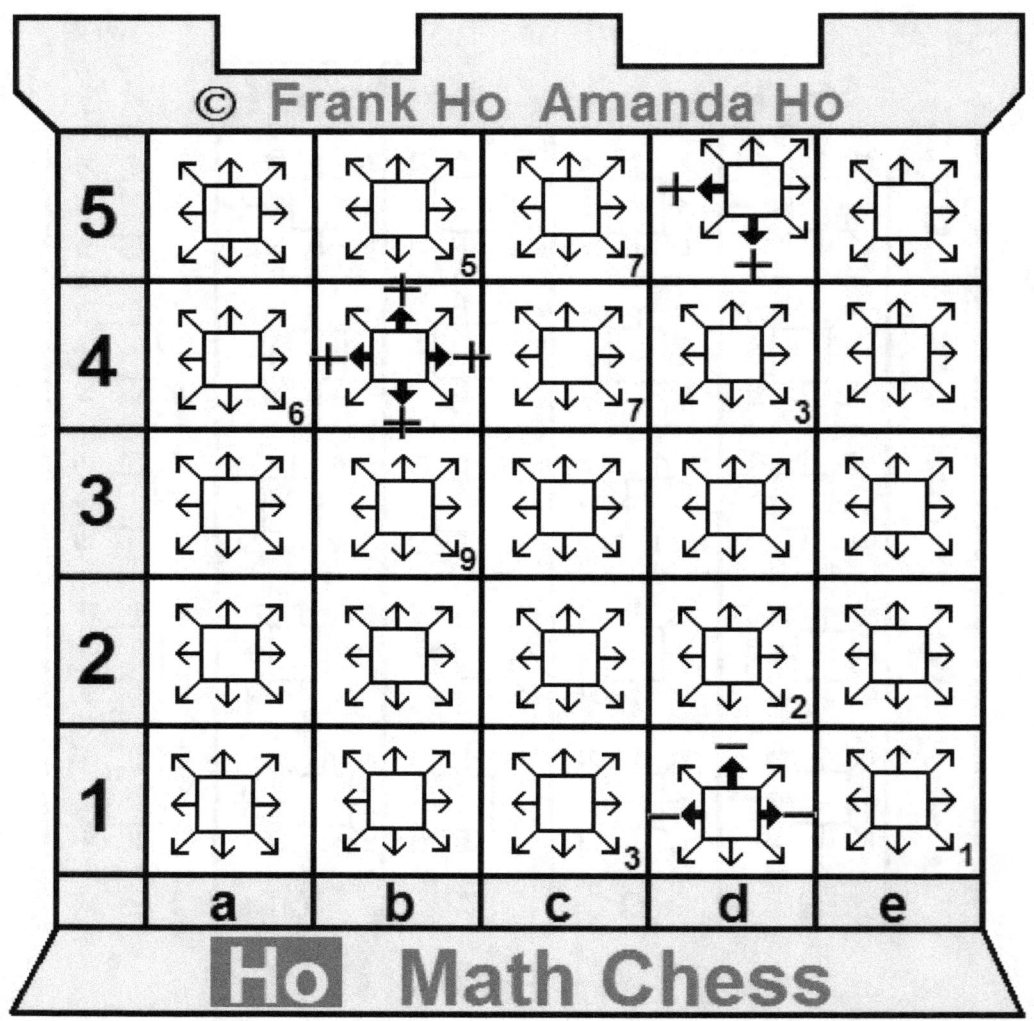

Ho Math Chess 何数棋谜 益智健脑非药物良方
Frankho Puzzle for KIDS – Brain Fitness Workbook
© 2007 — 2016 Frank Ho, Amanda Ho all rights reserved www.mathandchess.com

Frankho Puzzle™ # 77

Rule All the digits 1 to 5 must appear exactly once in every row and column. The number appears in the bottom right-hand corner is the end result calculated according to arithmetic operator(s) and chess move(s) as indicated by darker arrow(s).

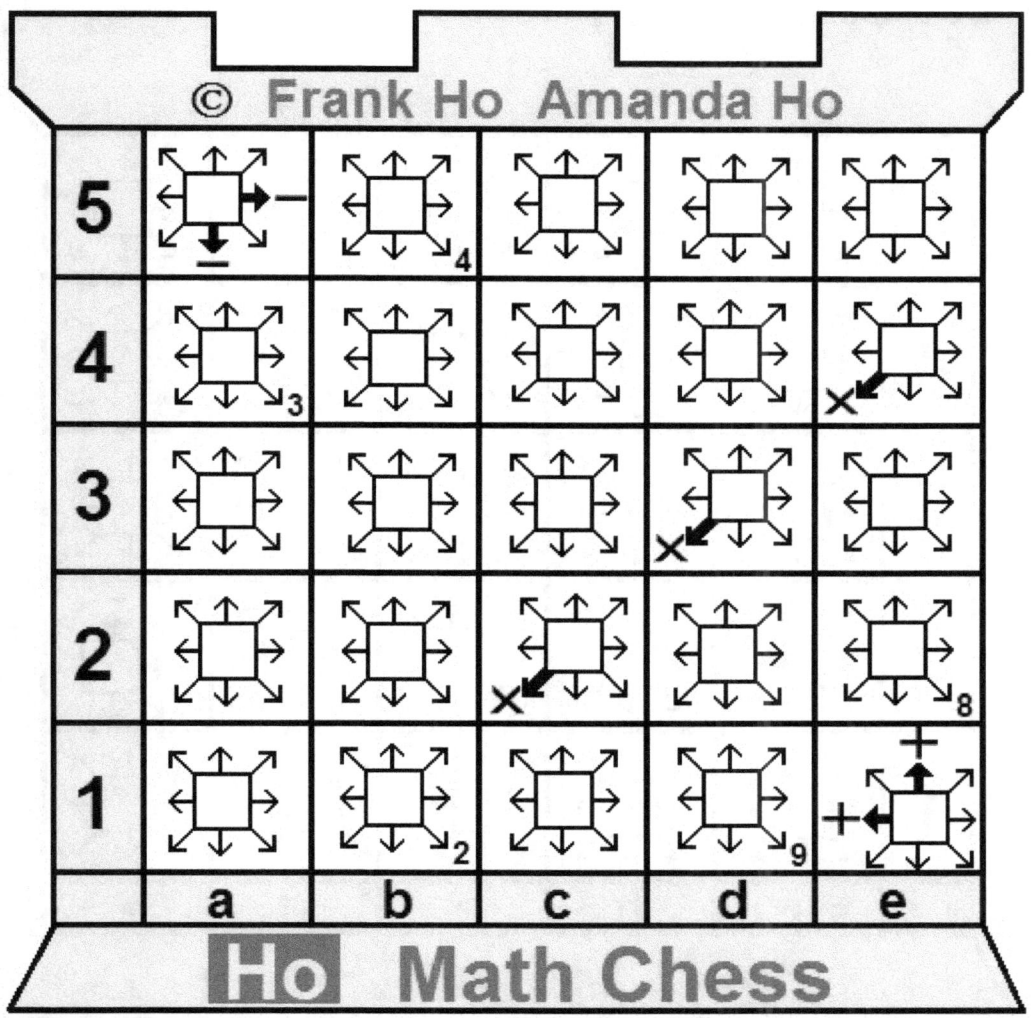

Ho Math Chess 何数棋谜 益智健脑非药物良方
Frankho Puzzle for KIDS – Brain Fitness Workbook
© 2007 — 2016 Frank Ho, Amanda Ho all rights reserved www.mathandchess.com

Frankho Puzzle™ # 78

Rule All the digits 1 to 5 must appear exactly once in every row and column. The number appears in the bottom right-hand corner is the end result calculated according to arithmetic operator(s) and chess move(s) as indicated by darker arrow(s).

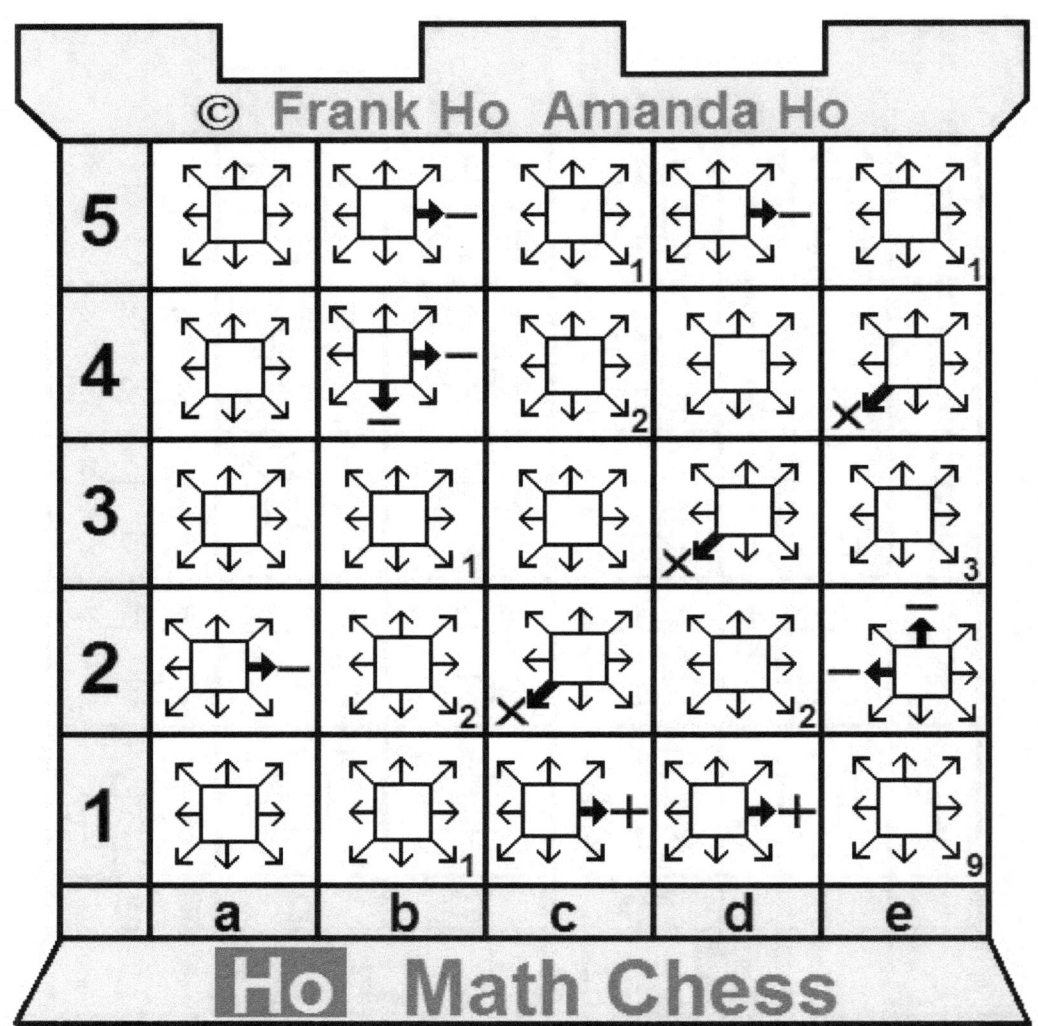

Ho Math Chess 何数棋谜 益智健脑非药物良方
Frankho Puzzle for KIDS – Brain Fitness Workbook
© 2007 — 2016 Frank Ho, Amanda Ho all rights reserved www.mathandchess.com

Frankho Puzzle™ # 79

Rule All the digits 1 to 5 must appear exactly once in every row and column. The number appears in the bottom right-hand corner is the end result calculated according to arithmetic operator(s) and chess move(s) as indicated by darker arrow(s).

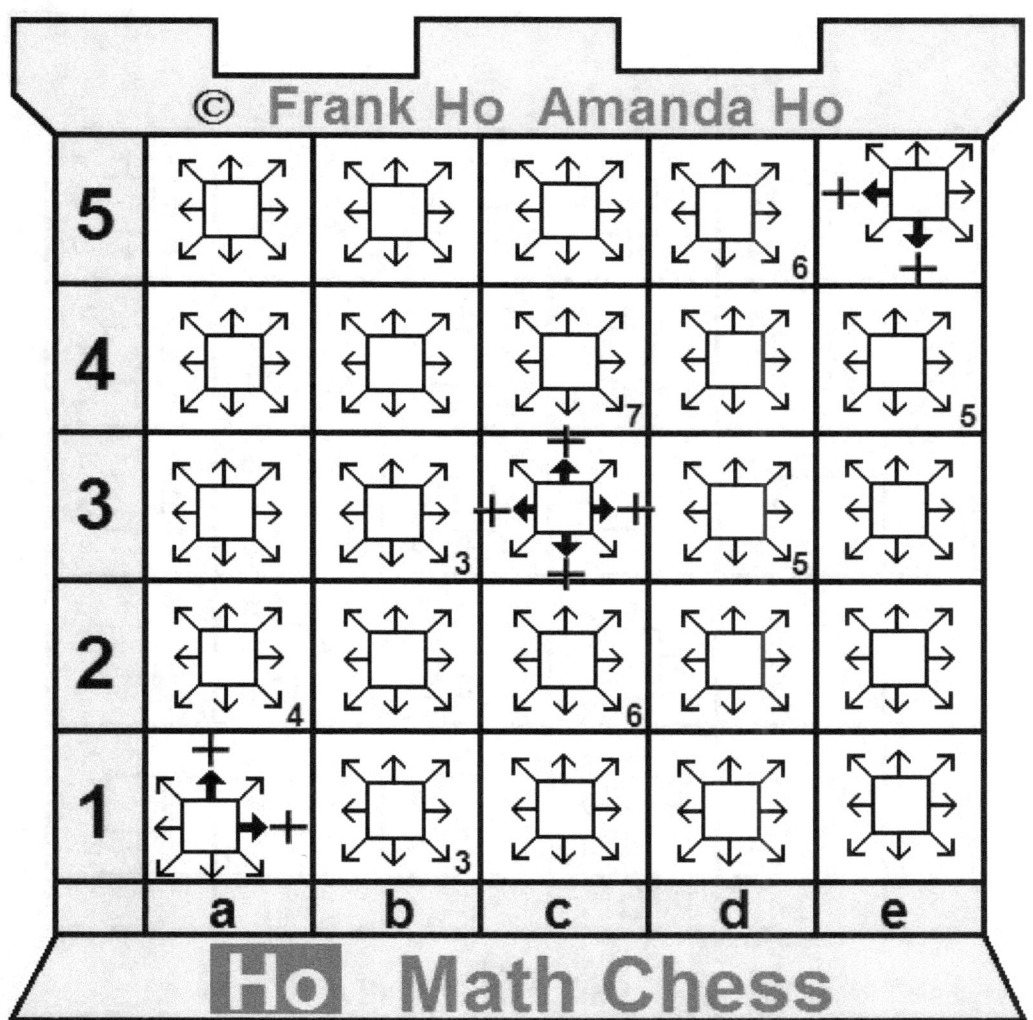

Ho Math Chess
何数棋谜 益智健脑非药物良方
Frankho Puzzle for KIDS – Brain Fitness Workbook
© 2007 — 2016 Frank Ho, Amanda Ho all rights reserved www.mathandchess.com

Frankho Puzzle™ # 80

Rule All the digits 1 to 5 must appear exactly once in every row and column. The number appears in the bottom right-hand corner is the end result calculated according to arithmetic operator(s) and chess move(s) as indicated by darker arrow(s).

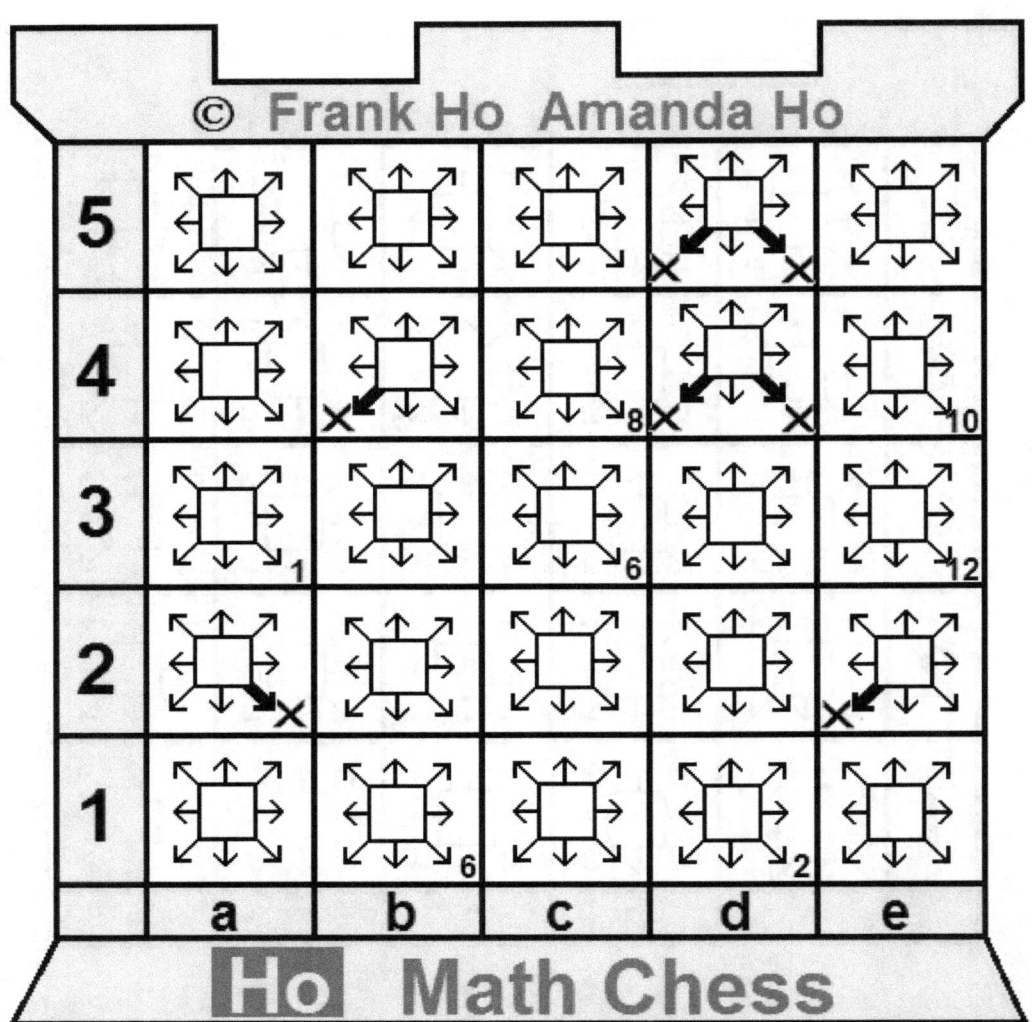

Ho Math Chess 何数棋谜 益智健脑非药物良方
Frankho Puzzle for KIDS – Brain Fitness Workbook
© 2007 – 2016 Frank Ho, Amanda Ho all rights reserved www.mathandchess.com

Frankho Puzzle™ # 81

Rule All the digits 1 to 5 must appear exactly once in every row and column. The number appears in the bottom right-hand corner is the end result calculated according to arithmetic operator(s) and chess move(s) as indicated by darker arrow(s).

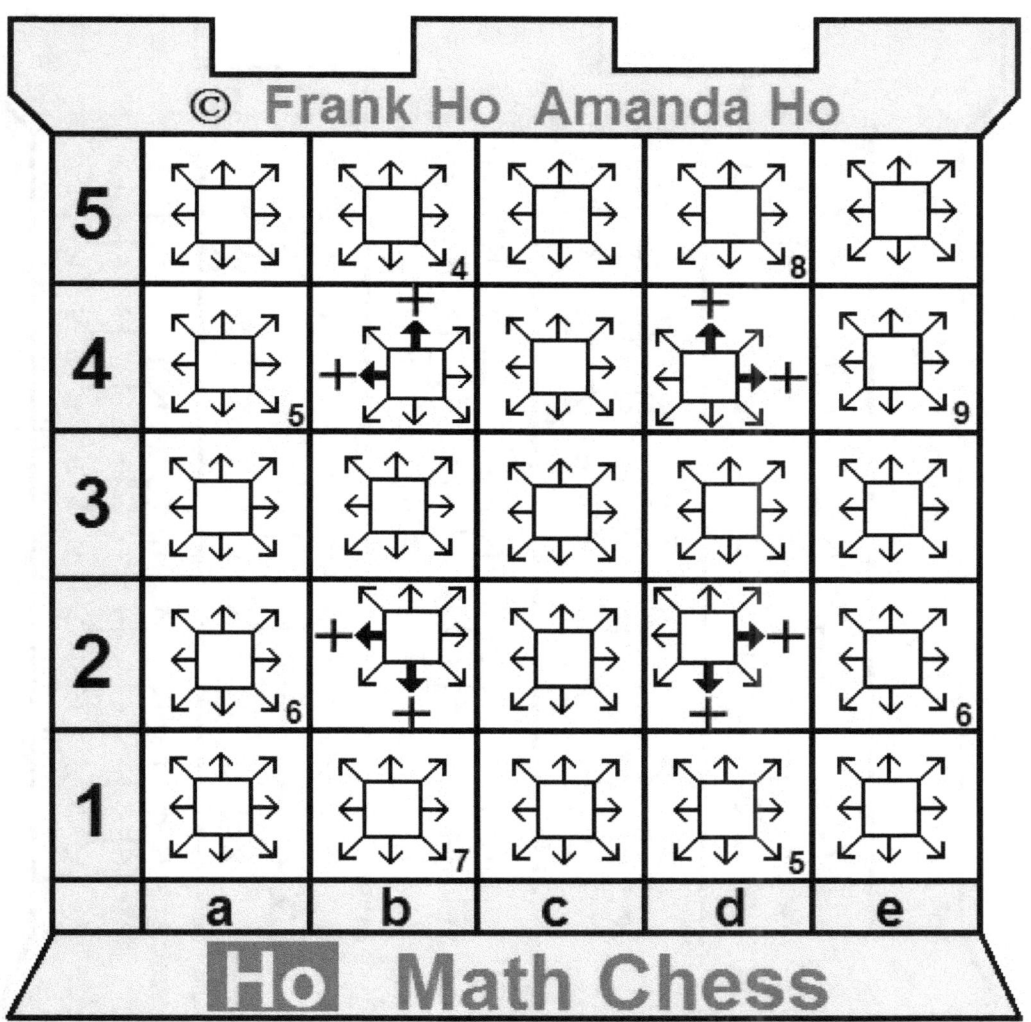

Frankho Puzzle™ # 82

Rule All the digits 1 to 5 must appear exactly once in every row and column. The number appears in the bottom right-hand corner is the end result calculated according to arithmetic operator(s) and chess move(s) as indicated by darker arrow(s).

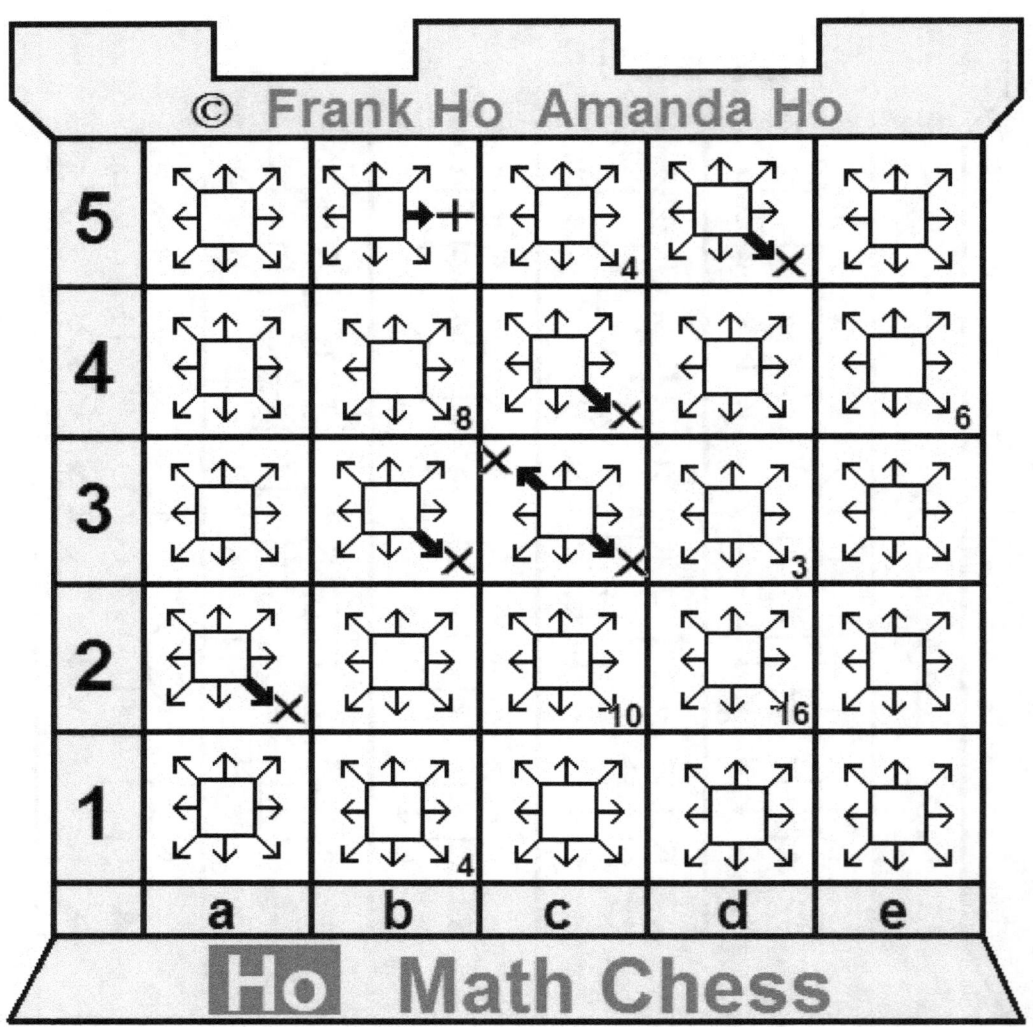

Ho Math Chess 何数棋谜 益智健脑非药物良方
Frankho Puzzle for KIDS – Brain Fitness Workbook
© 2007 — 2016 Frank Ho, Amanda Ho all rights reserved www.mathandchess.com

Frankho Puzzle™ # 83

Rule All the digits 1 to 5 must appear exactly once in every row and column. The number appears in the bottom right-hand corner is the end result calculated according to arithmetic operator(s) and chess move(s) as indicated by darker arrow(s).

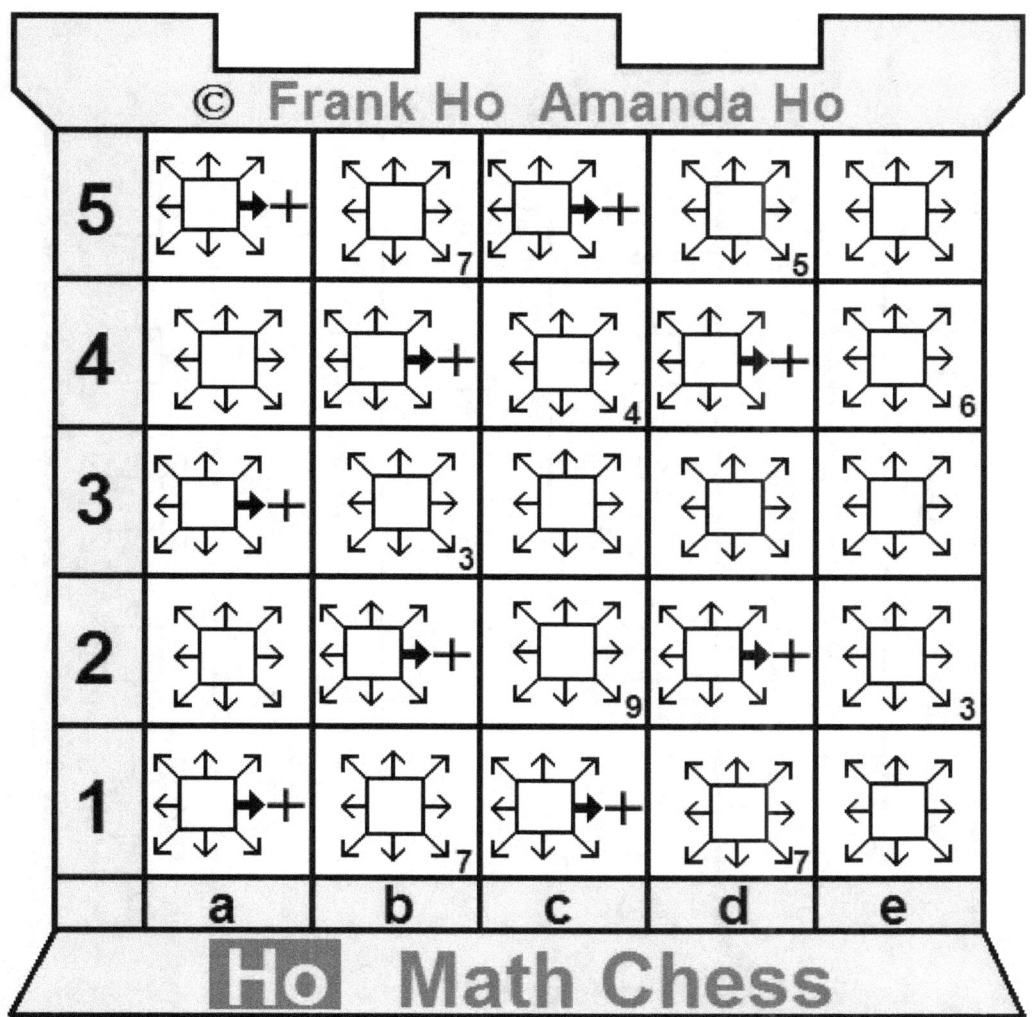

Ho Math Chess 何数棋谜 益智健脑非药物良方
Frankho Puzzle for KIDS – Brain Fitness Workbook

© 2007 — 2016 Frank Ho, Amanda Ho all rights reserved www.mathandchess.com

Frankho Puzzle™ # 84

Rule All the digits 1 to 5 must appear exactly once in every row and column. The number appears in the bottom right-hand corner is the end result calculated according to arithmetic operator(s) and chess move(s) as indicated by darker arrow(s).

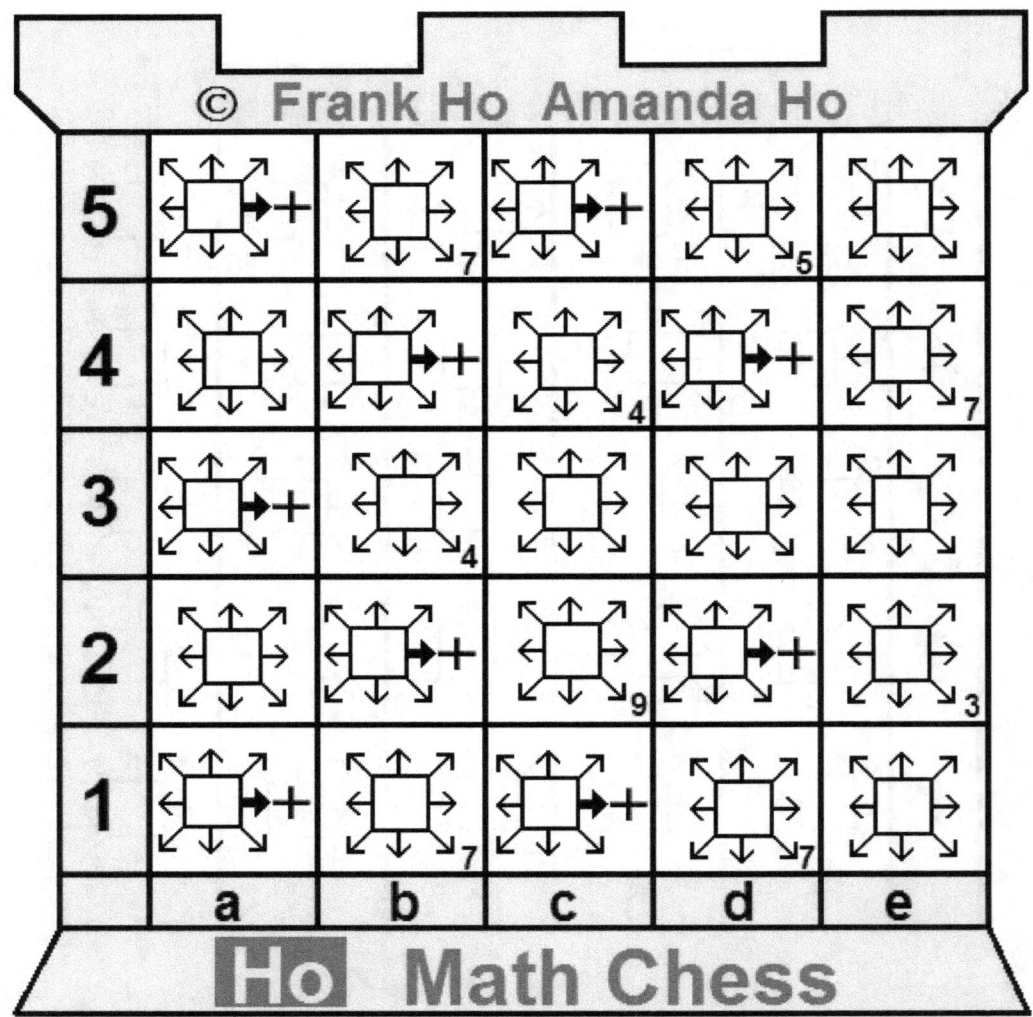

Ho Math Chess
何数棋谜 益智健脑非药物良方
Frankho Puzzle for KIDS – Brain Fitness Workbook
© 2007 – 2016 Frank Ho, Amanda Ho all rights reserved www.mathandchess.com

Frankho Puzzle™ # 85

Rule All the digits 1 to 5 must appear exactly once in every row and column. The number appears in the bottom right-hand corner is the end result calculated according to arithmetic operator(s) and chess move(s) as indicated by darker arrow(s).

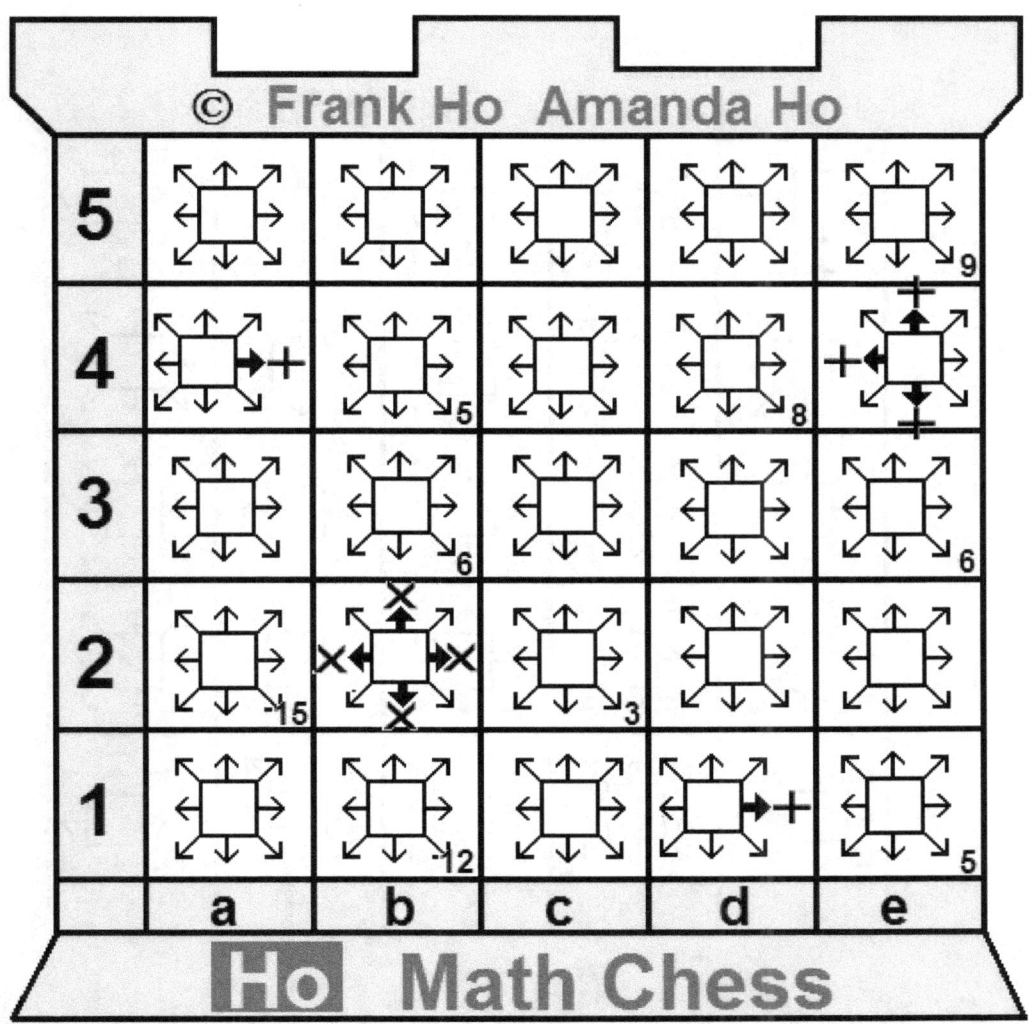

Frankho Puzzle™ # 86

Rule All the digits 1 to 5 must appear exactly once in every row and column. The number appears in the bottom right-hand corner is the end result calculated according to arithmetic operator(s) and chess move(s) as indicated by darker arrow(s).

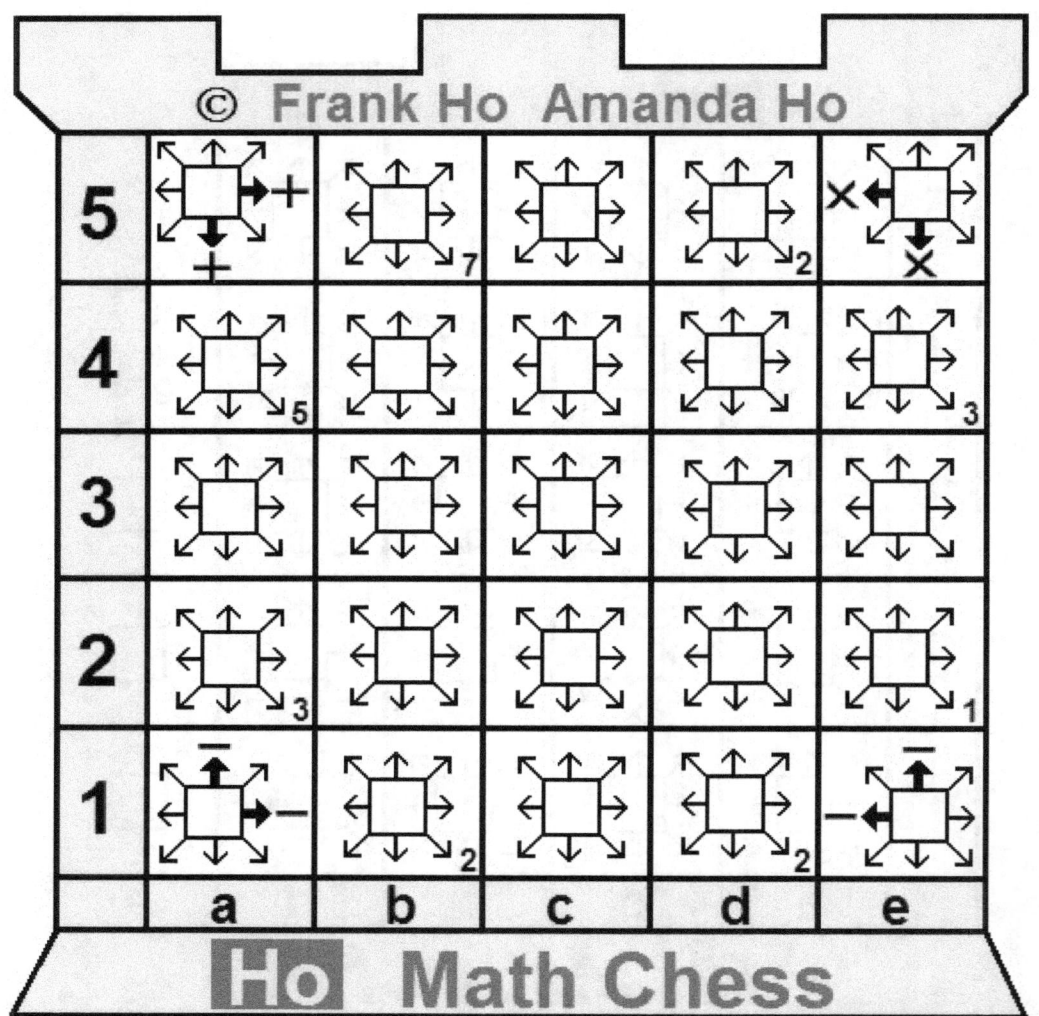

Ho Math Chess 何数棋谜 益智健脑非药物良方
Frankho Puzzle for KIDS – Brain Fitness Workbook

© 2007 — 2016 Frank Ho, Amanda Ho all rights reserved www.mathandchess.com

Frankho Puzzle™ # 87

Rule All the digits 1 to 5 must appear exactly once in every row and column. The number appears in the bottom right-hand corner is the end result calculated according to arithmetic operator(s) and chess move(s) as indicated by darker arrow(s).

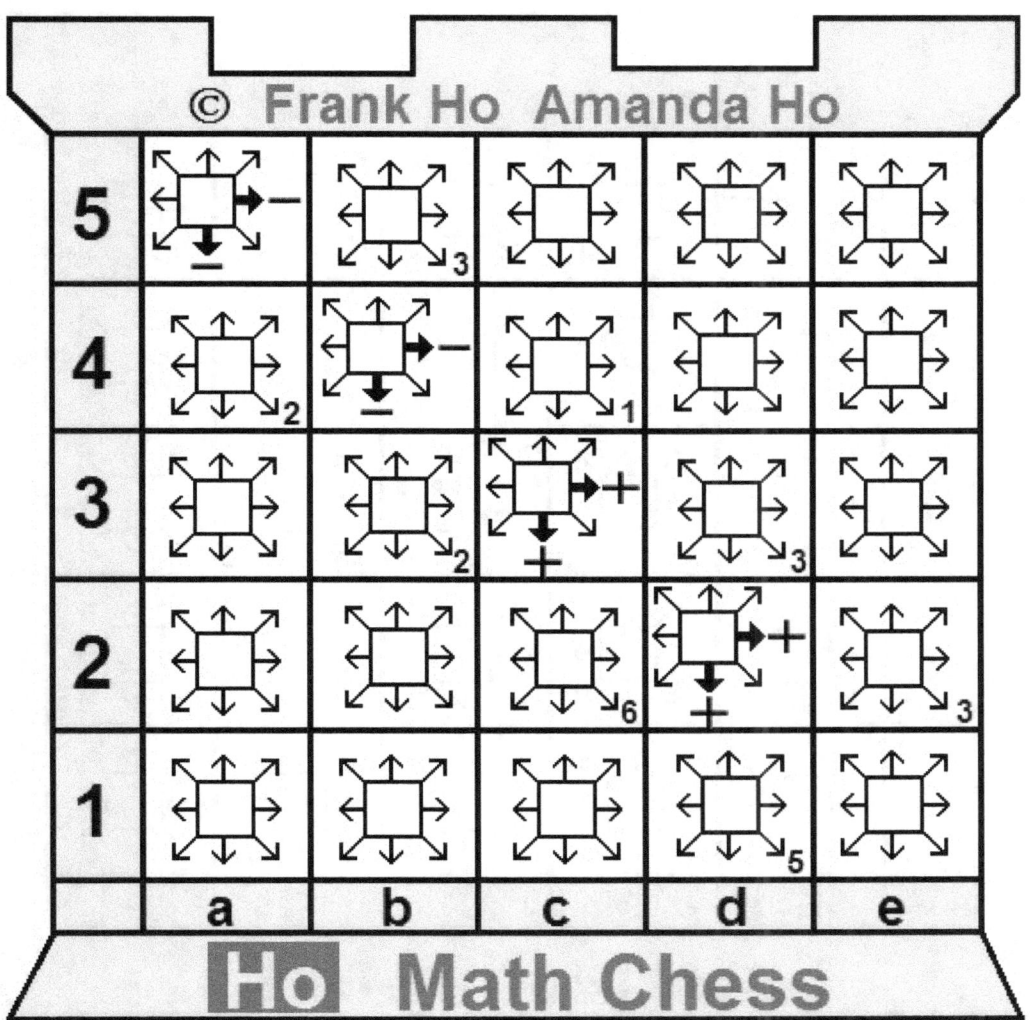

Frankho Puzzle™ # 88

Rule All the digits 1 to 5 must appear exactly once in every row and column. The number appears in the bottom right-hand corner is the end result calculated according to arithmetic operator(s) and chess move(s) as indicated by darker arrow(s).

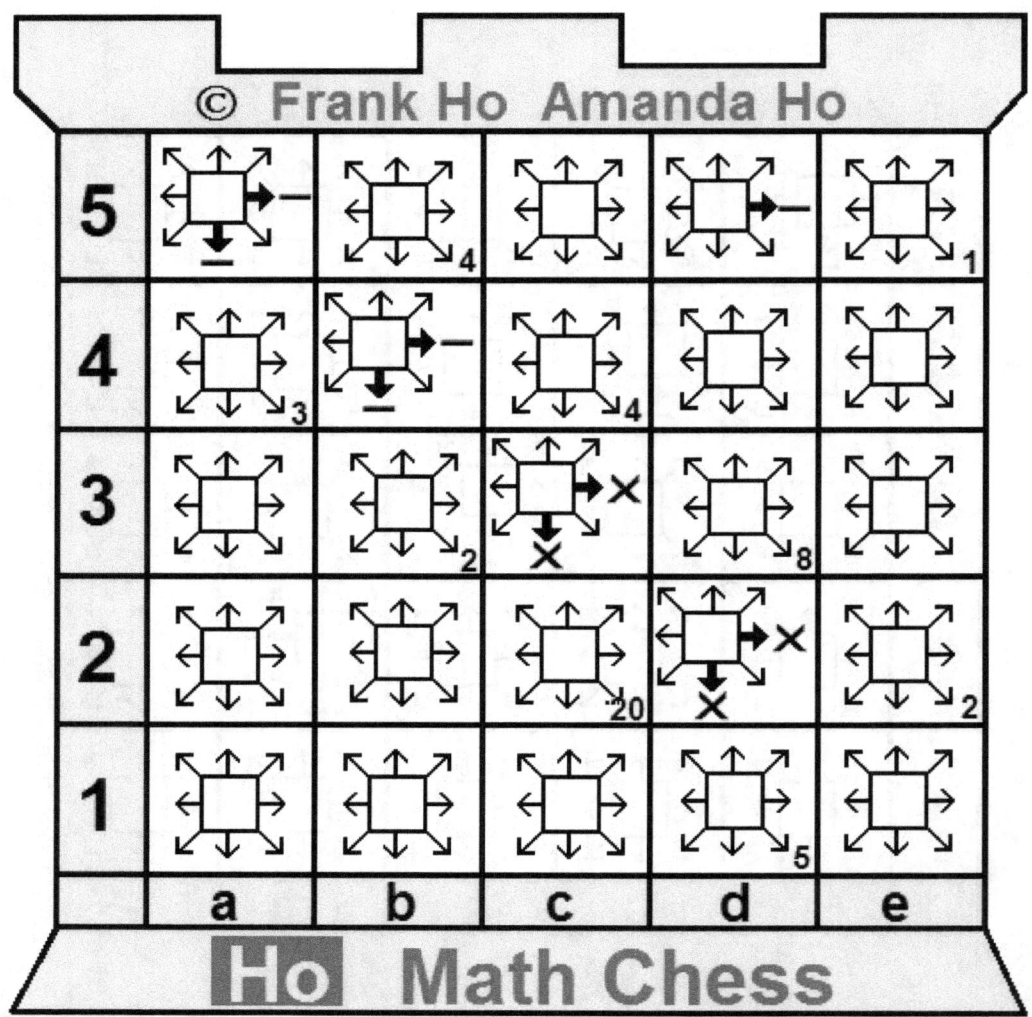

Ho Math Chess 何数棋谜 益智健脑非药物良方
Frankho Puzzle for KIDS – Brain Fitness Workbook
© 2007 – 2016 Frank Ho, Amanda Ho all rights reserved www.mathandchess.com

Frankho Puzzle™ # 89

Rule All the digits 1 to 5 must appear exactly once in every row and column. The number appears in the bottom right-hand corner is the end result calculated according to arithmetic operator(s) and chess move(s) as indicated by darker arrow(s).

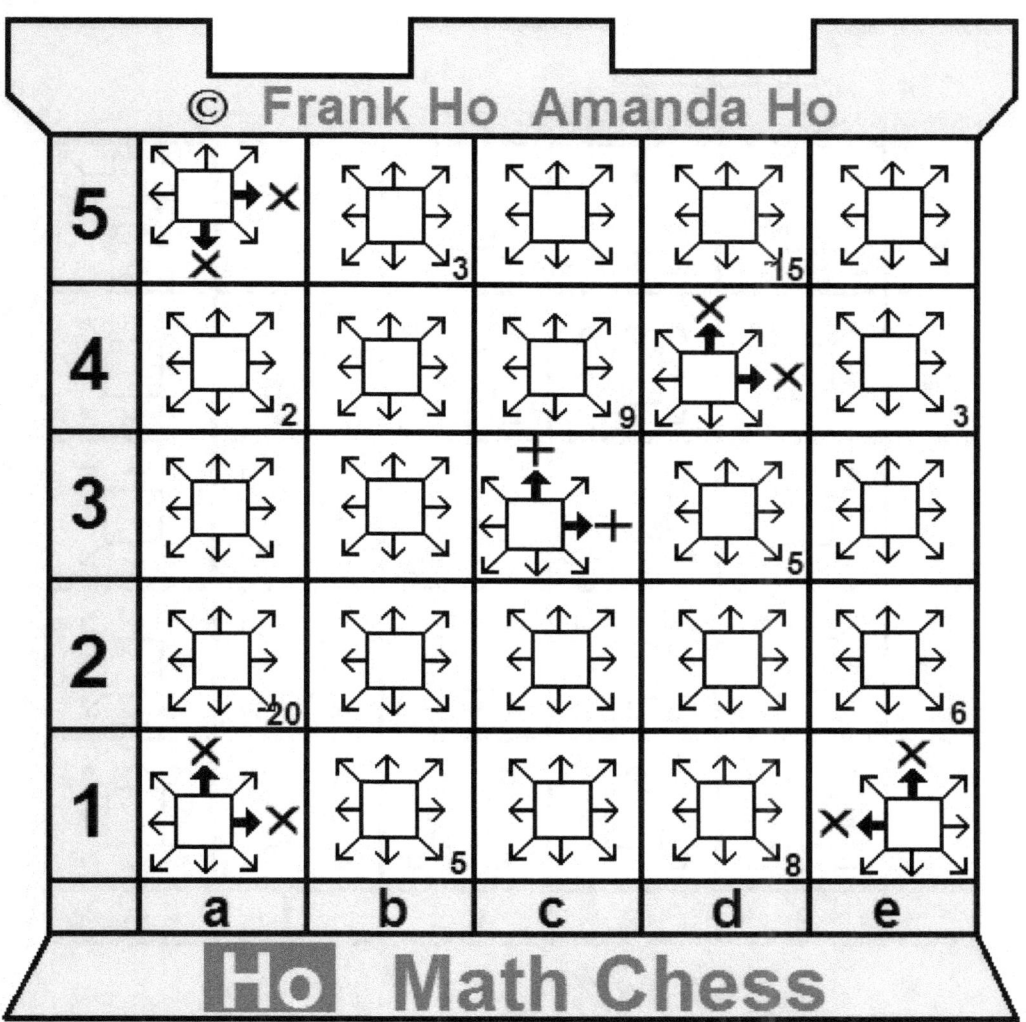

Frankho Puzzle™ # 90

Rule All the digits 1 to 5 must appear exactly once in every row and column. The number appears in the bottom right-hand corner is the end result calculated according to arithmetic operator(s) and chess move(s) as indicated by darker arrow(s).

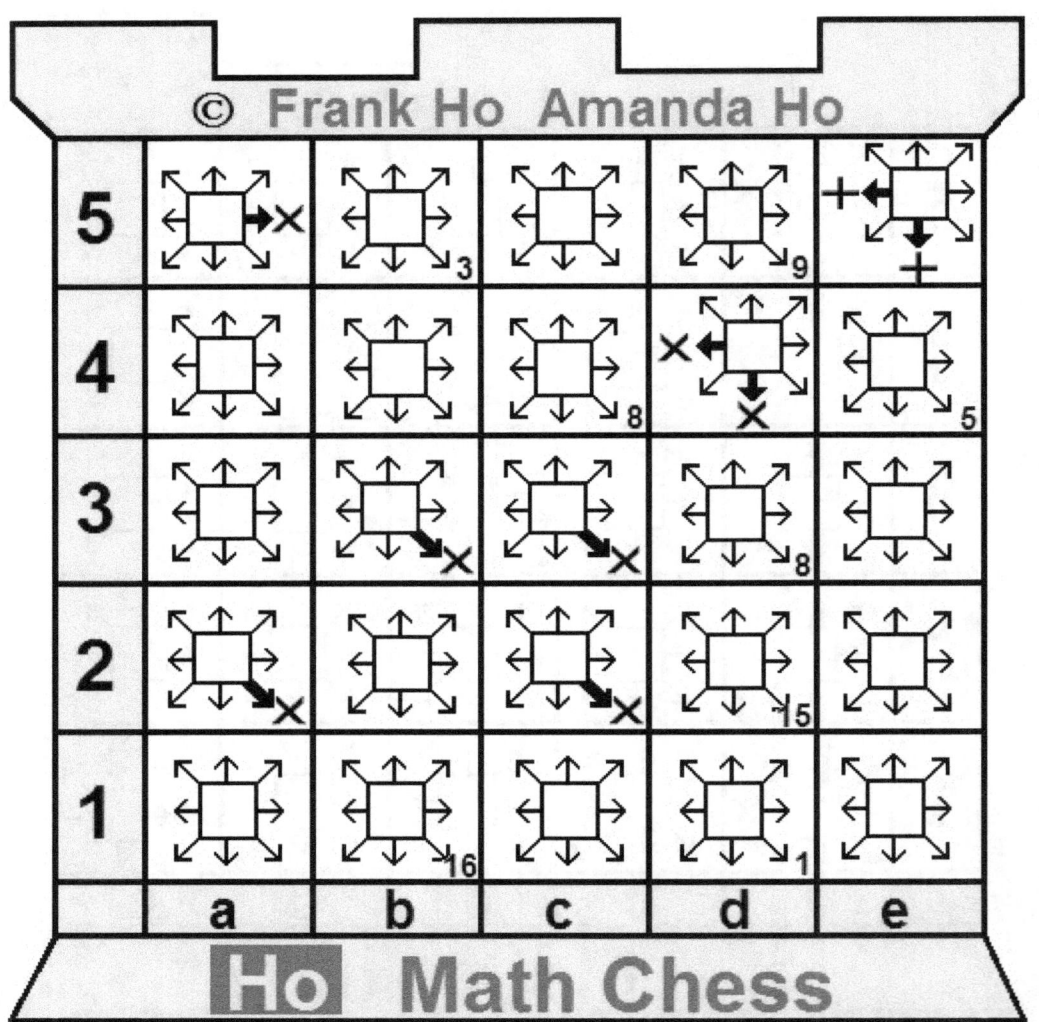

Ho Math Chess 何数棋谜 益智健脑非药物良方
Frankho Puzzle for KIDS – Brain Fitness Workbook
© 2007 — 2016 Frank Ho, Amanda Ho all rights reserved www.mathandchess.com

Frankho Puzzle™ # 91

Rule All the digits 1 to 5 must appear exactly once in every row and column. The number appears in the bottom right-hand corner is the end result calculated according to arithmetic operator(s) and chess move(s) as indicated by darker arrow(s).

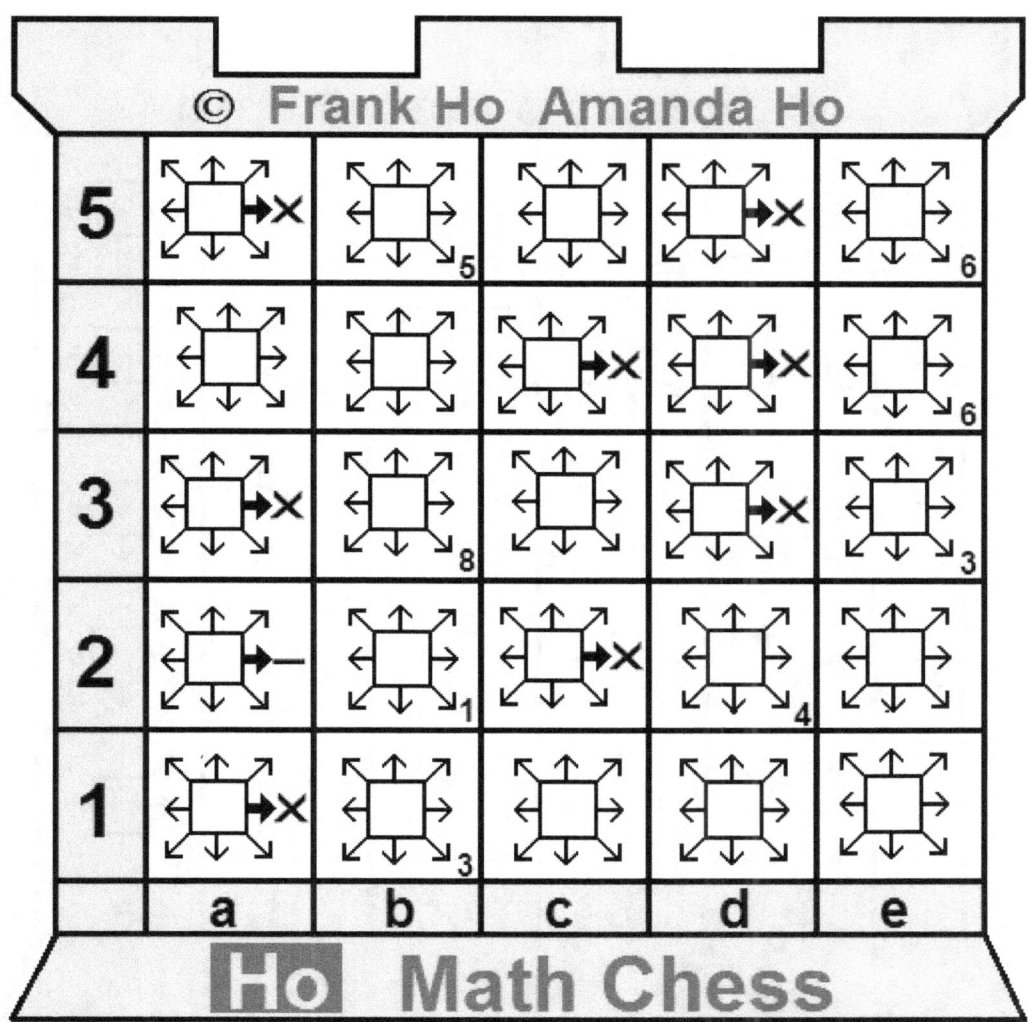

Ho Math Chess 何数棋谜 益智健脑非药物良方
Frankho Puzzle for KIDS – Brain Fitness Workbook
© 2007 — 2016 Frank Ho, Amanda Ho all rights reserved www.mathandchess.com

Frankho Puzzle™ # 92

Rule All the digits 1 to 5 must appear exactly once in every row and column. The number appears in the bottom right-hand corner is the end result calculated according to arithmetic operator(s) and chess move(s) as indicated by darker arrow(s).

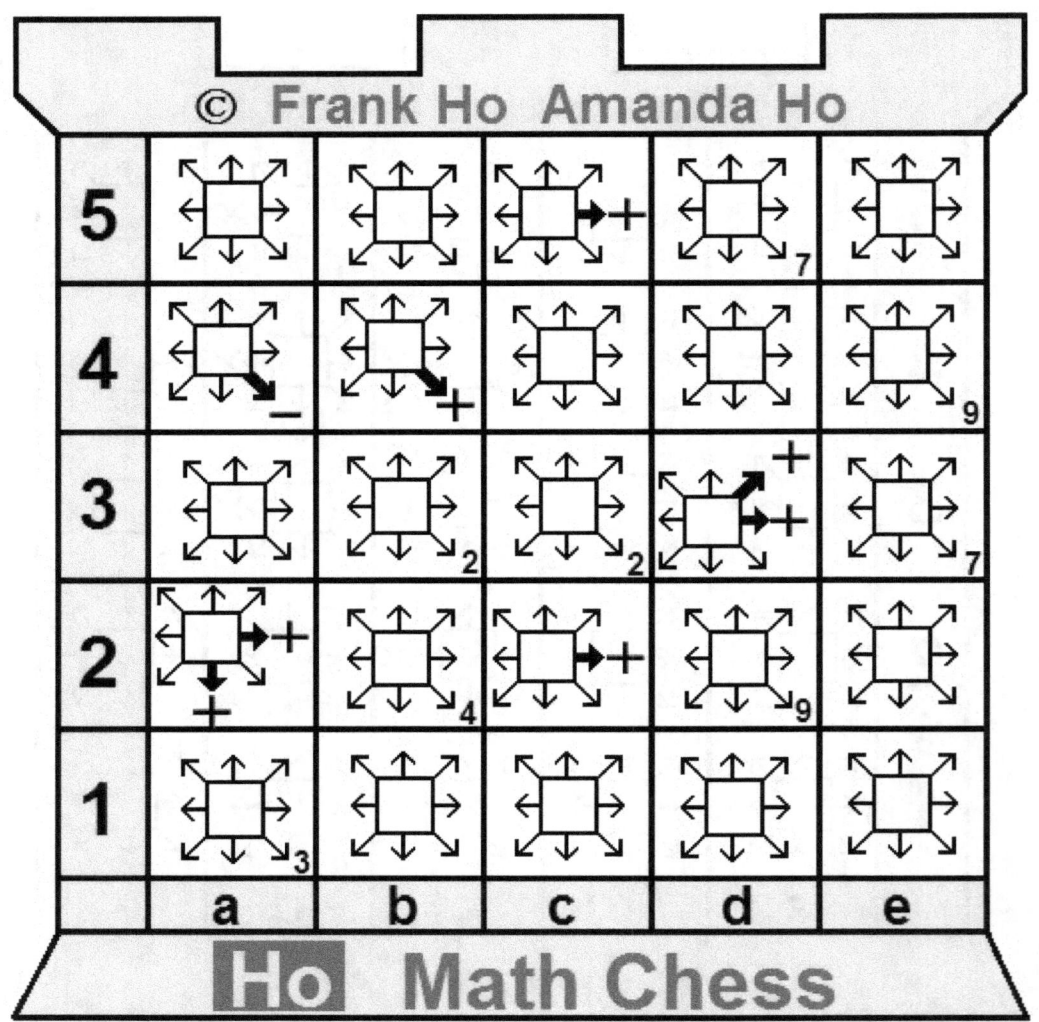

Frankho Puzzle™ # 93

Rule All the digits 1 to 5 must appear exactly once in every row and column. The number appears in the bottom right-hand corner is the end result calculated according to arithmetic operator(s) and chess move(s) as indicated by darker arrow(s).

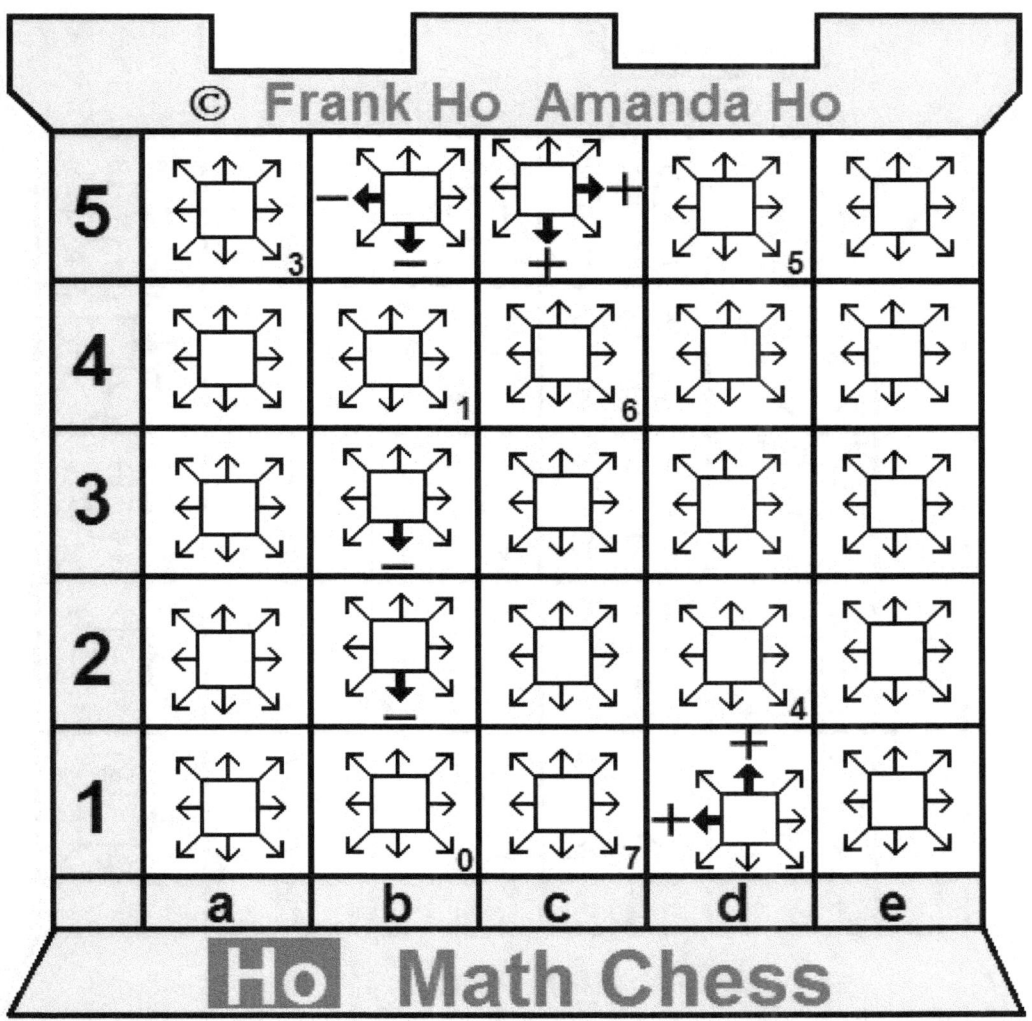

Frankho Puzzle™ # 94

Rule All the digits 1 to 5 must appear exactly once in every row and column. The number appears in the bottom right-hand corner is the end result calculated according to arithmetic operator(s) and chess move(s) as indicated by darker arrow(s).

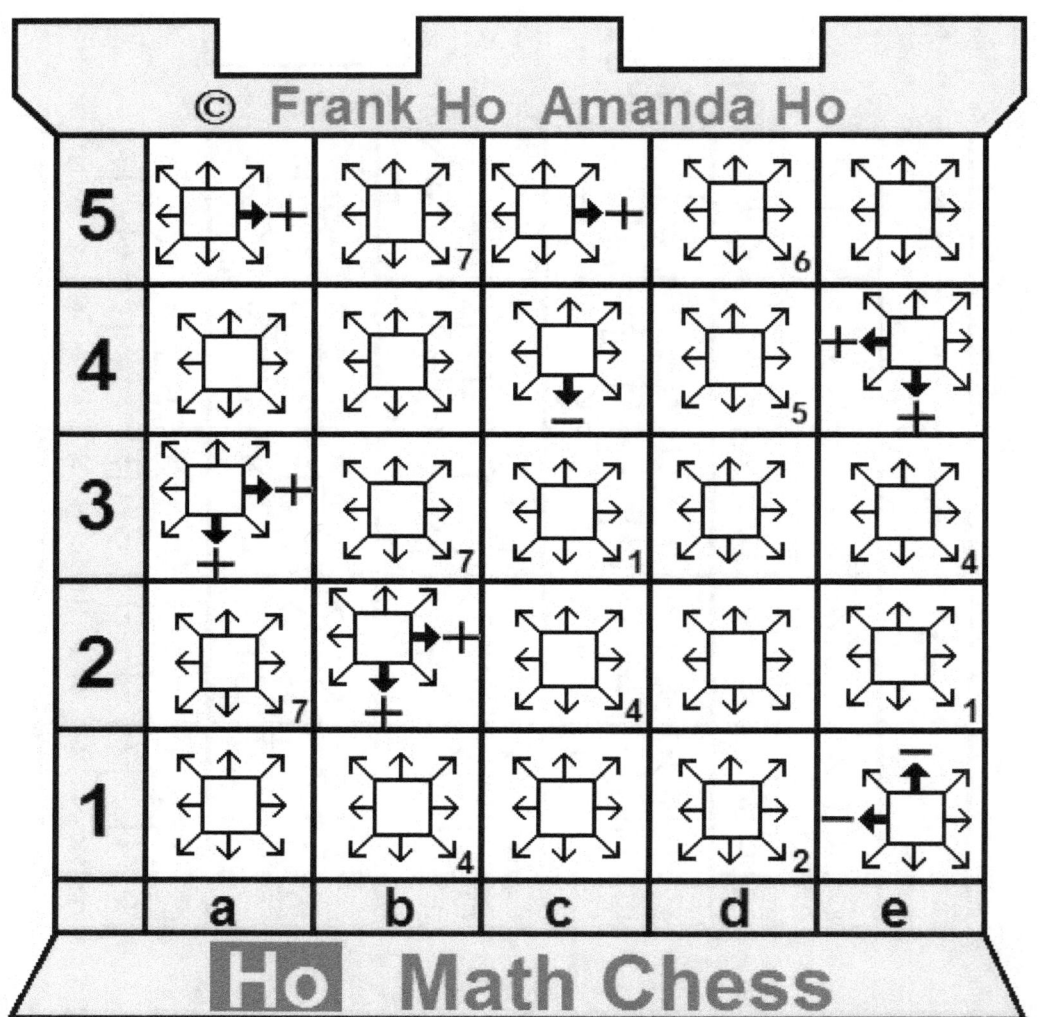

Ho Math Chess 何数棋谜 益智健脑非药物良方
Frankho Puzzle for KIDS – Brain Fitness Workbook
© 2007 – 2016 Frank Ho, Amanda Ho all rights reserved www.mathandchess.com

Frankho Puzzle™ # 95

Rule All the digits 1 to 5 must appear exactly once in every row and column. The number appears in the bottom right-hand corner is the end result calculated according to arithmetic operator(s) and chess move(s) as indicated by darker arrow(s).

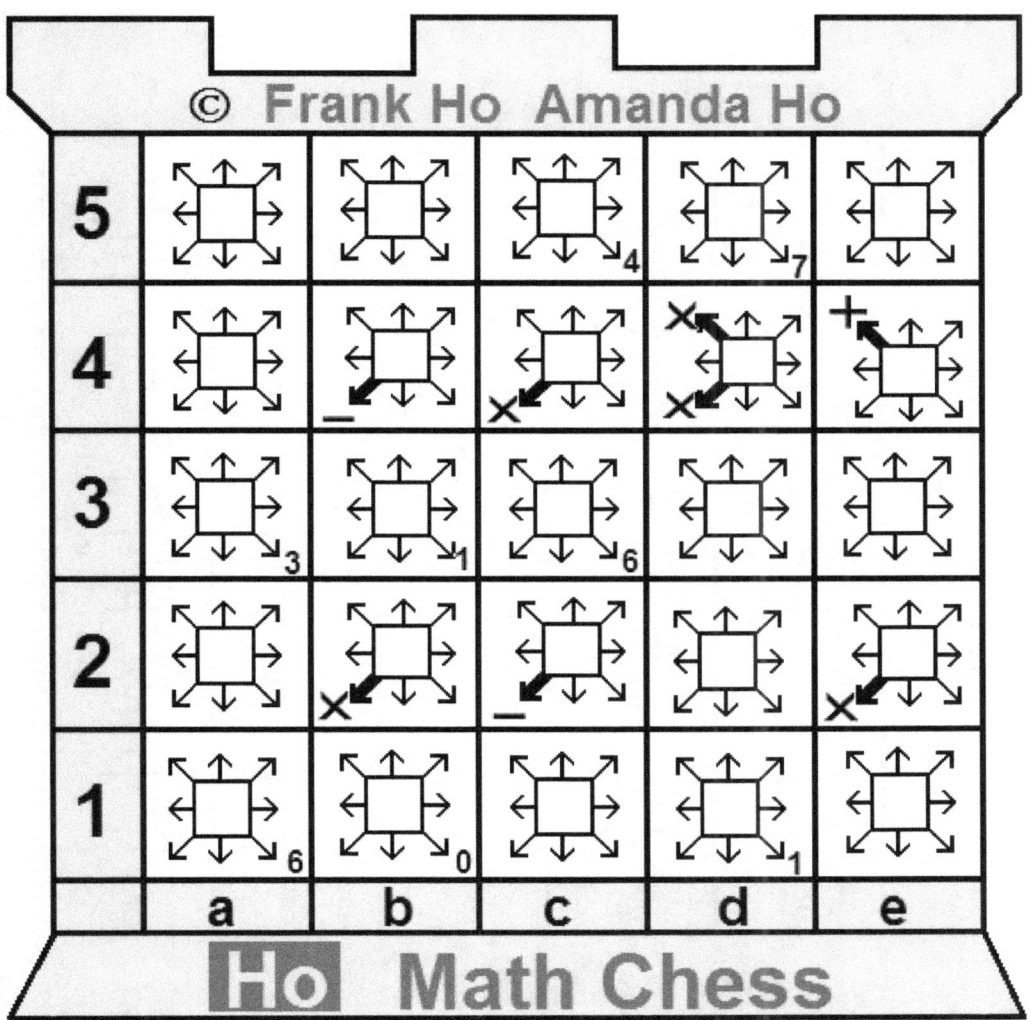

Frankho Puzzle™ # 96

Rule All the digits 1 to 5 must appear exactly once in every row and column. The number appears in the bottom right-hand corner is the end result calculated according to arithmetic operator(s) and chess move(s) as indicated by darker arrow(s).

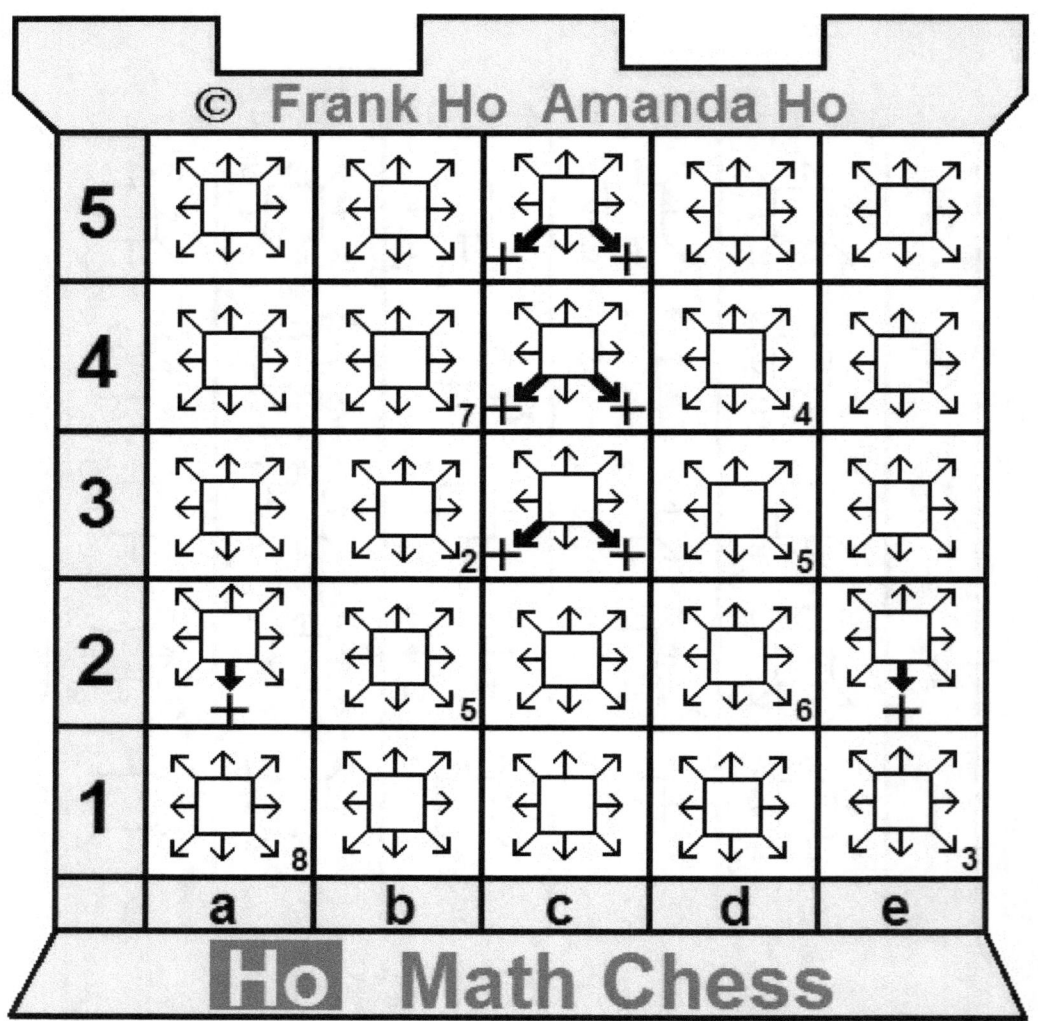

Ho Math Chess 何数棋谜 益智健脑非药物良方
Frankho Puzzle for KIDS – Brain Fitness Workbook
© 2007 — 2016 Frank Ho, Amanda Ho all rights reserved www.mathandchess.com

Frankho Puzzle™ # 97

Rule All the digits 1 to 5 must appear exactly once in every row and column. The number appears in the bottom right-hand corner is the end result calculated according to arithmetic operator(s) and chess move(s) as indicated by darker arrow(s).

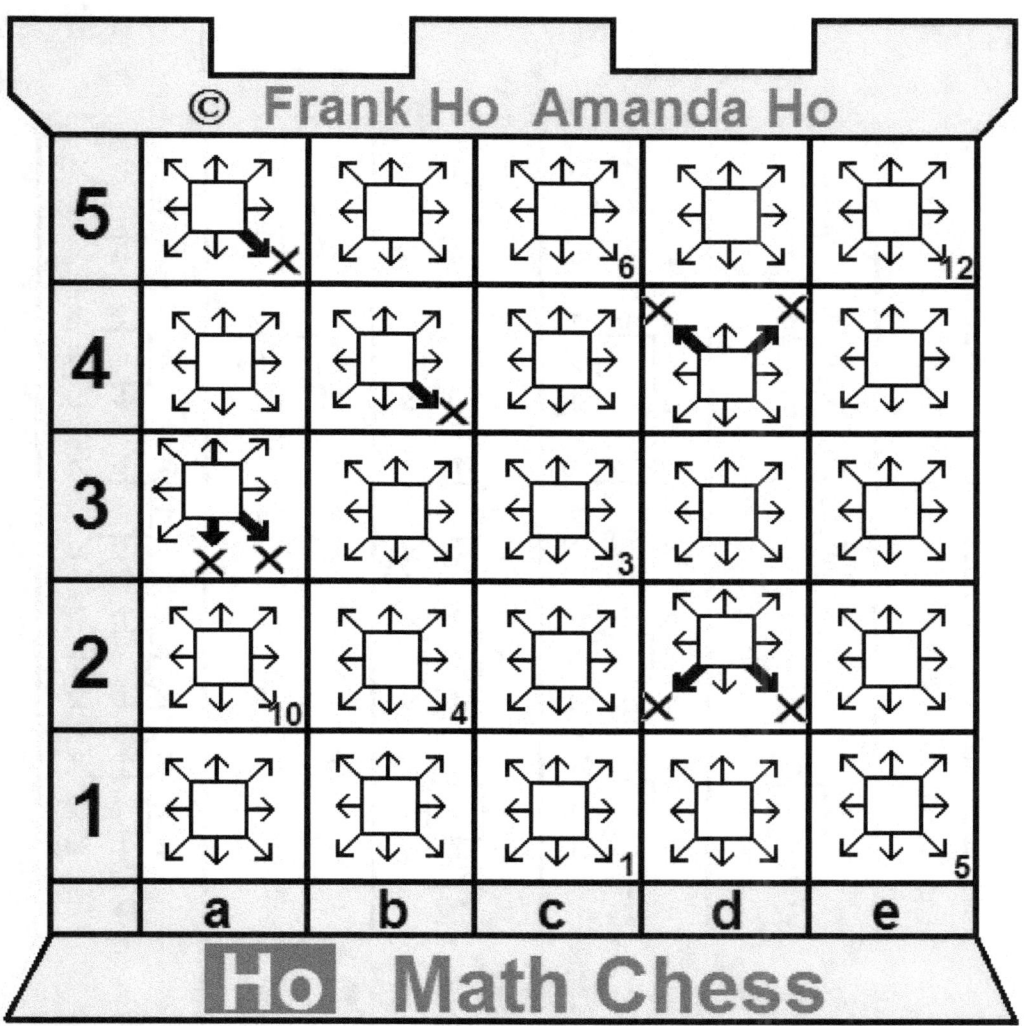

Frankho Puzzle™ # 98

Rule All the digits 1 to 5 must appear exactly once in every row and column. The number appears in the bottom right-hand corner is the end result calculated according to arithmetic operator(s) and chess move(s) as indicated by darker arrow(s).

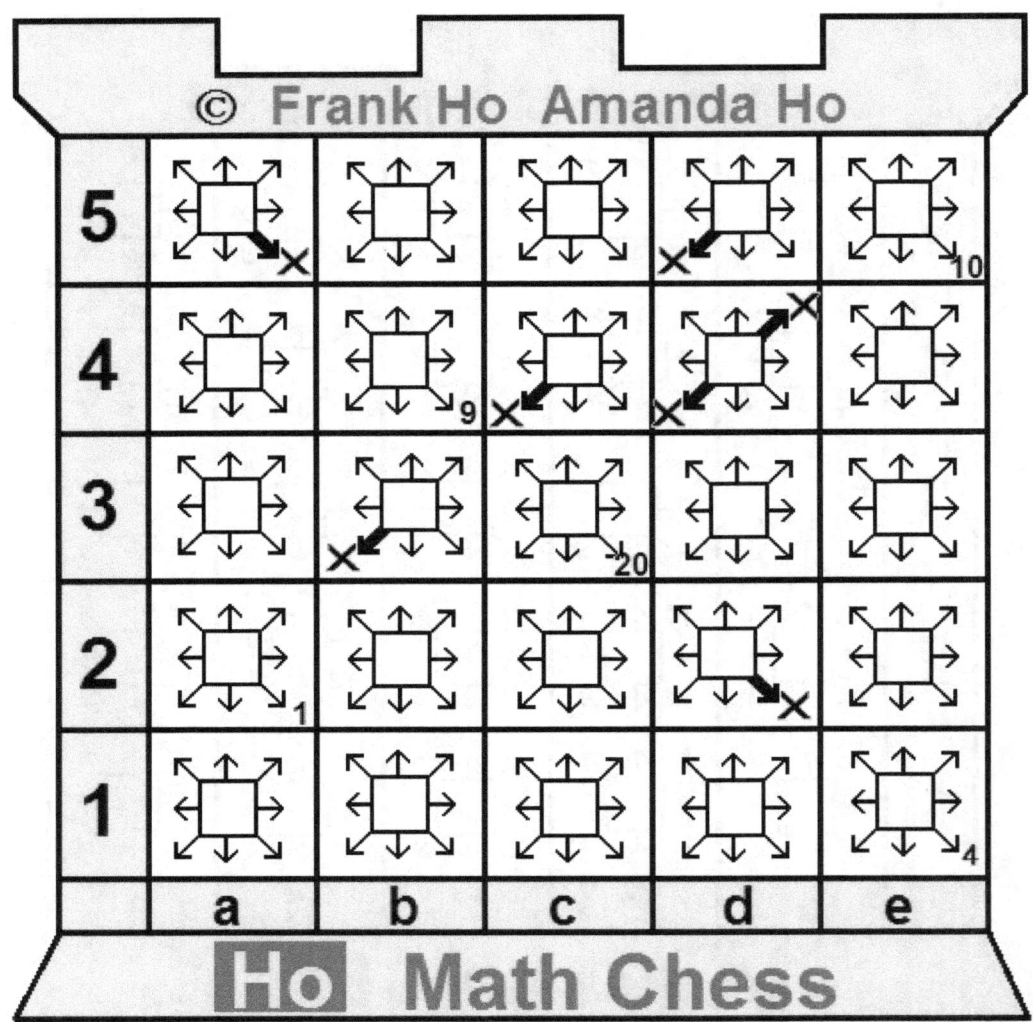

Ho Math Chess 何数棋谜 益智健脑非药物良方
Frankho Puzzle for KIDS – Brain Fitness Workbook
© 2007 — 2016 Frank Ho, Amanda Ho all rights reserved www.mathandchess.com

Frankho Puzzle™ # 99

Rule All the digits 1 to 5 must appear exactly once in every row and column. The number appears in the bottom right-hand corner is the end result calculated according to arithmetic operator(s) and chess move(s) as indicated by darker arrow(s).

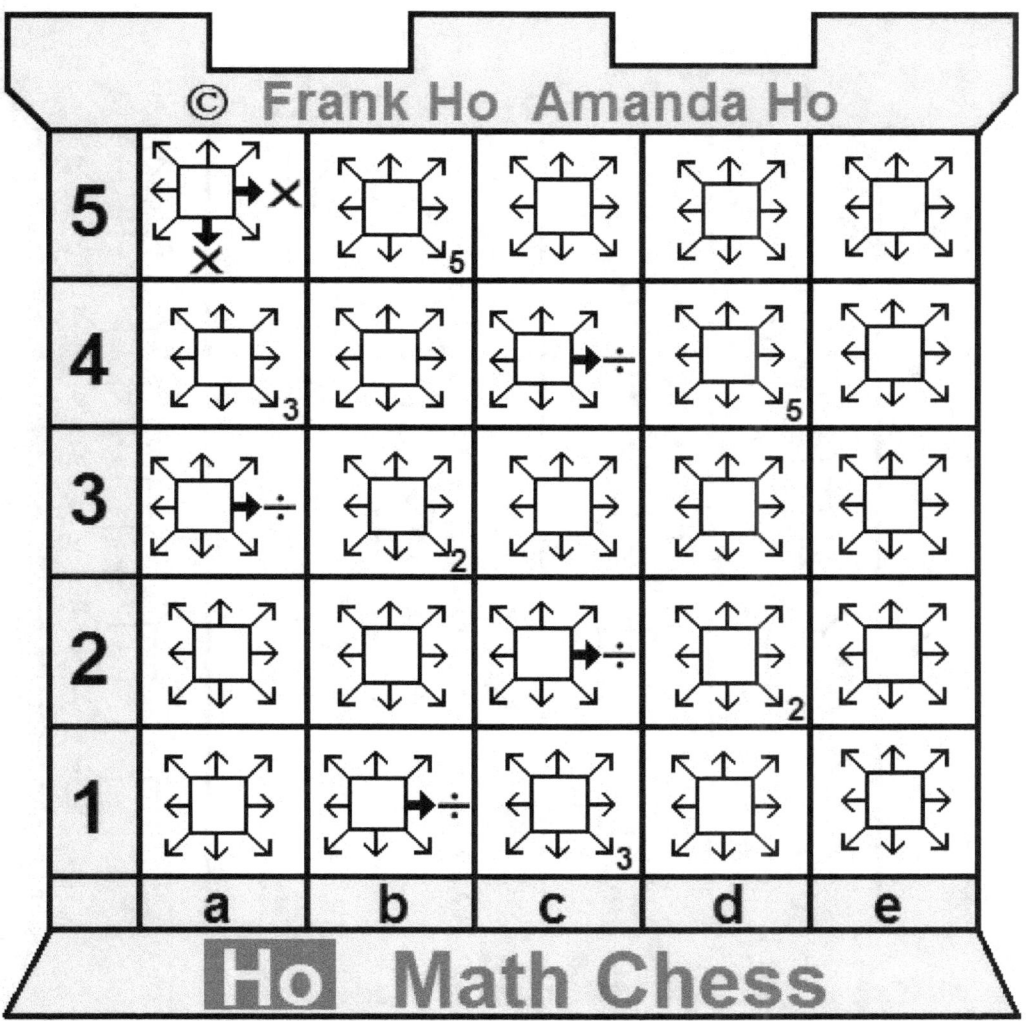

Ho Math Chess
何数棋谜 益智健脑非药物良方
Frankho Puzzle for KIDS – Brain Fitness Workbook
© 2007 — 2016 Frank Ho, Amanda Ho all rights reserved www.mathandchess.com

Frankho Puzzle™ # 100

Rule All the digits 1 to 5 must appear exactly once in every row and column. The number appears in the bottom right-hand corner is the end result calculated according to arithmetic operator(s) and chess move(s) as indicated by darker arrow(s).

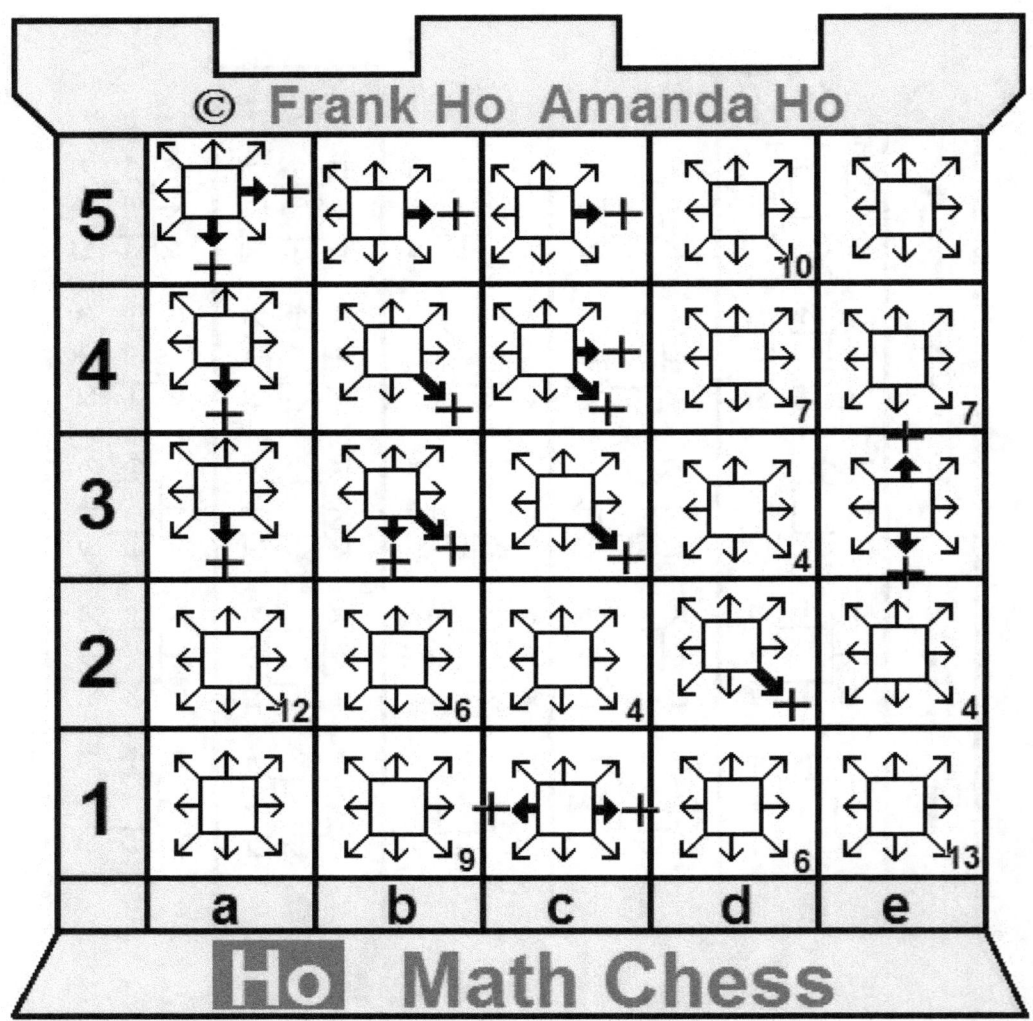

Ho Math Chess 何数棋谜 益智健脑非药物良方
Frankho Puzzle for KIDS – Brain Fitness Workbook
© 2007 — 2016 Frank Ho, Amanda Ho all rights reserved www.mathandchess.com

Frankho Puzzle™ # 101

Rule All the digits 1 to 5 must appear exactly once in every row and column. The number appears in the bottom right-hand corner is the end result calculated according to arithmetic operator(s) and chess move(s) as indicated by darker arrow(s).

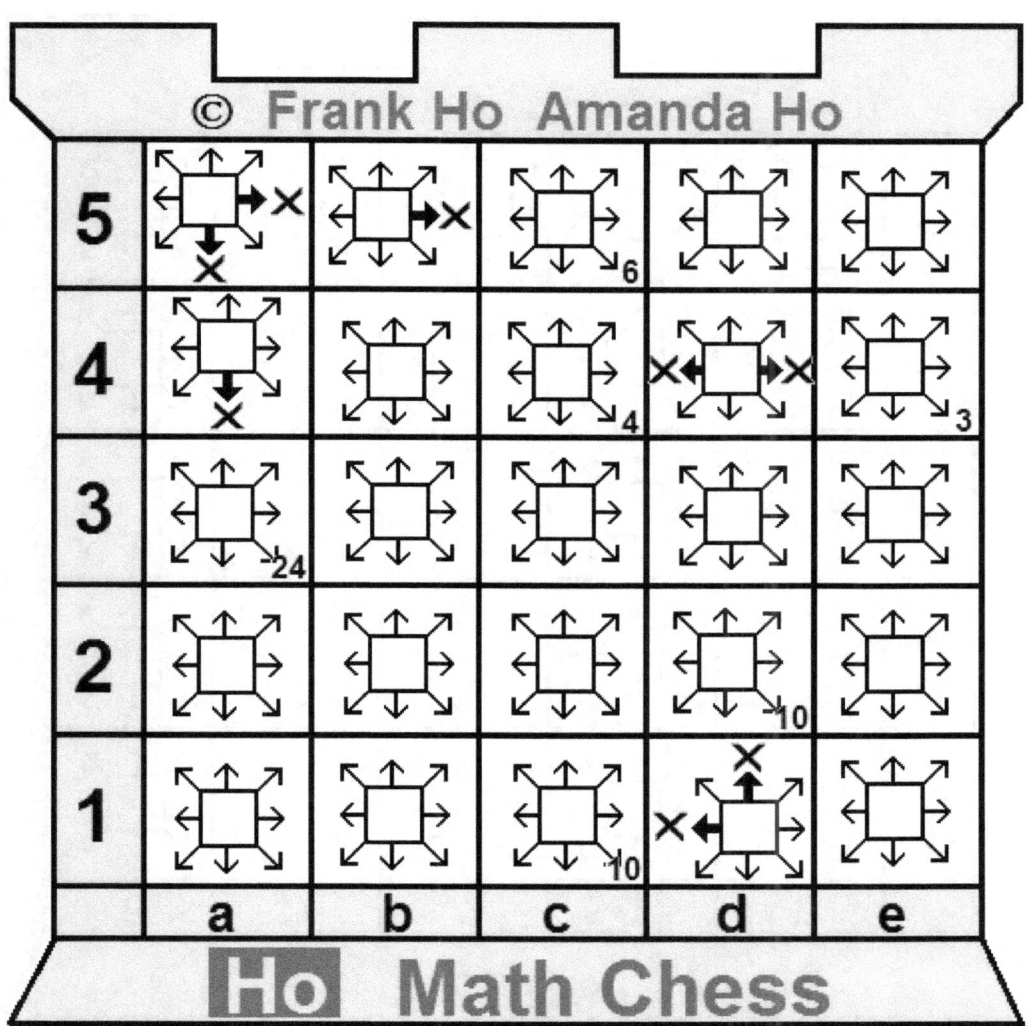

Ho Math Chess 何数棋谜 益智健脑非药物良方
Frankho Puzzle for KIDS – Brain Fitness Workbook

© 2007 — 2016 Frank Ho, Amanda Ho all rights reserved www.mathandchess.com

Frankho Puzzle™ # 102

Rule All the digits 1 to 5 must appear exactly once in every row and column. The number appears in the bottom right-hand corner is the end result calculated according to arithmetic operator(s) and chess move(s) as indicated by darker arrow(s).

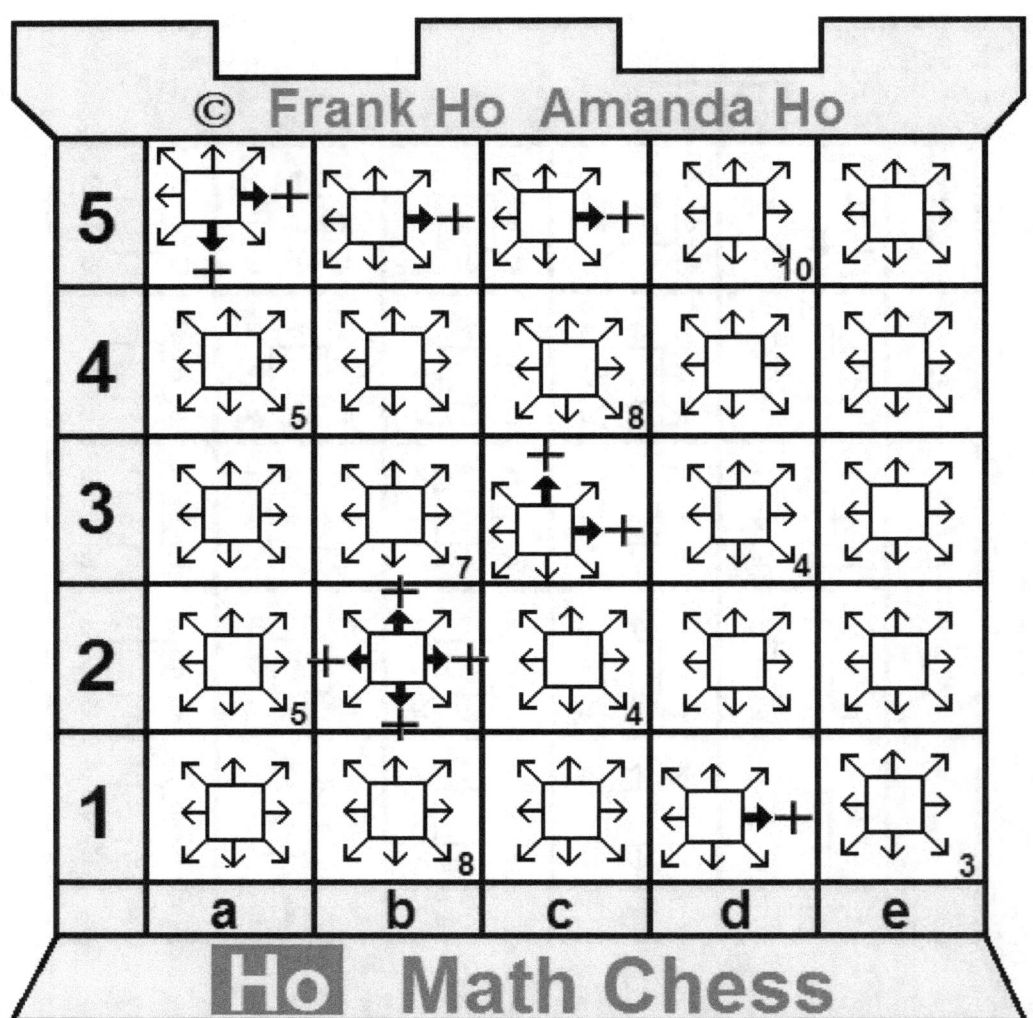

Ho Math Chess 何数棋谜 益智健脑非药物良方
Frankho Puzzle for KIDS – Brain Fitness Workbook
© 2007 – 2016 Frank Ho, Amanda Ho all rights reserved www.mathandchess.com

Frankho Puzzle™ # 103

Rule All the digits 1 to 5 must appear exactly once in every row and column. The number appears in the bottom right-hand corner is the end result calculated according to arithmetic operator(s) and chess move(s) as indicated by darker arrow(s).

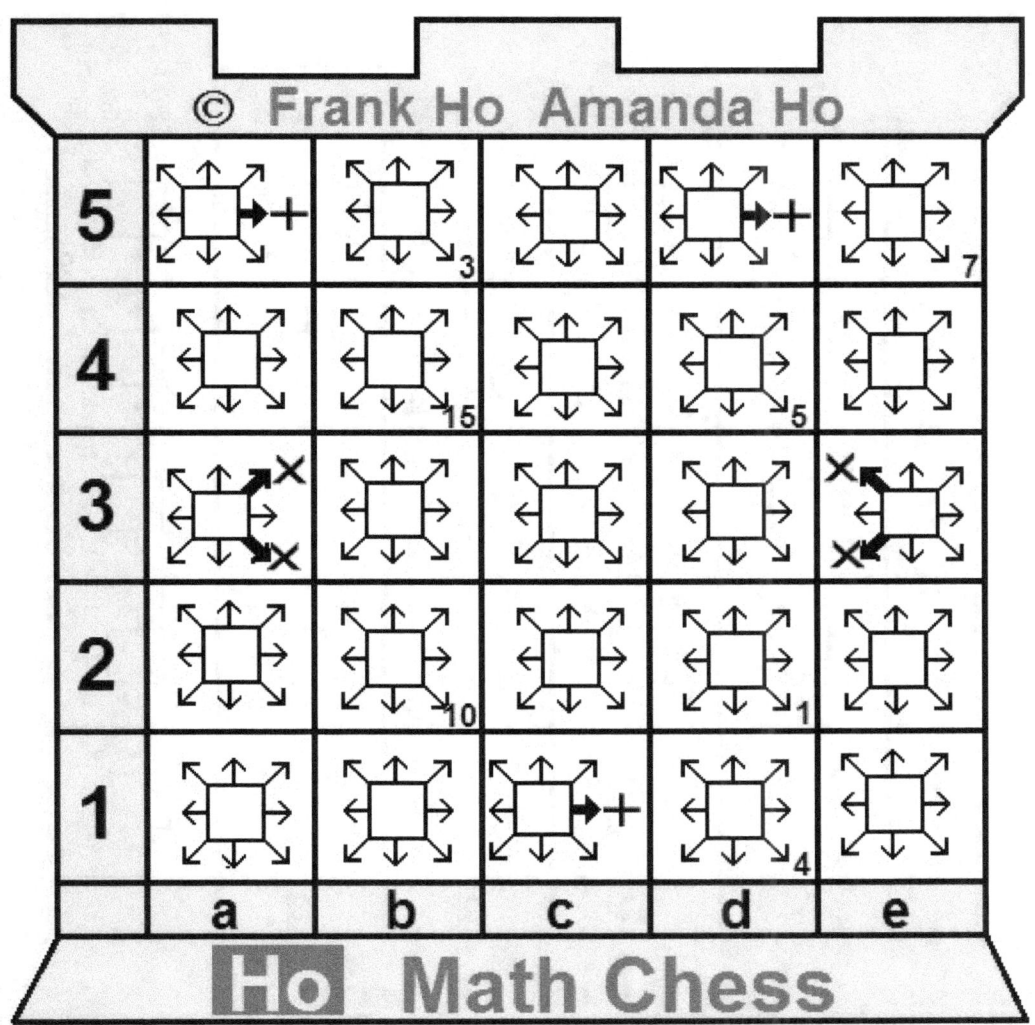

Frankho Puzzle™ # 104

Rule All the digits 1 to 5 must appear exactly once in every row and column. The number appears in the bottom right-hand corner is the end result calculated according to arithmetic operator(s) and chess move(s) as indicated by darker arrow(s).

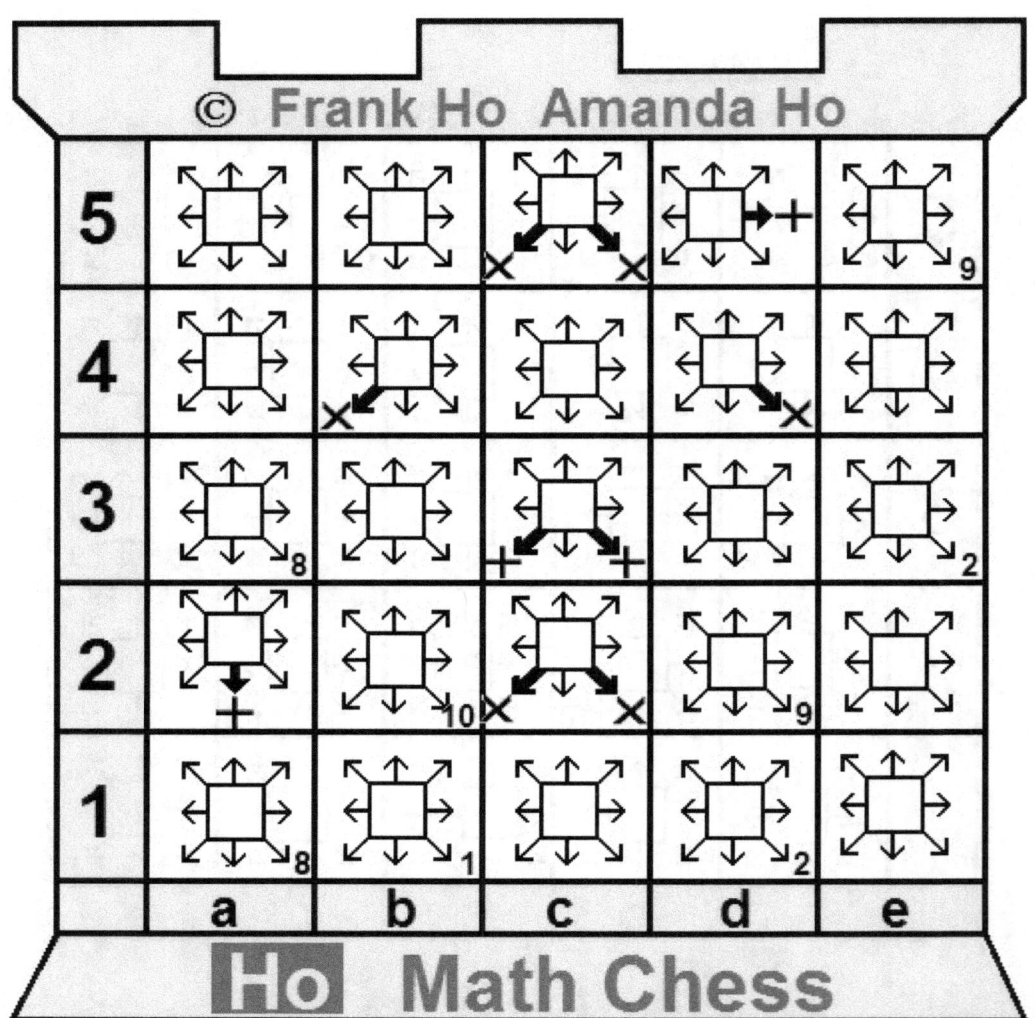

Ho Math Chess 何数棋谜 益智健脑非药物良方
Frankho Puzzle for KIDS – Brain Fitness Workbook
© 2007 – 2016 Frank Ho, Amanda Ho all rights reserved www.mathandchess.com

Frankho Puzzle™ # 105

Rule All the digits 1 to 5 must appear exactly once in every row and column. The number appears in the bottom right-hand corner is the end result calculated according to arithmetic operator(s) and chess move(s) as indicated by darker arrow(s).

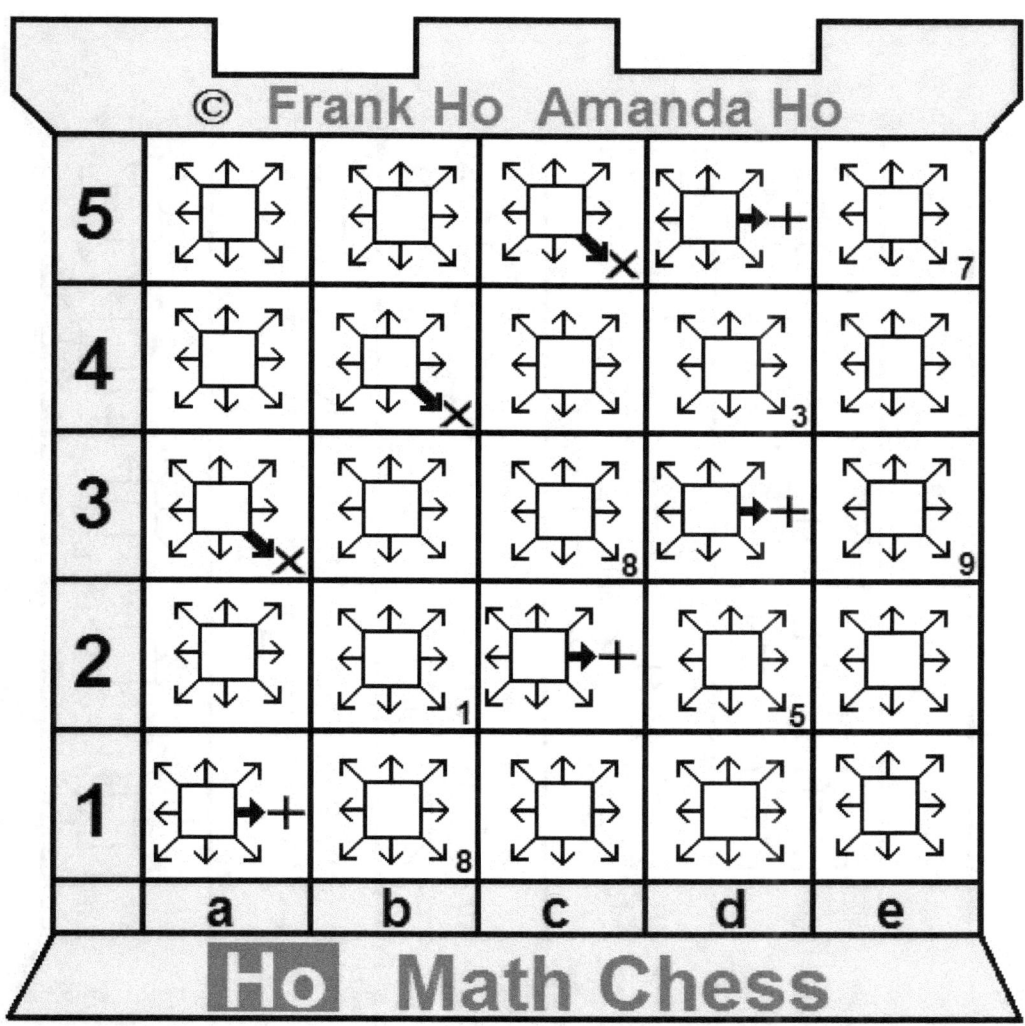

Frankho Puzzle™ # 106

Rule All the digits 1 to 5 must appear exactly once in every row and column. The number appears in the bottom right-hand corner is the end result calculated according to arithmetic operator(s) and chess move(s) as indicated by darker arrow(s).

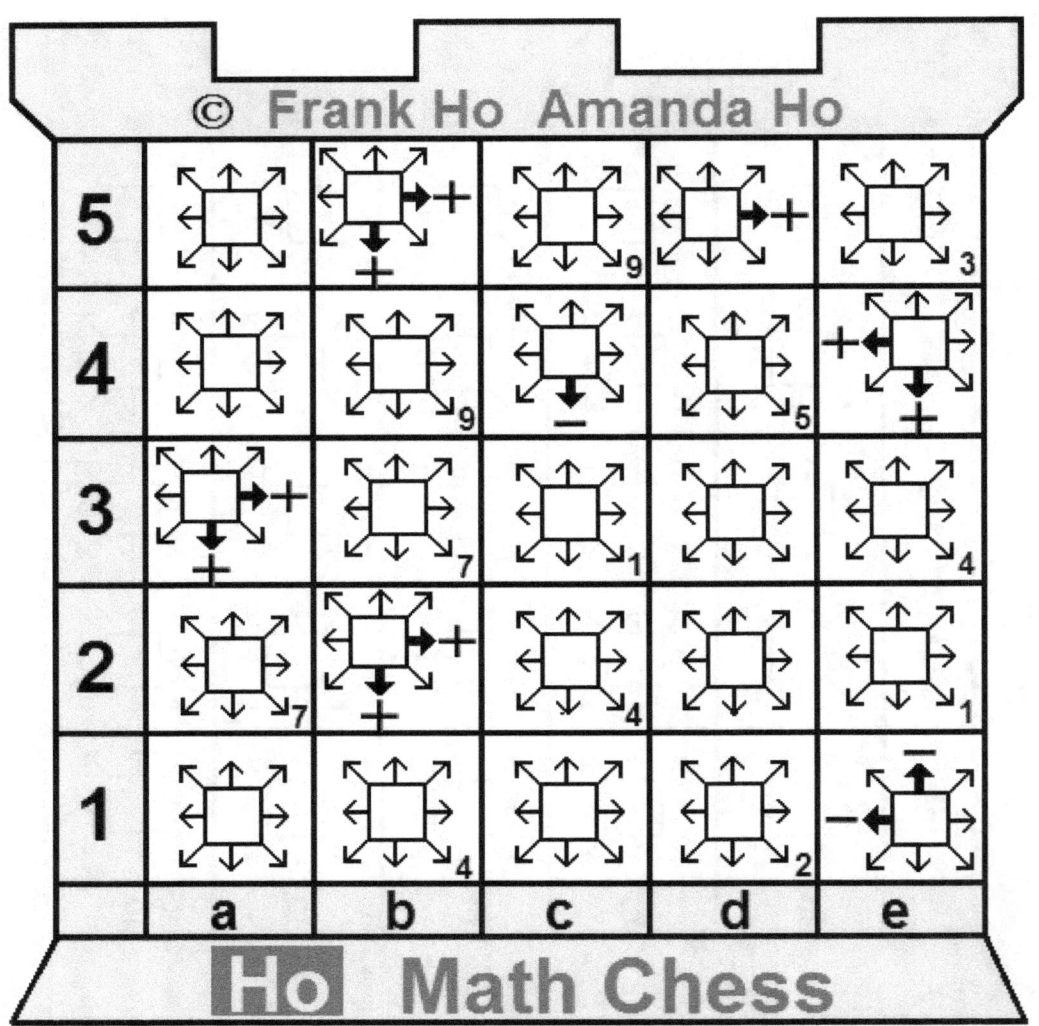

Ho Math Chess 何数棋谜 益智健脑非药物良方
Frankho Puzzle for KIDS – Brain Fitness Workbook

© 2007 — 2016 Frank Ho, Amanda Ho all rights reserved www.mathandchess.com

Frankho Puzzle™ # 107

Rule All the digits 1 to 5 must appear exactly once in every row and column. The number appears in the bottom right-hand corner is the end result calculated according to arithmetic operator(s) and chess move(s) as indicated by darker arrow(s).

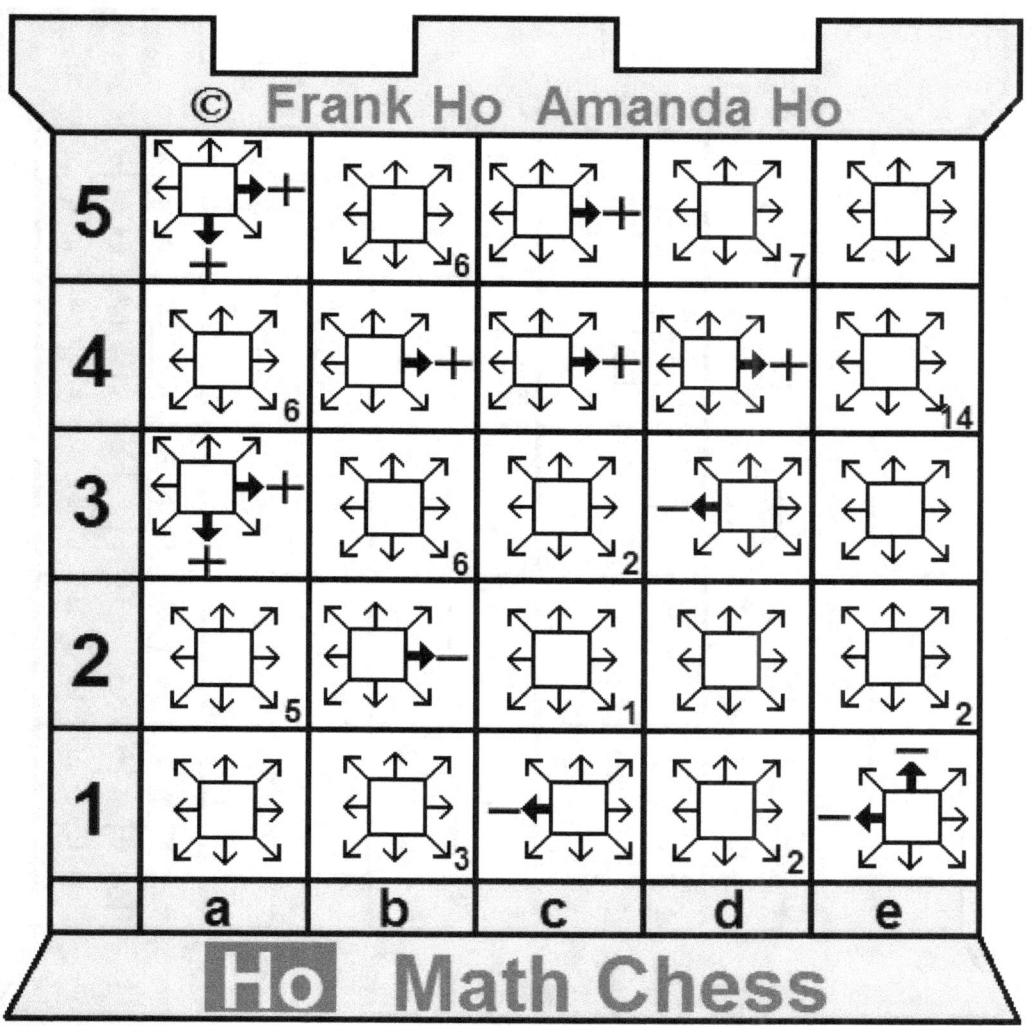

Ho Math Chess 何数棋谜 益智健脑非药物良方
Frankho Puzzle for KIDS – Brain Fitness Workbook
© 2007 — 2016 Frank Ho, Amanda Ho all rights reserved www.mathandchess.com

Frankho Puzzle™ # 108

Rule All the digits 1 to 5 must appear exactly once in every row and column. The number appears in the bottom right-hand corner is the end result calculated according to arithmetic operator(s) and chess move(s) as indicated by darker arrow(s).

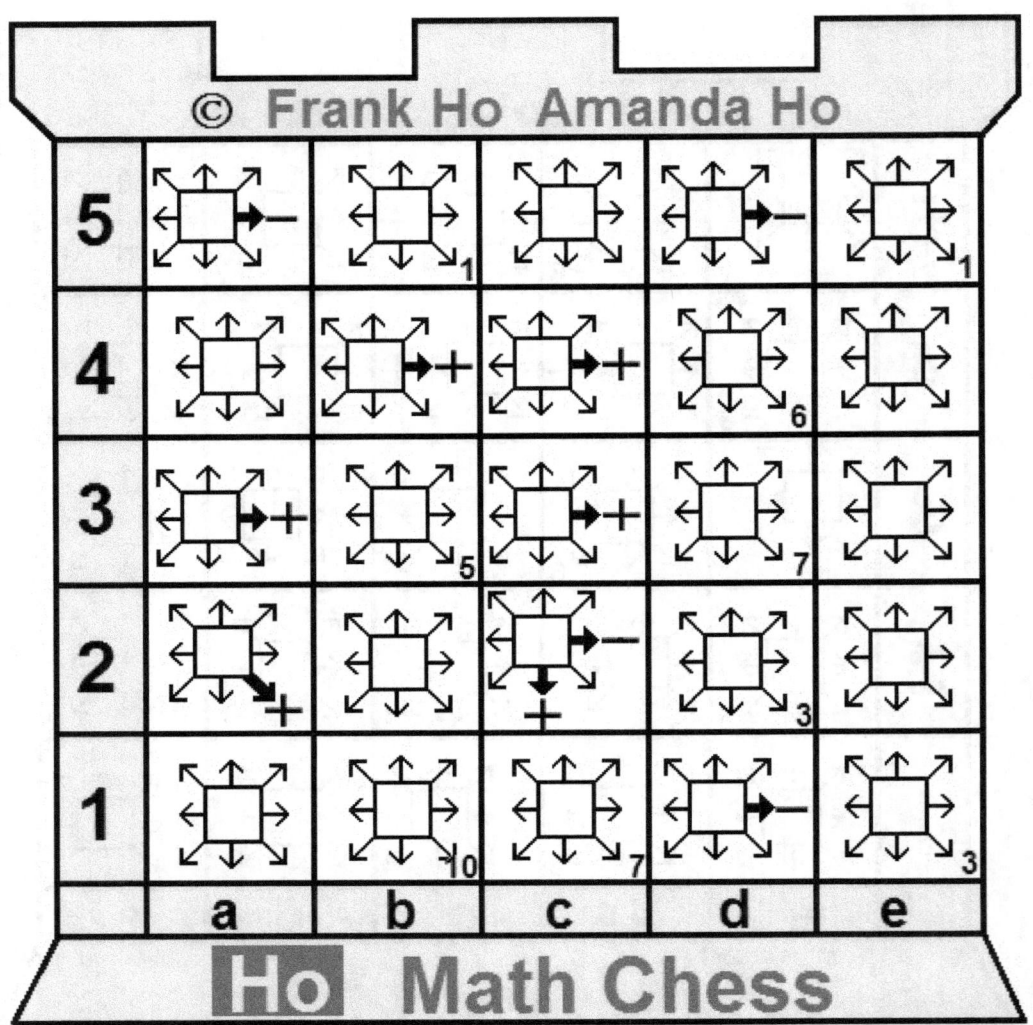

Frankho Puzzle™ # 109

Rule All the digits 1 to 5 must appear exactly once in every row and column. The number appears in the bottom right-hand corner is the end result calculated according to arithmetic operator(s) and chess move(s) as indicated by darker arrow(s).

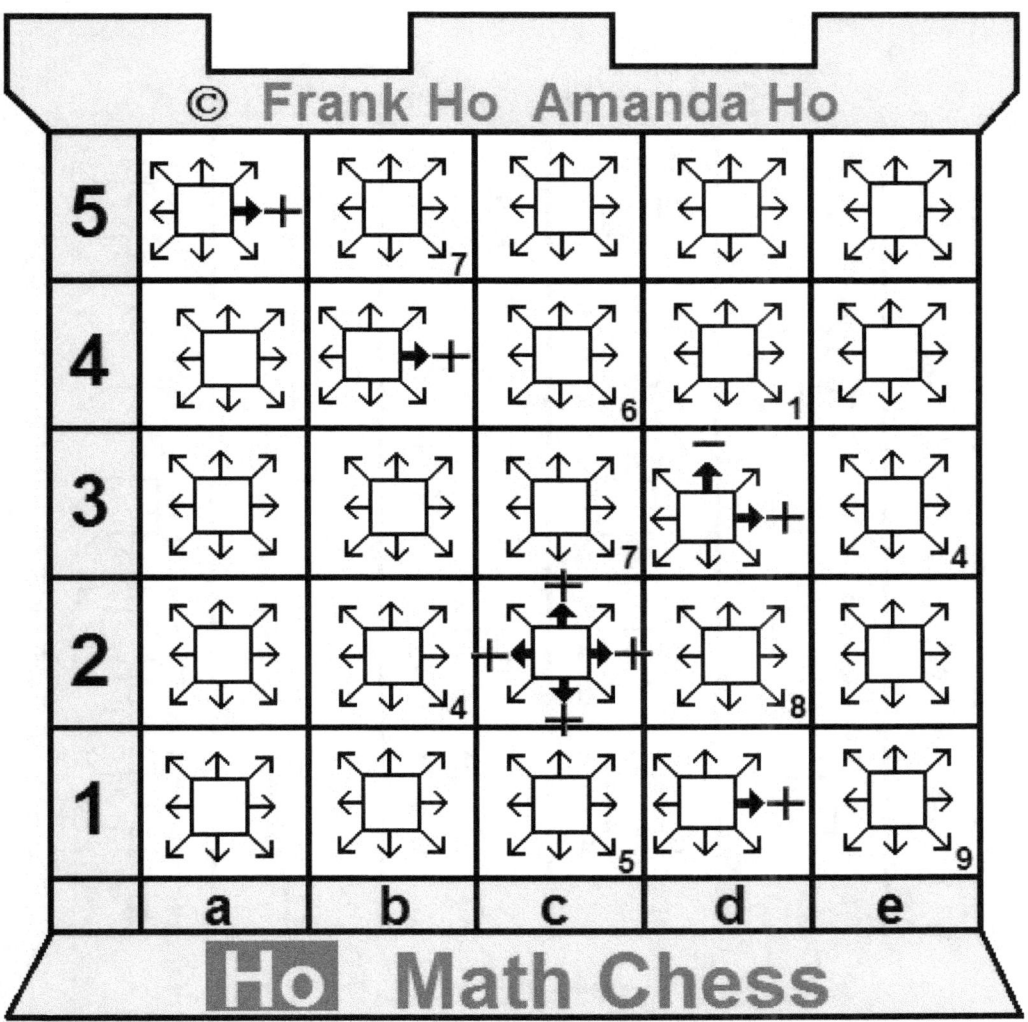

Ho Math Chess
Frankho Puzzle for KIDS – Brain Fitness Workbook
© 2007 — 2016 Frank Ho, Amanda Ho all rights reserved www.mathandchess.com

Frankho Puzzle™ # 110

Rule All the digits 1 to 5 must appear exactly once in every row and column. The number appears in the bottom right-hand corner is the end result calculated according to arithmetic operator(s) and chess move(s) as indicated by darker arrow(s).

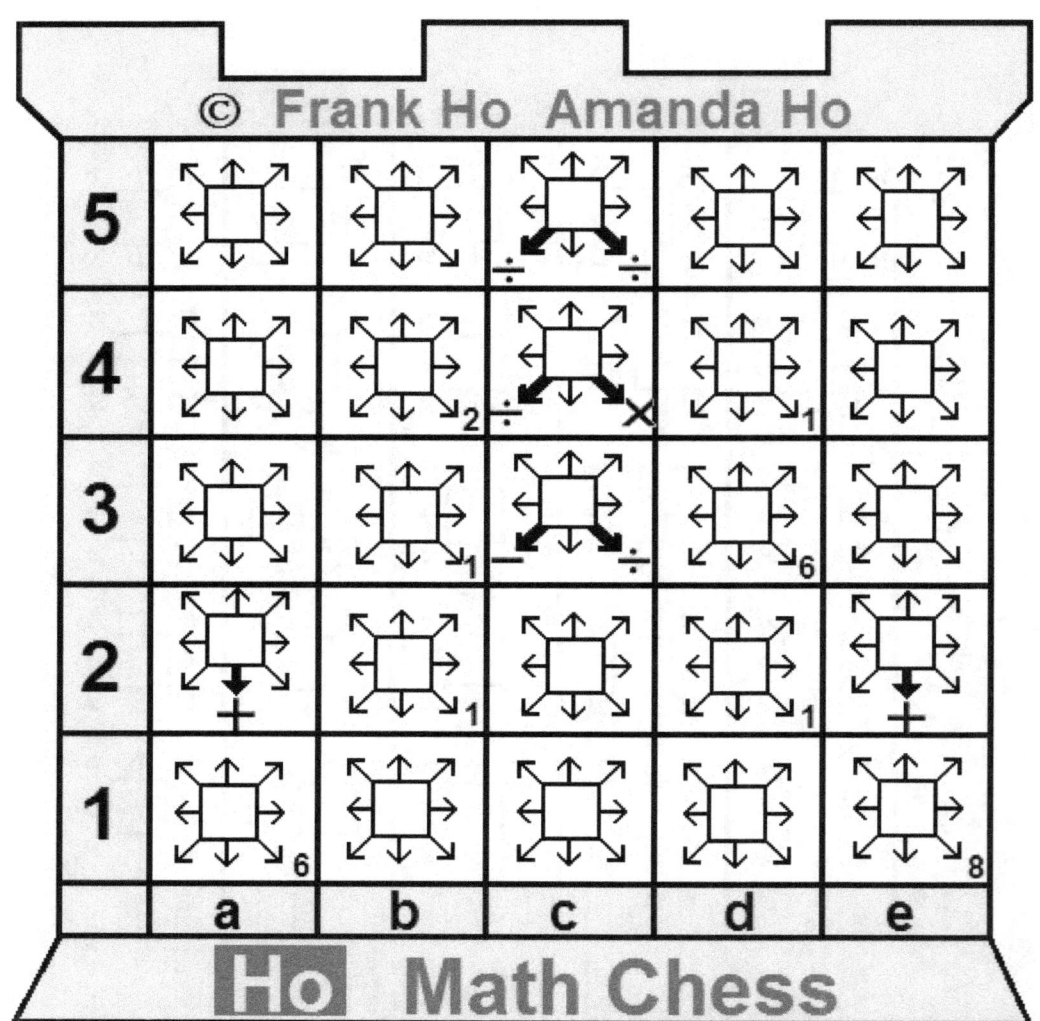

Frankho Puzzle™ # 111

Rule All the digits 1 to 5 must appear exactly once in every row and column. The number appears in the bottom right-hand corner is the end result calculated according to arithmetic operator(s) and chess move(s) as indicated by darker arrow(s).

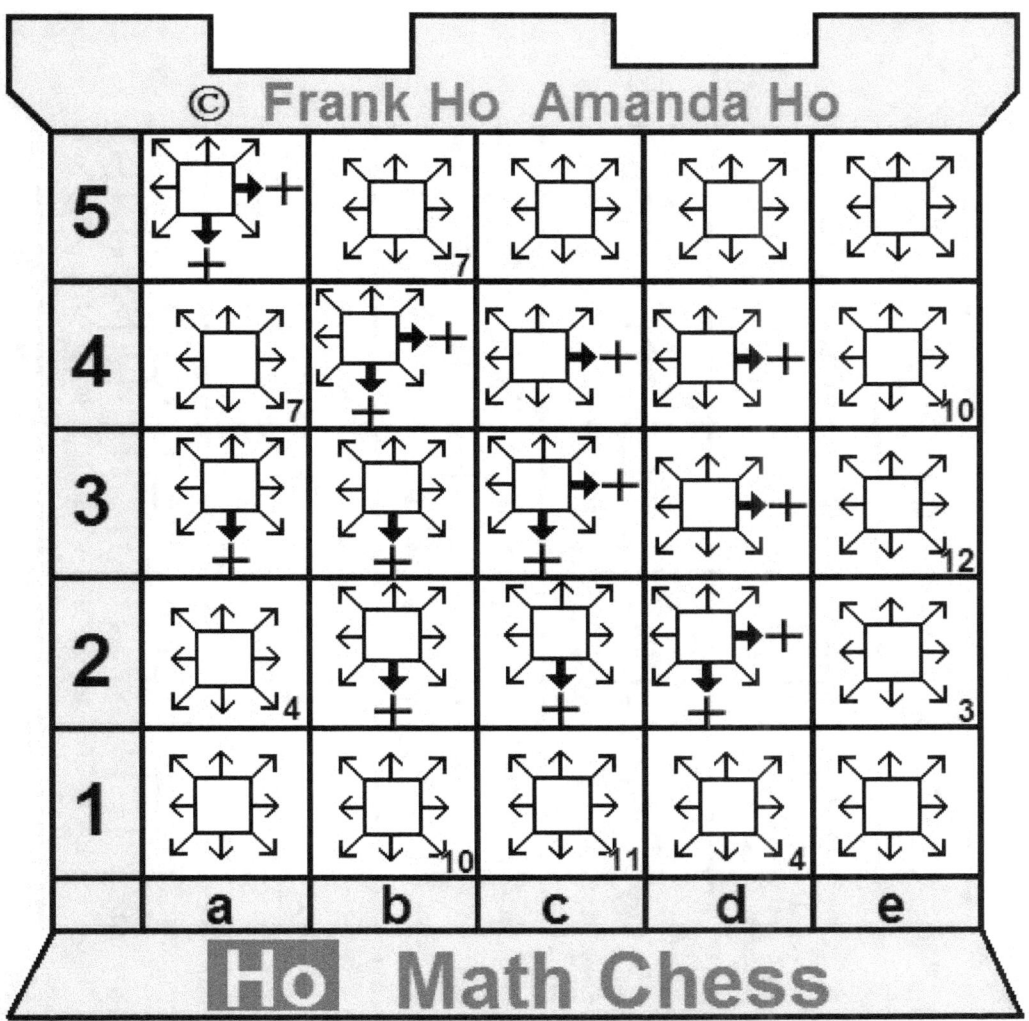

Ho Math Chess 何数棋谜 益智健脑非药物良方
Frankho Puzzle for KIDS – Brain Fitness Workbook
© 2007 — 2016 Frank Ho, Amanda Ho all rights reserved www.mathandchess.com

Frankho Puzzle™ # 112

Rule All the digits 1 to 5 must appear exactly once in every row and column. The number appears in the bottom right-hand corner is the end result calculated according to arithmetic operator(s) and chess move(s) as indicated by darker arrow(s).

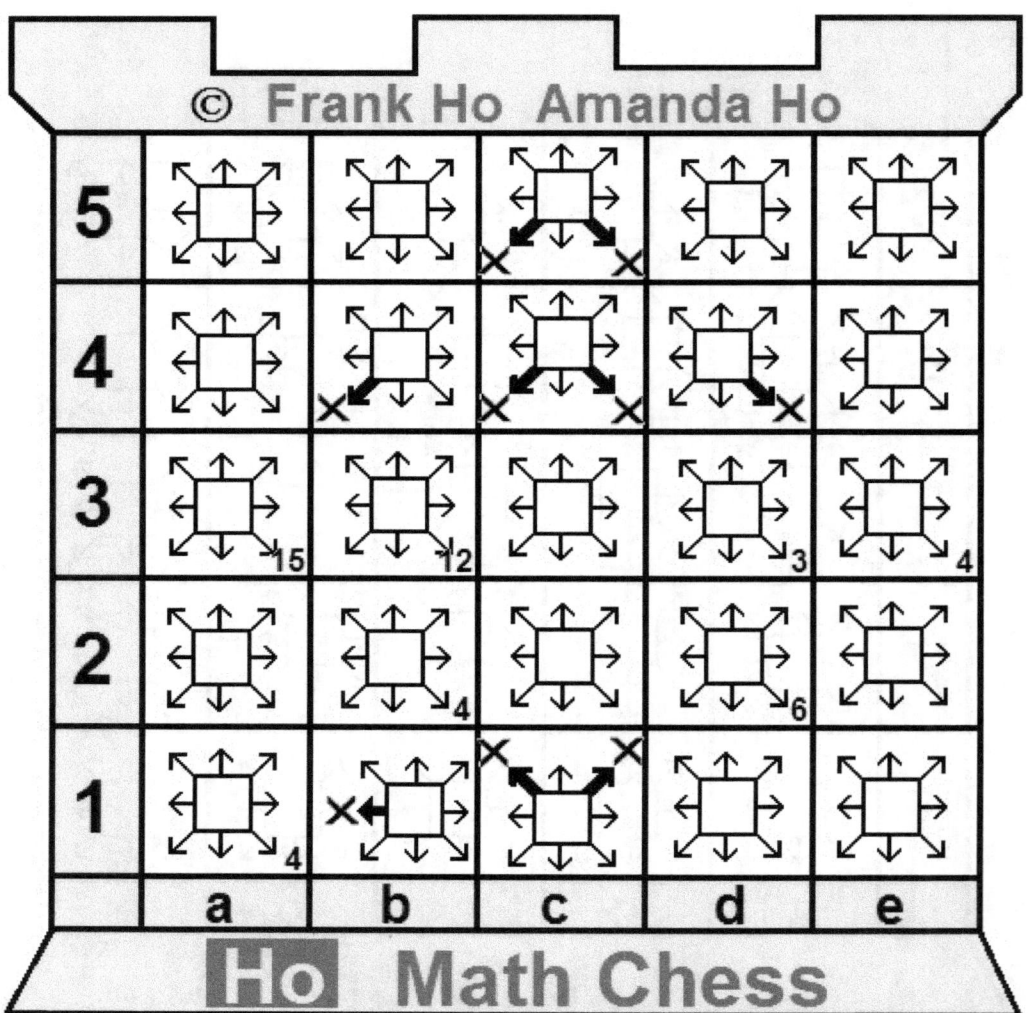

Frankho Puzzle™ # 113

Rule All the digits 1 to 5 must appear exactly once in every row and column. The number appears in the bottom right-hand corner is the end result calculated according to arithmetic operator(s) and chess move(s) as indicated by darker arrow(s).

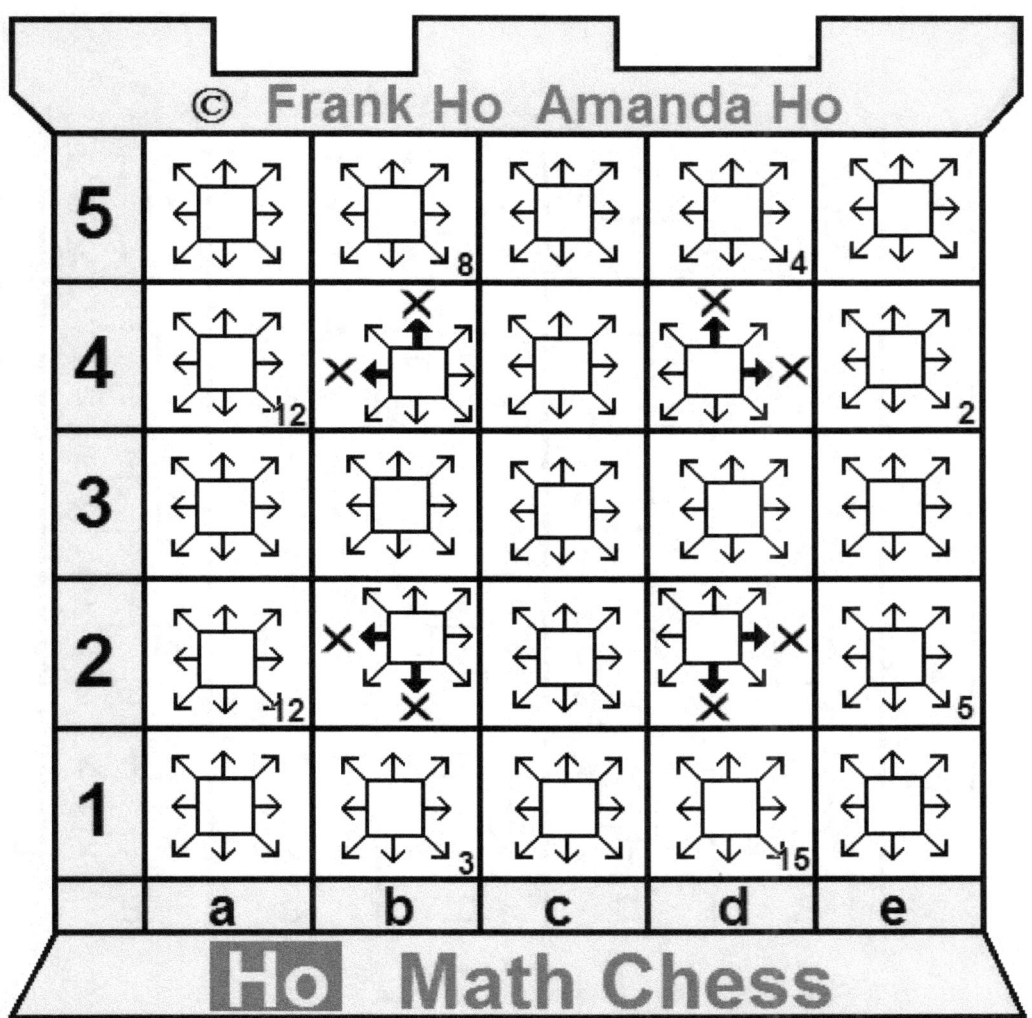

Frankho Puzzle™ # 114

Rule All the digits 1 to 5 must appear exactly once in every row and column. The number appears in the bottom right-hand corner is the end result calculated according to arithmetic operator(s) and chess move(s) as indicated by darker arrow(s).

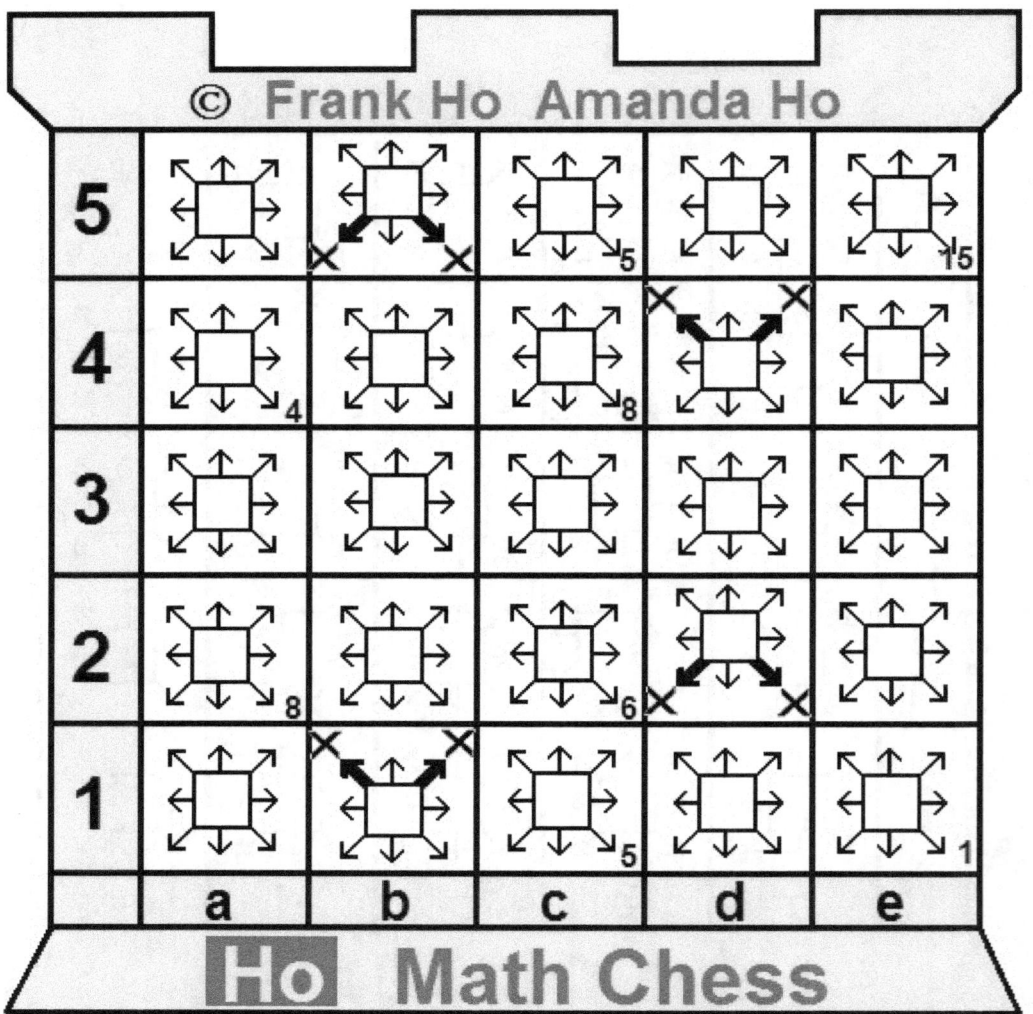

Ho Math Chess 何数棋谜 益智健脑非药物良方
Frankho Puzzle for KIDS – Brain Fitness Workbook
© 2007 — 2016 Frank Ho, Amanda Ho all rights reserved www.mathandchess.com

Frankho Puzzle™ # 115

Rule All the digits 1 to 5 must appear exactly once in every row and column. The number appears in the bottom right-hand corner is the end result calculated according to arithmetic operator(s) and chess move(s) as indicated by darker arrow(s).

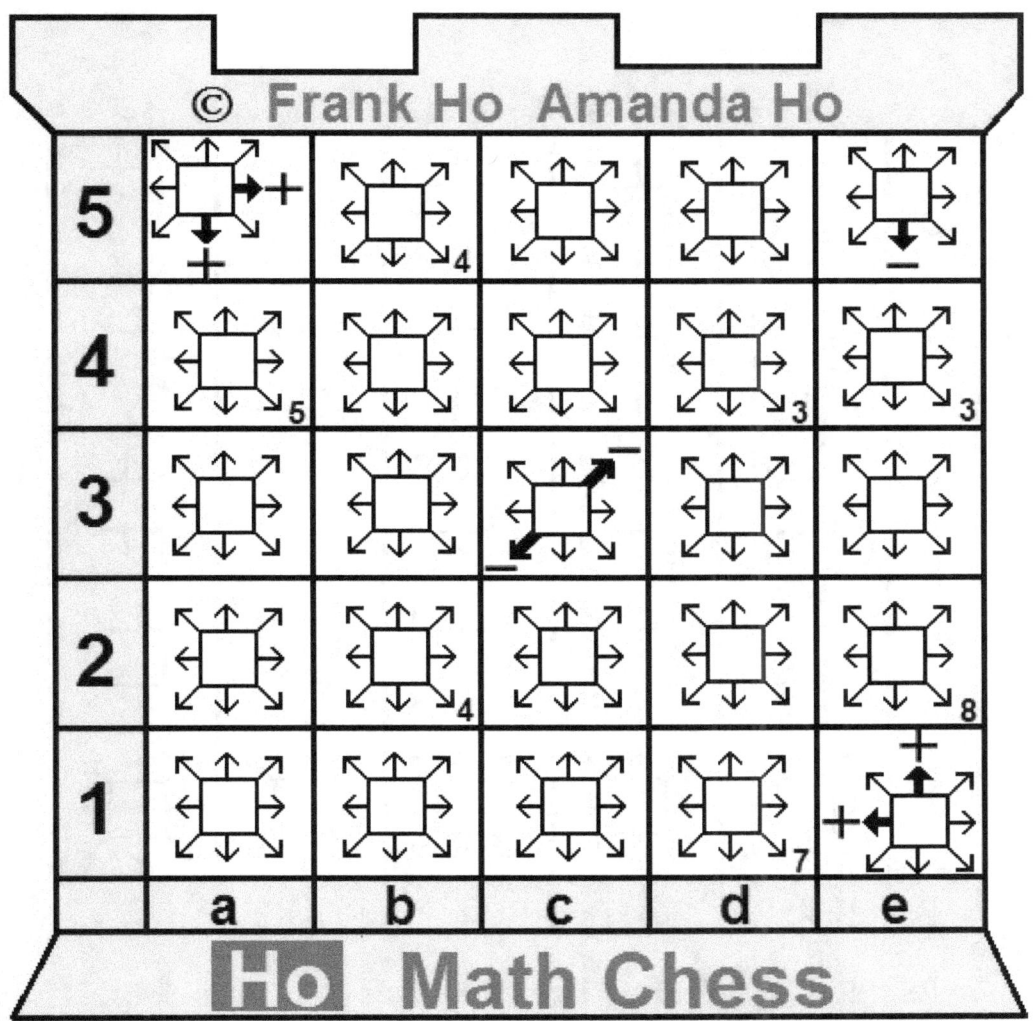

Ho Math Chess 何数棋谜 益智健脑非药物良方
Frankho Puzzle for KIDS – Brain Fitness Workbook

© 2007 — 2016 Frank Ho, Amanda Ho all rights reserved www.mathandchess.com

Frankho Puzzle™ # 116

Rule All the digits 1 to 5 must appear exactly once in every row and column. The number appears in the bottom right-hand corner is the end result calculated according to arithmetic operator(s) and chess move(s) as indicated by darker arrow(s).

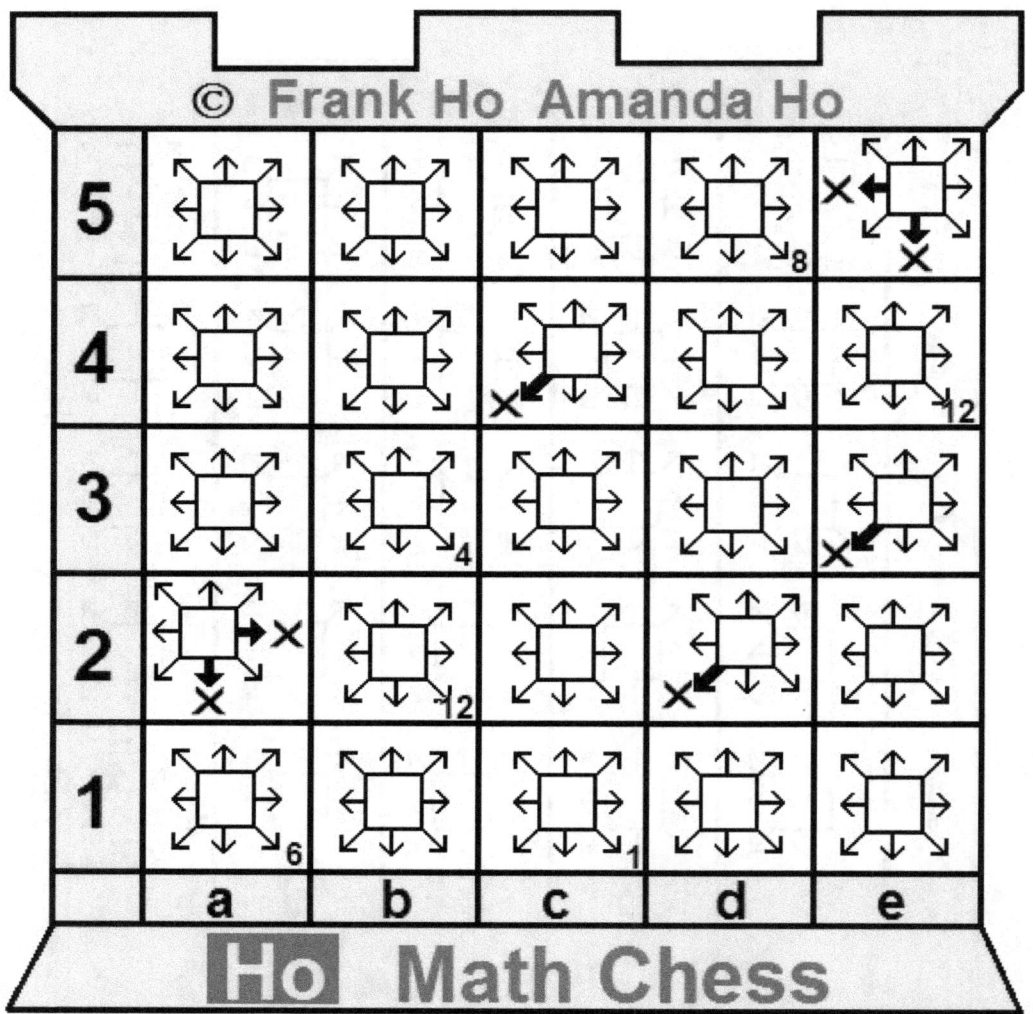

Ho Math Chess 何数棋谜 益智健脑非药物良方
Frankho Puzzle for KIDS – Brain Fitness Workbook
© 2007 — 2016 Frank Ho, Amanda Ho all rights reserved www.mathandchess.com

Frankho Puzzle™ # 117

Rule All the digits 1 to 5 must appear exactly once in every row and column. The number appears in the bottom right-hand corner is the end result calculated according to arithmetic operator(s) and chess move(s) as indicated by darker arrow(s).

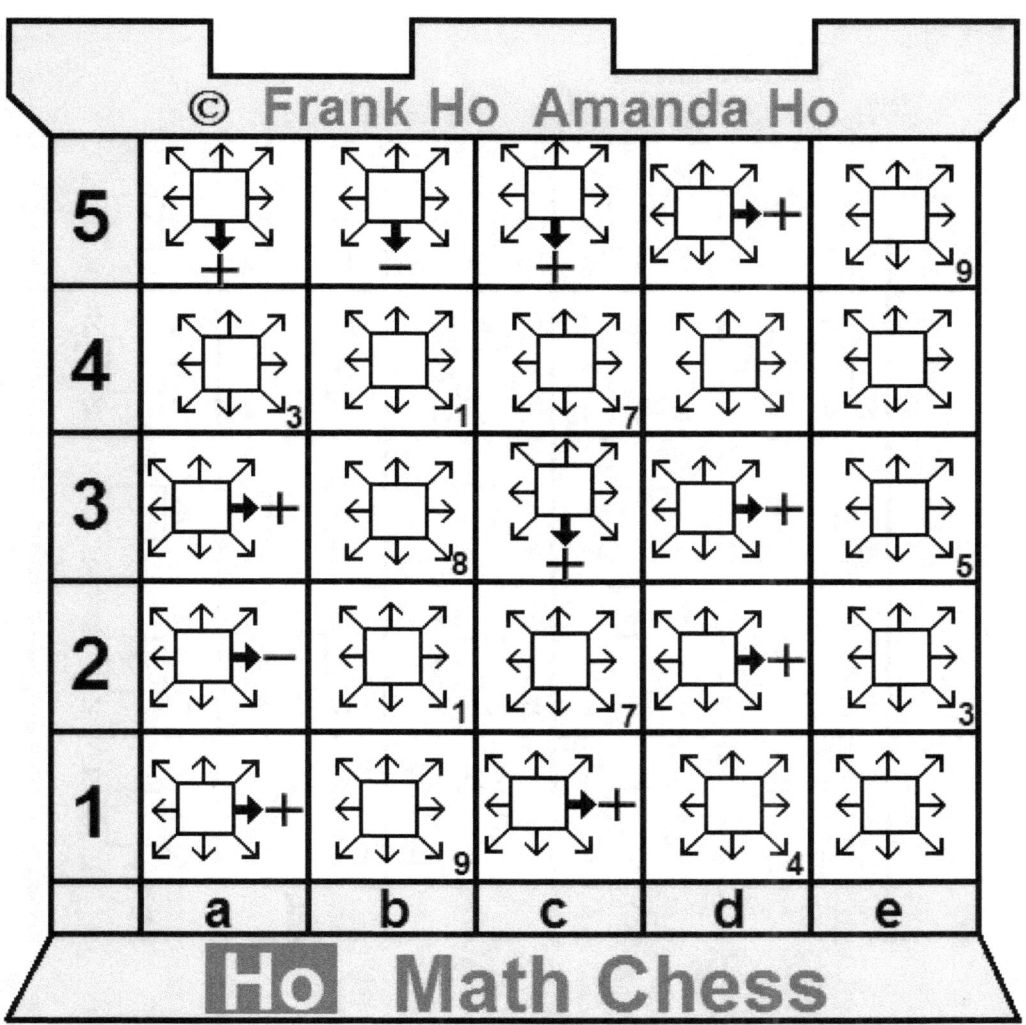

121

Ho Math Chess 何数棋谜 益智健脑非药物良方
Frankho Puzzle for KIDS – Brain Fitness Workbook

© 2007 — 2016 Frank Ho, Amanda Ho all rights reserved www.mathandchess.com

Frankho Puzzle™ # 118

Rule All the digits 1 to 5 must appear exactly once in every row and column. The number appears in the bottom right-hand corner is the end result calculated according to arithmetic operator(s) and chess move(s) as indicated by darker arrow(s).

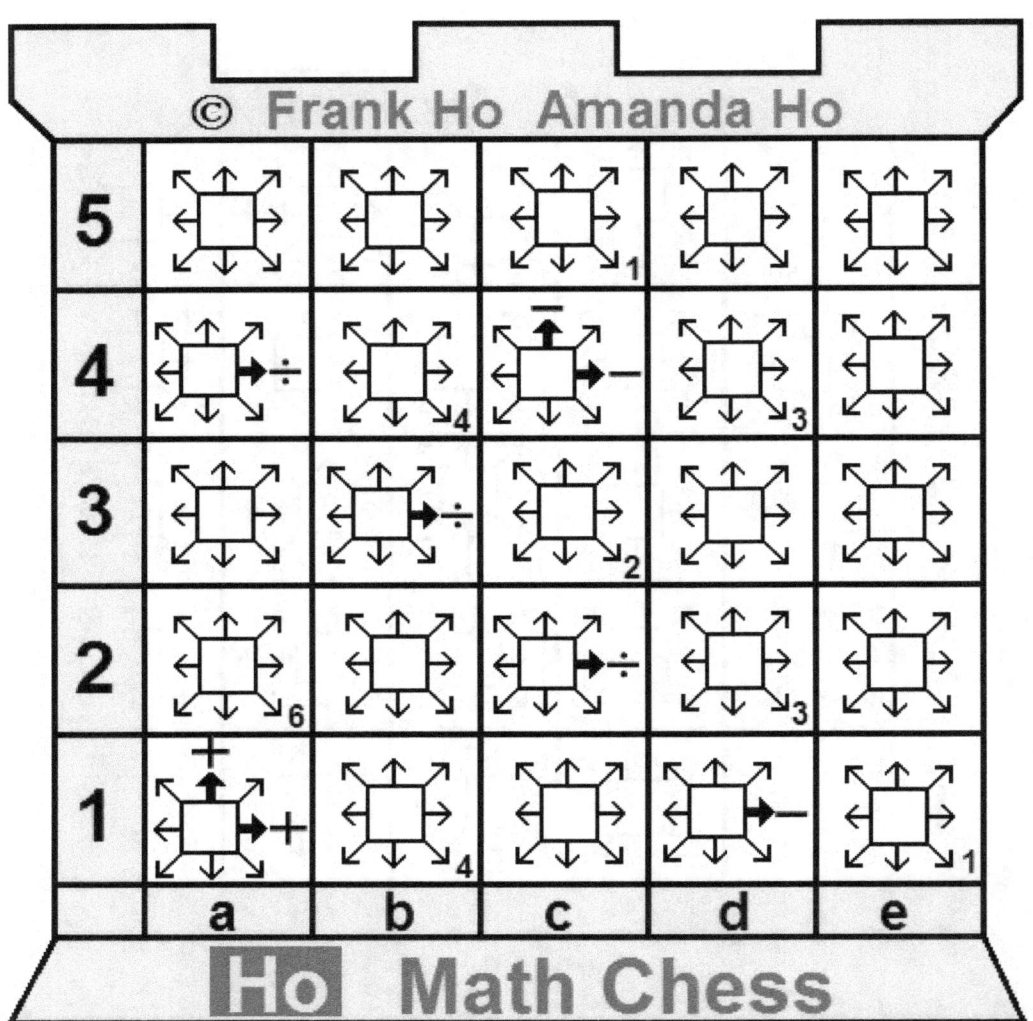

Ho Math Chess 何数棋谜 益智健脑非药物良方
Frankho Puzzle for KIDS – Brain Fitness Workbook
© 2007 — 2016 Frank Ho, Amanda Ho all rights reserved www.mathandchess.com

Frankho Puzzle™ # 119

Rule All the digits 1 to 5 must appear exactly once in every row and column. The number appears in the bottom right-hand corner is the end result calculated according to arithmetic operator(s) and chess move(s) as indicated by darker arrow(s).

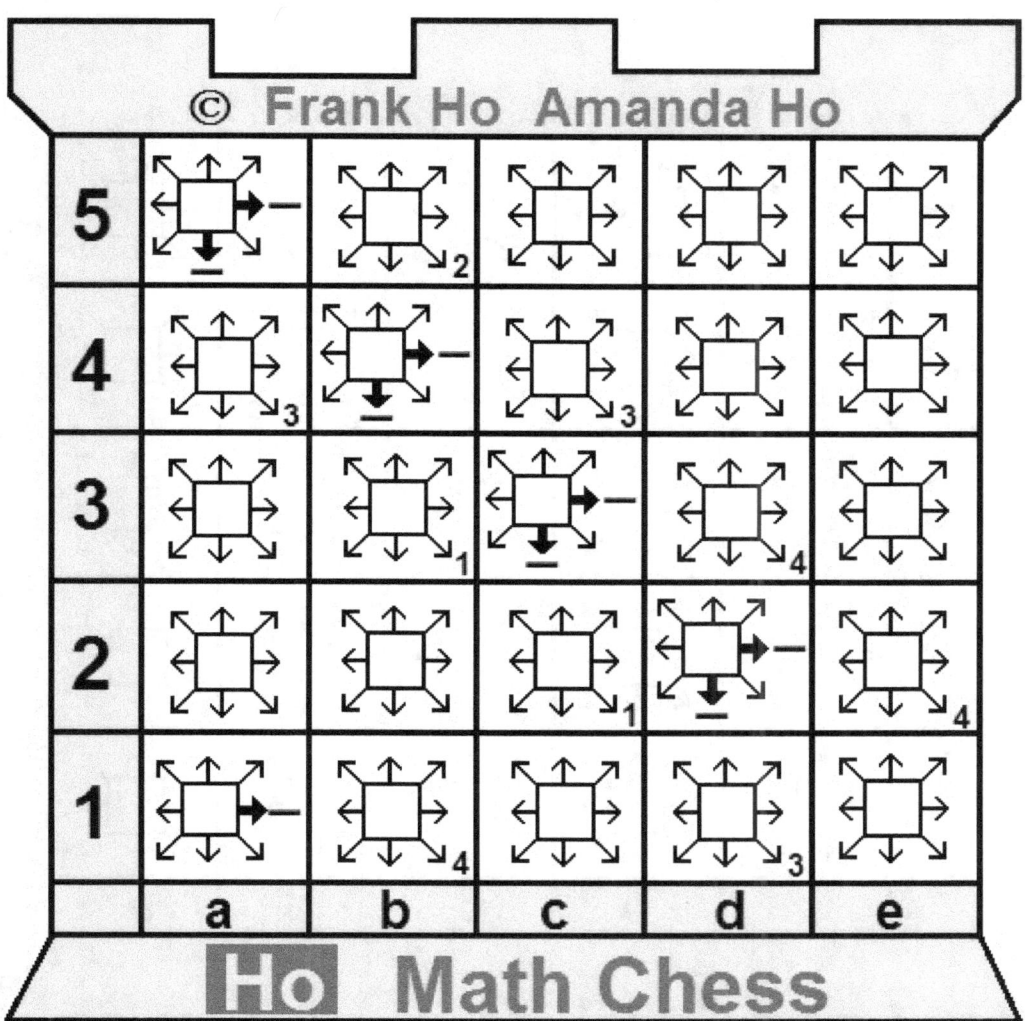

Frankho Puzzle™ # 120

Rule All the digits 1 to 5 must appear exactly once in every row and column. The number appears in the bottom right-hand corner is the end result calculated according to arithmetic operator(s) and chess move(s) as indicated by darker arrow(s).

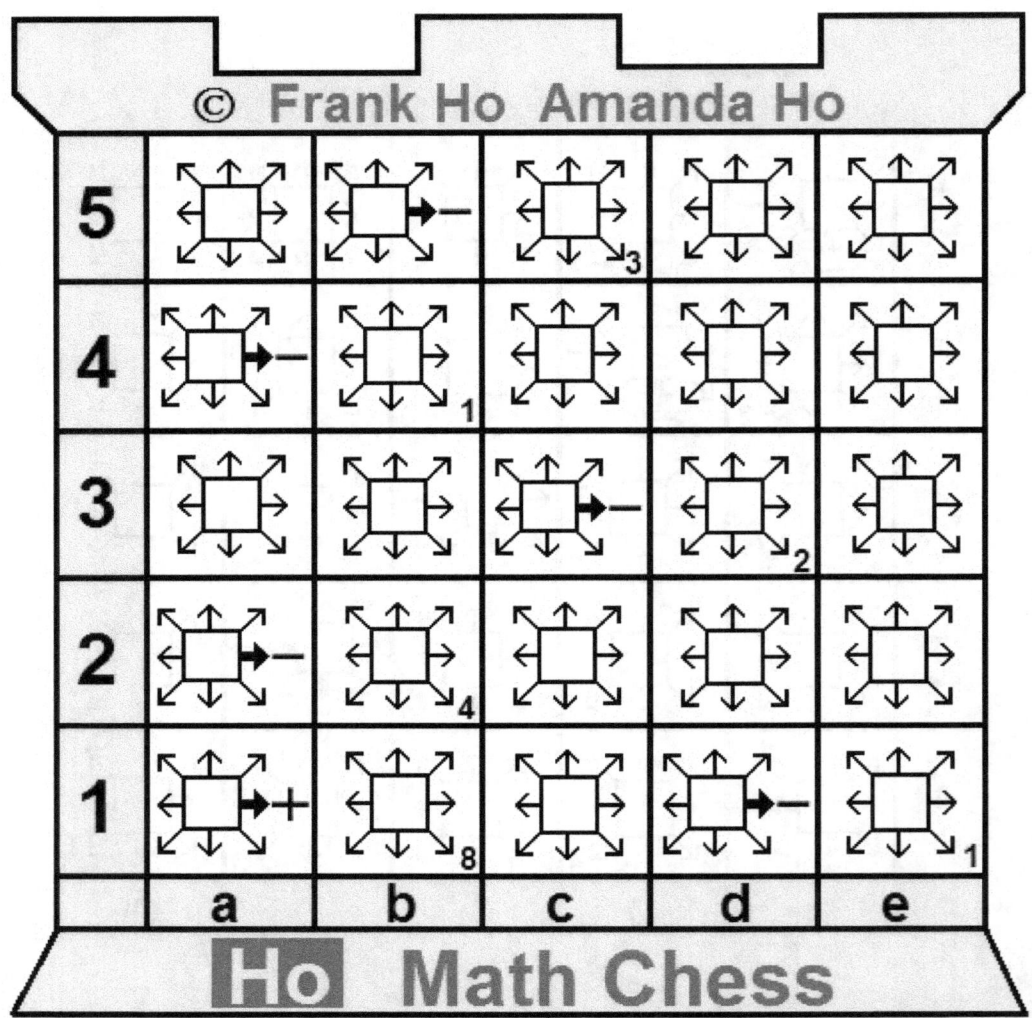

Ho Math Chess 何数棋谜 益智健脑非药物良方
Frankho Puzzle for KIDS – Brain Fitness Workbook
© 2007 — 2016 Frank Ho, Amanda Ho all rights reserved www.mathandchess.com

Frankho Puzzle™ # 121

Rule All the digits 1 to 5 must appear exactly once in every row and column. The number appears in the bottom right-hand corner is the end result calculated according to arithmetic operator(s) and chess move(s) as indicated by darker arrow(s).

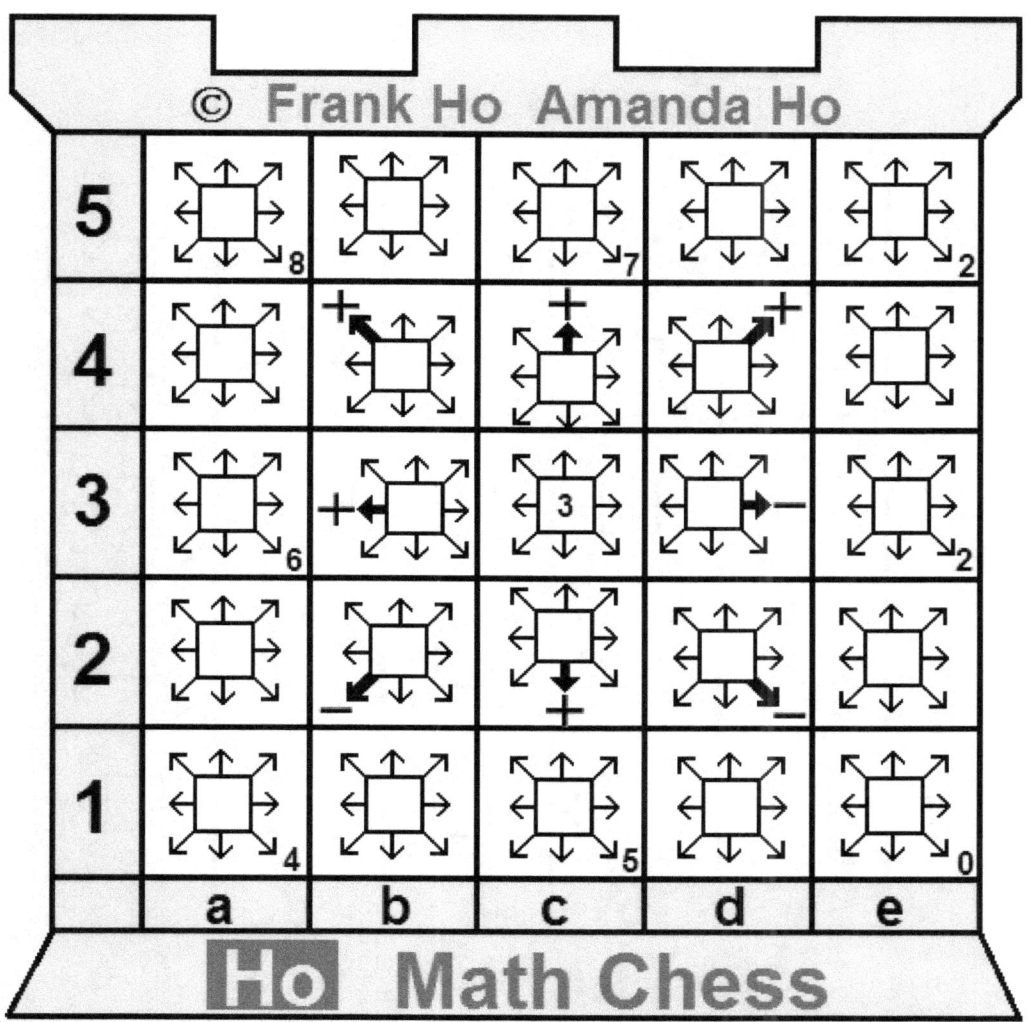

125

Frankho Puzzle™ # 122

Rule All the digits 1 to 5 must appear exactly once in every row and column. The number appears in the bottom right-hand corner is the end result calculated according to arithmetic operator(s) and chess move(s) as indicated by darker arrow(s).

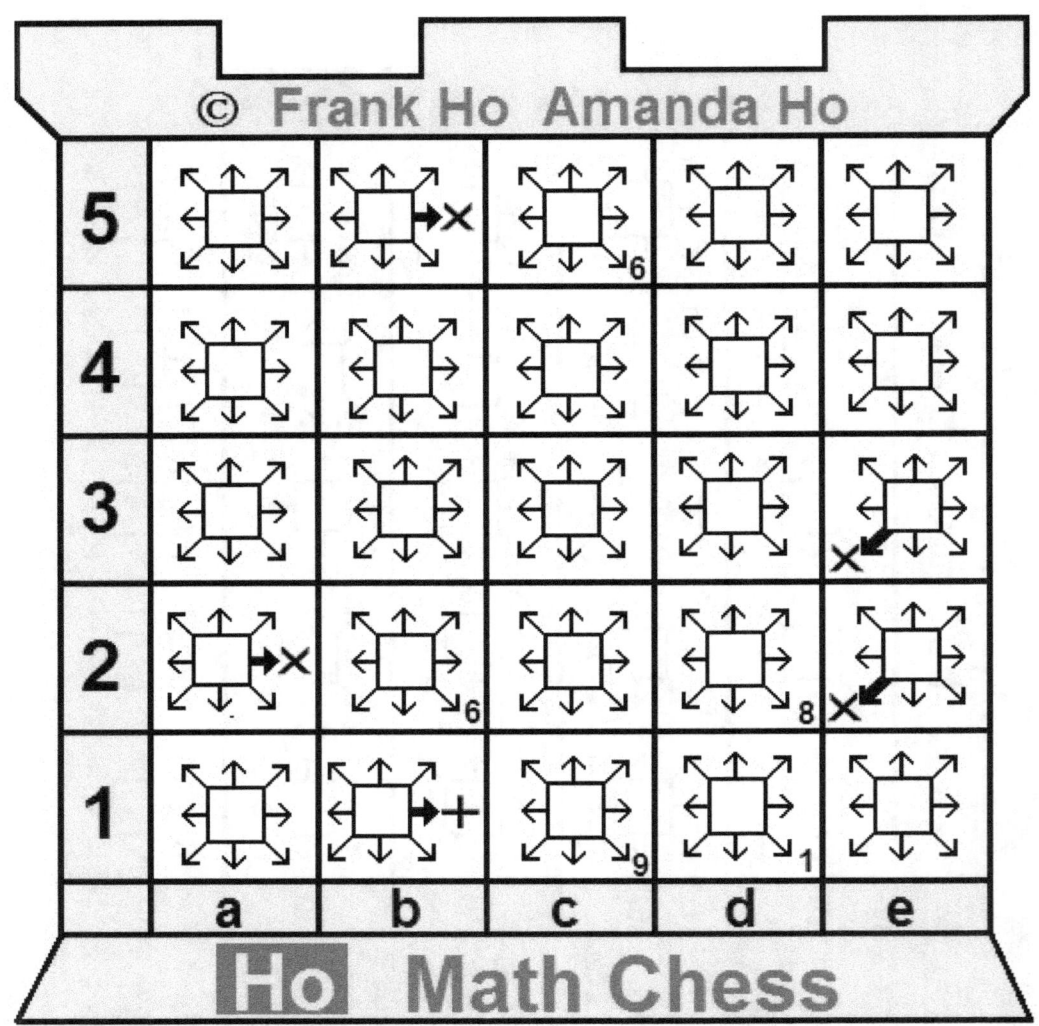

Ho Math Chess 何数棋谜 益智健脑非药物良方
Frankho Puzzle for KIDS – Brain Fitness Workbook

© 2007 — 2016 Frank Ho, Amanda Ho all rights reserved www.mathandchess.com

Frankho Puzzle™ # 123

Rule All the digits 1 to 5 must appear exactly once in every row and column. The number appears in the bottom right-hand corner is the end result calculated according to arithmetic operator(s) and chess move(s) as indicated by darker arrow(s).

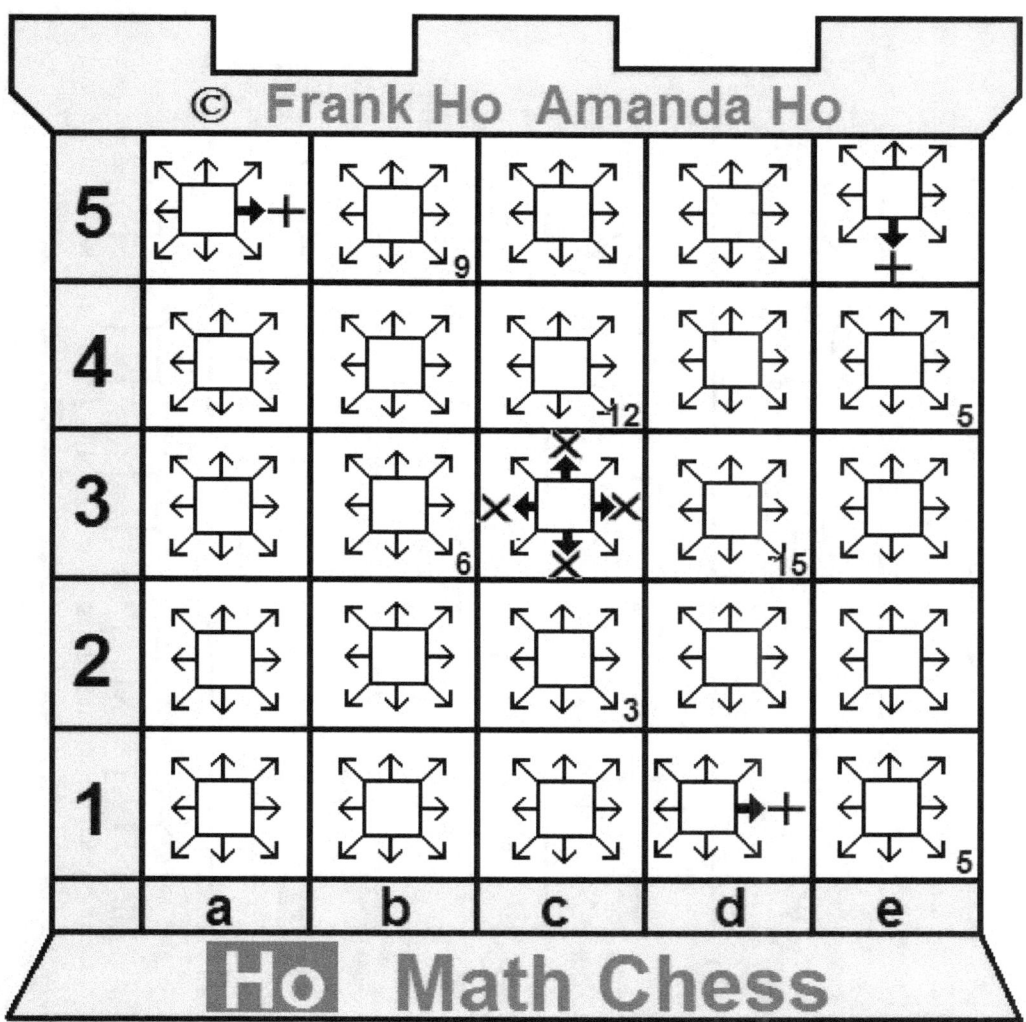

127

Frankho Puzzle™ # 124

Rule All the digits 1 to 5 must appear exactly once in every row and column. The number appears in the bottom right-hand corner is the end result calculated according to arithmetic operator(s) and chess move(s) as indicated by darker arrow(s).

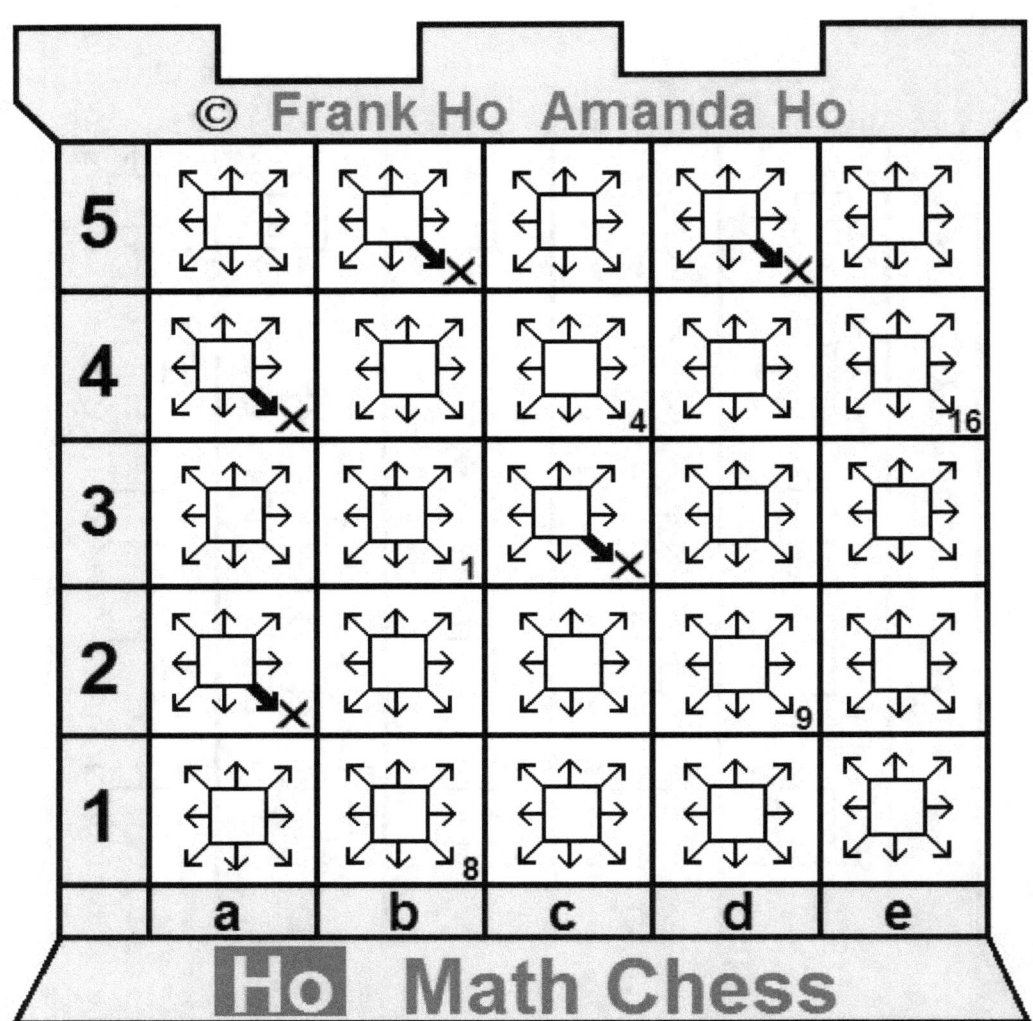

Frankho Puzzle™ # 125

Rule All the digits 1 to 5 must appear exactly once in every row and column. The number appears in the bottom right-hand corner is the end result calculated according to arithmetic operator(s) and chess move(s) as indicated by darker arrow(s).

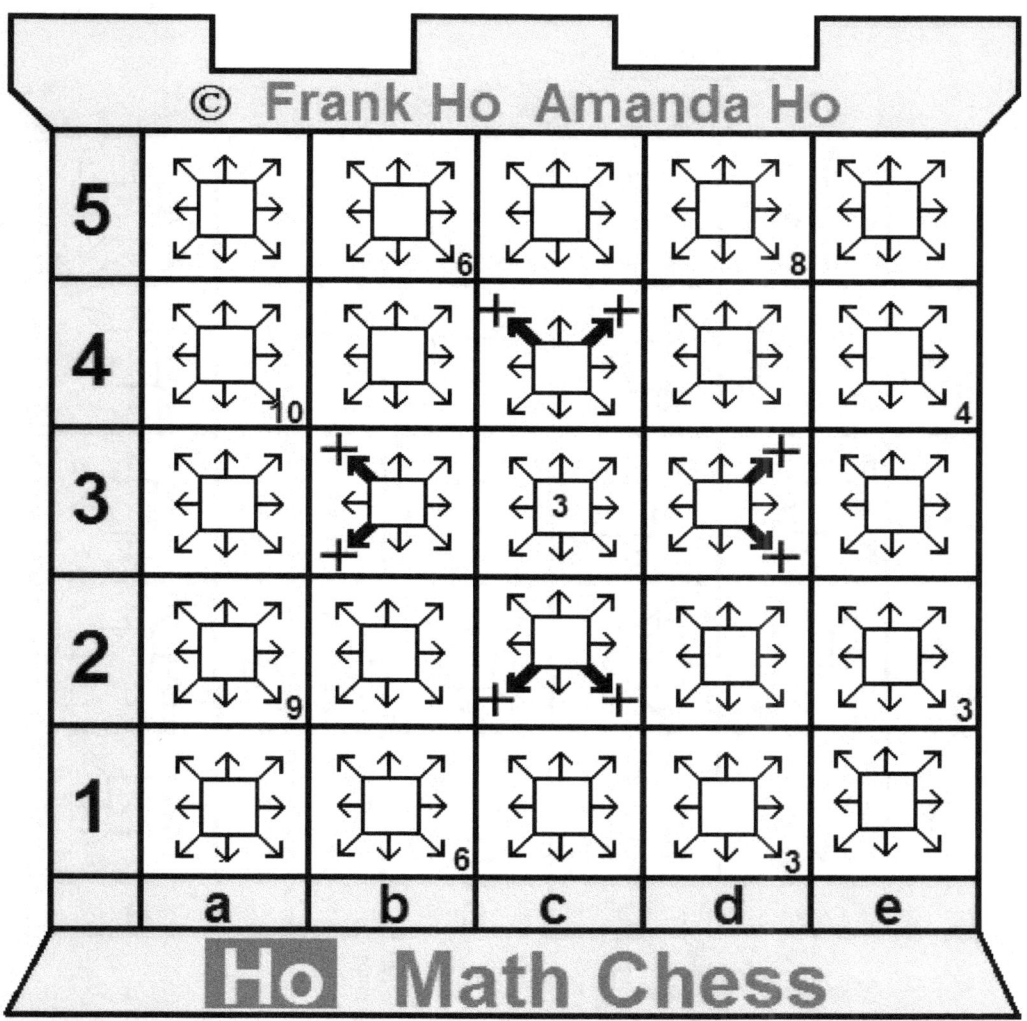

Frankho Puzzle™ # 126

Rule All the digits 1 to 5 must appear exactly once in every row and column. The number appears in the bottom right-hand corner is the end result calculated according to arithmetic operator(s) and chess move(s) as indicated by darker arrow(s).

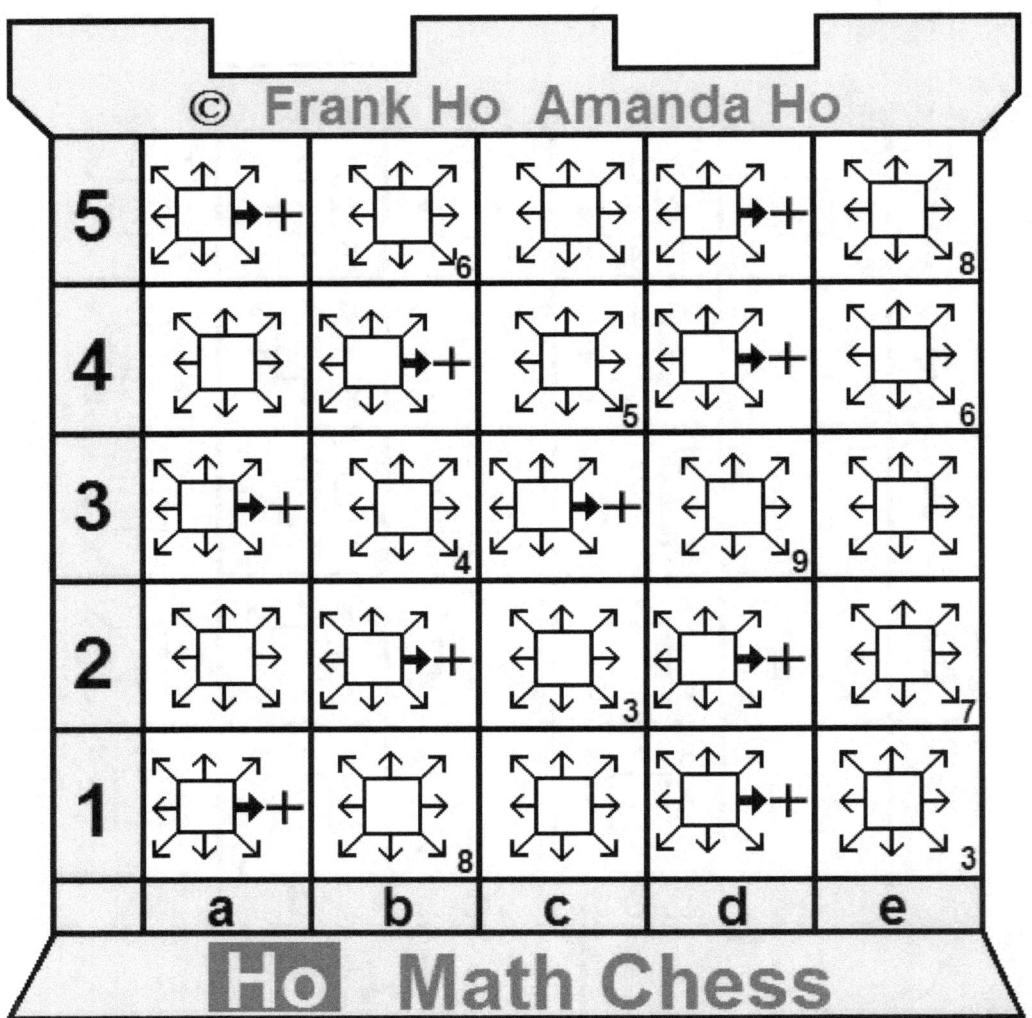

Ho Math Chess 何数棋谜 益智健脑非药物良方
Frankho Puzzle for KIDS – Brain Fitness Workbook

© 2007 — 2016 Frank Ho, Amanda Ho all rights reserved www.mathandchess.com

Frankho Puzzle™ # 127

Rule All the digits 1 to 5 must appear exactly once in every row and column. The number appears in the bottom right-hand corner is the end result calculated according to arithmetic operator(s) and chess move(s) as indicated by darker arrow(s).

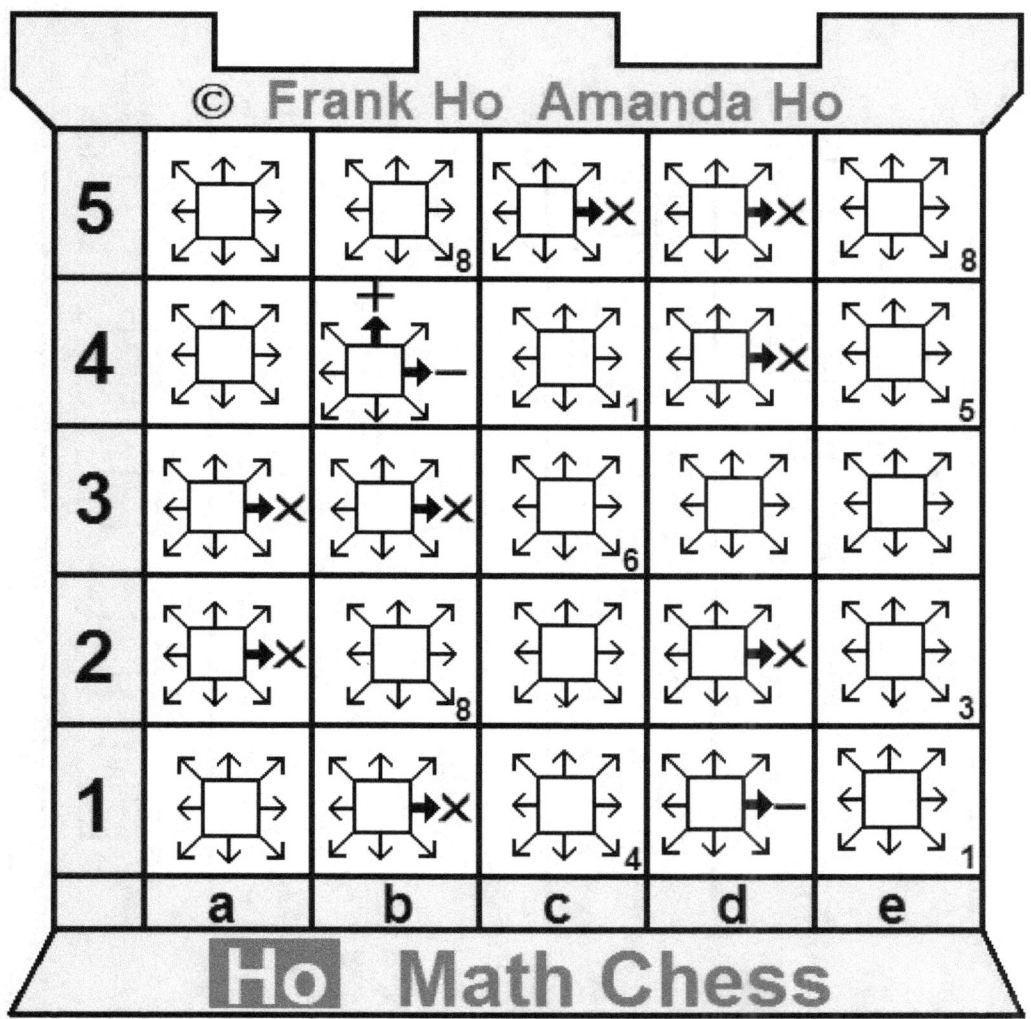

Frankho Puzzle™ # 128

Rule All the digits 1 to 5 must appear exactly once in every row and column. The number appears in the bottom right-hand corner is the end result calculated according to arithmetic operator(s) and chess move(s) as indicated by darker arrow(s).

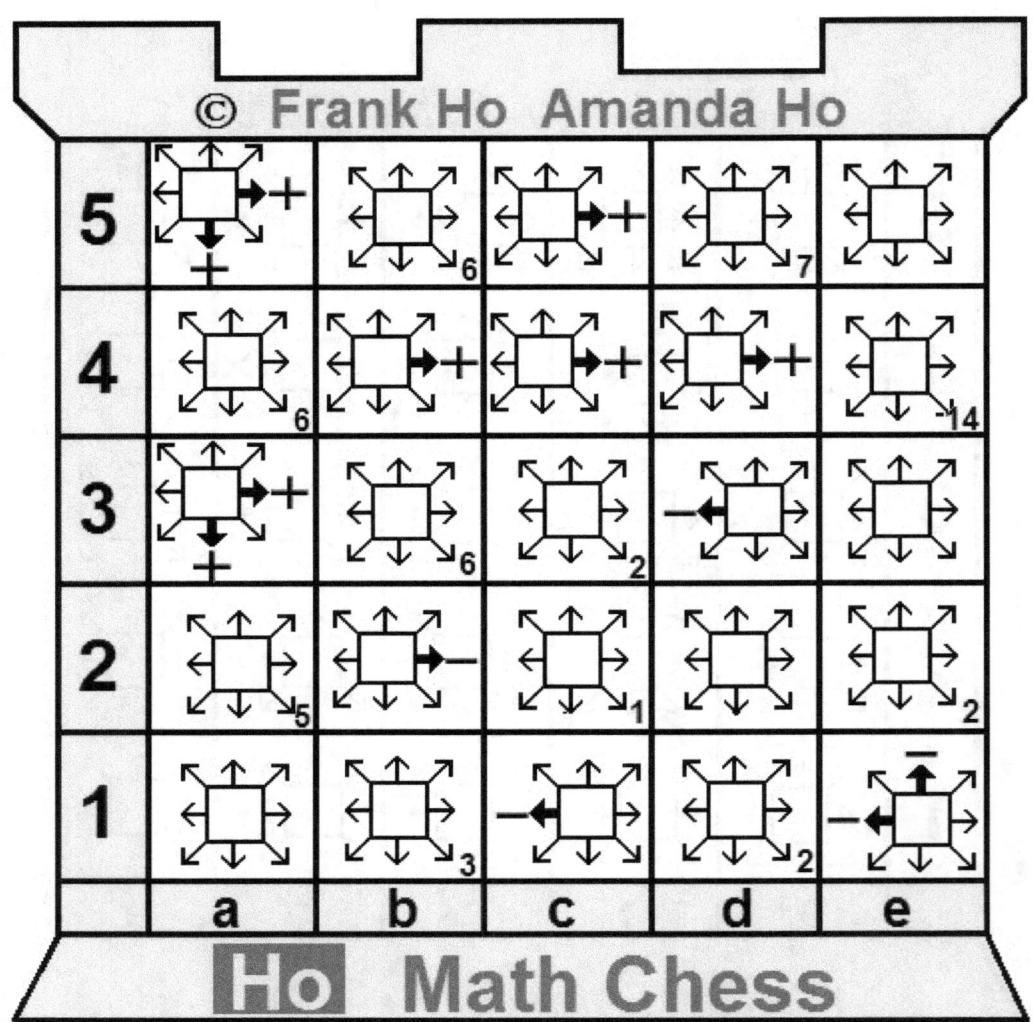

Frankho Puzzle™ # 129

Rule All the digits 1 to 5 must appear exactly once in every row and column. The number appears in the bottom right-hand corner is the end result calculated according to arithmetic operator(s) and chess move(s) as indicated by darker arrow(s).

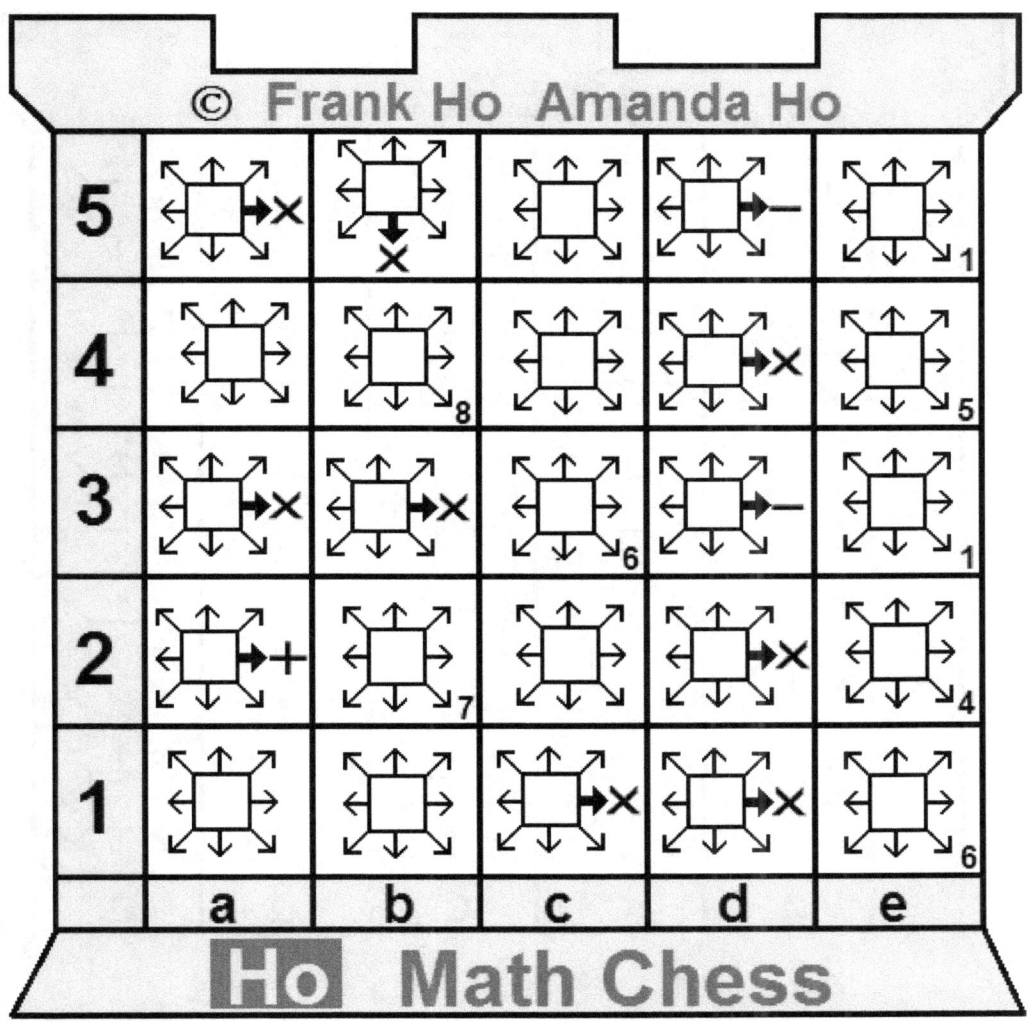

Frankho Puzzle™ # 130

Rule All the digits 1 to 5 must appear exactly once in every row and column. The number appears in the bottom right-hand corner is the end result calculated according to arithmetic operator(s) and chess move(s) as indicated by darker arrow(s).

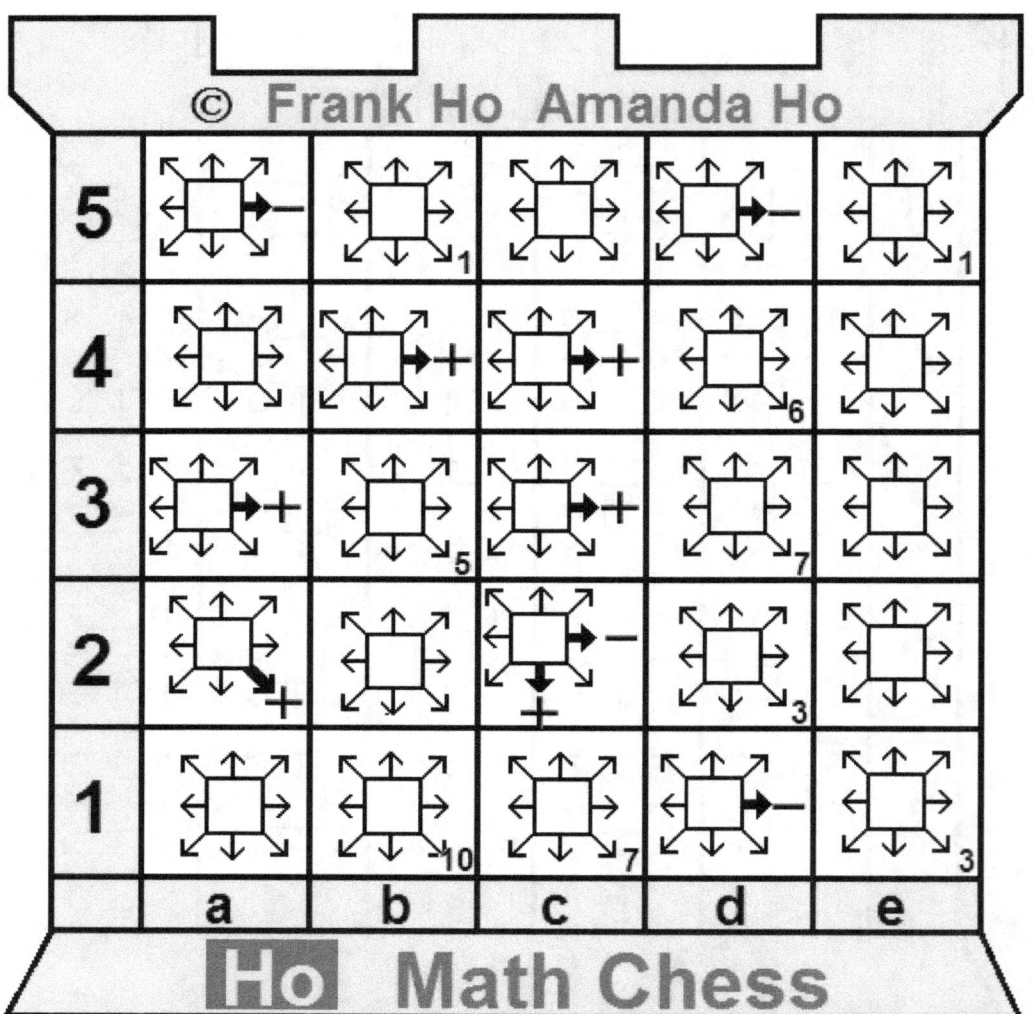

Ho Math Chess 何数棋谜 益智健脑非药物良方
Frankho Puzzle for KIDS – Brain Fitness Workbook
© 2007 — 2016 Frank Ho, Amanda Ho all rights reserved www.mathandchess.com

Frankho Puzzle™ # 131

Rule All the digits 1 to 5 must appear exactly once in every row and column. The number appears in the bottom right-hand corner is the end result calculated according to arithmetic operator(s) and chess move(s) as indicated by darker arrow(s).

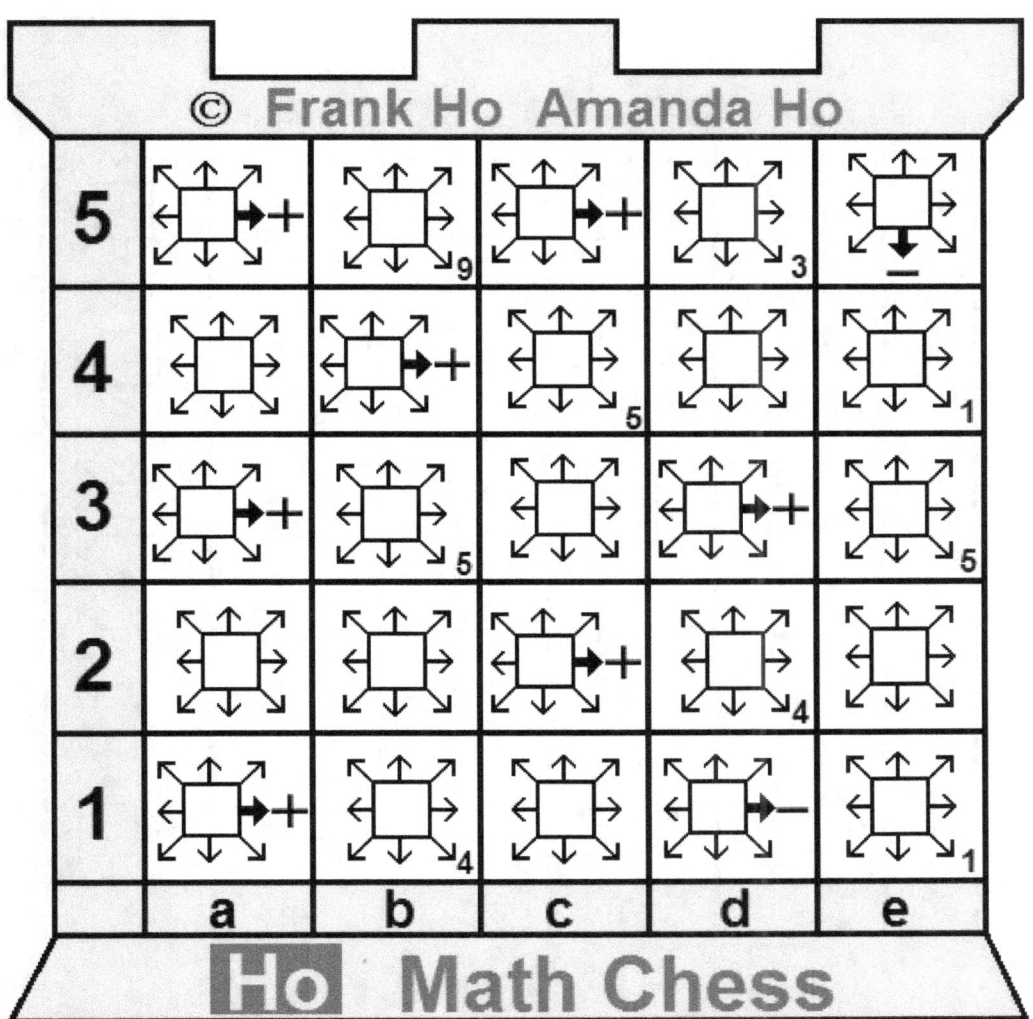

Ho Math Chess 何数棋谜 益智健脑非药物良方
Frankho Puzzle for KIDS – Brain Fitness Workbook
© 2007 — 2016 Frank Ho, Amanda Ho all rights reserved www.mathandchess.com

Frankho Puzzle™ # 132

Rule All the digits 1 to 5 must appear exactly once in every row and column. The number appears in the bottom right-hand corner is the end result calculated according to arithmetic operator(s) and chess move(s) as indicated by darker arrow(s).

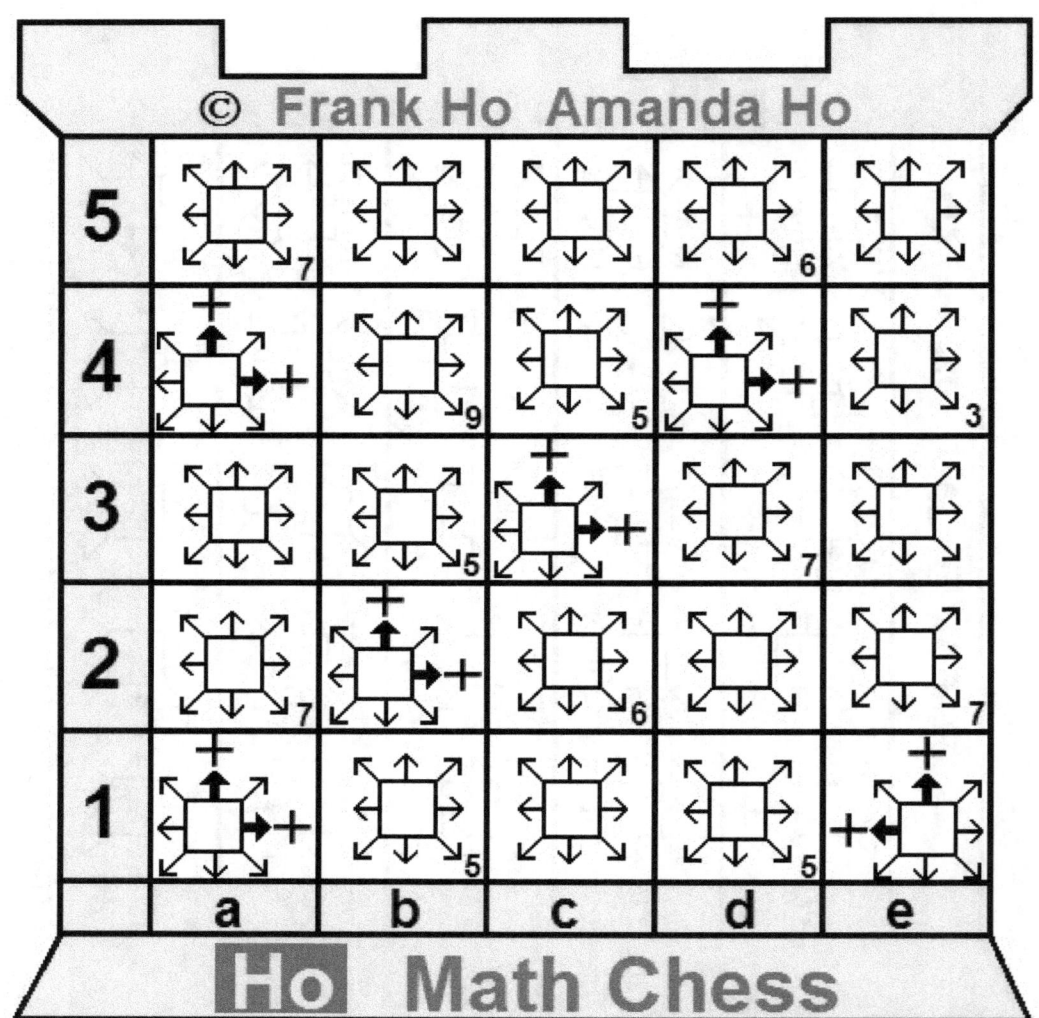

Ho Math Chess 何数棋谜 益智健脑非药物良方
Frankho Puzzle for KIDS – Brain Fitness Workbook

© 2007 — 2016 Frank Ho, Amanda Ho all rights reserved www.mathandchess.com

Frankho Puzzle™ # 133

Rule All the digits 1 to 5 must appear exactly once in every row and column. The number appears in the bottom right-hand corner is the end result calculated according to arithmetic operator(s) and chess move(s) as indicated by darker arrow(s).

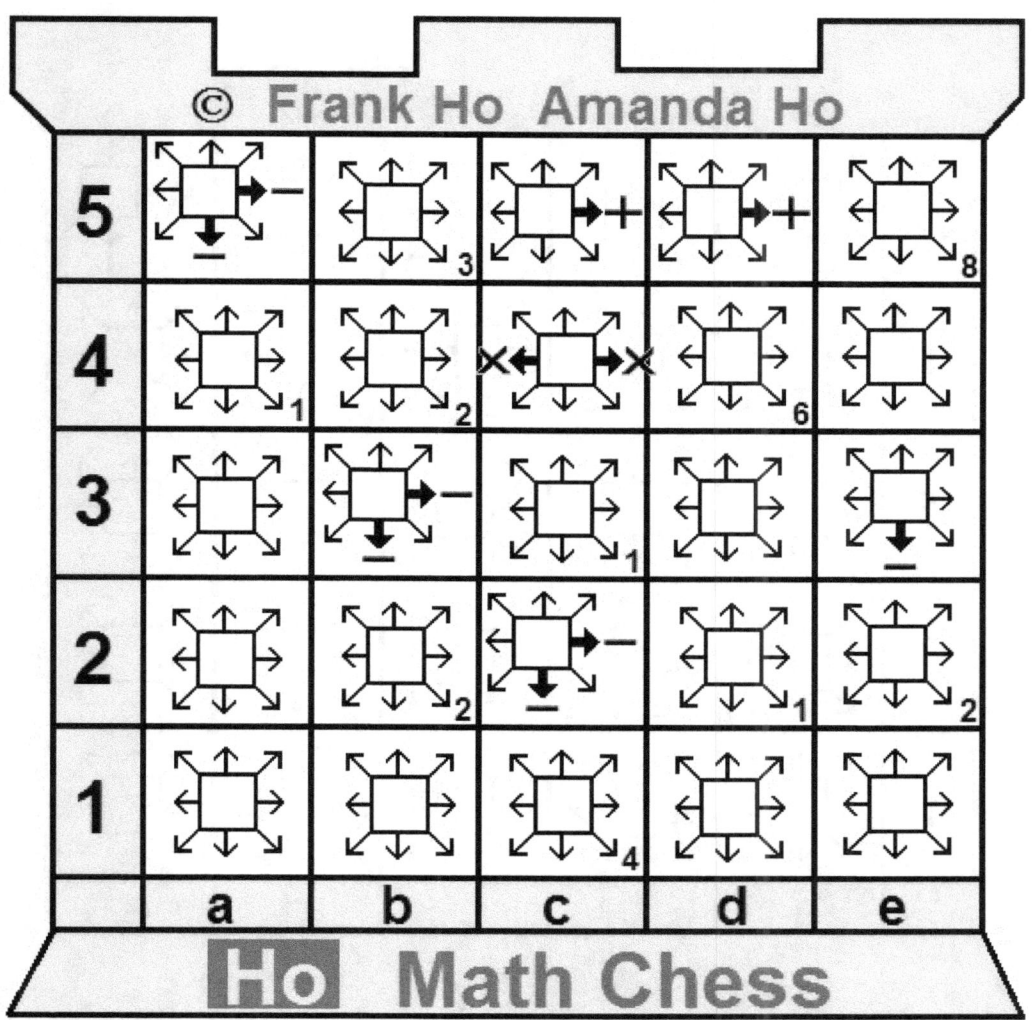

Frankho Puzzle™ # 134

Rule All the digits 1 to 5 must appear exactly once in every row and column. The number appears in the bottom right-hand corner is the end result calculated according to arithmetic operator(s) and chess move(s) as indicated by darker arrow(s).

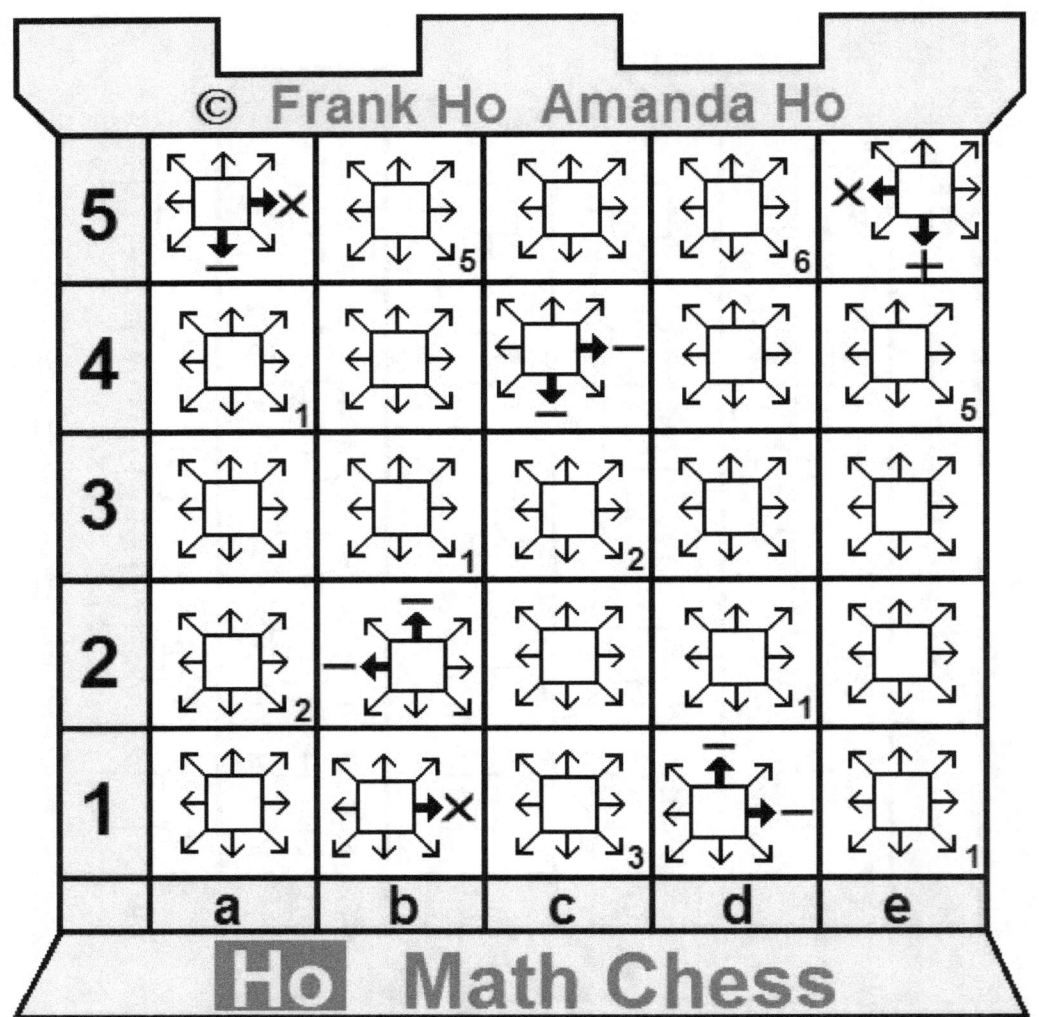

Ho Math Chess 何数棋谜 益智健脑非药物良方
Frankho Puzzle for KIDS – Brain Fitness Workbook
© 2007 — 2016 Frank Ho, Amanda Ho all rights reserved www.mathandchess.com

Frankho Puzzle™ # 135

Rule All the digits 1 to 5 must appear exactly once in every row and column. The number appears in the bottom right-hand corner is the end result calculated according to arithmetic operator(s) and chess move(s) as indicated by darker arrow(s).

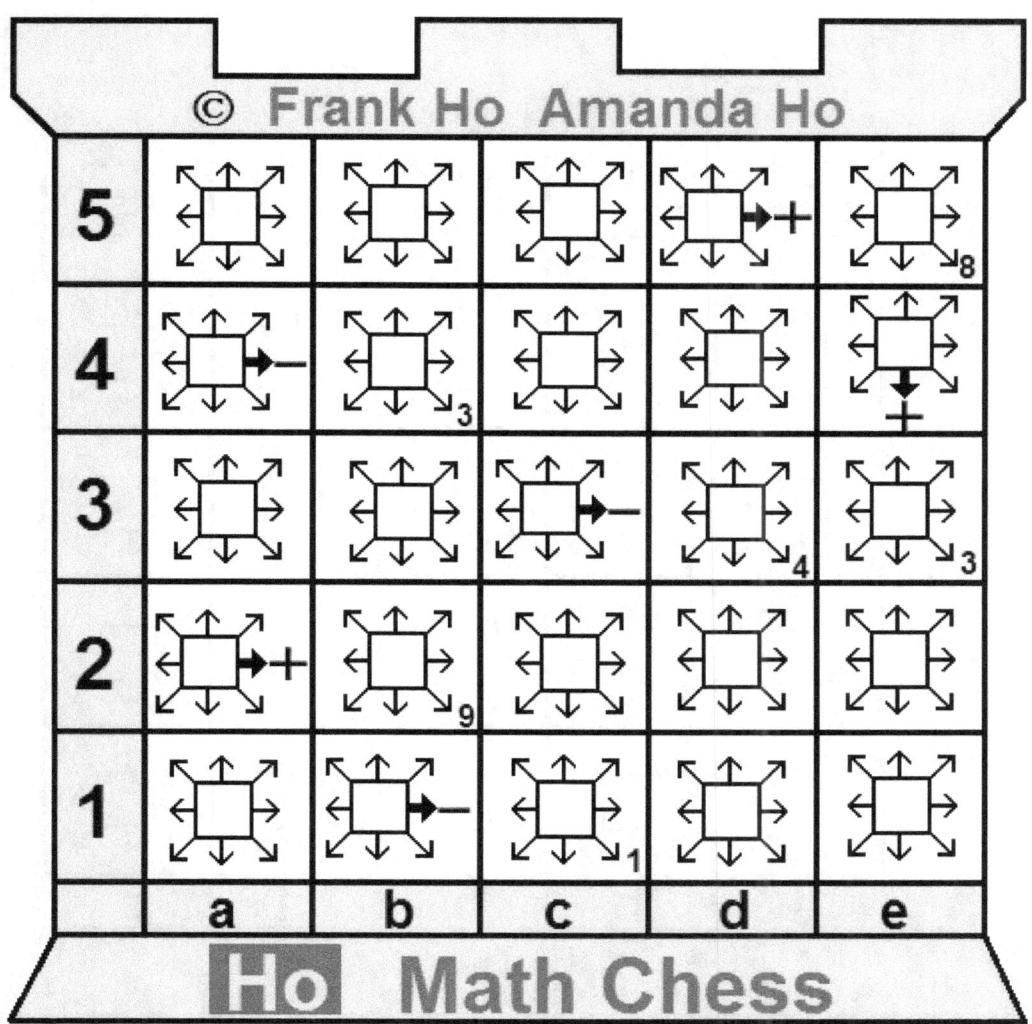

Frankho Puzzle™ # 136

Rule All the digits 1 to 5 must appear exactly once in every row and column. The number appears in the bottom right-hand corner is the end result calculated according to arithmetic operator(s) and chess move(s) as indicated by darker arrow(s).

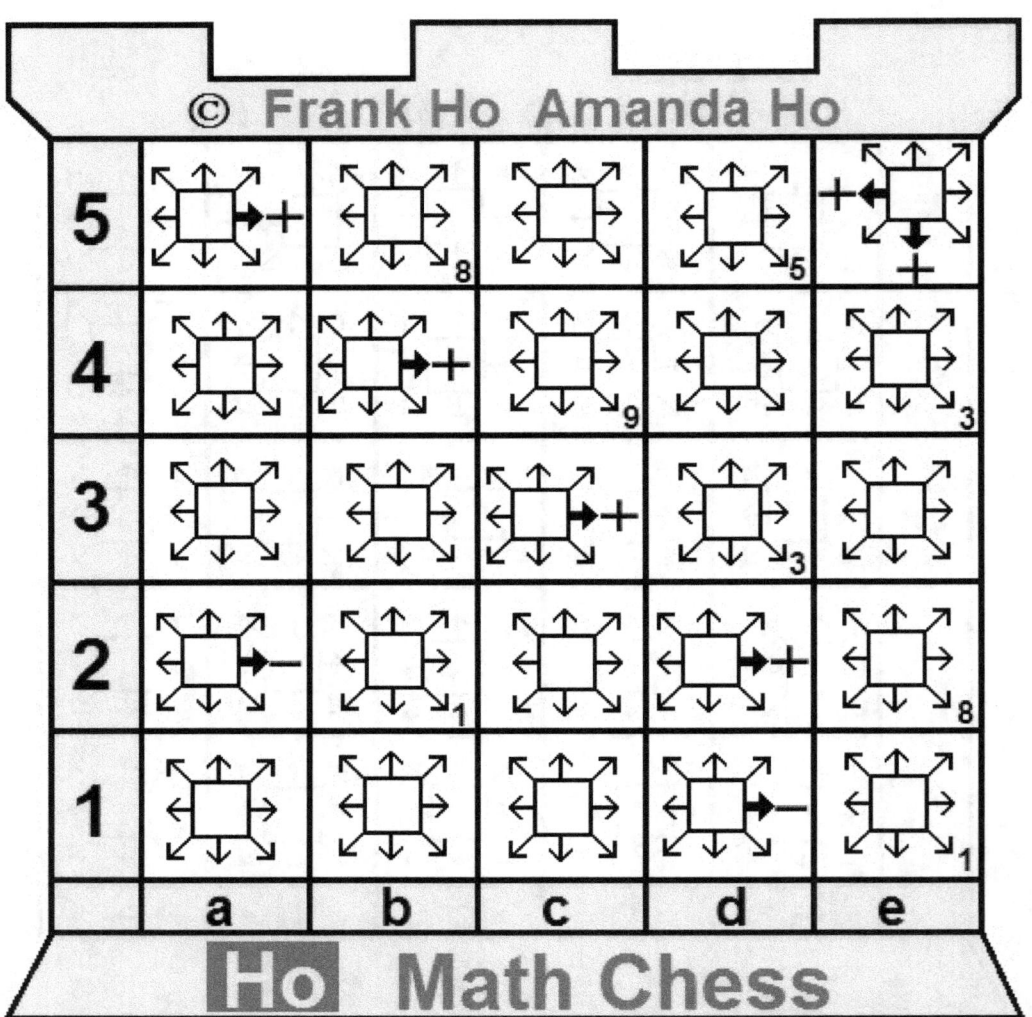

Ho Math Chess 何数棋谜 益智健脑非药物良方
Frankho Puzzle for KIDS – Brain Fitness Workbook
© 2007 – 2016 Frank Ho, Amanda Ho all rights reserved www.mathandchess.com

Frankho Puzzle™ # 137

Rule All the digits 1 to 5 must appear exactly once in every row and column. The number appears in the bottom right-hand corner is the end result calculated according to arithmetic operator(s) and chess move(s) as indicated by darker arrow(s).

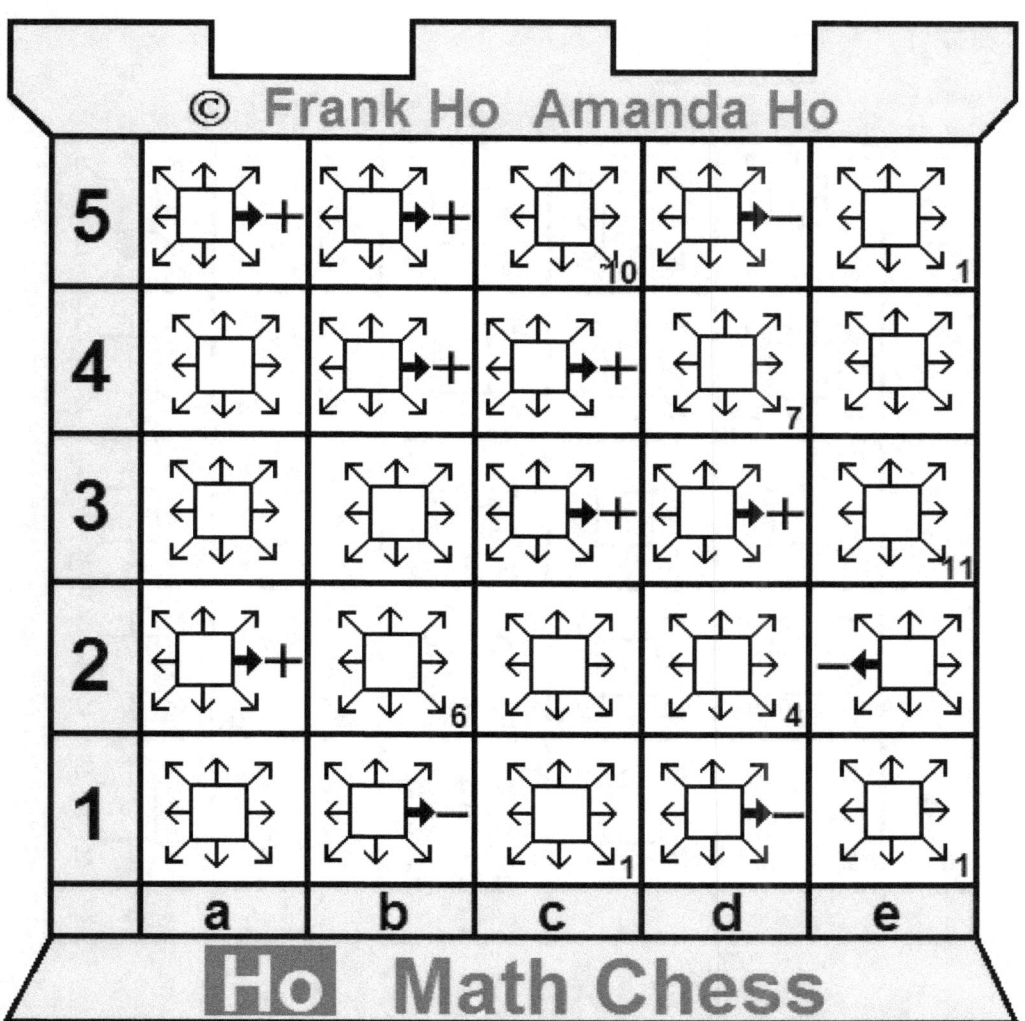

Frankho Puzzle™ # 138

Rule All the digits 1 to 5 must appear exactly once in every row and column. The number appears in the bottom right-hand corner is the end result calculated according to arithmetic operator(s) and chess move(s) as indicated by darker arrow(s).

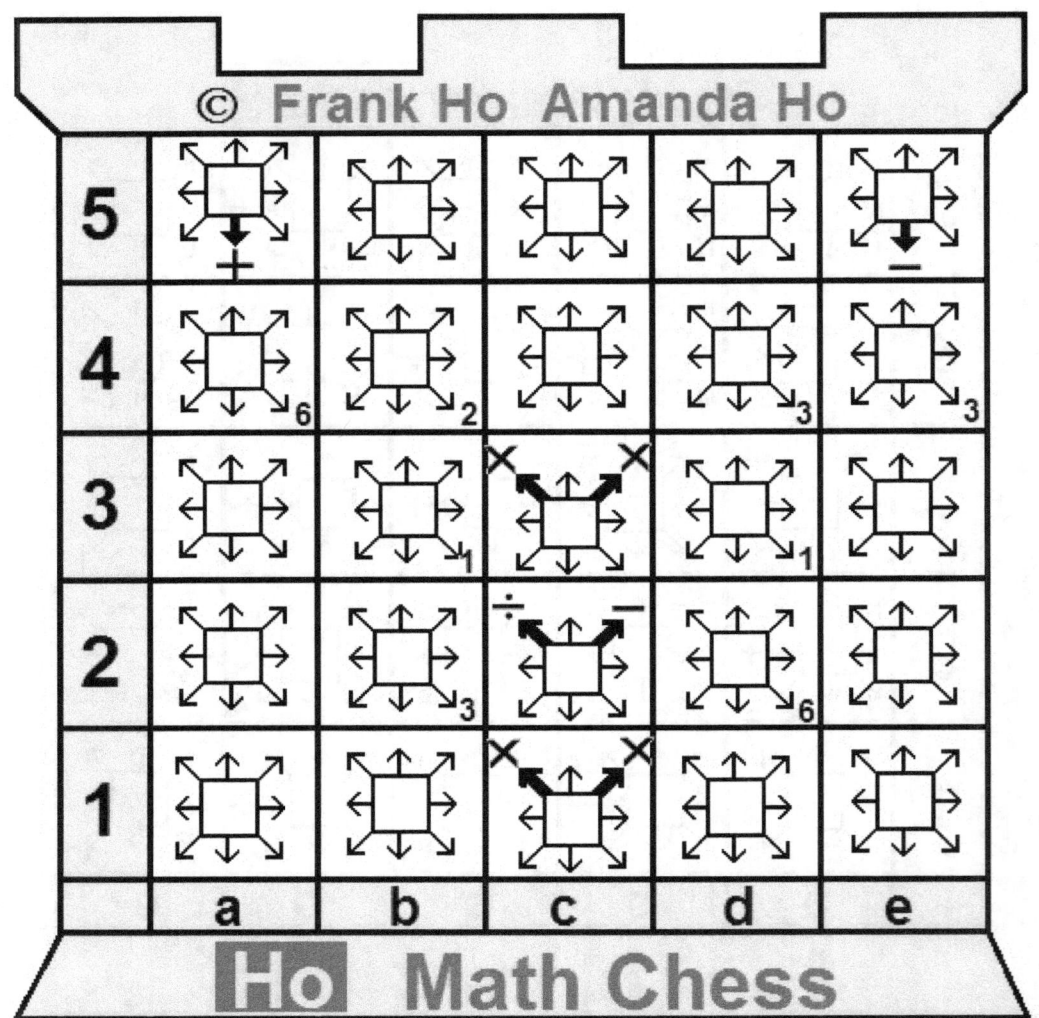

Ho Math Chess 何数棋谜 益智健脑非药物良方
Frankho Puzzle for KIDS – Brain Fitness Workbook

© 2007 — 2016 Frank Ho, Amanda Ho all rights reserved www.mathandchess.com

Frankho Puzzle™ # 139

Rule All the digits 1 to 5 must appear exactly once in every row and column. The number appears in the bottom right-hand corner is the end result calculated according to arithmetic operator(s) and chess move(s) as indicated by darker arrow(s).

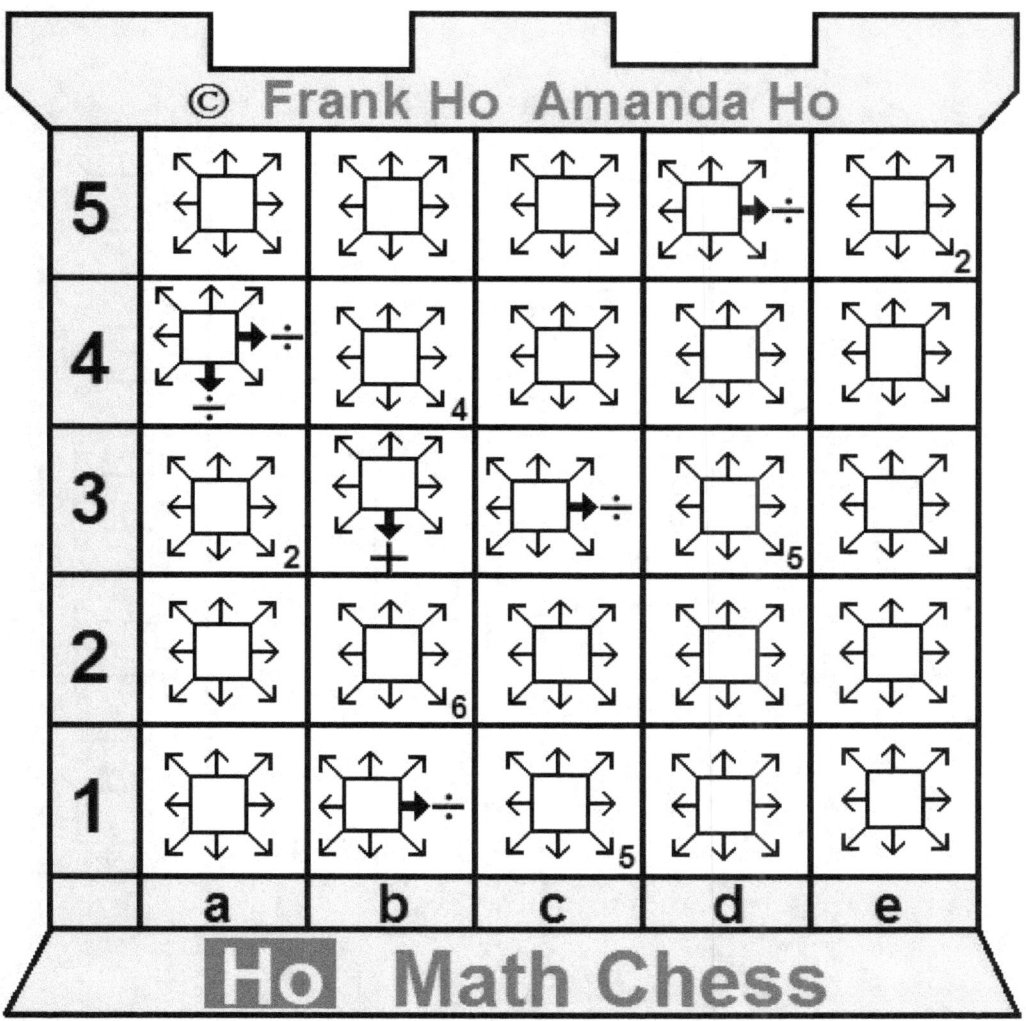

Frankho Puzzle™ # 140

Rule All the digits 1 to 5 must appear exactly once in every row and column. The number appears in the bottom right-hand corner is the end result calculated according to arithmetic operator(s) and chess move(s) as indicated by darker arrow(s).

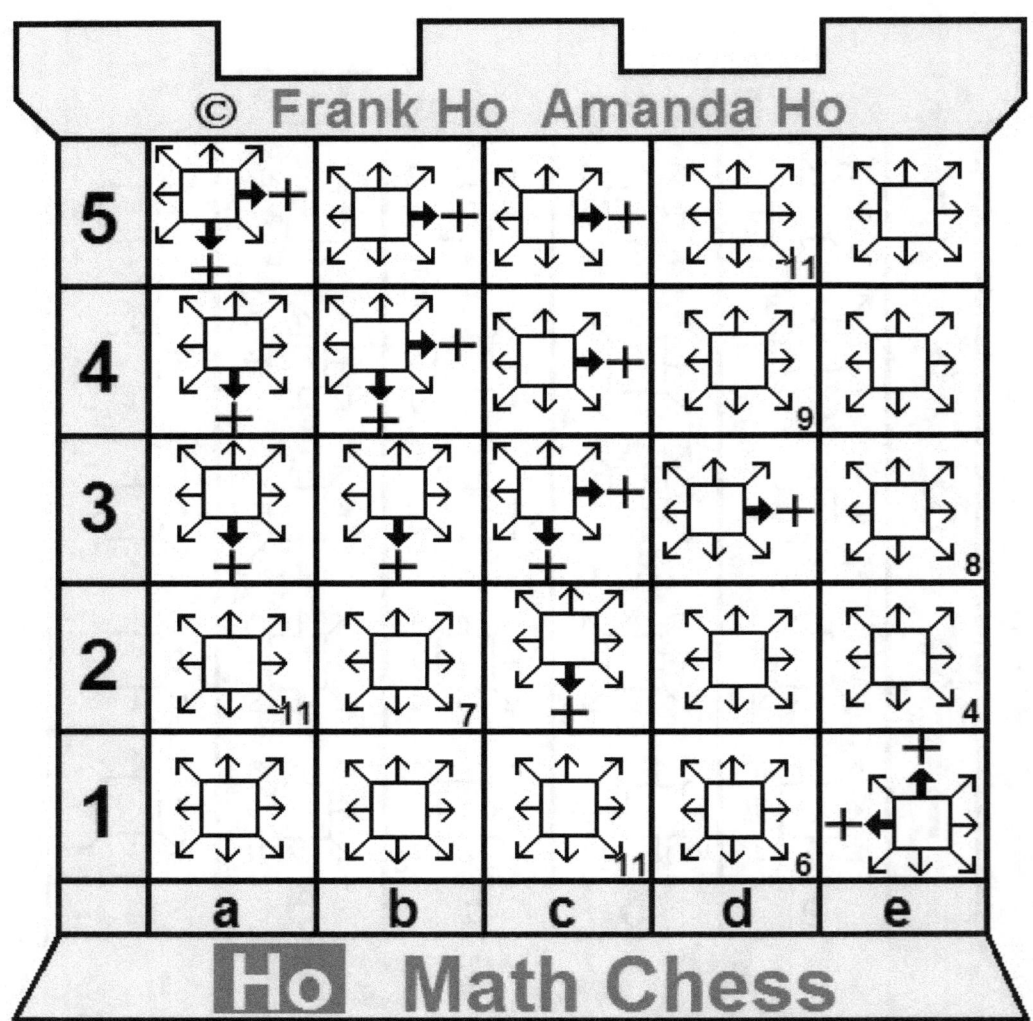

Ho Math Chess 何数棋谜 益智健脑非药物良方
Frankho Puzzle for KIDS – Brain Fitness Workbook
© 2007 – 2016 Frank Ho, Amanda Ho all rights reserved www.mathandchess.com

Frankho Puzzle™ # 141

Rule All the digits 1 to 5 must appear exactly once in every row and column. The number appears in the bottom right-hand corner is the end result calculated according to arithmetic operator(s) and chess move(s) as indicated by darker arrow(s).

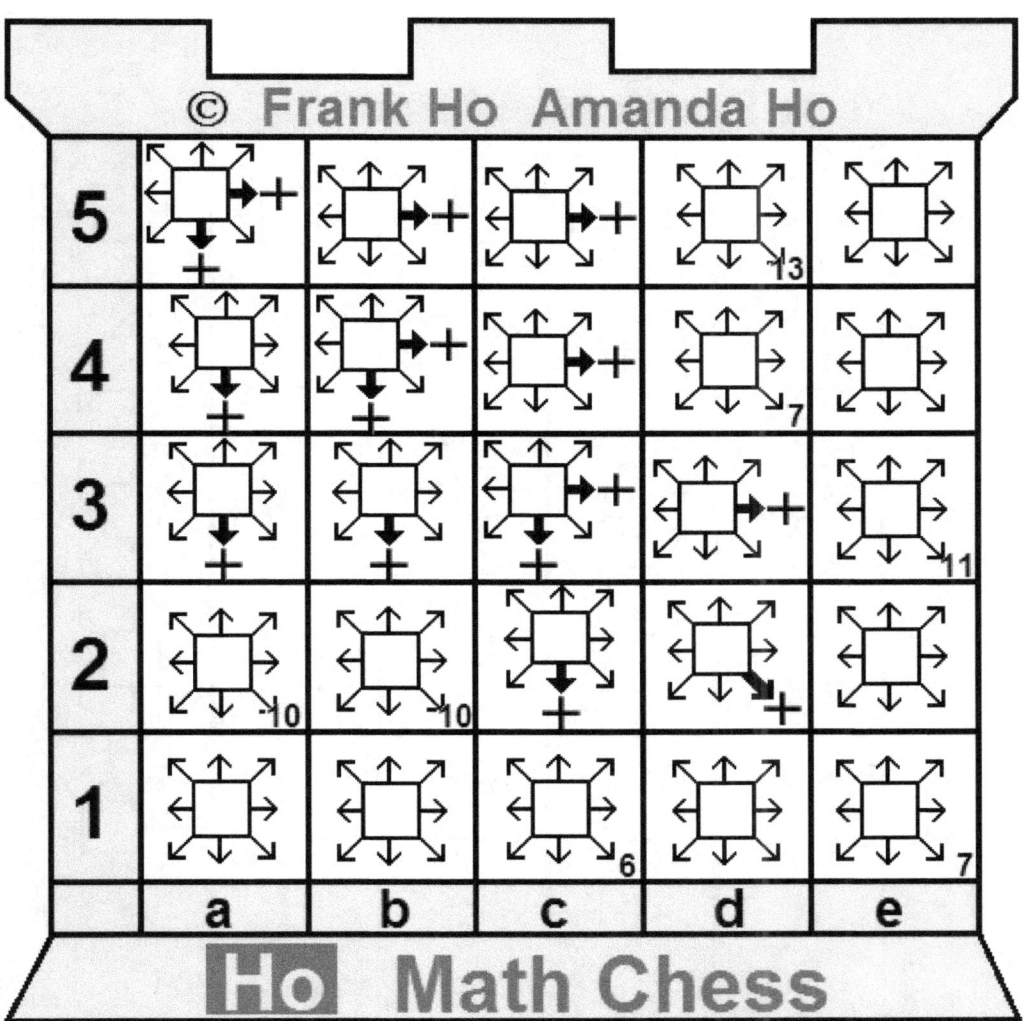

Frankho Puzzle™ # 142

Rule All the digits 1 to 5 must appear exactly once in every row and column. The number appears in the bottom right-hand corner is the end result calculated according to arithmetic operator(s) and chess move(s) as indicated by darker arrow(s).

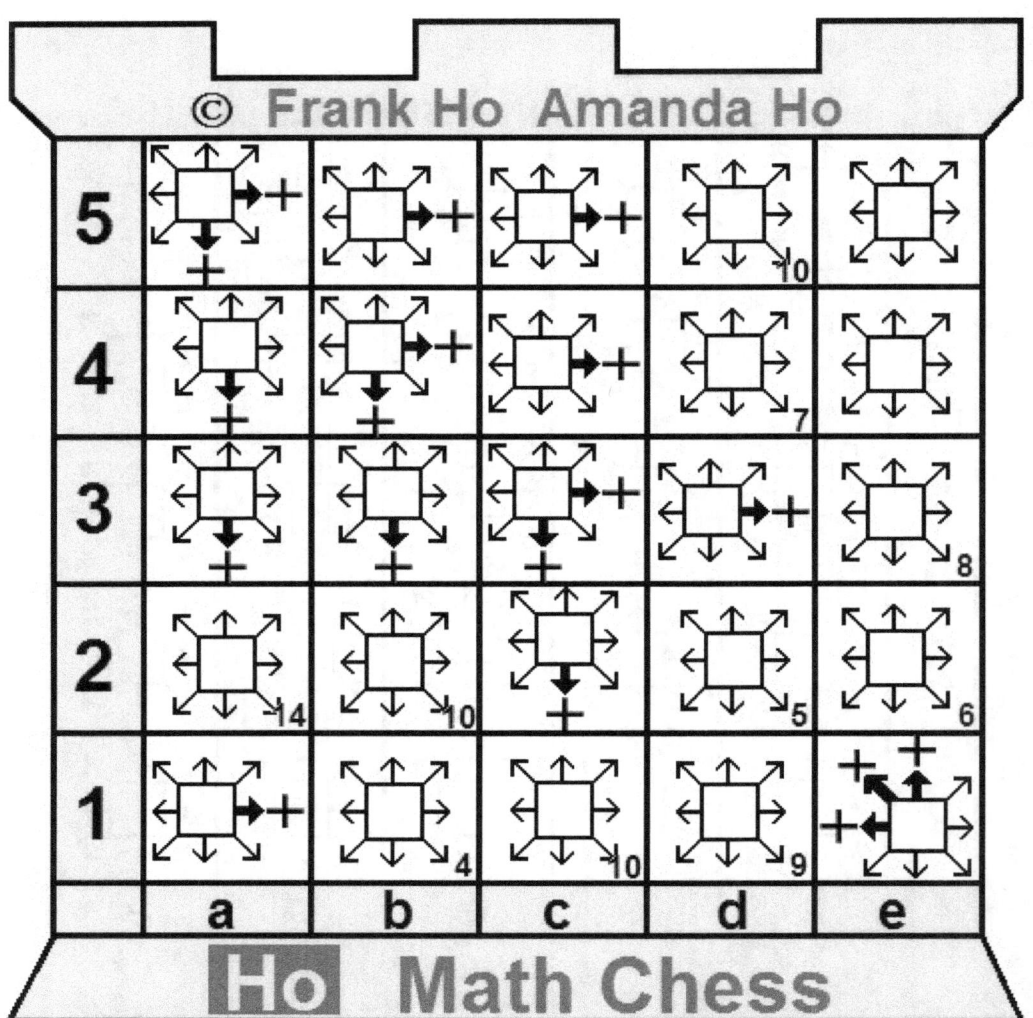

Ho Math Chess 何数棋谜 益智健脑非药物良方
Frankho Puzzle for KIDS – Brain Fitness Workbook

© 2007 — 2016 Frank Ho, Amanda Ho all rights reserved www.mathandchess.com

Frankho Puzzle™ # 143

Rule All the digits 1 to 5 must appear exactly once in every row and column. The number appears in the bottom right-hand corner is the end result calculated according to arithmetic operator(s) and chess move(s) as indicated by darker arrow(s).

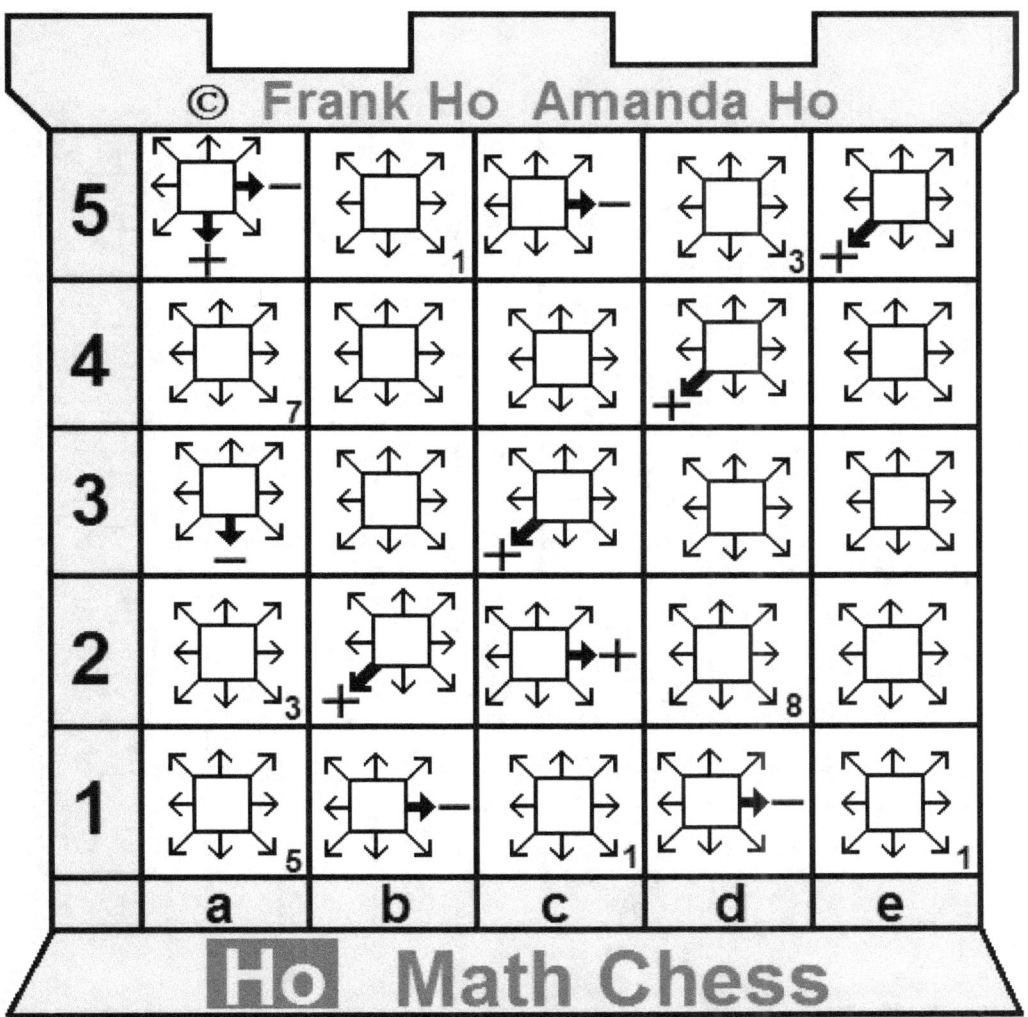

Frankho Puzzle™ # 144

Rule All the digits 1 to 5 must appear exactly once in every row and column. The number appears in the bottom right-hand corner is the end result calculated according to arithmetic operator(s) and chess move(s) as indicated by darker arrow(s).

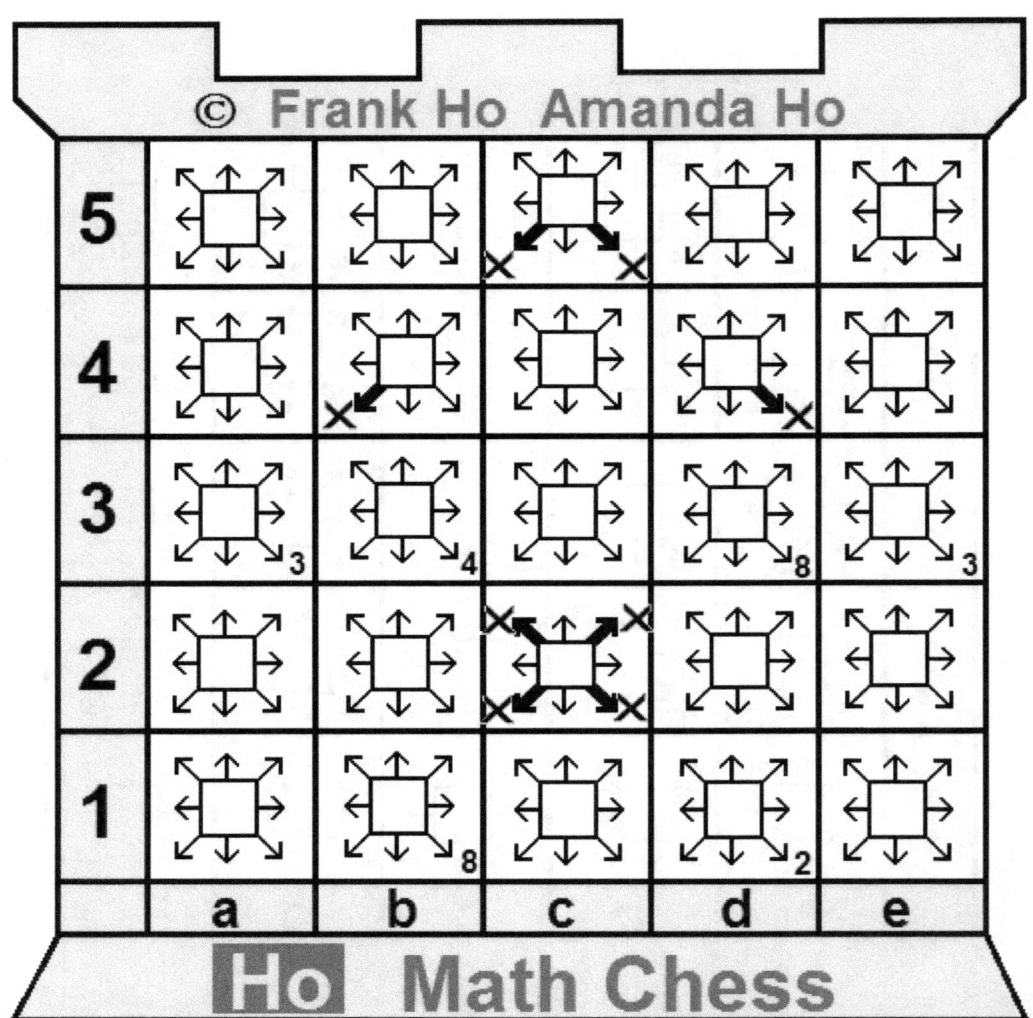

Ho Math Chess 何数棋谜 益智健脑非药物良方
Frankho Puzzle for KIDS – Brain Fitness Workbook
© 2007 – 2016 Frank Ho, Amanda Ho all rights reserved www.mathandchess.com

Frankho Puzzle™ # 145

Rule All the digits 1 to 5 must appear exactly once in every row and column. The number appears in the bottom right-hand corner is the end result calculated according to arithmetic operator(s) and chess move(s) as indicated by darker arrow(s).

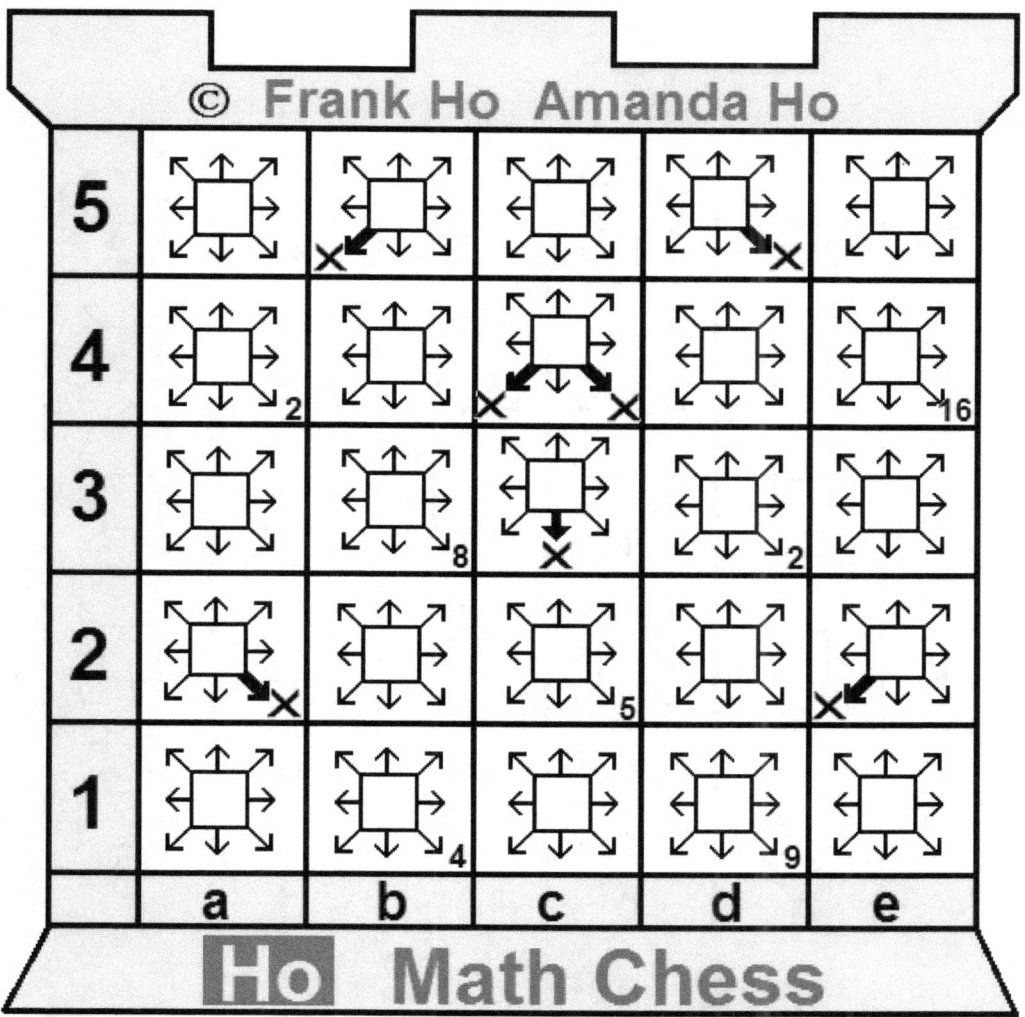

Frankho Puzzle™ # 146

Rule All the digits 1 to 5 must appear exactly once in every row and column. The number appears in the bottom right-hand corner is the end result calculated according to arithmetic operator(s) and chess move(s) as indicated by darker arrow(s).

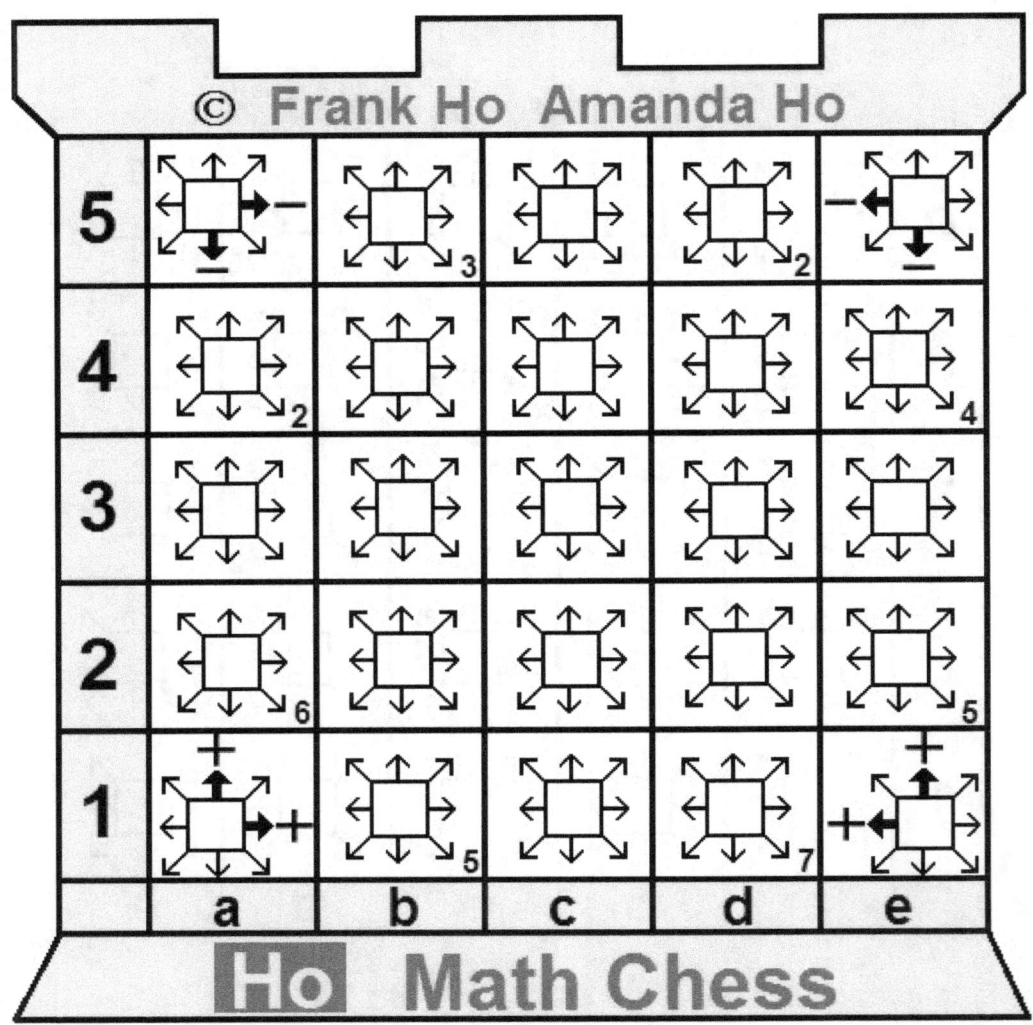

Ho Math Chess 何数棋谜 益智健脑非药物良方
Frankho Puzzle for KIDS – Brain Fitness Workbook

© 2007 — 2016 Frank Ho, Amanda Ho all rights reserved www.mathandchess.com

Frankho Puzzle™ # 147

Rule All the digits 1 to 5 must appear exactly once in every row and column. The number appears in the bottom right-hand corner is the end result calculated according to arithmetic operator(s) and chess move(s) as indicated by darker arrow(s).

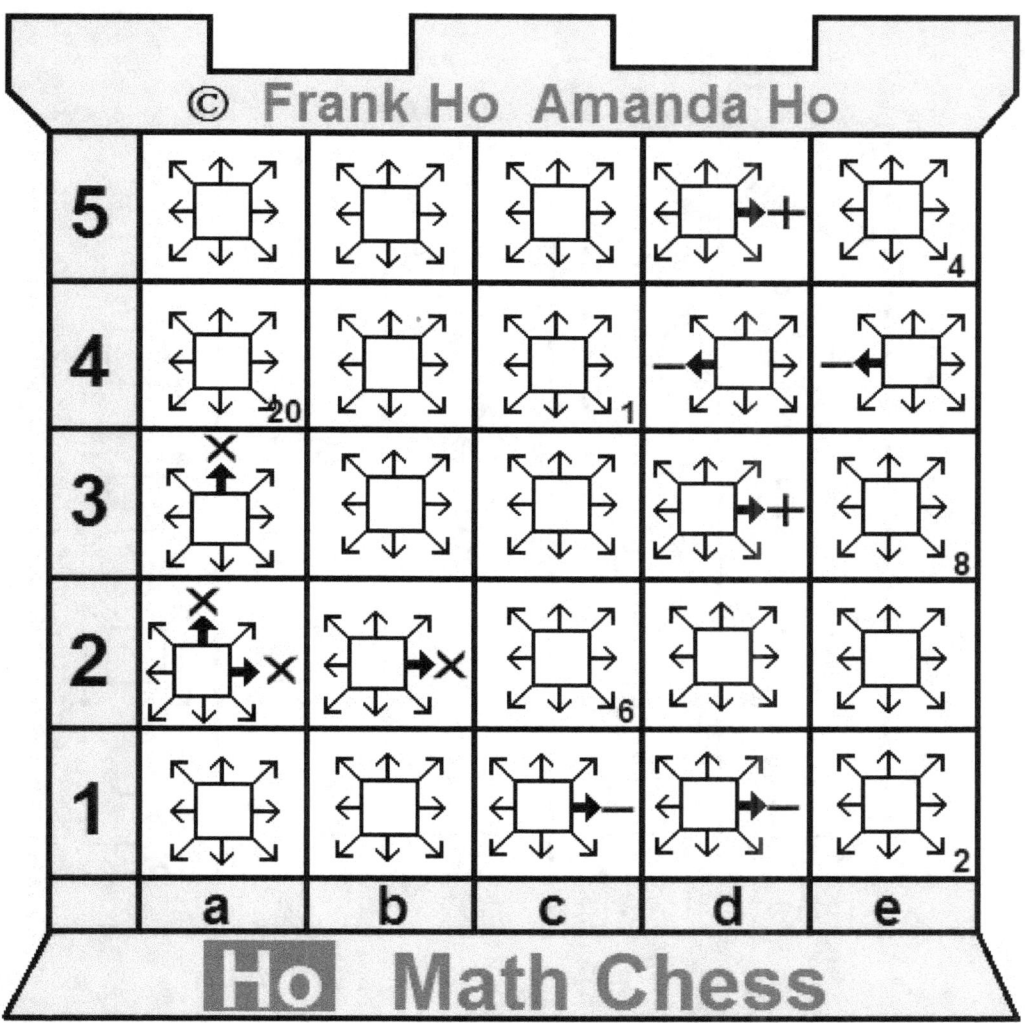

Ho Math Chess 何数棋谜 益智健脑非药物良方
Frankho Puzzle for KIDS – Brain Fitness Workbook
© 2007 – 2016 Frank Ho, Amanda Ho all rights reserved www.mathandchess.com

Frankho Puzzle™ # 148

Rule All the digits 1 to 5 must appear exactly once in every row and column. The number appears in the bottom right-hand corner is the end result calculated according to arithmetic operator(s) and chess move(s) as indicated by darker arrow(s).

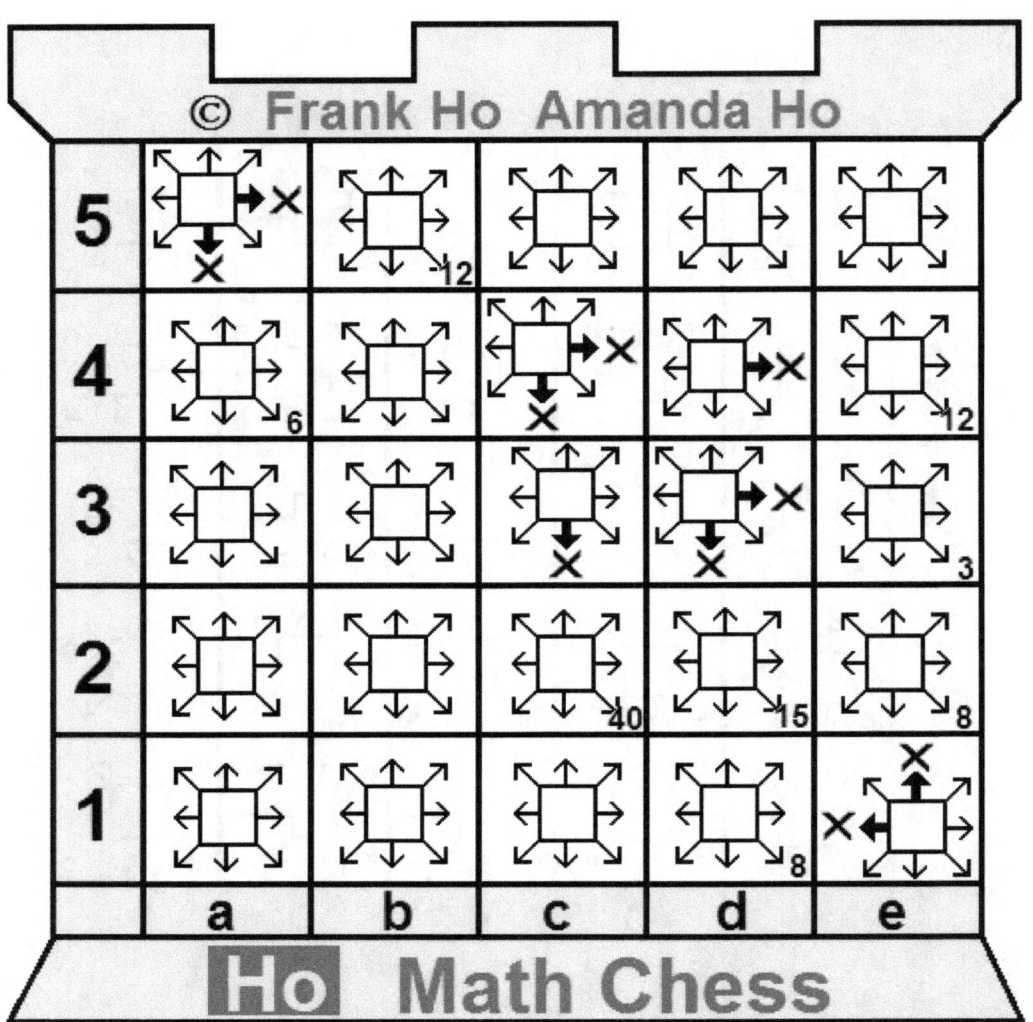

152

Ho Math Chess 何数棋谜 益智健脑非药物良方
Frankho Puzzle for KIDS – Brain Fitness Workbook
© 2007 — 2016 Frank Ho, Amanda Ho all rights reserved www.mathandchess.com

Frankho Puzzle™ # 149

Rule All the digits 1 to 5 must appear exactly once in every row and column. The number appears in the bottom right-hand corner is the end result calculated according to arithmetic operator(s) and chess move(s) as indicated by darker arrow(s).

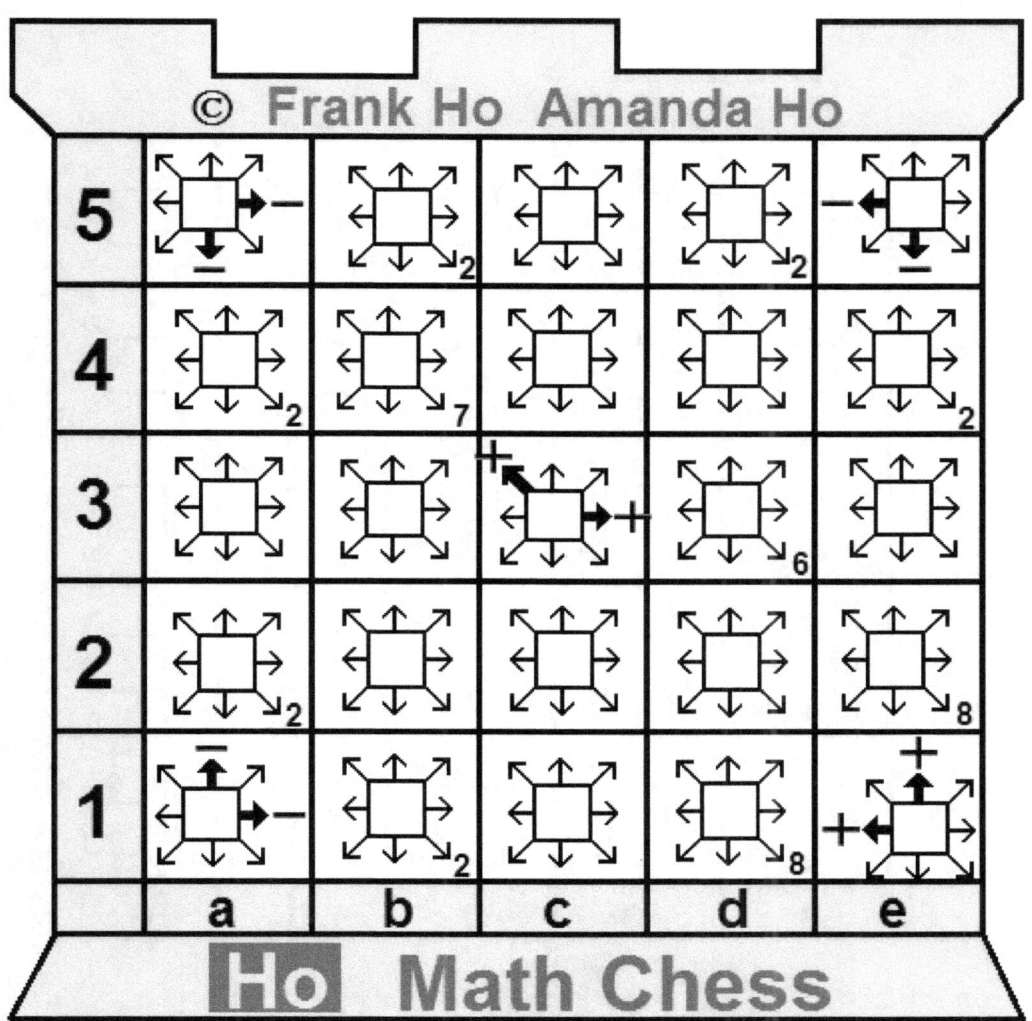

Frankho Puzzle™ # 150

Rule All the digits 1 to 5 must appear exactly once in every row and column. The number appears in the bottom right-hand corner is the end result calculated according to arithmetic operator(s) and chess move(s) as indicated by darker arrow(s).

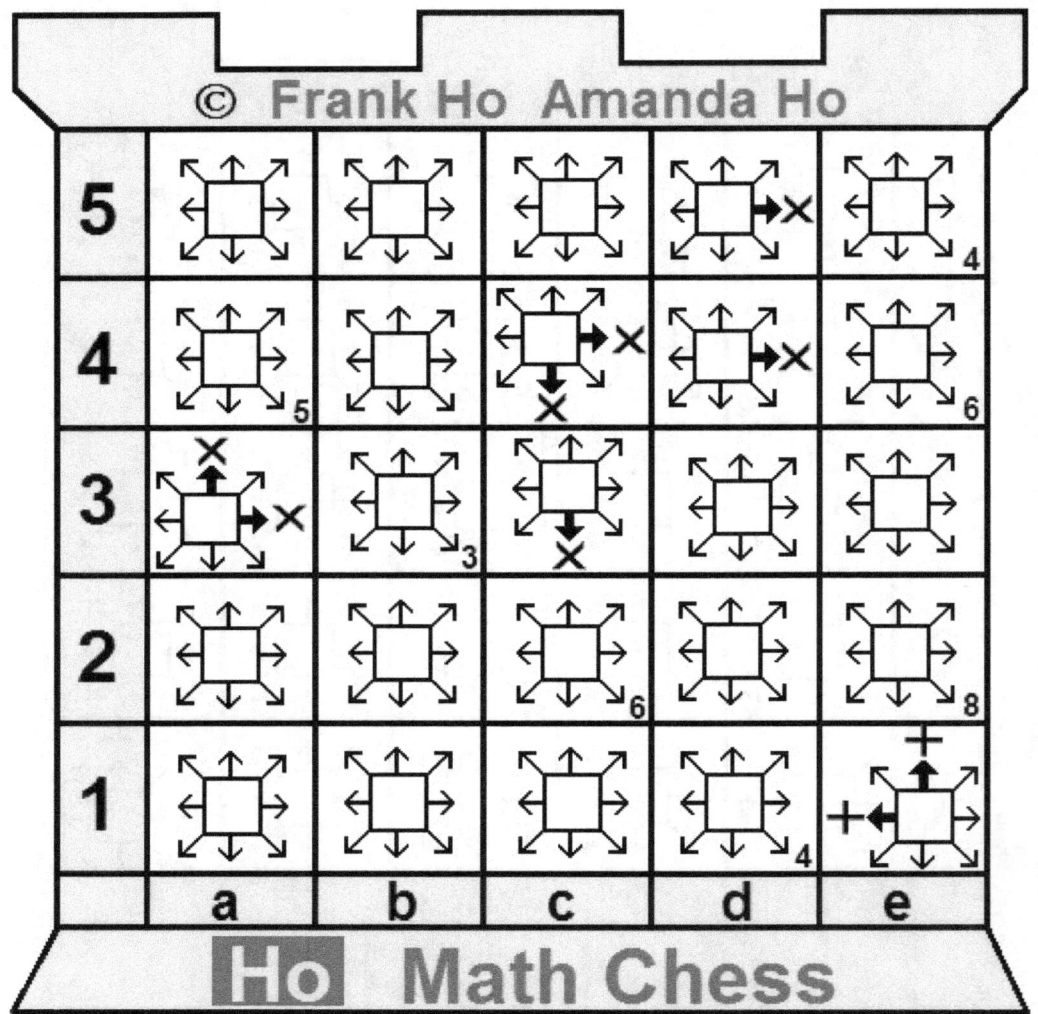

Frankho Puzzle™ # 151

Rule All the digits 1 to 5 must appear exactly once in every row and column. The number appears in the bottom right-hand corner is the end result calculated according to arithmetic operator(s) and chess move(s) as indicated by darker arrow(s).

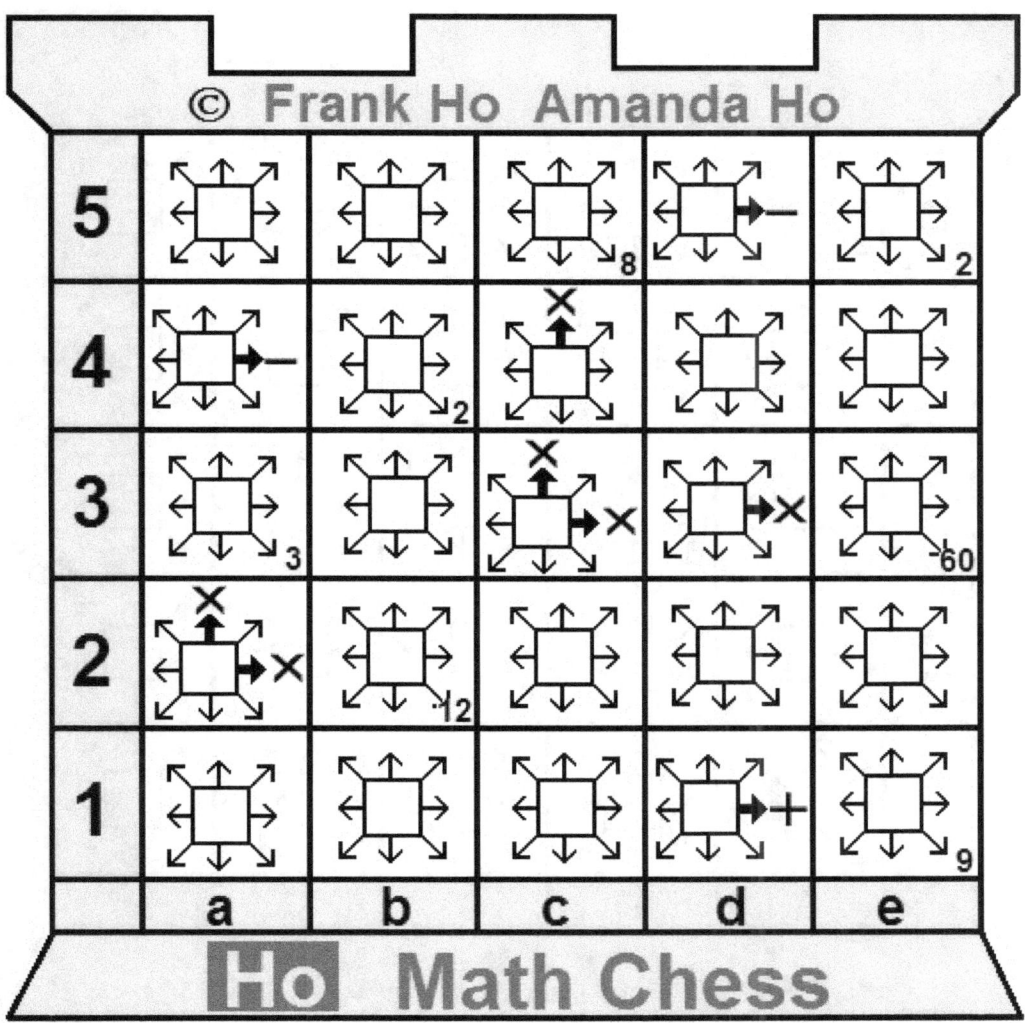

Ho Math Chess 何数棋谜 益智健脑非药物良方
Frankho Puzzle for KIDS – Brain Fitness Workbook

© 2007 — 2016 Frank Ho, Amanda Ho all rights reserved www.mathandchess.com

Frankho Puzzle™ # 152

Rule All the digits 1 to 5 must appear exactly once in every row and column. The number appears in the bottom right-hand corner is the end result calculated according to arithmetic operator(s) and chess move(s) as indicated by darker arrow(s).

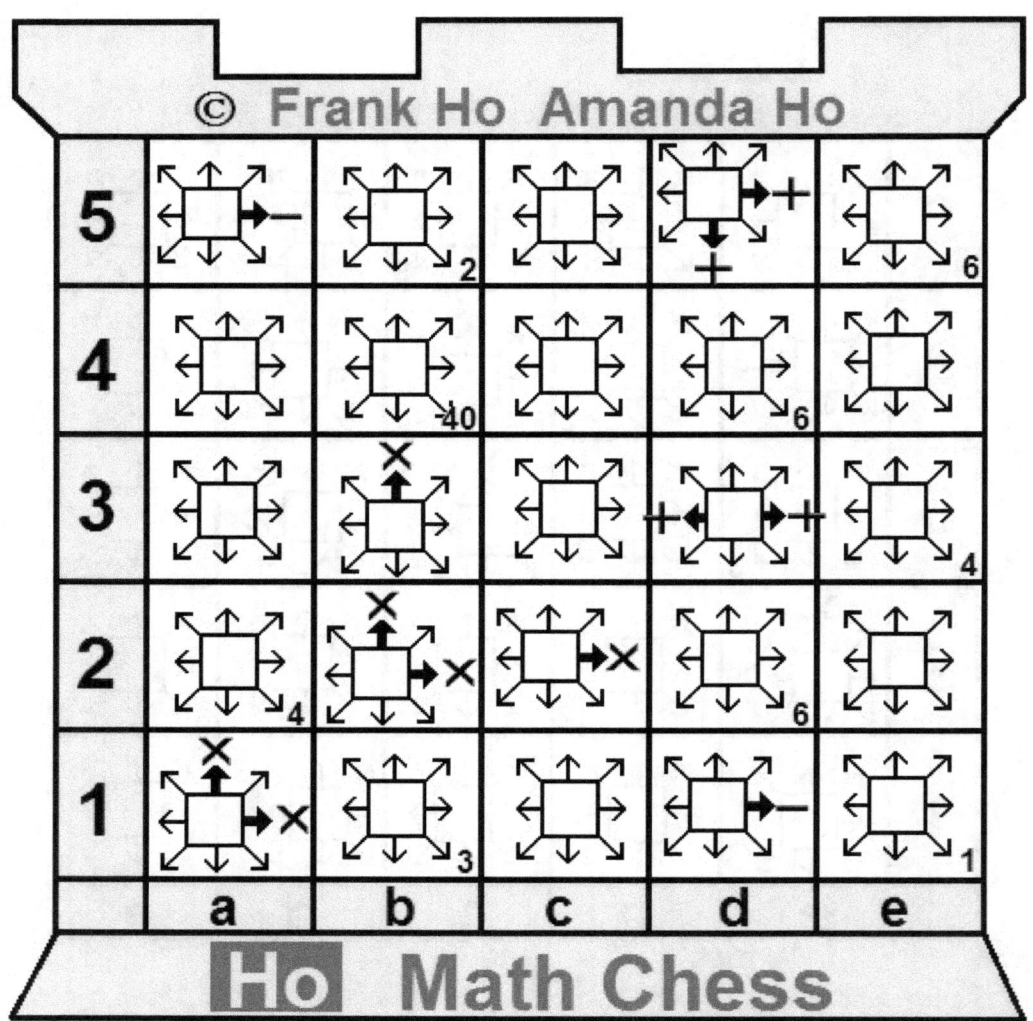

156

Ho Math Chess 何数棋谜 益智健脑非药物良方
Frankho Puzzle for KIDS – Brain Fitness Workbook
© 2007 – 2016 Frank Ho, Amanda Ho all rights reserved www.mathandchess.com

Frankho Puzzle™ # 153

Rule All the digits 1 to 5 must appear exactly once in every row and column. The number appears in the bottom right-hand corner is the end result calculated according to arithmetic operator(s) and chess move(s) as indicated by darker arrow(s).

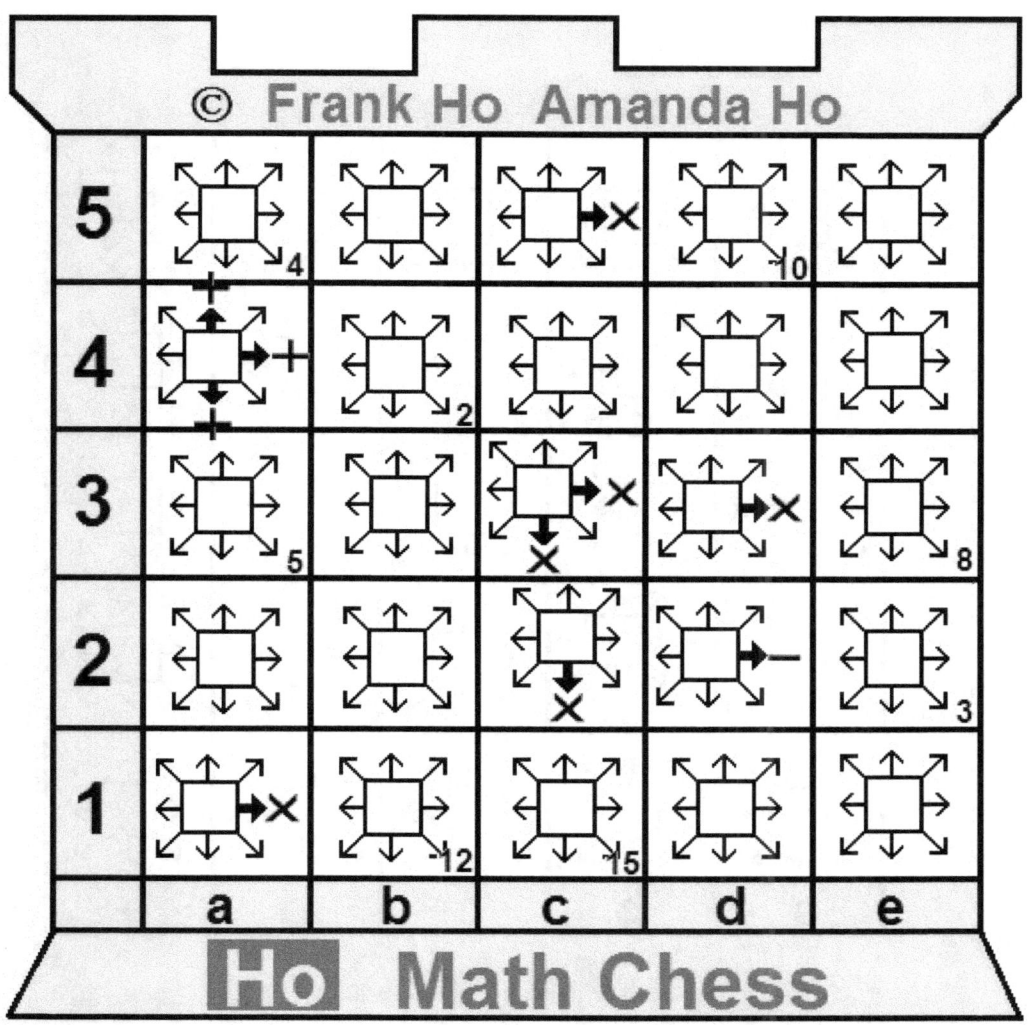

Frankho Puzzle™ # 154

Rule All the digits 1 to 5 must appear exactly once in every row and column. The number appears in the bottom right-hand corner is the end result calculated according to arithmetic operator(s) and chess move(s) as indicated by darker arrow(s).

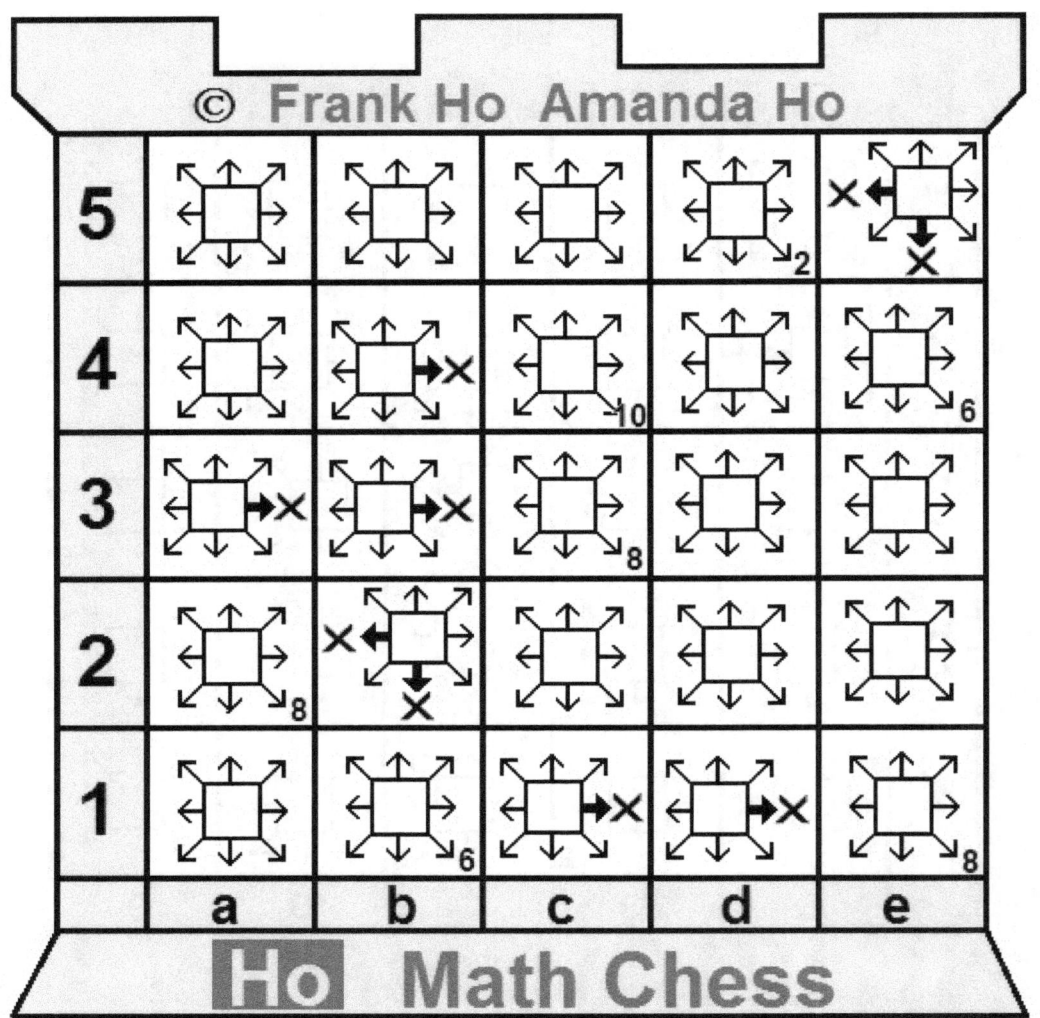

Ho Math Chess 何数棋谜 益智健脑非药物良方
Frankho Puzzle for KIDS – Brain Fitness Workbook
© 2007 — 2016 Frank Ho, Amanda Ho all rights reserved www.mathandchess.com

Frankho Puzzle™ # 155

Rule All the digits 1 to 5 must appear exactly once in every row and column. The number appears in the bottom right-hand corner is the end result calculated according to arithmetic operator(s) and chess move(s) as indicated by darker arrow(s).

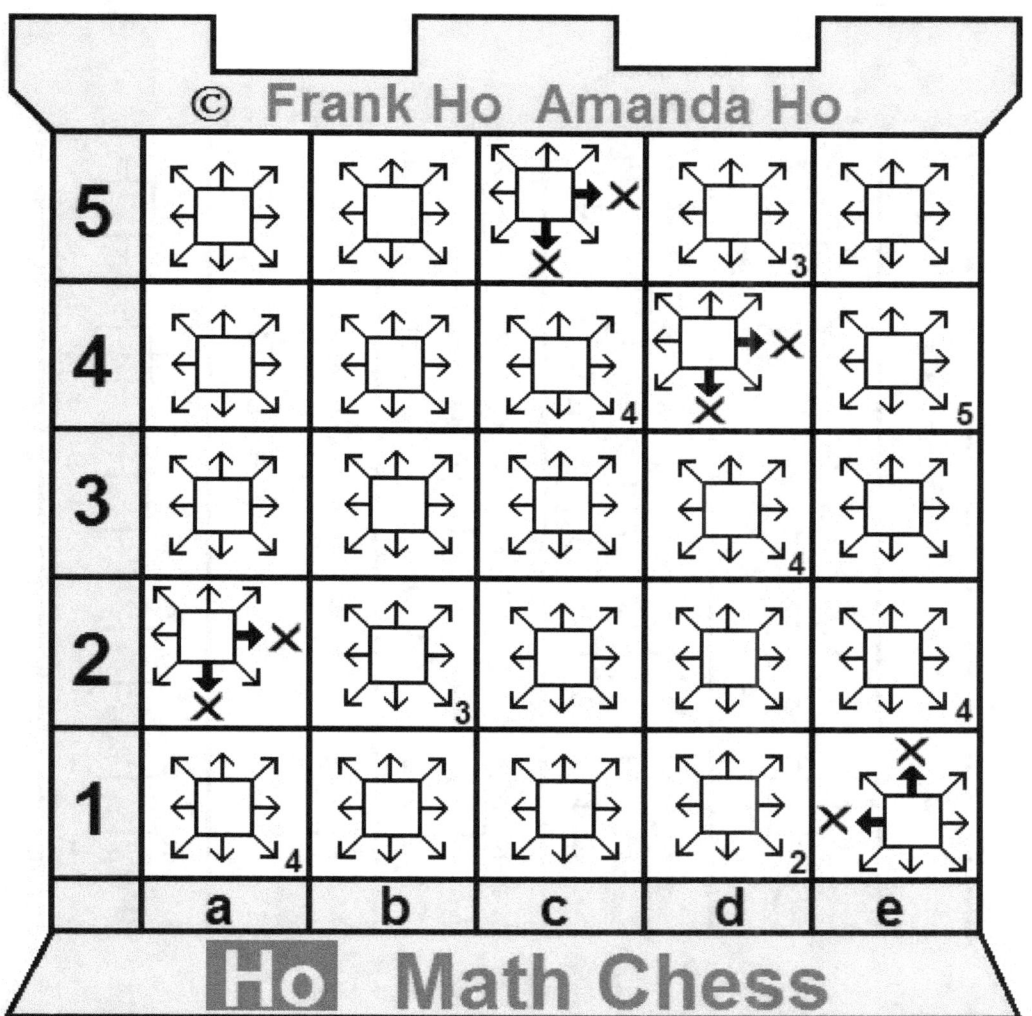

Ho Math Chess 何数棋谜 益智健脑非药物良方
Frankho Puzzle for KIDS – Brain Fitness Workbook
© 2007 — 2016 Frank Ho, Amanda Ho all rights reserved www.mathandchess.com

Frankho Puzzle™ # 156

Rule All the digits 1 to 5 must appear exactly once in every row and column. The number appears in the bottom right-hand corner is the end result calculated according to arithmetic operator(s) and chess move(s) as indicated by darker arrow(s).

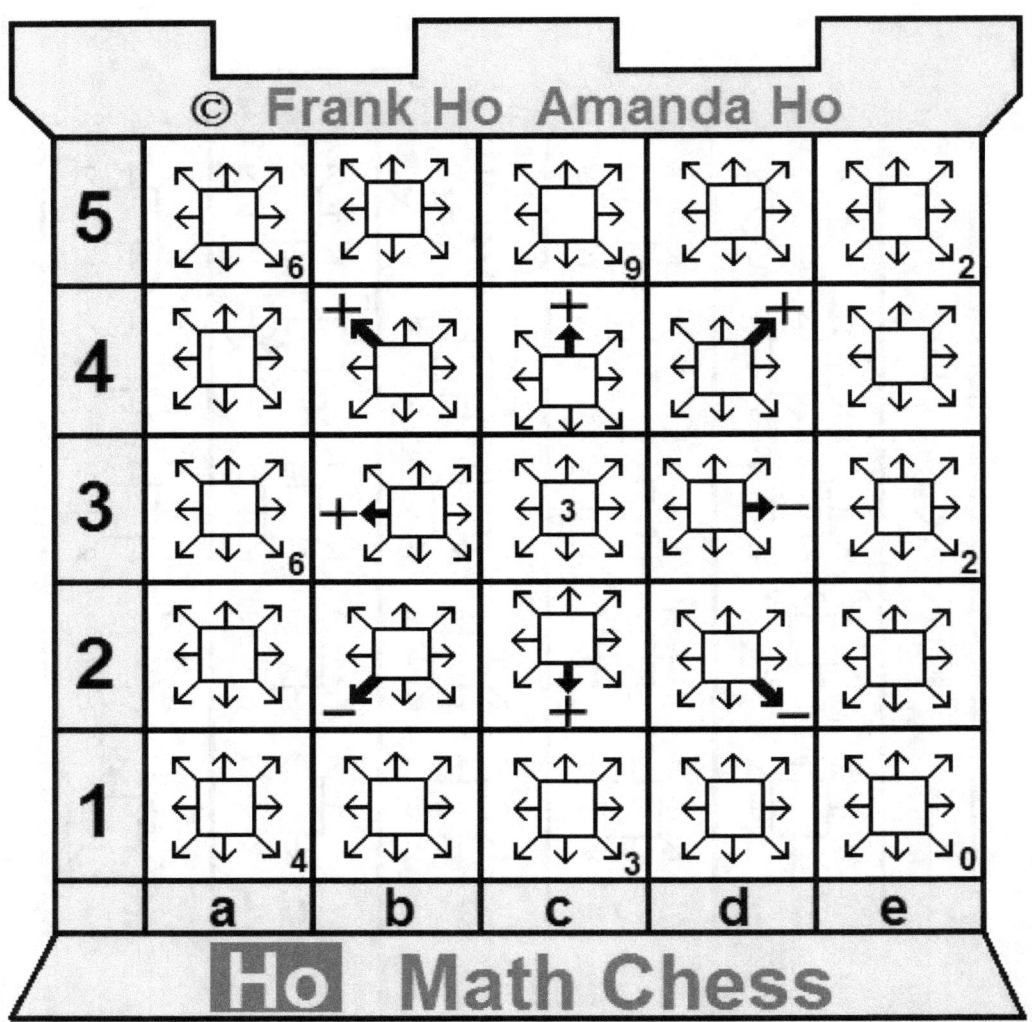

Frankho Puzzle™ # 157

Rule All the digits 1 to 5 must appear exactly once in every row and column. The number appears in the bottom right-hand corner is the end result calculated according to arithmetic operator(s) and chess move(s) as indicated by darker arrow(s).

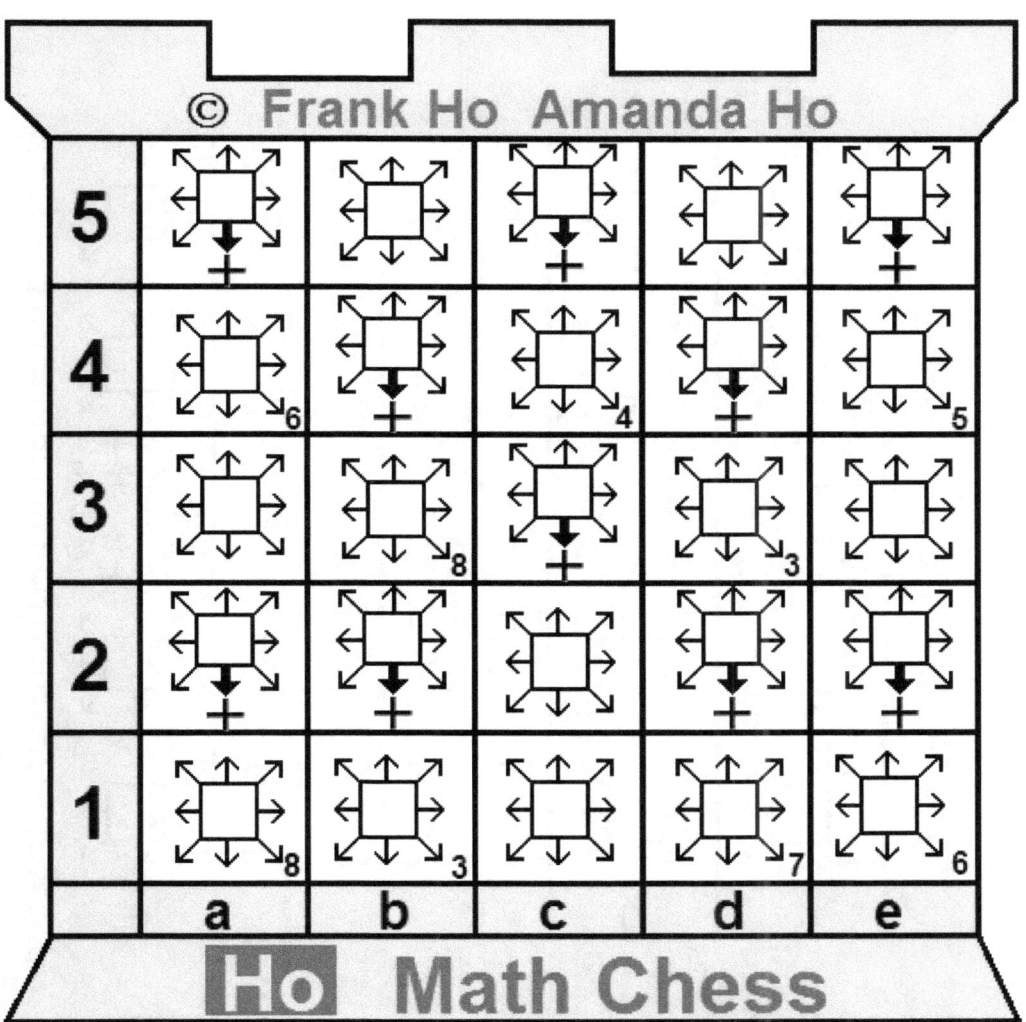

Frankho Puzzle™ # 158

Rule All the digits 1 to 5 must appear exactly once in every row and column. The number appears in the bottom right-hand corner is the end result calculated according to arithmetic operator(s) and chess move(s) as indicated by darker arrow(s).

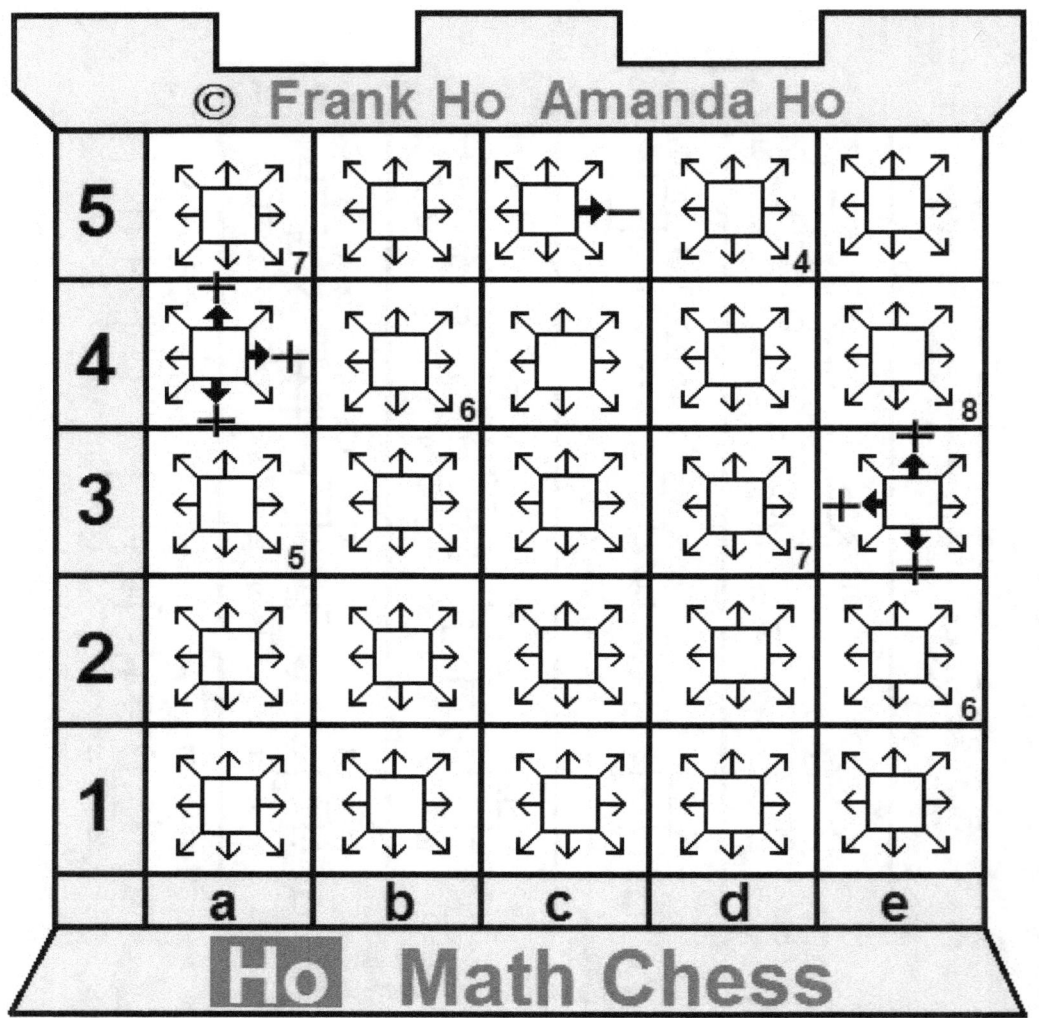

Ho Math Chess 何数棋谜 益智健脑非药物良方
Frankho Puzzle for KIDS – Brain Fitness Workbook

© 2007 — 2016 Frank Ho, Amanda Ho all rights reserved www.mathandchess.com

Frankho Puzzle™ # 159

Rule All the digits 1 to 5 must appear exactly once in every row and column. The number appears in the bottom right-hand corner is the end result calculated according to arithmetic operator(s) and chess move(s) as indicated by darker arrow(s).

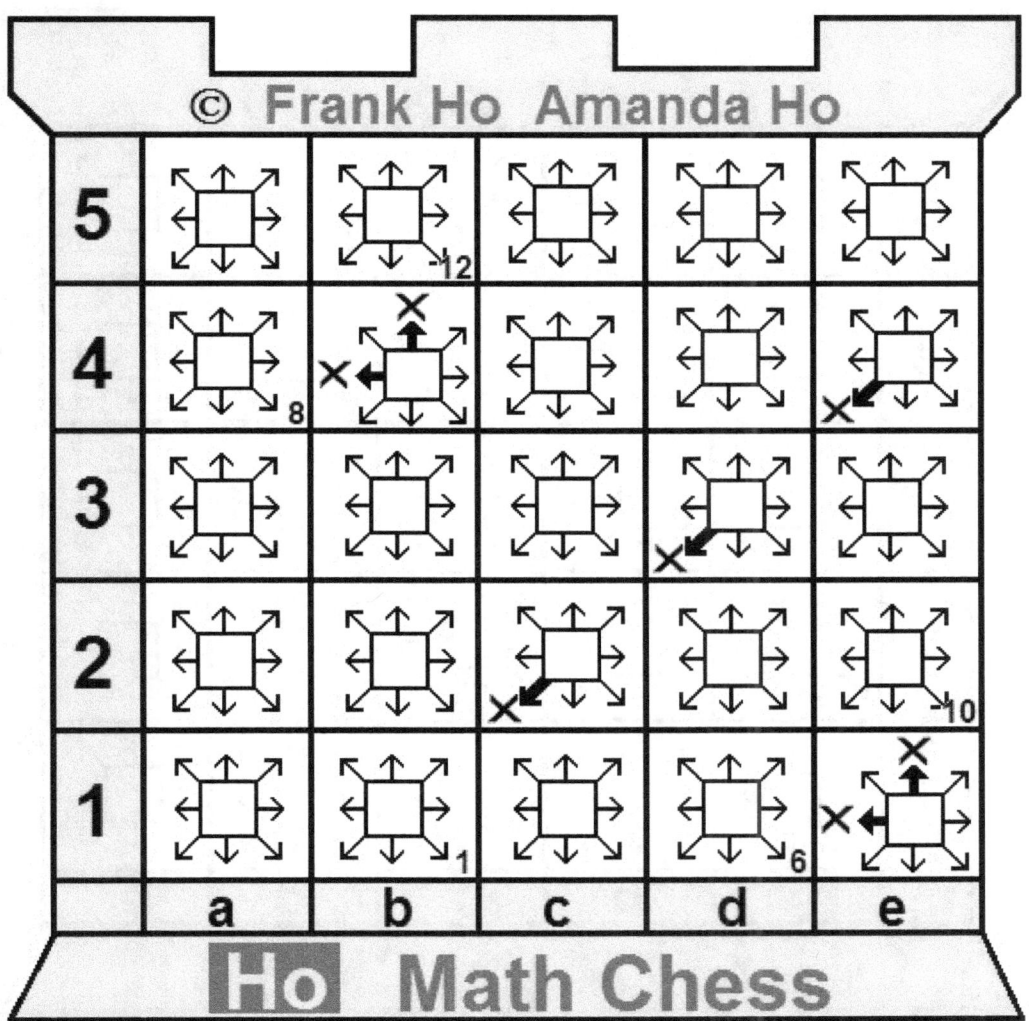

Ho Math Chess 何数棋谜 益智健脑非药物良方
Frankho Puzzle for KIDS – Brain Fitness Workbook
© 2007 — 2016 Frank Ho, Amanda Ho all rights reserved www.mathandchess.com

Frankho Puzzle™ # 160

Rule All the digits 1 to 5 must appear exactly once in every row and column. The number appears in the bottom right-hand corner is the end result calculated according to arithmetic operator(s) and chess move(s) as indicated by darker arrow(s).

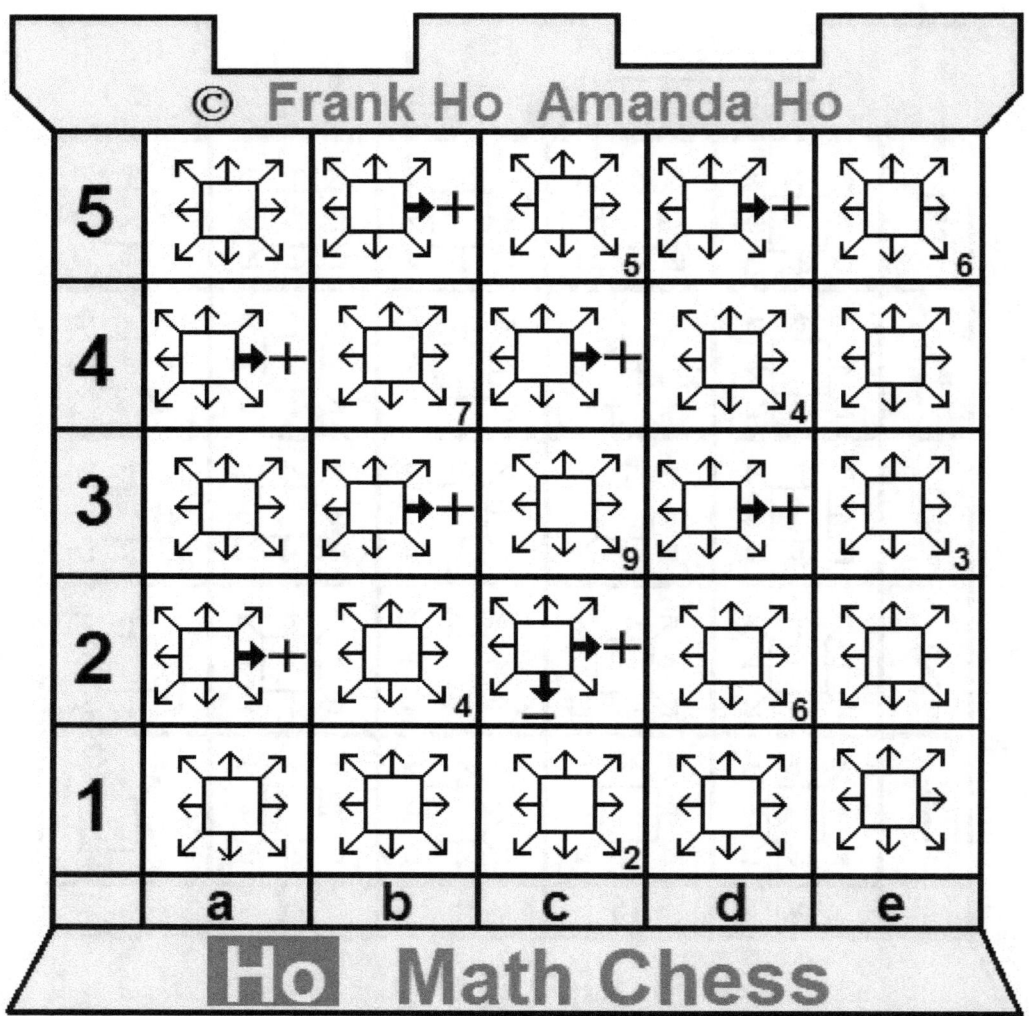

Ho Math Chess 何数棋谜 益智健脑非药物良方
Frankho Puzzle for KIDS – Brain Fitness Workbook
© 2007 — 2016 Frank Ho, Amanda Ho all rights reserved www.mathandchess.com

Frankho Puzzle™ # 161

Rule All the digits 1 to 5 must appear exactly once in every row and column. The number appears in the bottom right-hand corner is the end result calculated according to arithmetic operator(s) and chess move(s) as indicated by darker arrow(s).

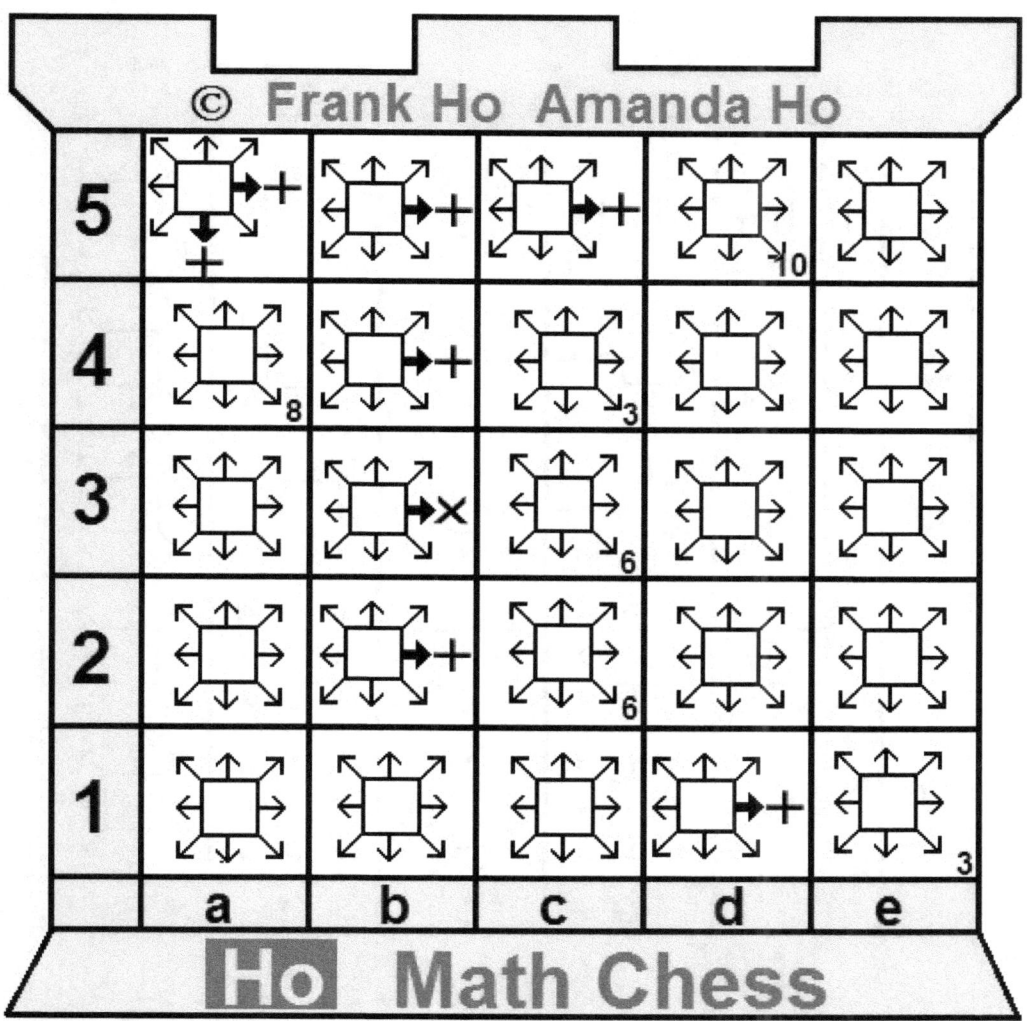

Ho Math Chess 何数棋谜 益智健脑非药物良方
Frankho Puzzle for KIDS – Brain Fitness Workbook
© 2007 — 2016 Frank Ho, Amanda Ho all rights reserved www.mathandchess.com

Frankho Puzzle™ # 162

Rule All the digits 1 to 5 must appear exactly once in every row and column. The number appears in the bottom right-hand corner is the end result calculated according to arithmetic operator(s) and chess move(s) as indicated by darker arrow(s).

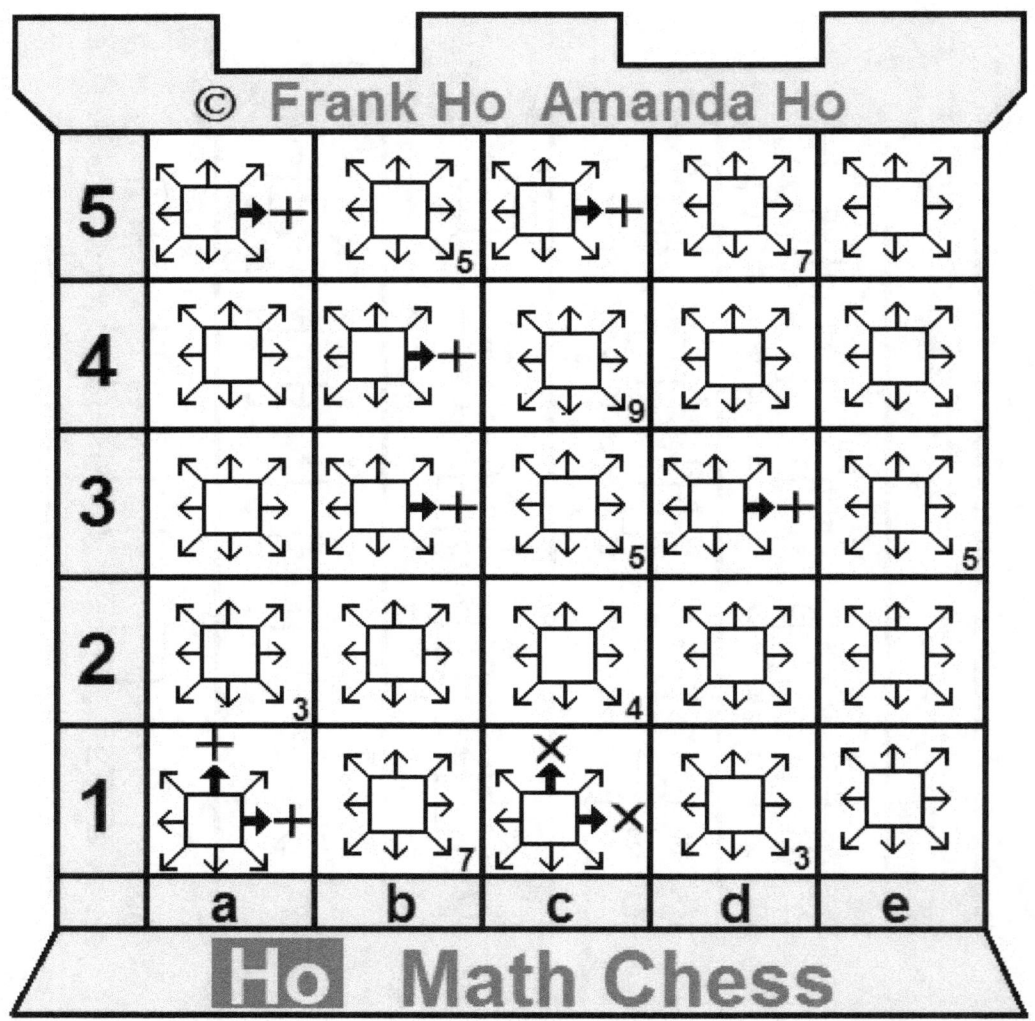

Ho Math Chess 何数棋谜 益智健脑非药物良方
Frankho Puzzle for KIDS – Brain Fitness Workbook
© 2007 — 2016 Frank Ho, Amanda Ho all rights reserved www.mathandchess.com

Frankho Puzzle™ # 163

Rule All the digits 1 to 5 must appear exactly once in every row and column. The number appears in the bottom right-hand corner is the end result calculated according to arithmetic operator(s) and chess move(s) as indicated by darker arrow(s).

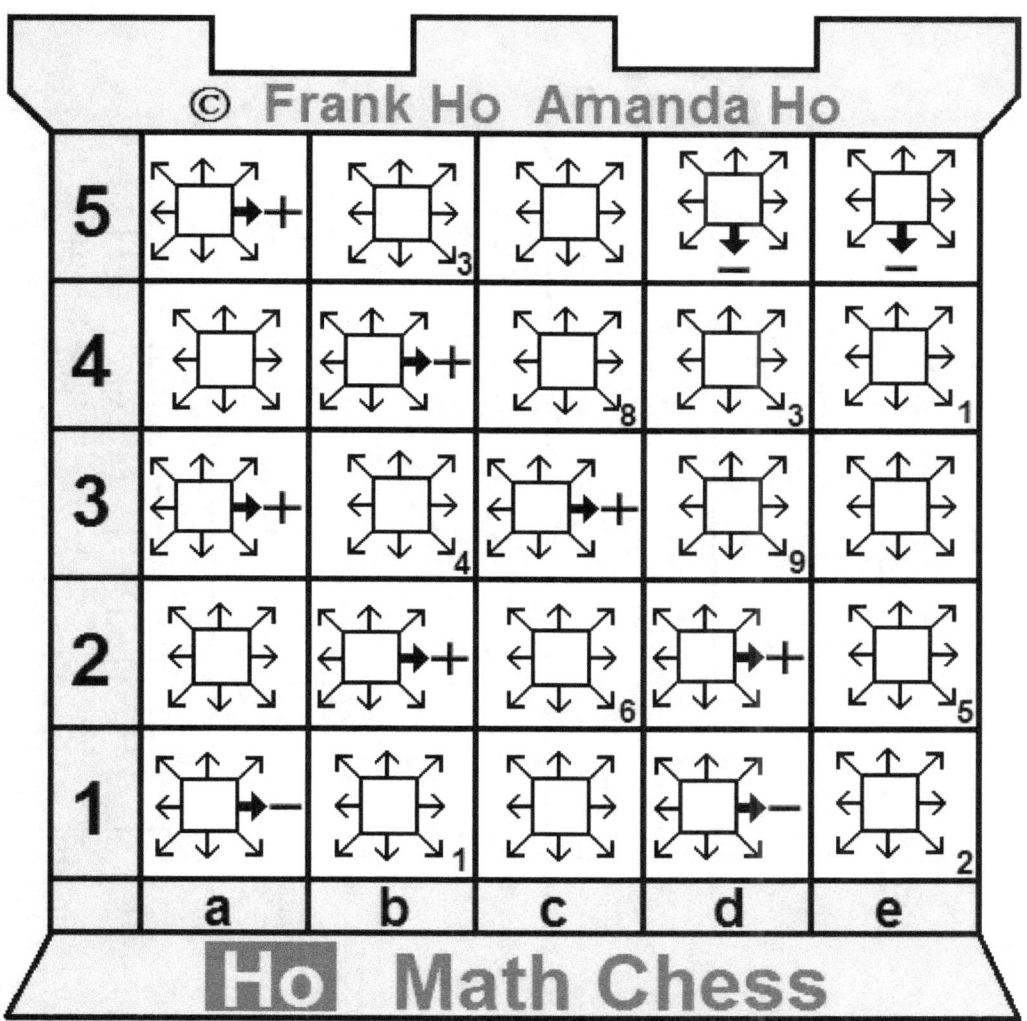

Ho Math Chess 何数棋谜 益智健脑非药物良方
Frankho Puzzle for KIDS – Brain Fitness Workbook
© 2007 — 2016 Frank Ho, Amanda Ho all rights reserved www.mathandchess.com

Frankho Puzzle™ # 164

Rule All the digits 1 to 5 must appear exactly once in every row and column. The number appears in the bottom right-hand corner is the end result calculated according to arithmetic operator(s) and chess move(s) as indicated by darker arrow(s).

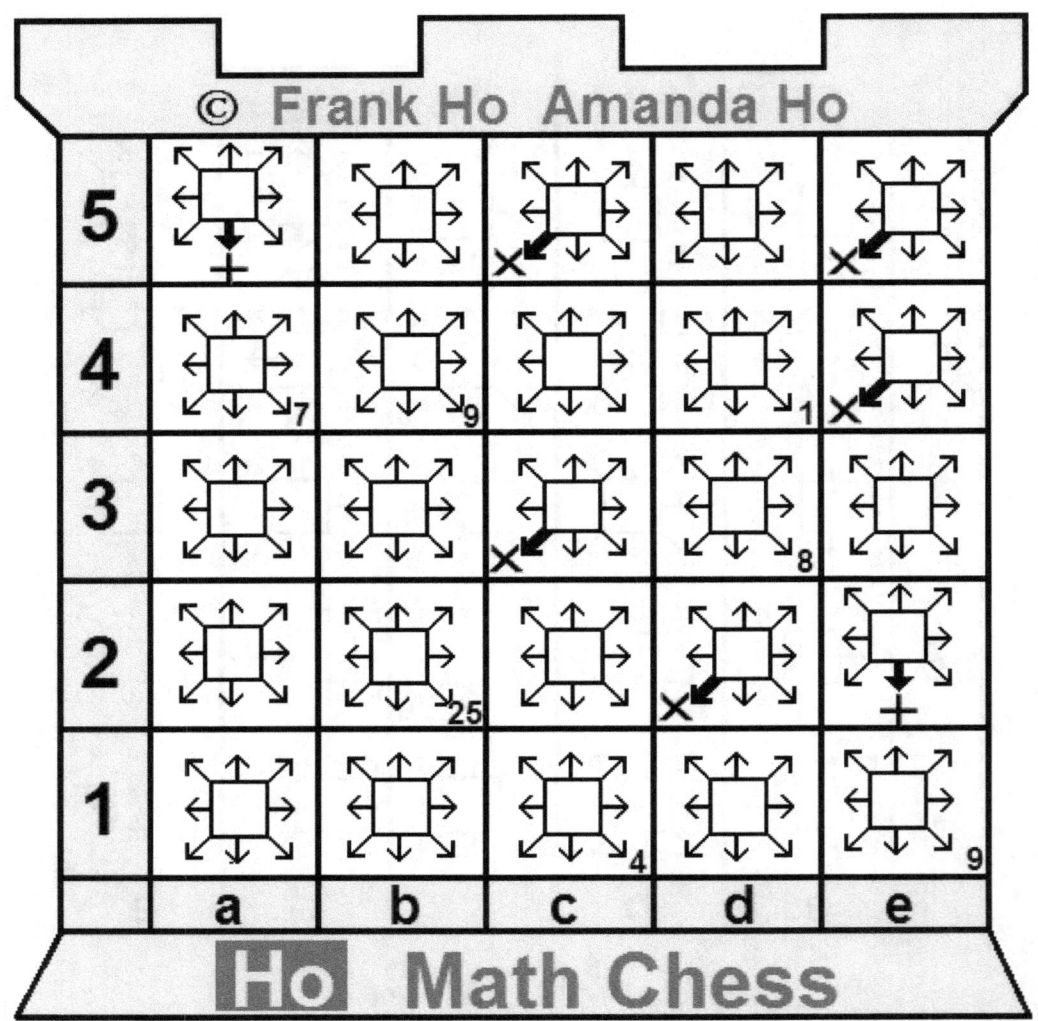

Ho Math Chess 何数棋谜 益智健脑非药物良方
Frankho Puzzle for KIDS – Brain Fitness Workbook
© 2007 — 2016 Frank Ho, Amanda Ho all rights reserved www.mathandchess.com

Frankho Puzzle™ # 165

Rule All the digits 1 to 5 must appear exactly once in every row and column. The number appears in the bottom right-hand corner is the end result calculated according to arithmetic operator(s) and chess move(s) as indicated by darker arrow(s).

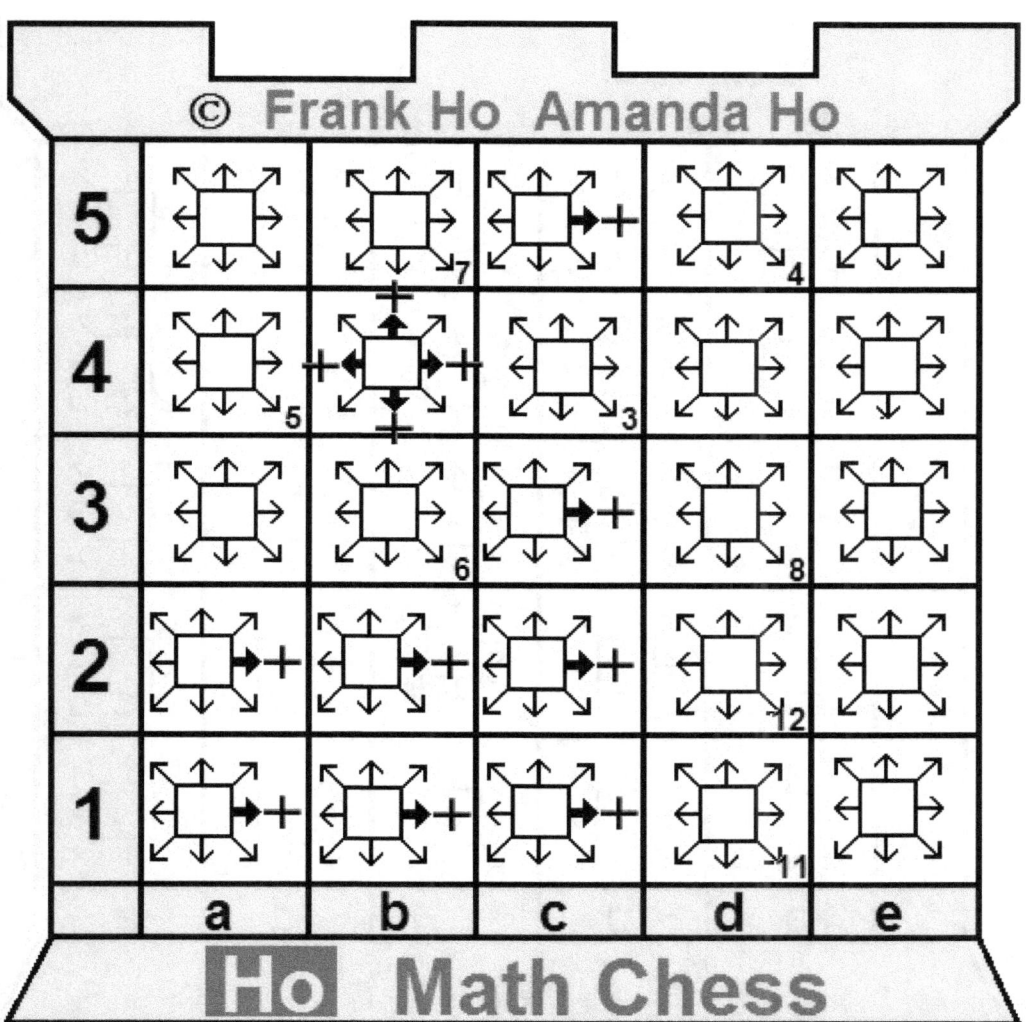

Frankho Puzzle™ # 166

Rule All the digits 1 to 5 must appear exactly once in every row and column. The number appears in the bottom right-hand corner is the end result calculated according to arithmetic operator(s) and chess move(s) as indicated by darker arrow(s).

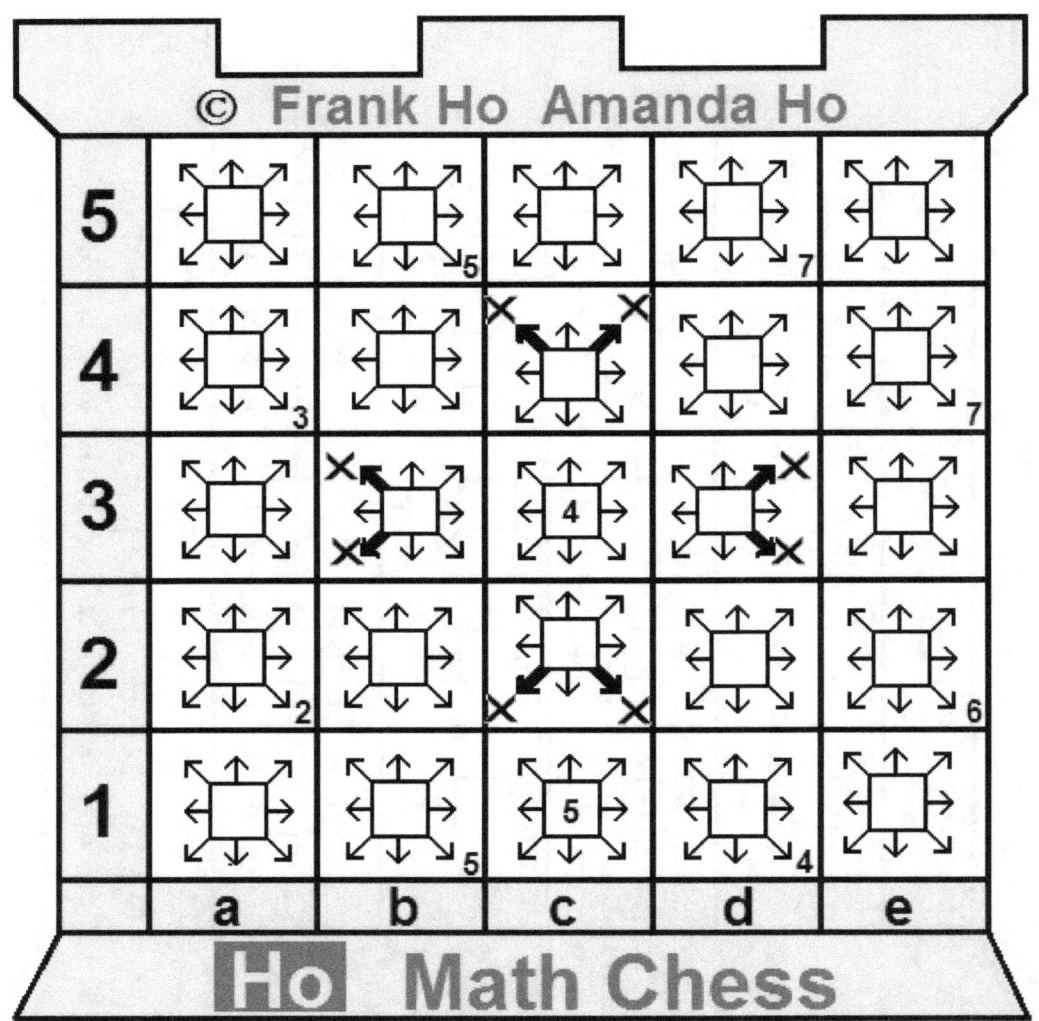

170

Ho Math Chess 何数棋谜 益智健脑非药物良方
Frankho Puzzle for KIDS – Brain Fitness Workbook
© 2007 – 2016 Frank Ho, Amanda Ho all rights reserved www.mathandchess.com

Frankho Puzzle™ # 167

Rule All the digits 1 to 5 must appear exactly once in every row and column. The number appears in the bottom right-hand corner is the end result calculated according to arithmetic operator(s) and chess move(s) as indicated by darker arrow(s).

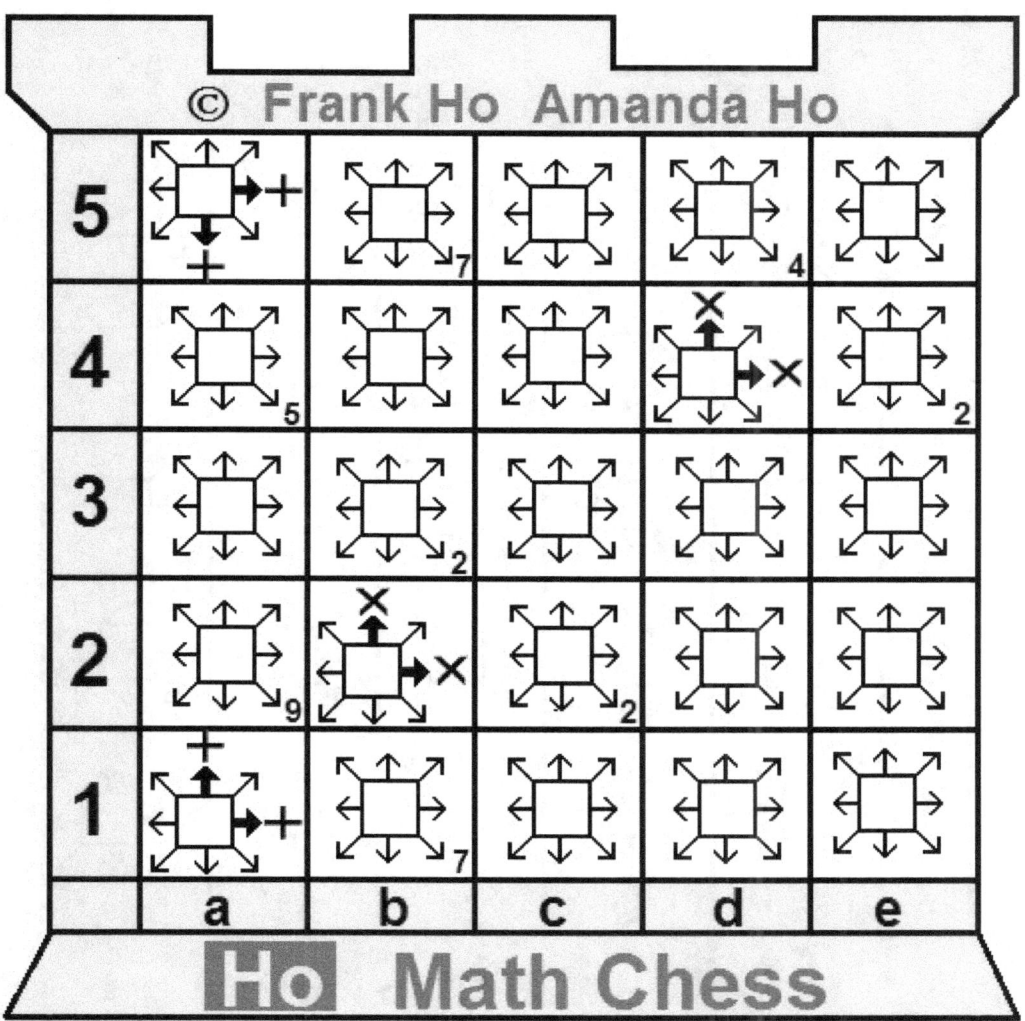

Ho Math Chess 何数棋谜 益智健脑非药物良方
Frankho Puzzle for KIDS – Brain Fitness Workbook
© 2007 — 2016 Frank Ho, Amanda Ho all rights reserved www.mathandchess.com

Frankho Puzzle™ # 168

Rule All the digits 1 to 5 must appear exactly once in every row and column. The number appears in the bottom right-hand corner is the end result calculated according to arithmetic operator(s) and chess move(s) as indicated by darker arrow(s).

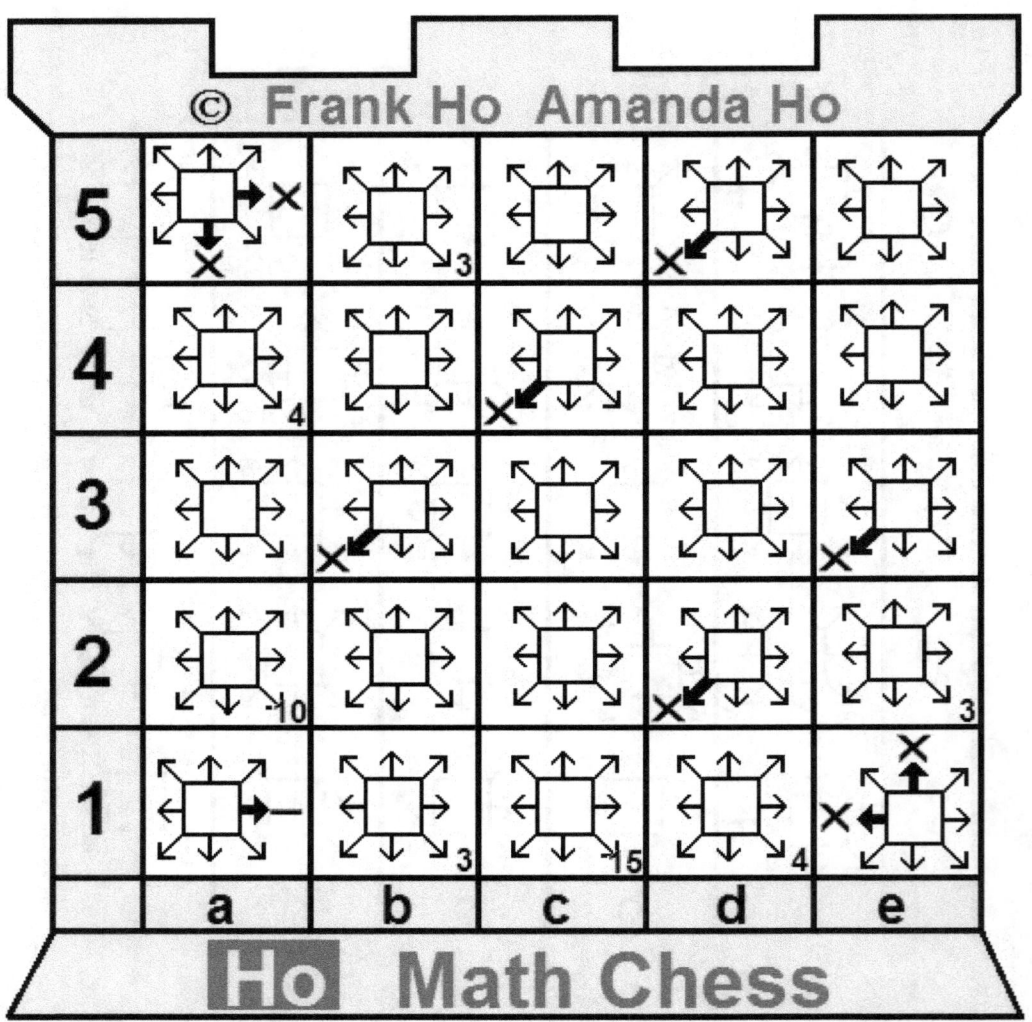

Ho Math Chess 何数棋谜 益智健脑非药物良方
Frankho Puzzle for KIDS – Brain Fitness Workbook
© 2007 — 2016 Frank Ho, Amanda Ho all rights reserved www.mathandchess.com

Frankho Puzzle™ # 169

Rule All the digits 1 to 5 must appear exactly once in every row and column. The number appears in the bottom right-hand corner is the end result calculated according to arithmetic operator(s) and chess move(s) as indicated by darker arrow(s).

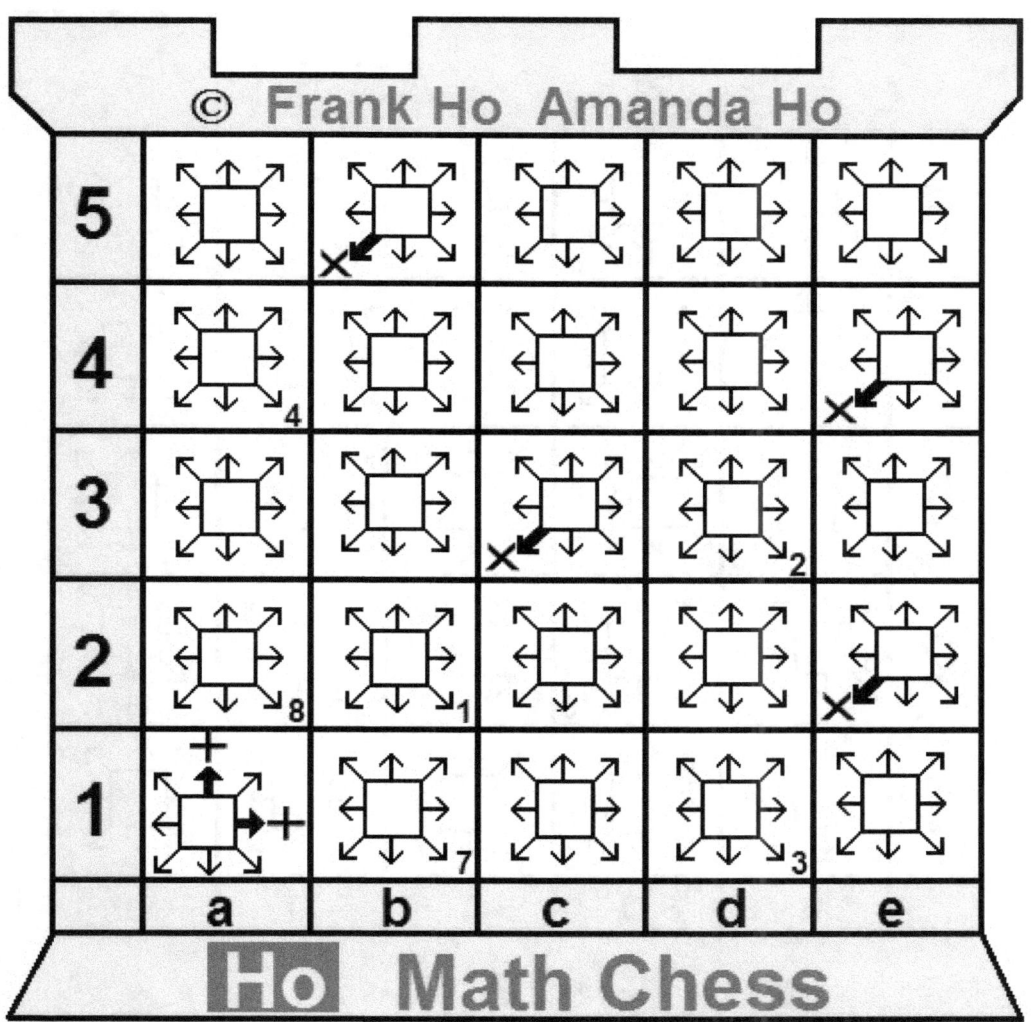

Ho Math Chess 何数棋谜 益智健脑非药物良方
Frankho Puzzle for KIDS – Brain Fitness Workbook
© 2007 – 2016 Frank Ho, Amanda Ho all rights reserved www.mathandchess.com

Frankho Puzzle™ # 170

Rule All the digits 1 to 5 must appear exactly once in every row and column. The number appears in the bottom right-hand corner is the end result calculated according to arithmetic operator(s) and chess move(s) as indicated by darker arrow(s).

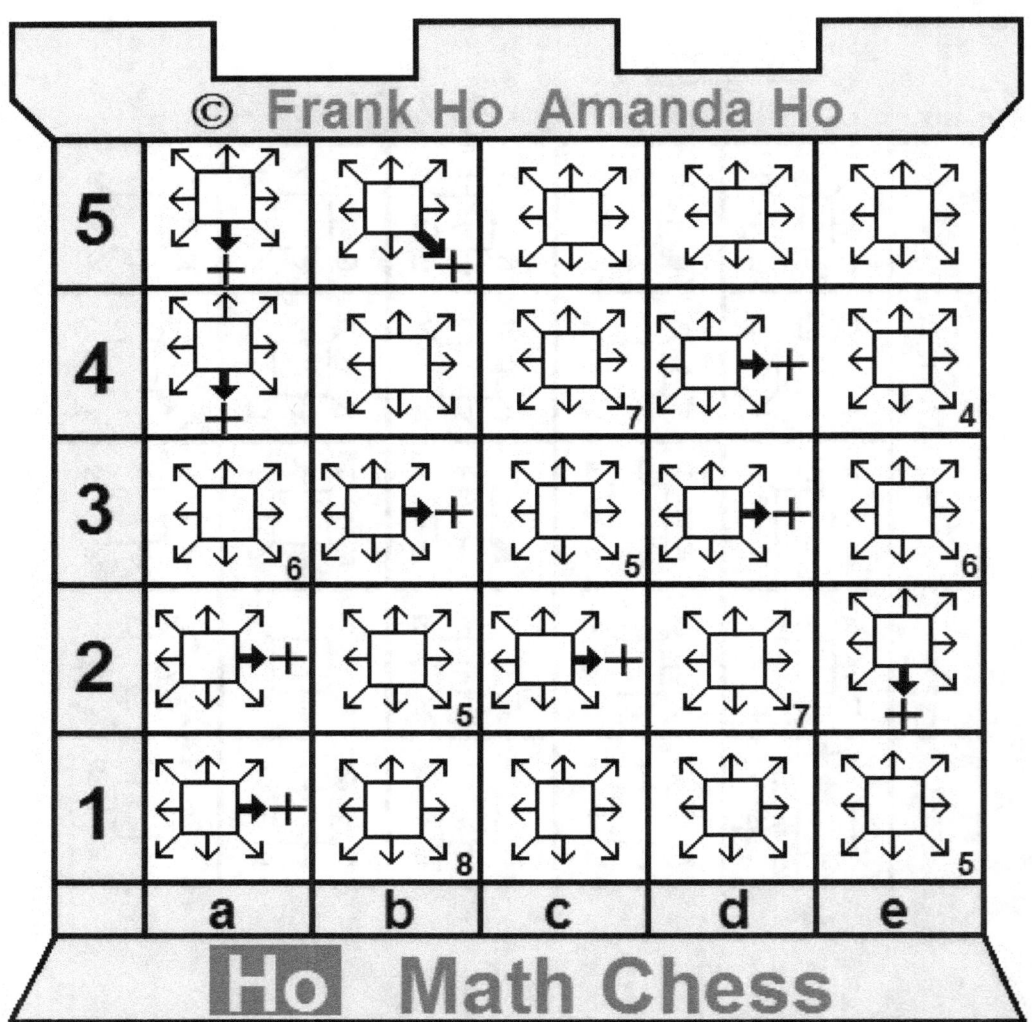

Ho Math Chess 何数棋谜 益智健脑非药物良方
Frankho Puzzle for KIDS – Brain Fitness Workbook

© 2007 — 2016 Frank Ho, Amanda Ho all rights reserved www.mathandchess.com

Frankho Puzzle™ # 171

Rule All the digits 1 to 5 must appear exactly once in every row and column. The number appears in the bottom right-hand corner is the end result calculated according to arithmetic operator(s) and chess move(s) as indicated by darker arrow(s).

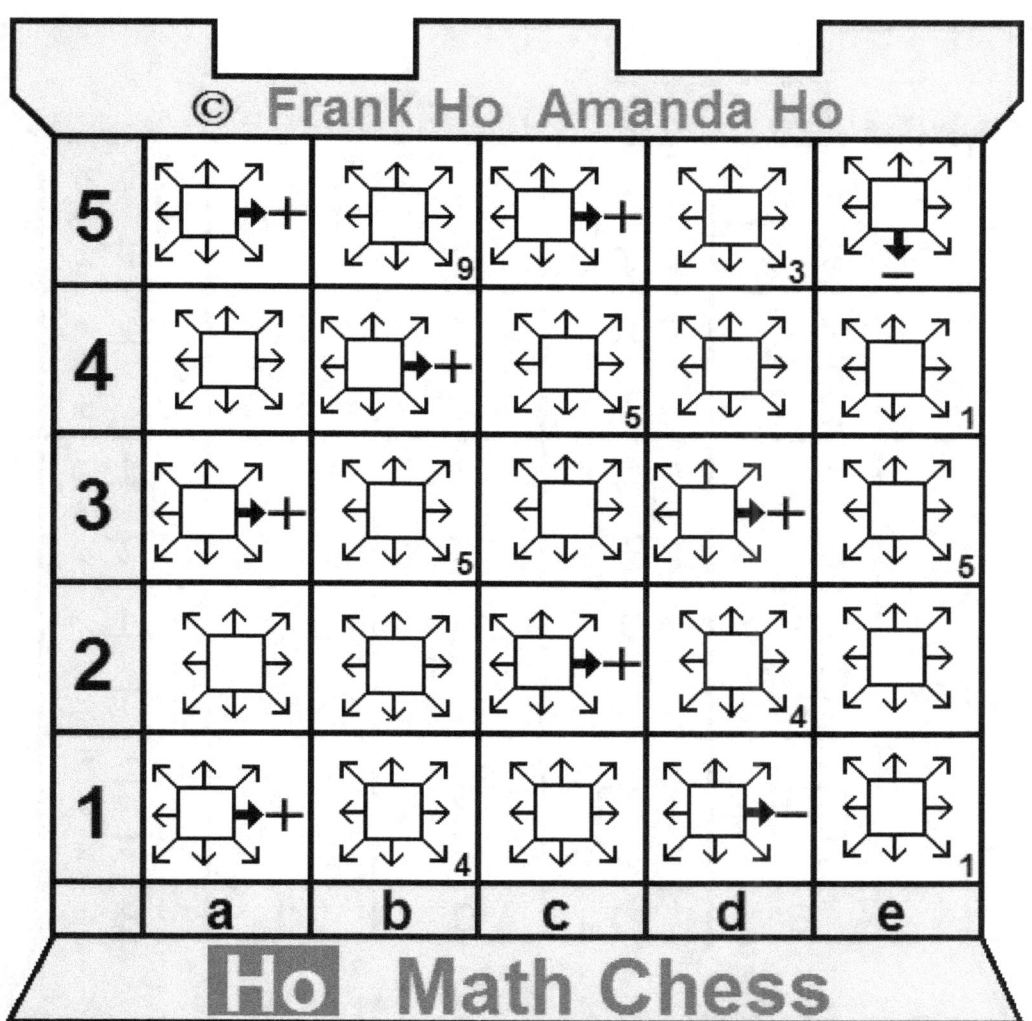

Ho Math Chess 何数棋谜 益智健脑非药物良方
Frankho Puzzle for KIDS – Brain Fitness Workbook
© 2007 — 2016 Frank Ho, Amanda Ho all rights reserved www.mathandchess.com

Frankho Puzzle™ # 172

Rule All the digits 1 to 5 must appear exactly once in every row and column. The number appears in the bottom right-hand corner is the end result calculated according to arithmetic operator(s) and chess move(s) as indicated by darker arrow(s).

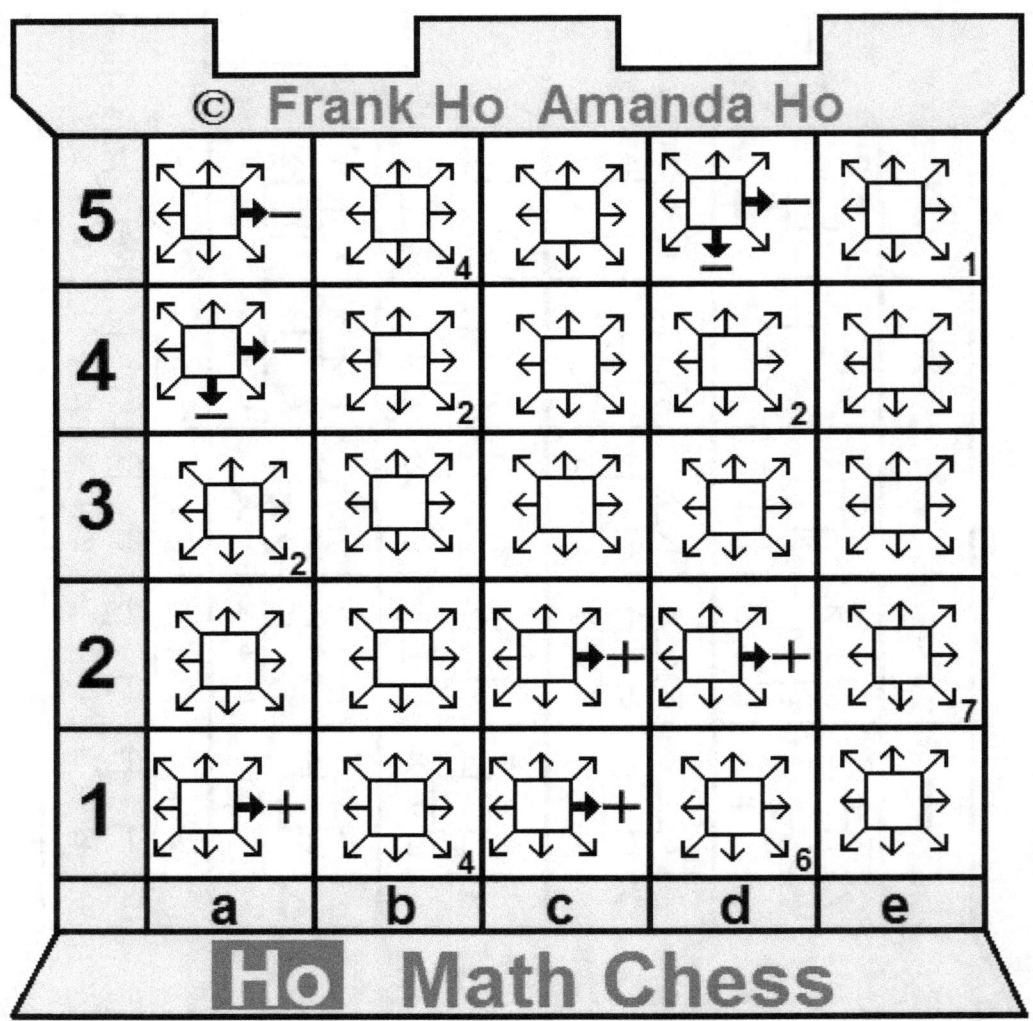

Ho Math Chess 何数棋谜 益智健脑非药物良方
Frankho Puzzle for KIDS – Brain Fitness Workbook

© 2007 — 2016 Frank Ho, Amanda Ho all rights reserved www.mathandchess.com

Frankho Puzzle™ # 173

Rule All the digits 1 to 5 must appear exactly once in every row and column. The number appears in the bottom right-hand corner is the end result calculated according to arithmetic operator(s) and chess move(s) as indicated by darker arrow(s).

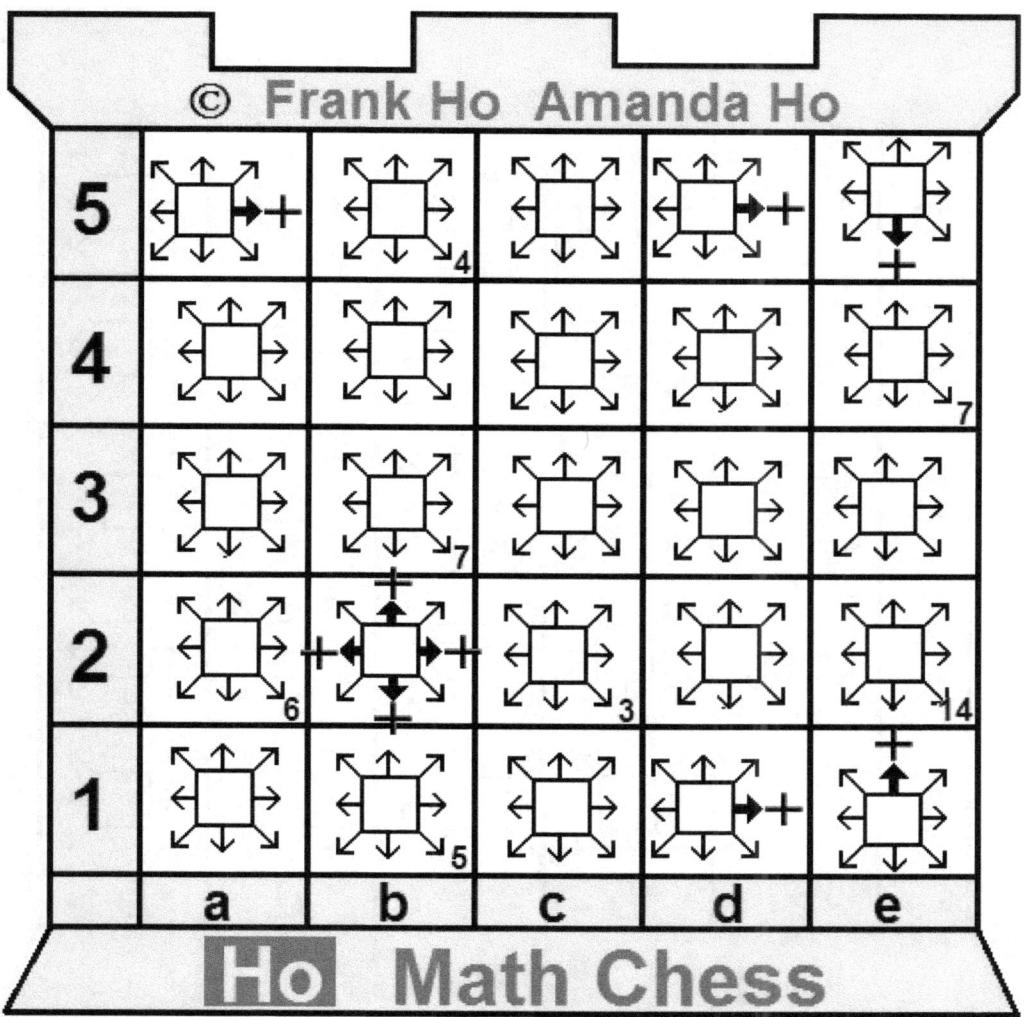

Frankho Puzzle™ # 174

Rule All the digits 1 to 5 must appear exactly once in every row and column. The number appears in the bottom right-hand corner is the end result calculated according to arithmetic operator(s) and chess move(s) as indicated by darker arrow(s).

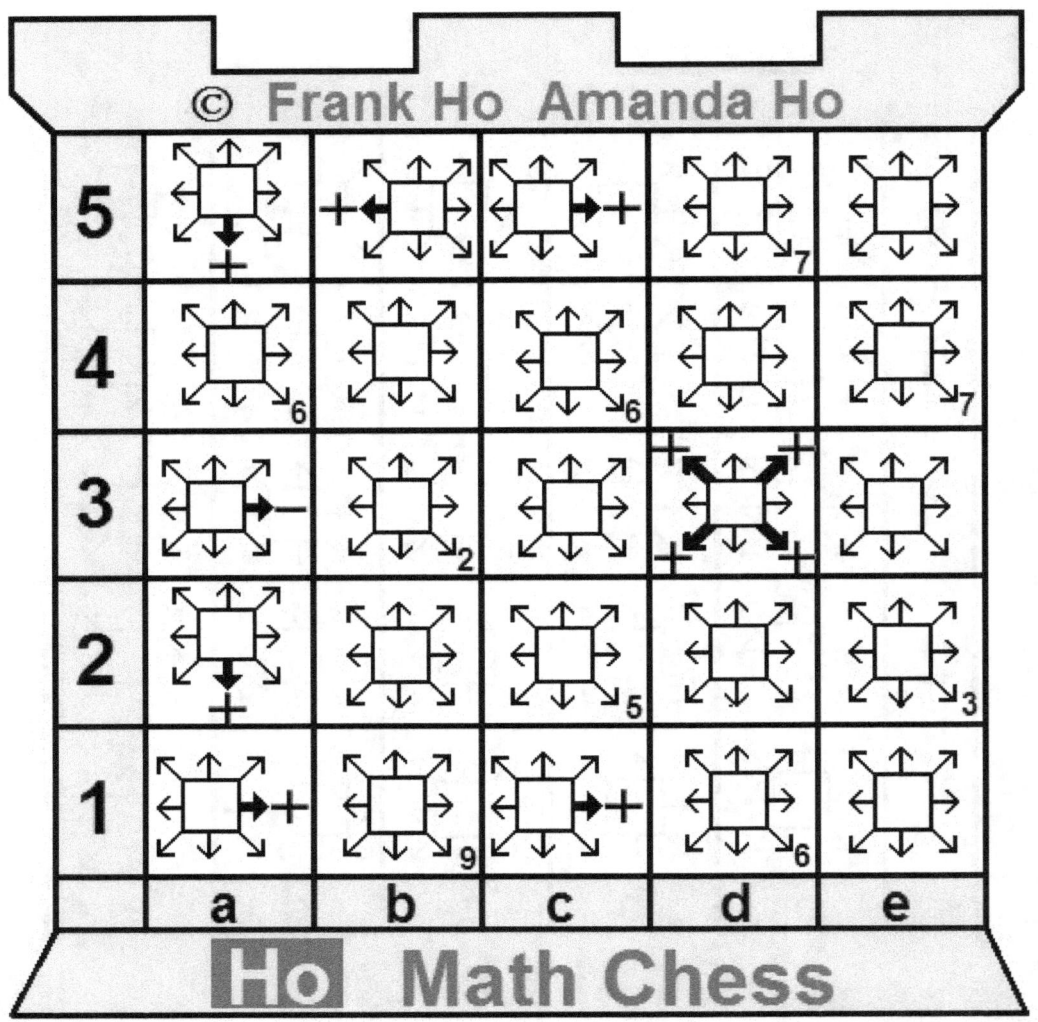

Ho Math Chess 何数棋谜 益智健脑非药物良方
Frankho Puzzle for KIDS – Brain Fitness Workbook
© 2007 — 2016 Frank Ho, Amanda Ho all rights reserved www.mathandchess.com

Frankho Puzzle™ # 175

Rule All the digits 1 to 5 must appear exactly once in every row and column. The number appears in the bottom right-hand corner is the end result calculated according to arithmetic operator(s) and chess move(s) as indicated by darker arrow(s).

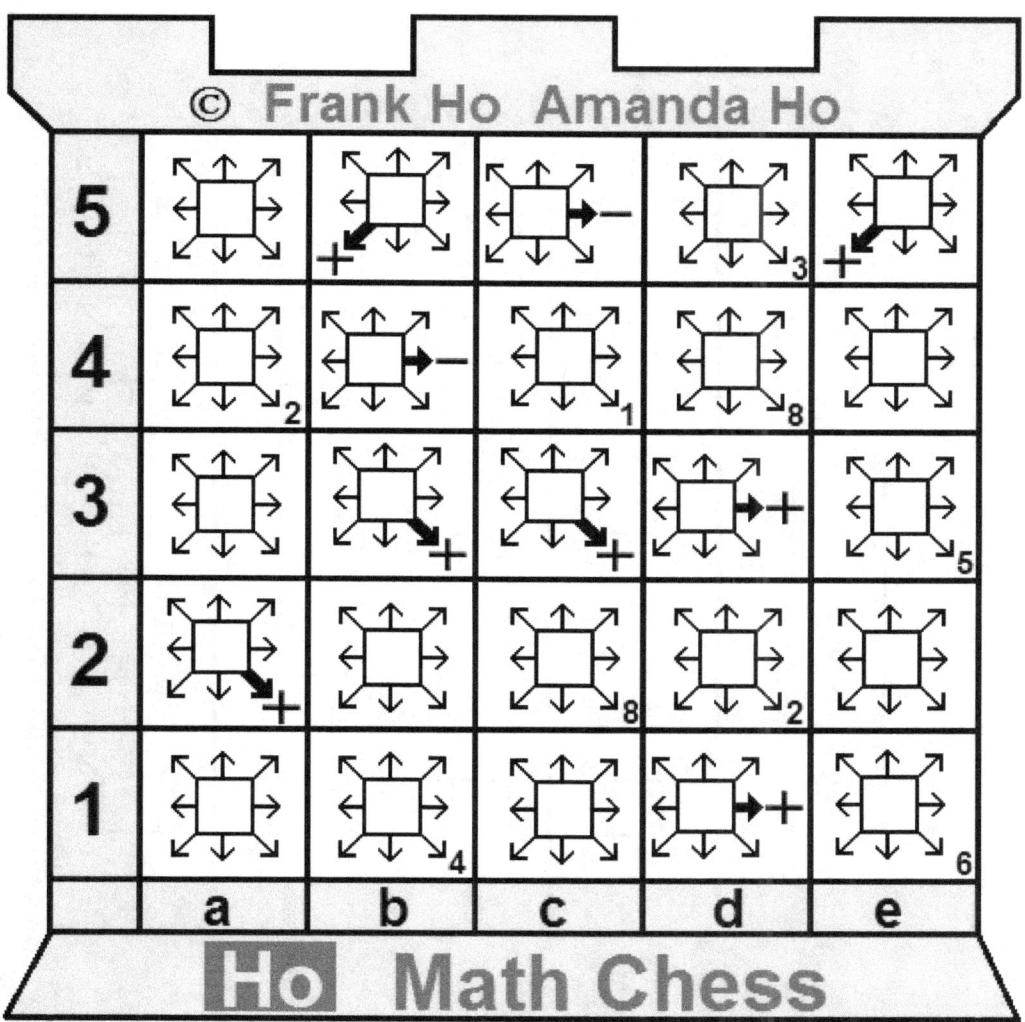

Ho Math Chess
何数棋谜 益智健脑非药物良方
Frankho Puzzle for KIDS – Brain Fitness Workbook
© 2007 — 2016 Frank Ho, Amanda Ho all rights reserved www.mathandchess.com

Frankho Puzzle™ # 176

Rule All the digits 1 to 5 must appear exactly once in every row and column. The number appears in the bottom right-hand corner is the end result calculated according to arithmetic operator(s) and chess move(s) as indicated by darker arrow(s).

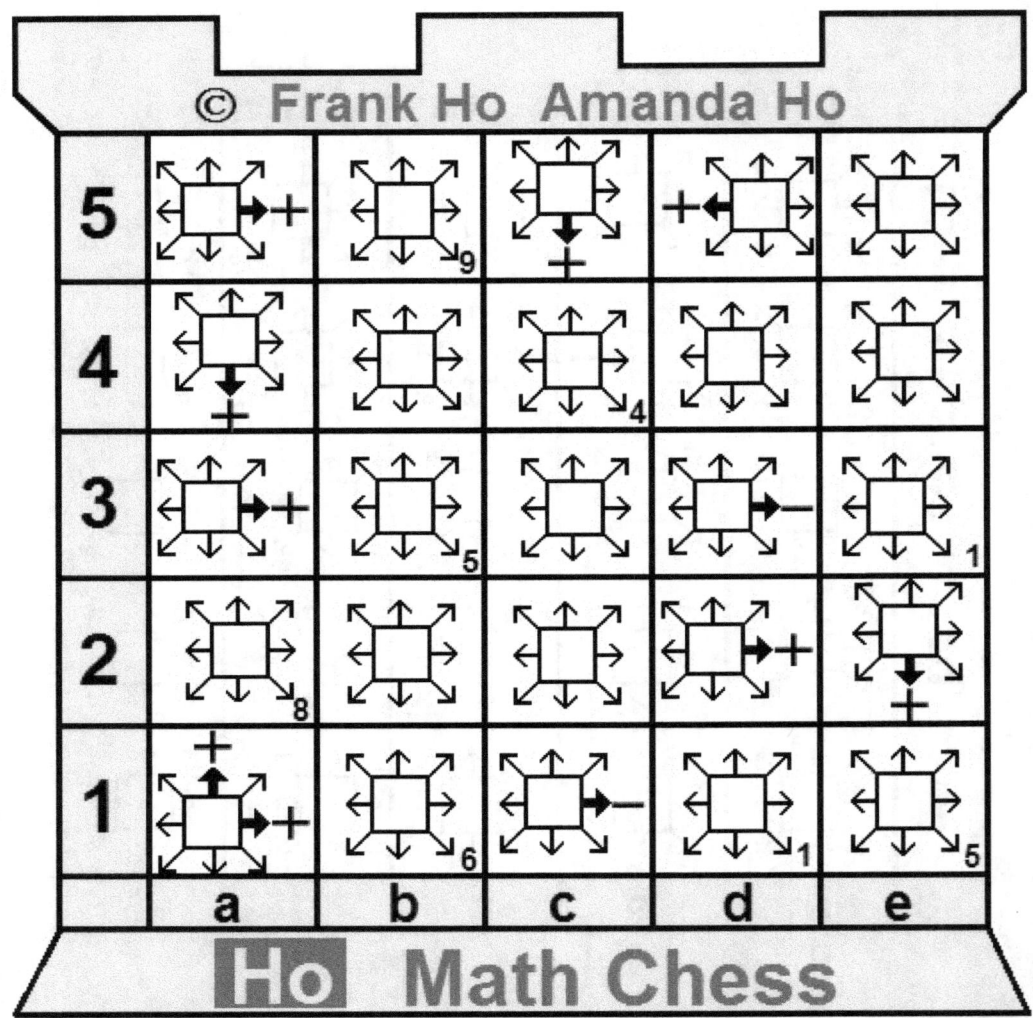

180

Ho Math Chess 何数棋谜 益智健脑非药物良方
Frankho Puzzle for KIDS – Brain Fitness Workbook
© 2007 – 2016 Frank Ho, Amanda Ho all rights reserved www.mathandchess.com

Frankho Puzzle™ # 177

Rule All the digits 1 to 5 must appear exactly once in every row and column. The number appears in the bottom right-hand corner is the end result calculated according to arithmetic operator(s) and chess move(s) as indicated by darker arrow(s).

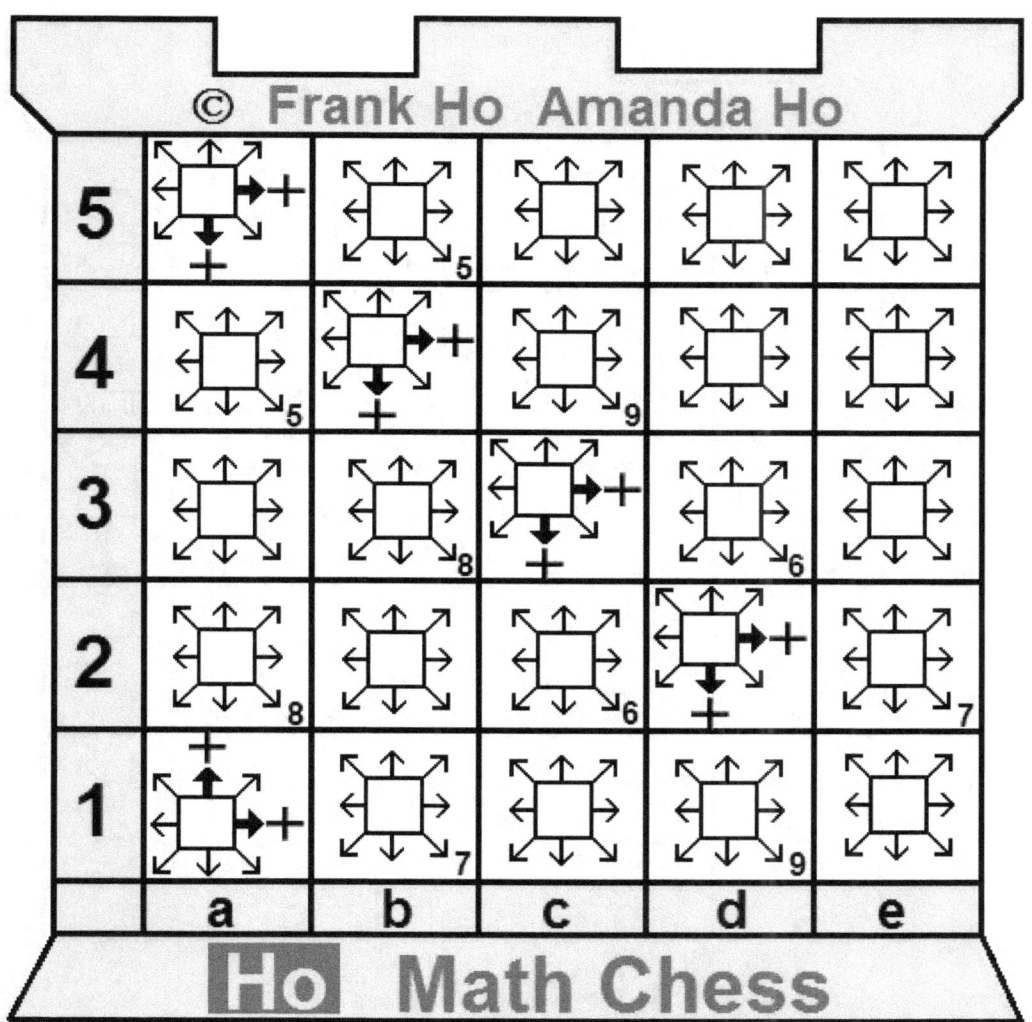

Ho Math Chess 何数棋谜 益智健脑非药物良方
Frankho Puzzle for KIDS – Brain Fitness Workbook
© 2007 — 2016 Frank Ho, Amanda Ho all rights reserved www.mathandchess.com

Frankho Puzzle™ # 178

Rule All the digits 1 to 5 must appear exactly once in every row and column. The number appears in the bottom right-hand corner is the end result calculated according to arithmetic operator(s) and chess move(s) as indicated by darker arrow(s).

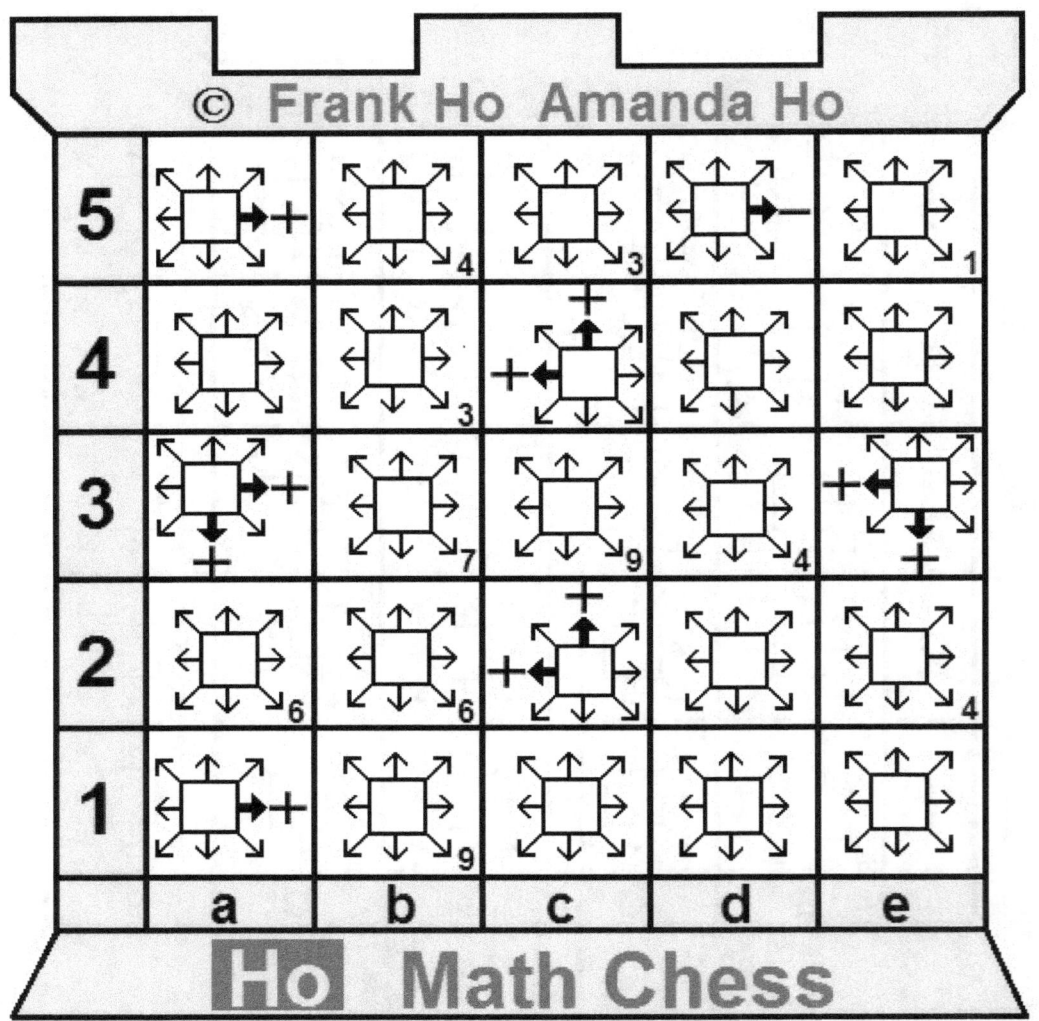

Ho Math Chess 何数棋谜 益智健脑非药物良方
Frankho Puzzle for KIDS – Brain Fitness Workbook
© 2007 — 2016 Frank Ho, Amanda Ho all rights reserved www.mathandchess.com

Frankho Puzzle™ # 179

Rule All the digits 1 to 5 must appear exactly once in every row and column. The number appears in the bottom right-hand corner is the end result calculated according to arithmetic operator(s) and chess move(s) as indicated by darker arrow(s).

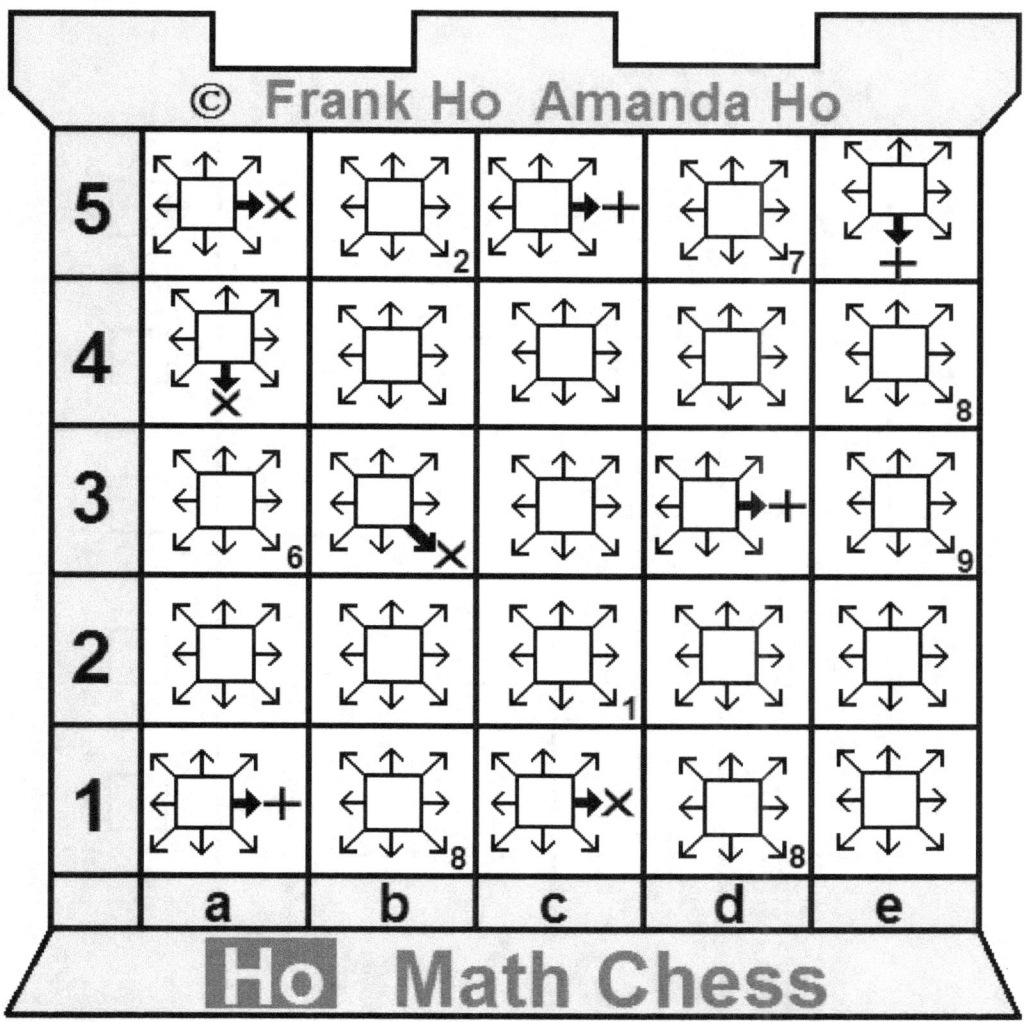

Frankho Puzzle™ # 180

Rule All the digits 1 to 5 must appear exactly once in every row and column. The number appears in the bottom right-hand corner is the end result calculated according to arithmetic operator(s) and chess move(s) as indicated by darker arrow(s).

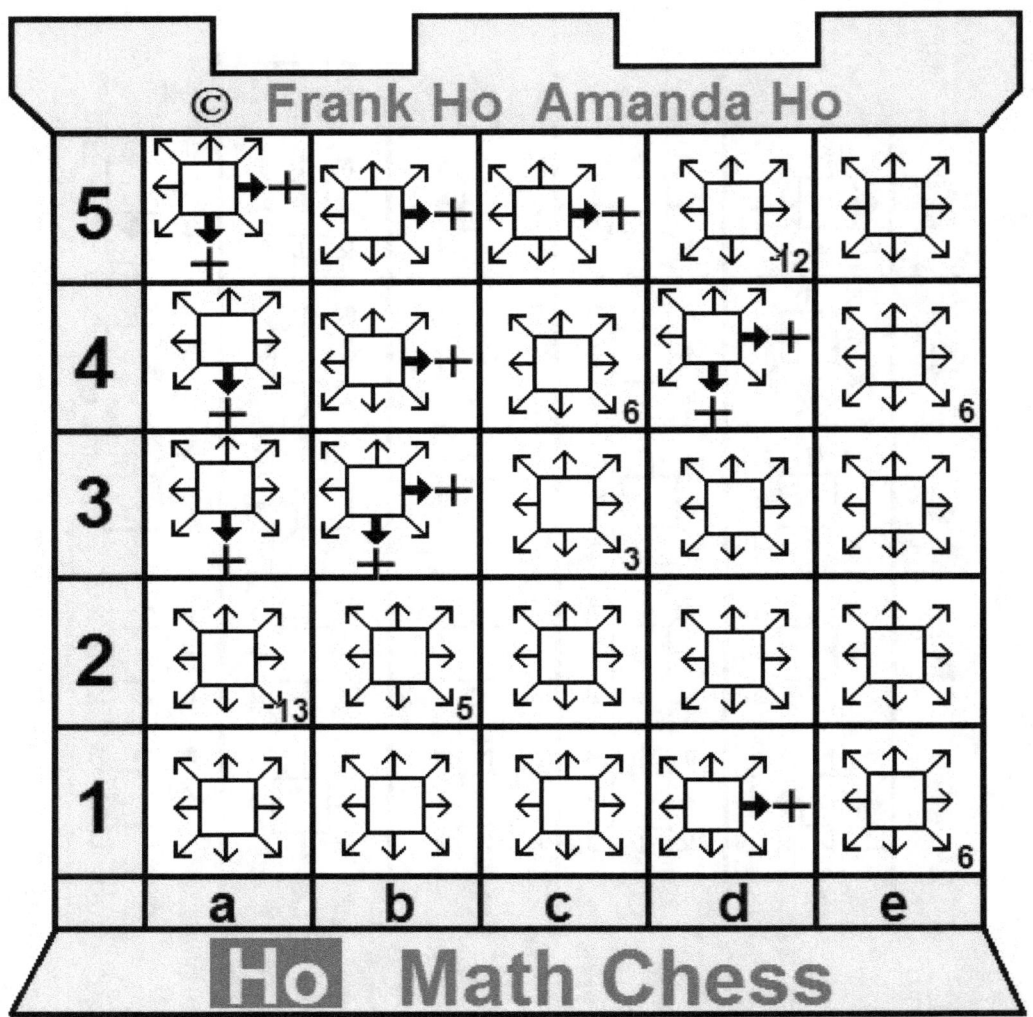

Ho Math Chess 何数棋谜 益智健脑非药物良方
Frankho Puzzle for KIDS – Brain Fitness Workbook
© 2007 — 2016 Frank Ho, Amanda Ho all rights reserved www.mathandchess.com

Frankho Puzzle™ # 181

Rule All the digits 1 to 5 must appear exactly once in every row and column. The number appears in the bottom right-hand corner is the end result calculated according to arithmetic operator(s) and chess move(s) as indicated by darker arrow(s).

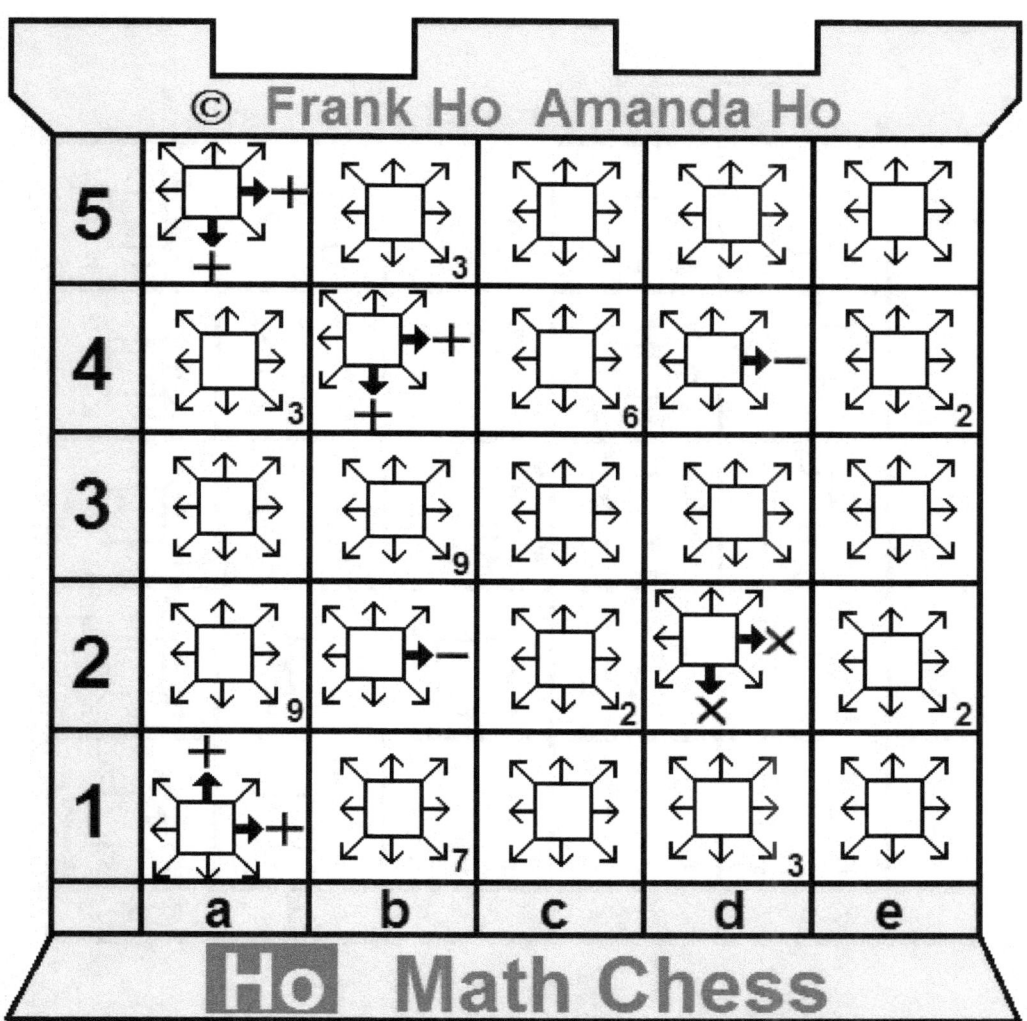

Frankho Puzzle™ # 182

Rule All the digits 1 to 5 must appear exactly once in every row and column. The number appears in the bottom right-hand corner is the end result calculated according to arithmetic operator(s) and chess move(s) as indicated by darker arrow(s).

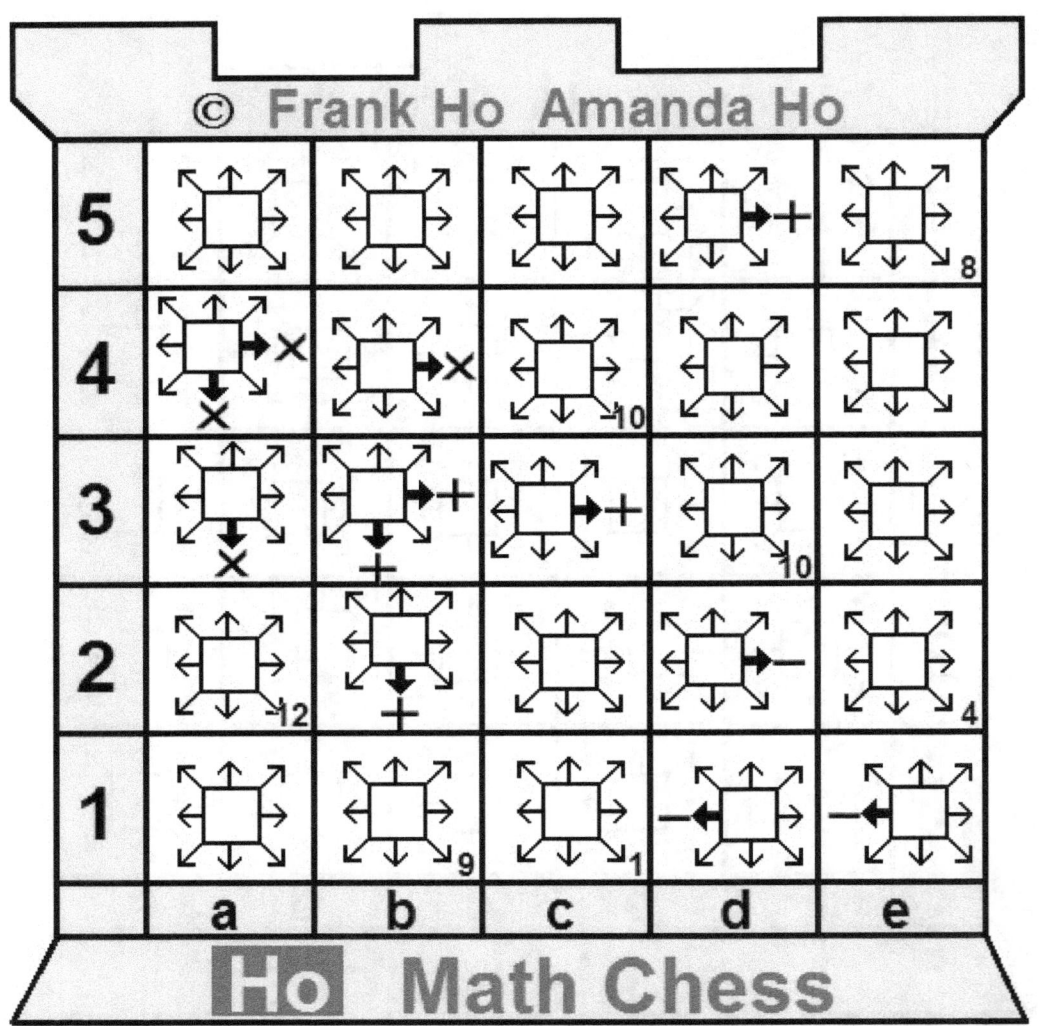

Ho Math Chess 何数棋谜 益智健脑非药物良方
Frankho Puzzle for KIDS – Brain Fitness Workbook
© 2007 — 2016 Frank Ho, Amanda Ho all rights reserved www.mathandchess.com

Frankho Puzzle™ # 183

Rule All the digits 1 to 5 must appear exactly once in every row and column. The number appears in the bottom right-hand corner is the end result calculated according to arithmetic operator(s) and chess move(s) as indicated by darker arrow(s).

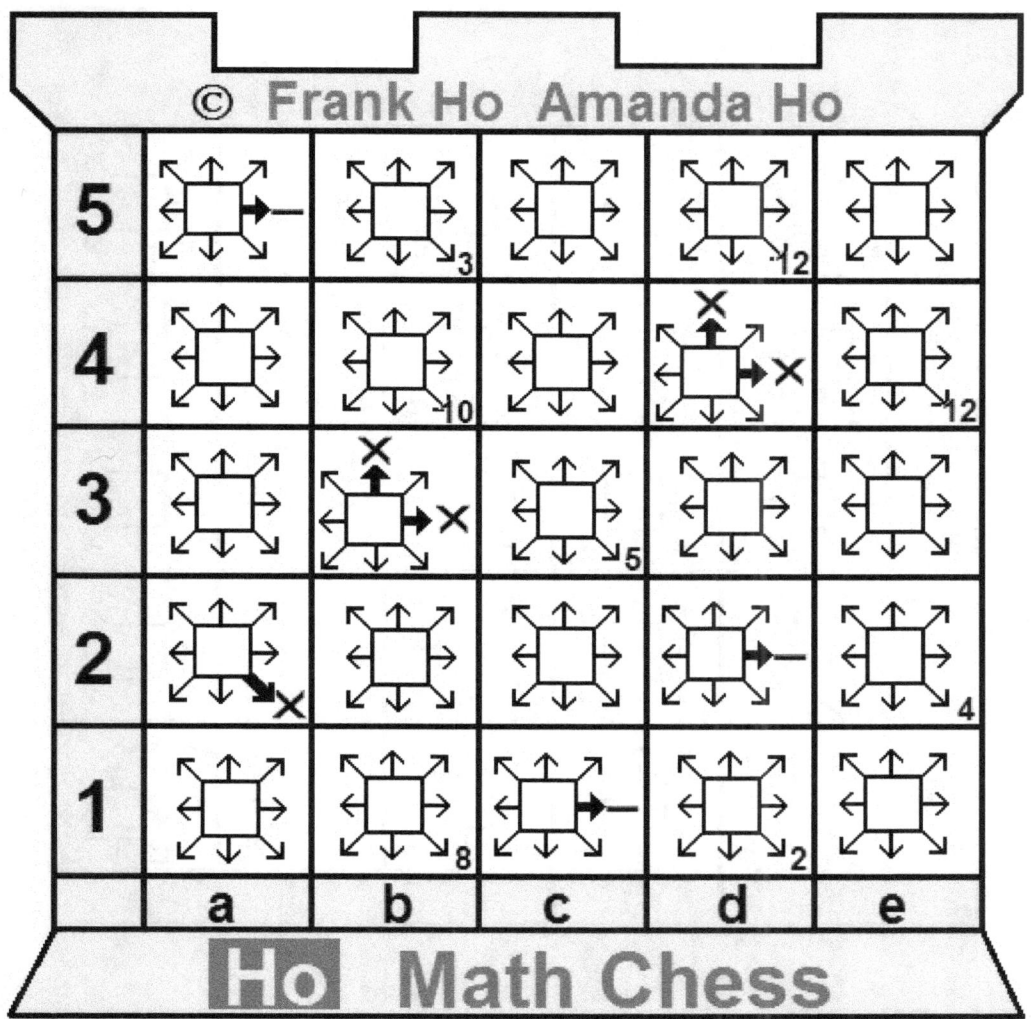

Ho Math Chess 何数棋谜 益智健脑非药物良方
Frankho Puzzle for KIDS – Brain Fitness Workbook
© 2007 — 2016 Frank Ho, Amanda Ho all rights reserved www.mathandchess.com

Frankho Puzzle™ # 184

Rule All the digits 1 to 5 must appear exactly once in every row and column. The number appears in the bottom right-hand corner is the end result calculated according to arithmetic operator(s) and chess move(s) as indicated by darker arrow(s).

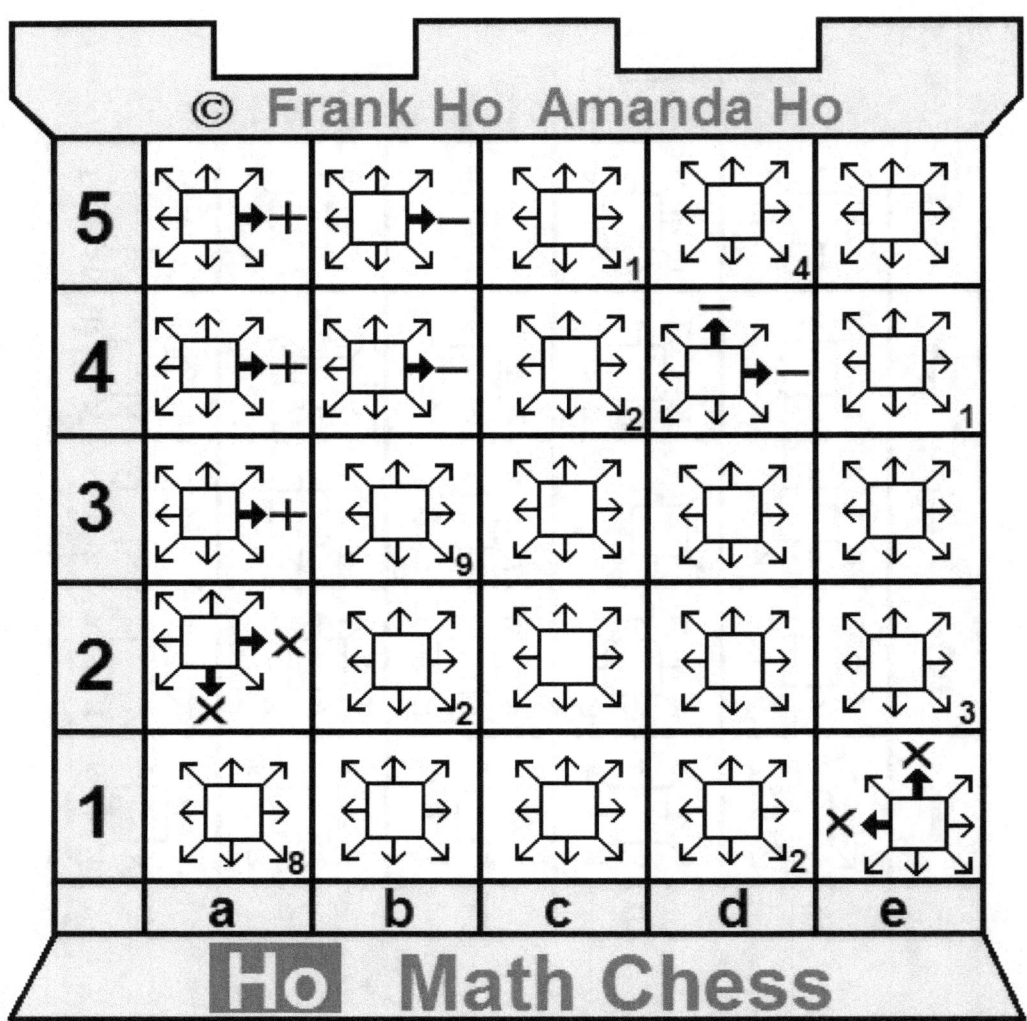

Ho Math Chess 何数棋谜 益智健脑非药物良方
Frankho Puzzle for KIDS – Brain Fitness Workbook
© 2007 — 2016 Frank Ho, Amanda Ho all rights reserved www.mathandchess.com

Frankho Puzzle™ # 185

Rule All the digits 1 to 5 must appear exactly once in every row and column. The number appears in the bottom right-hand corner is the end result calculated according to arithmetic operator(s) and chess move(s) as indicated by darker arrow(s).

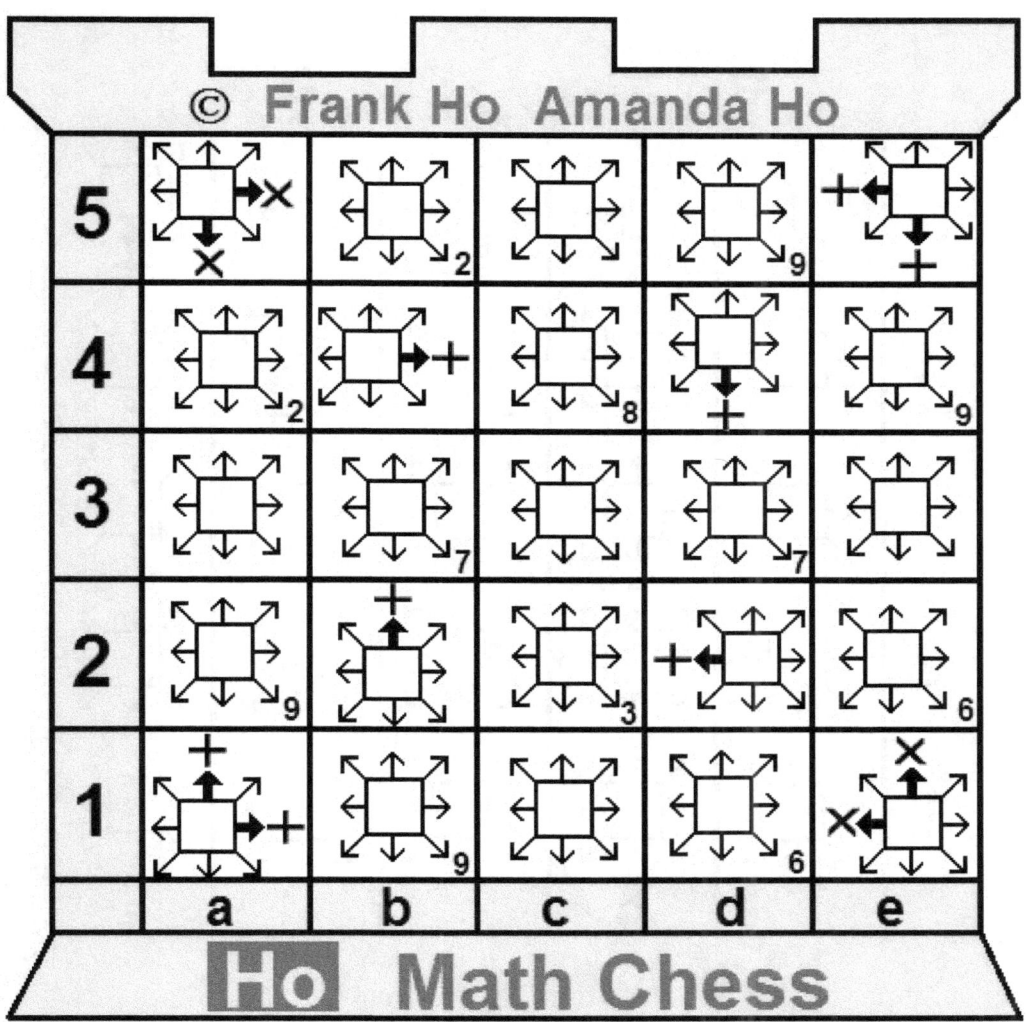

Frankho Puzzle™ # 186

Rule All the digits 1 to 5 must appear exactly once in every row and column. The number appears in the bottom right-hand corner is the end result calculated according to arithmetic operator(s) and chess move(s) as indicated by darker arrow(s).

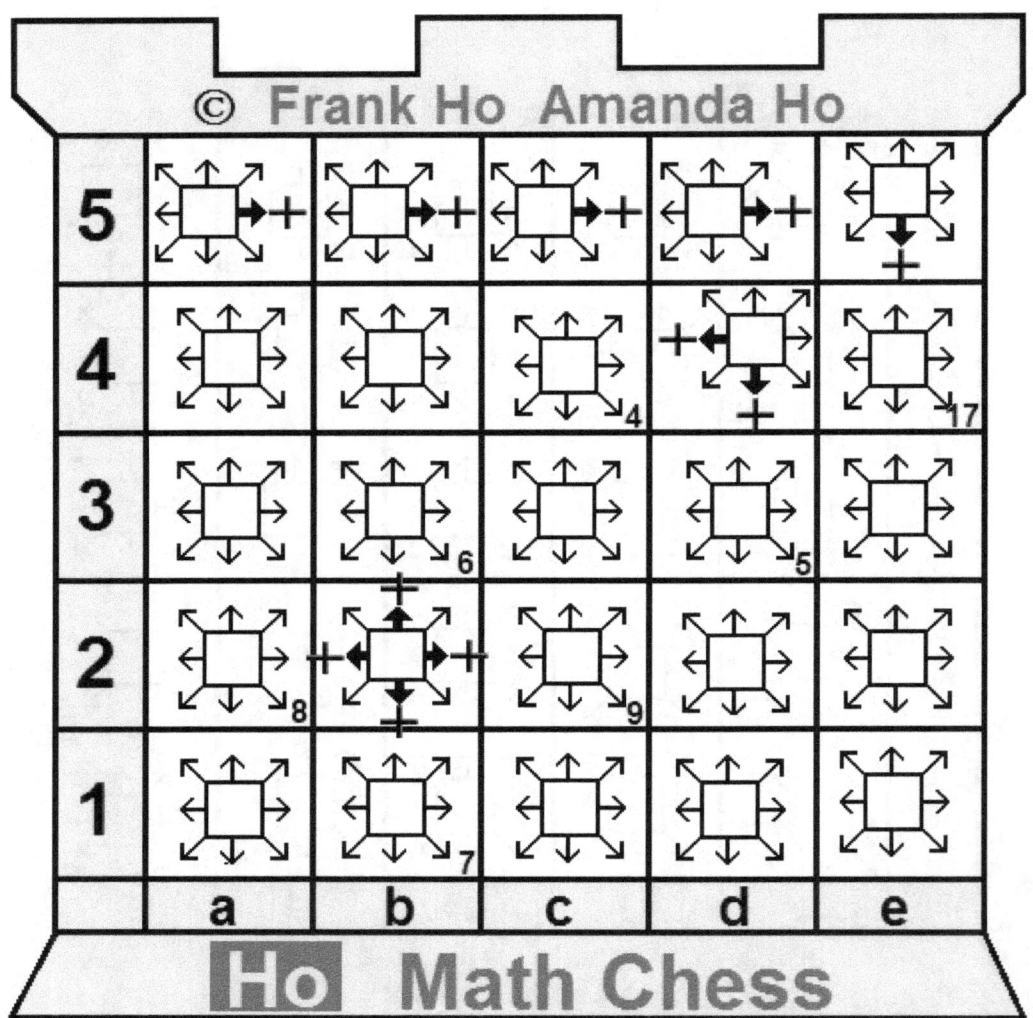

Ho Math Chess 何数棋谜 益智健脑非药物良方
Frankho Puzzle for KIDS – Brain Fitness Workbook
© 2007 — 2016 Frank Ho, Amanda Ho all rights reserved www.mathandchess.com

Frankho Puzzle™ # 187

Rule All the digits 1 to 5 must appear exactly once in every row and column. The number appears in the bottom right-hand corner is the end result calculated according to arithmetic operator(s) and chess move(s) as indicated by darker arrow(s).

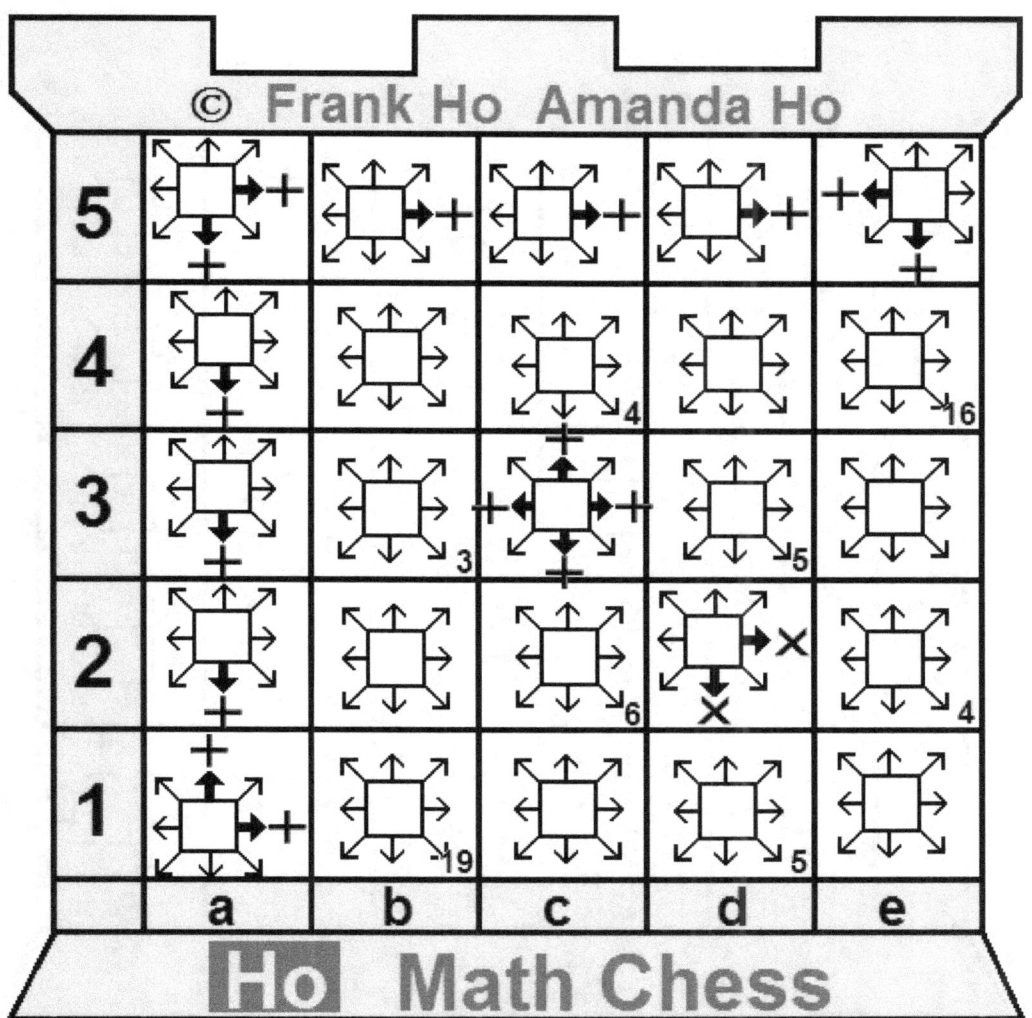

Ho Math Chess 何数棋谜 益智健脑非药物良方
Frankho Puzzle for KIDS – Brain Fitness Workbook
© 2007 — 2016 Frank Ho, Amanda Ho all rights reserved www.mathandchess.com

Frankho Puzzle™ # 188

Rule All the digits 1 to 5 must appear exactly once in every row and column. The number appears in the bottom right-hand corner is the end result calculated according to arithmetic operator(s) and chess move(s) as indicated by darker arrow(s).

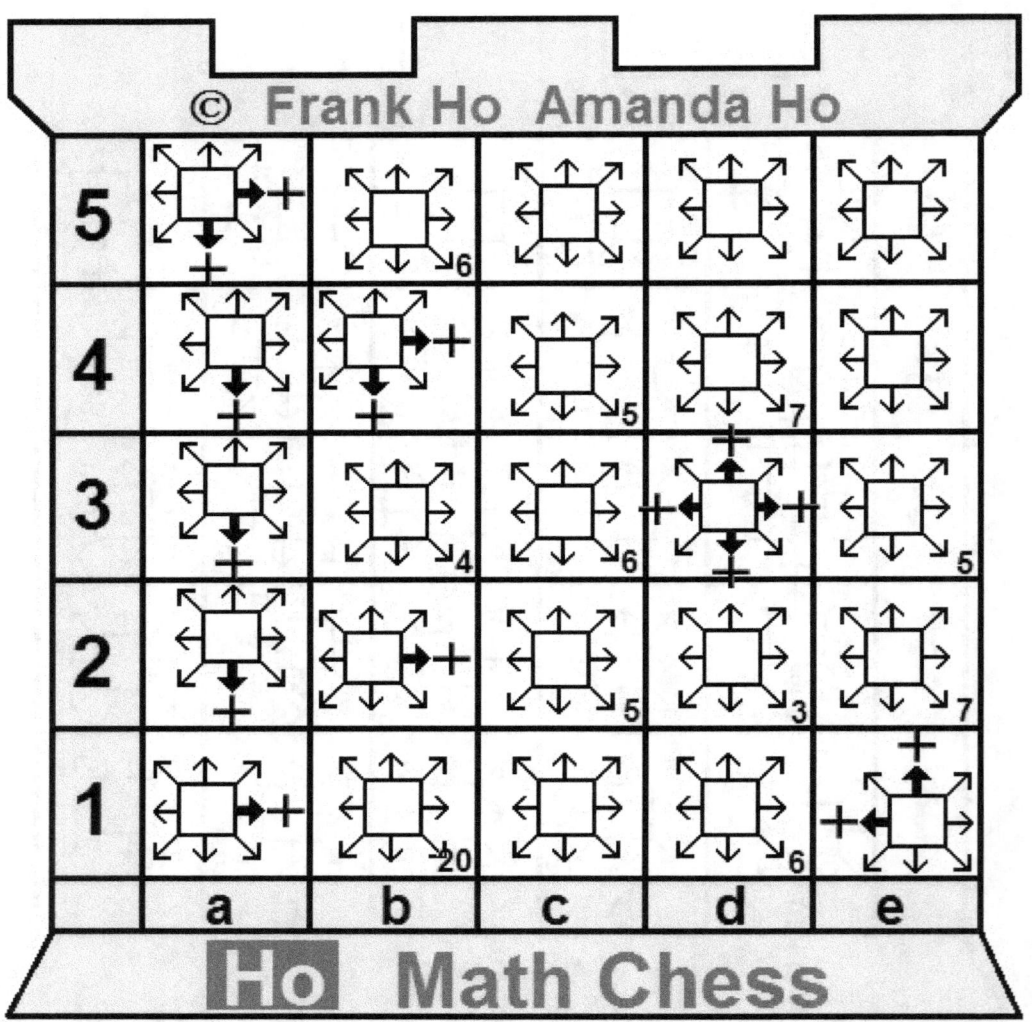

Ho Math Chess 何数棋谜 益智健脑非药物良方
Frankho Puzzle for KIDS – Brain Fitness Workbook
© 2007 — 2016 Frank Ho, Amanda Ho all rights reserved www.mathandchess.com

Frankho Puzzle™ # 189

Rule All the digits 1 to 5 must appear exactly once in every row and column. The number appears in the bottom right-hand corner is the end result calculated according to arithmetic operator(s) and chess move(s) as indicated by darker arrow(s).

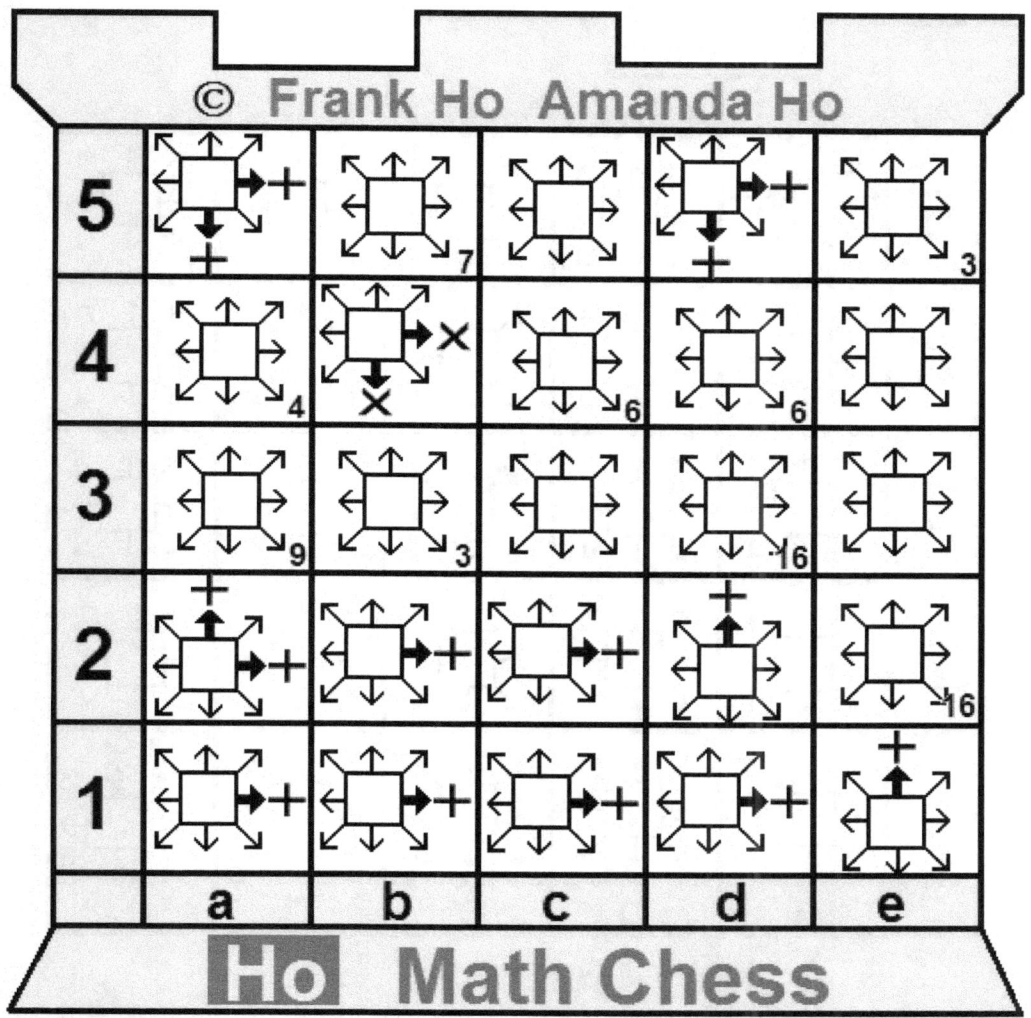

Frankho Puzzle™ # 190

Rule All the digits 1 to 5 must appear exactly once in every row and column. The number appears in the bottom right-hand corner is the end result calculated according to arithmetic operator(s) and chess move(s) as indicated by darker arrow(s).

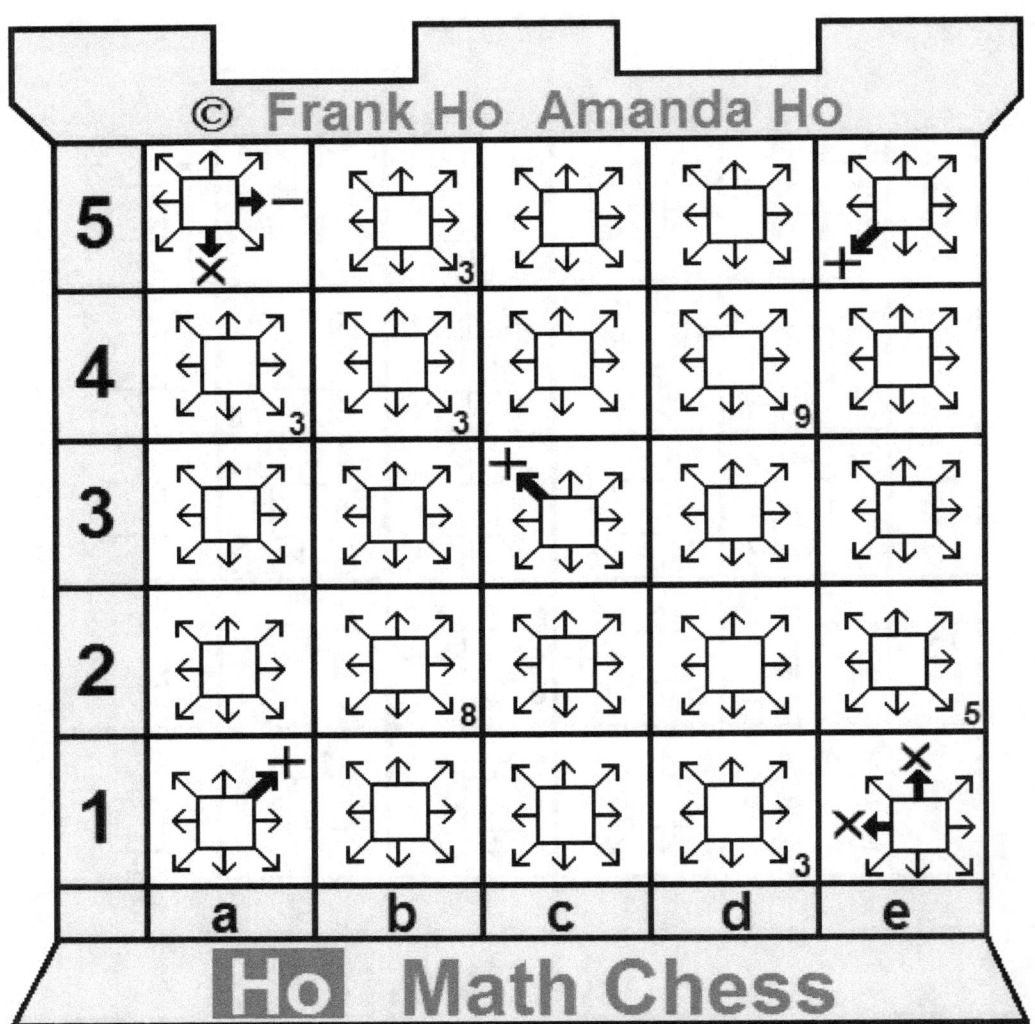

194

Ho Math Chess 何数棋谜 益智健脑非药物良方
Frankho Puzzle for KIDS – Brain Fitness Workbook
© 2007 — 2016 Frank Ho, Amanda Ho all rights reserved www.mathandchess.com

Frankho Puzzle™ # 191

Rule All the digits 1 to 5 must appear exactly once in every row and column. The number appears in the bottom right-hand corner is the end result calculated according to arithmetic operator(s) and chess move(s) as indicated by darker arrow(s).

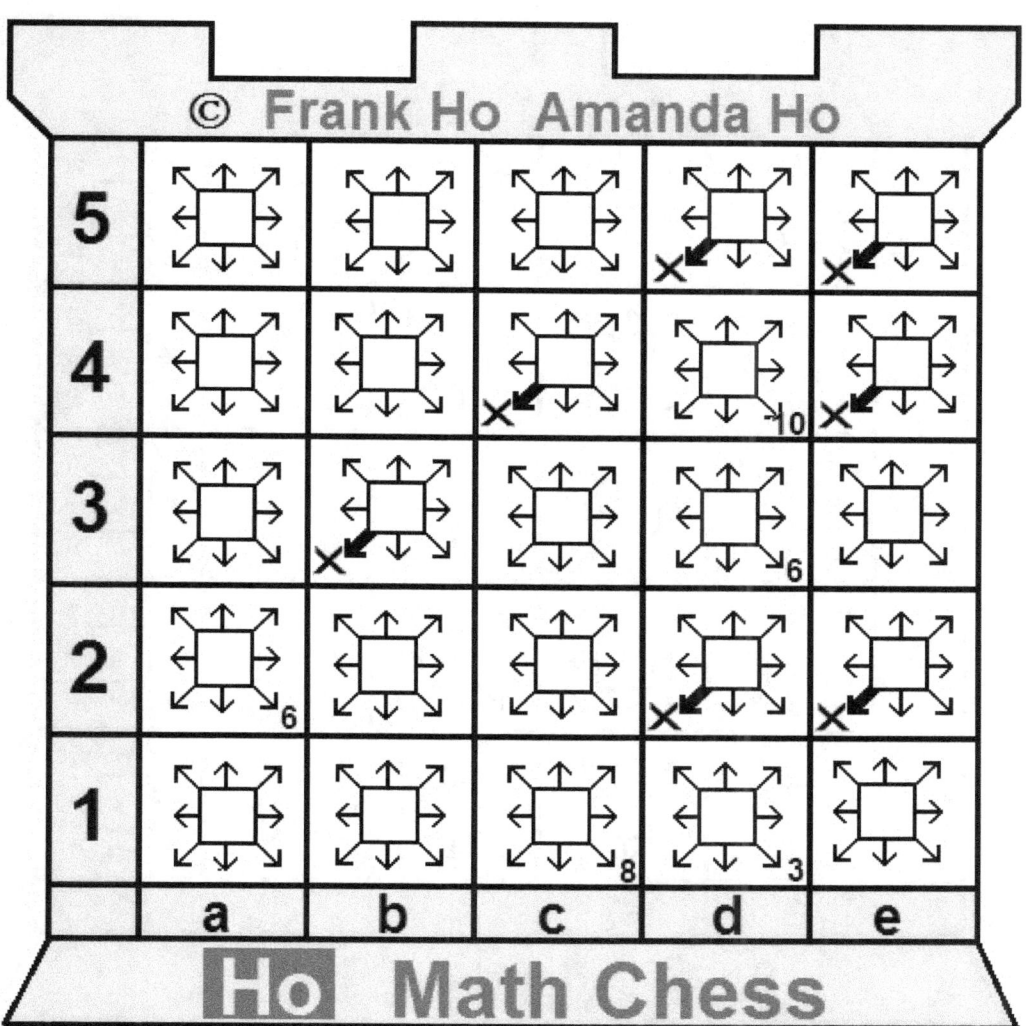

Ho Math Chess 何数棋谜 益智健脑非药物良方
Frankho Puzzle for KIDS – Brain Fitness Workbook
© 2007 — 2016 Frank Ho, Amanda Ho all rights reserved www.mathandchess.com

Frankho Puzzle™ # 192

Rule All the digits 1 to 5 must appear exactly once in every row and column. The number appears in the bottom right-hand corner is the end result calculated according to arithmetic operator(s) and chess move(s) as indicated by darker arrow(s).

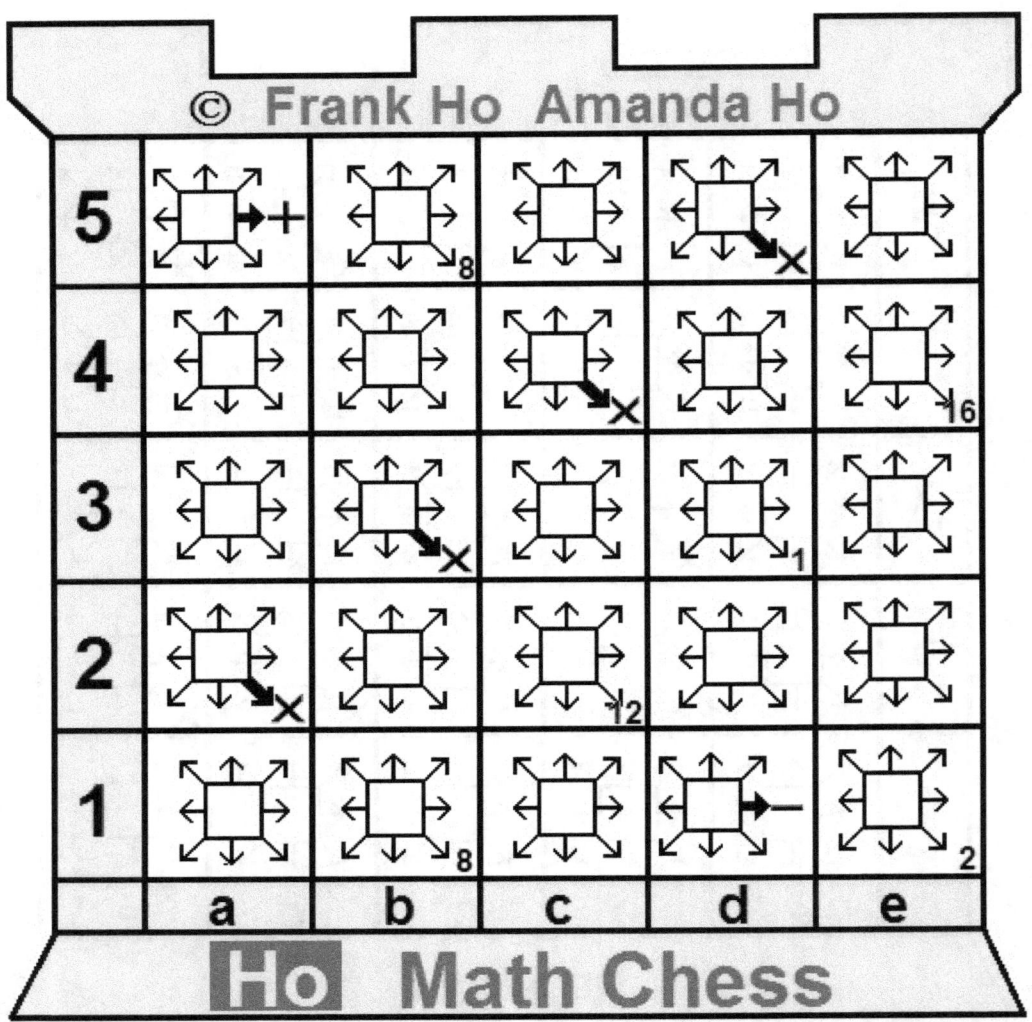

Ho Math Chess 何数棋谜 益智健脑非药物良方
Frankho Puzzle for KIDS – Brain Fitness Workbook
© 2007 — 2016 Frank Ho, Amanda Ho all rights reserved www.mathandchess.com

Frankho Puzzle™ # 193

Rule All the digits 1 to 5 must appear exactly once in every row and column. The number appears in the bottom right-hand corner is the end result calculated according to arithmetic operator(s) and chess move(s) as indicated by darker arrow(s).

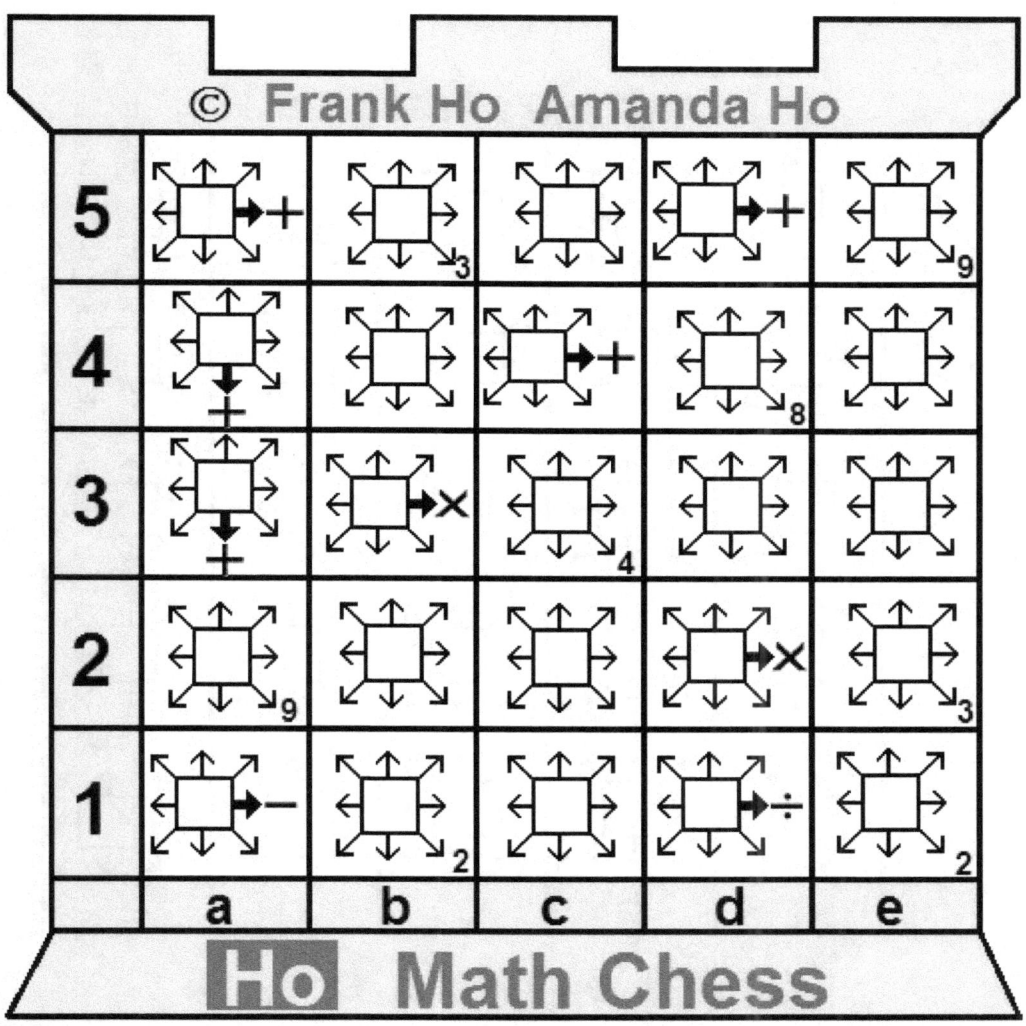

Ho Math Chess 何数棋谜 益智健脑非药物良方
Frankho Puzzle for KIDS – Brain Fitness Workbook

© 2007 – 2016 Frank Ho, Amanda Ho all rights reserved www.mathandchess.com

Frankho Puzzle™ # 194

Rule All the digits 1 to 5 must appear exactly once in every row and column. The number appears in the bottom right-hand corner is the end result calculated according to arithmetic operator(s) and chess move(s) as indicated by darker arrow(s).

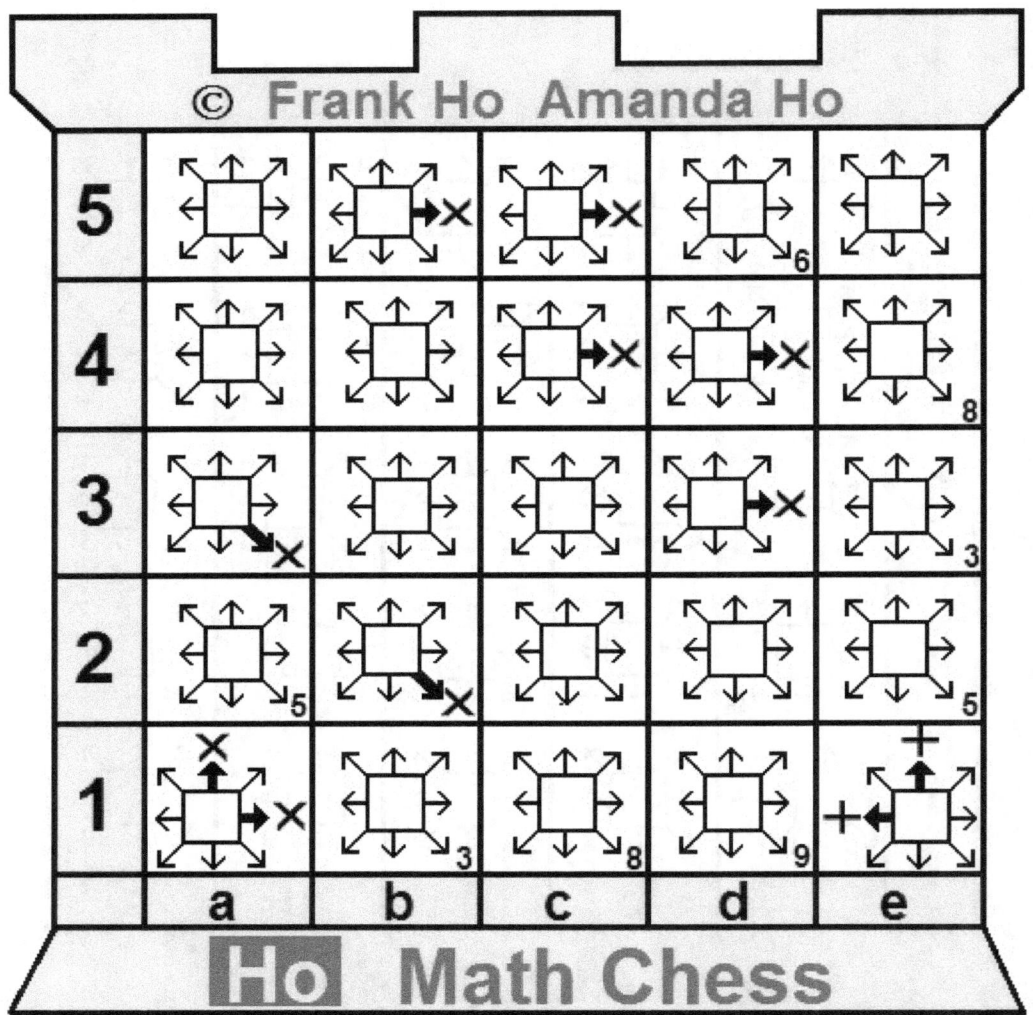

Frankho Puzzle™ # 195

Rule All the digits 1 to 5 must appear exactly once in every row and column. The number appears in the bottom right-hand corner is the end result calculated according to arithmetic operator(s) and chess move(s) as indicated by darker arrow(s).

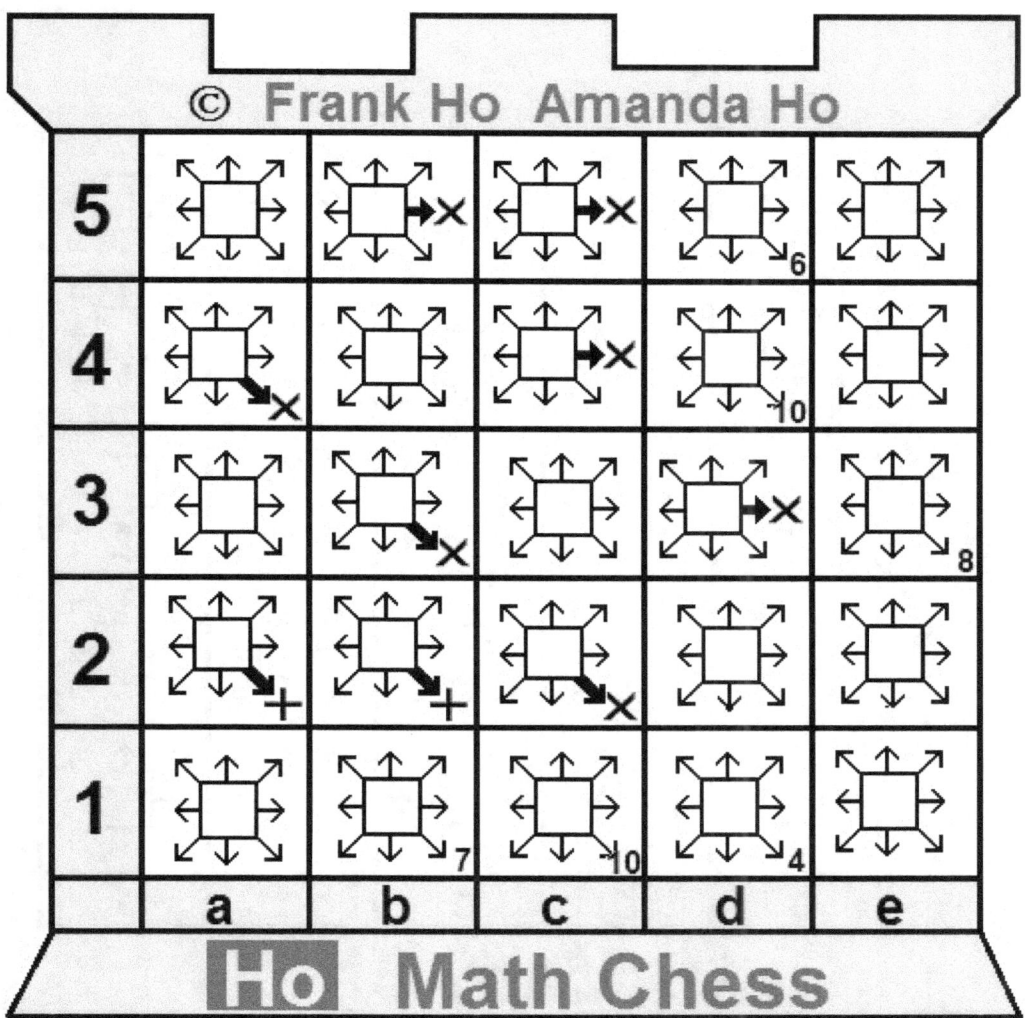

Ho Math Chess 何数棋谜 益智健脑非药物良方
Frankho Puzzle for KIDS – Brain Fitness Workbook
© 2007 – 2016 Frank Ho, Amanda Ho all rights reserved www.mathandchess.com

Frankho Puzzle™ # 196

Rule All the digits 1 to 5 must appear exactly once in every row and column. The number appears in the bottom right-hand corner is the end result calculated according to arithmetic operator(s) and chess move(s) as indicated by darker arrow(s).

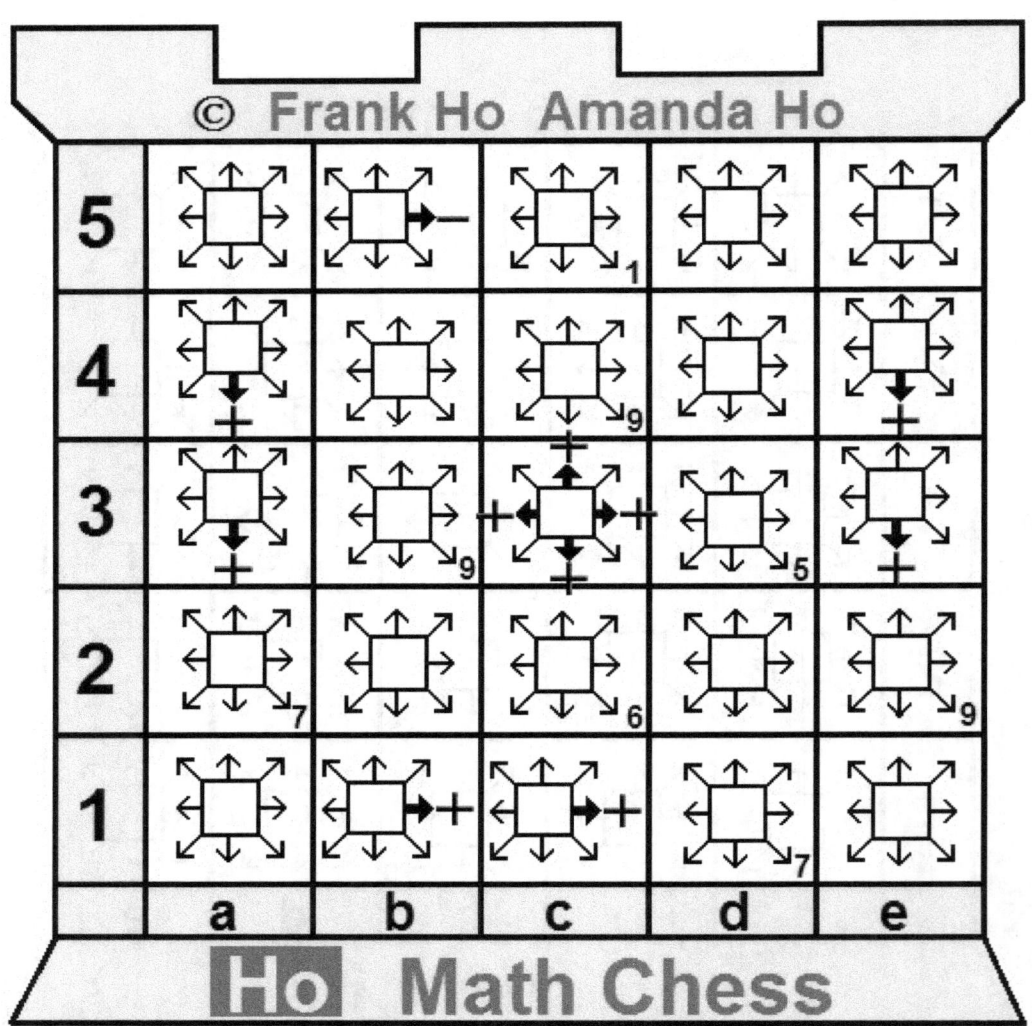

Ho Math Chess 何数棋谜 益智健脑非药物良方
Frankho Puzzle for KIDS – Brain Fitness Workbook
© 2007 – 2016 Frank Ho, Amanda Ho all rights reserved www.mathandchess.com

Frankho Puzzle™ # 197

Rule All the digits 1 to 5 must appear exactly once in every row and column. The number appears in the bottom right-hand corner is the end result calculated according to arithmetic operator(s) and chess move(s) as indicated by darker arrow(s).

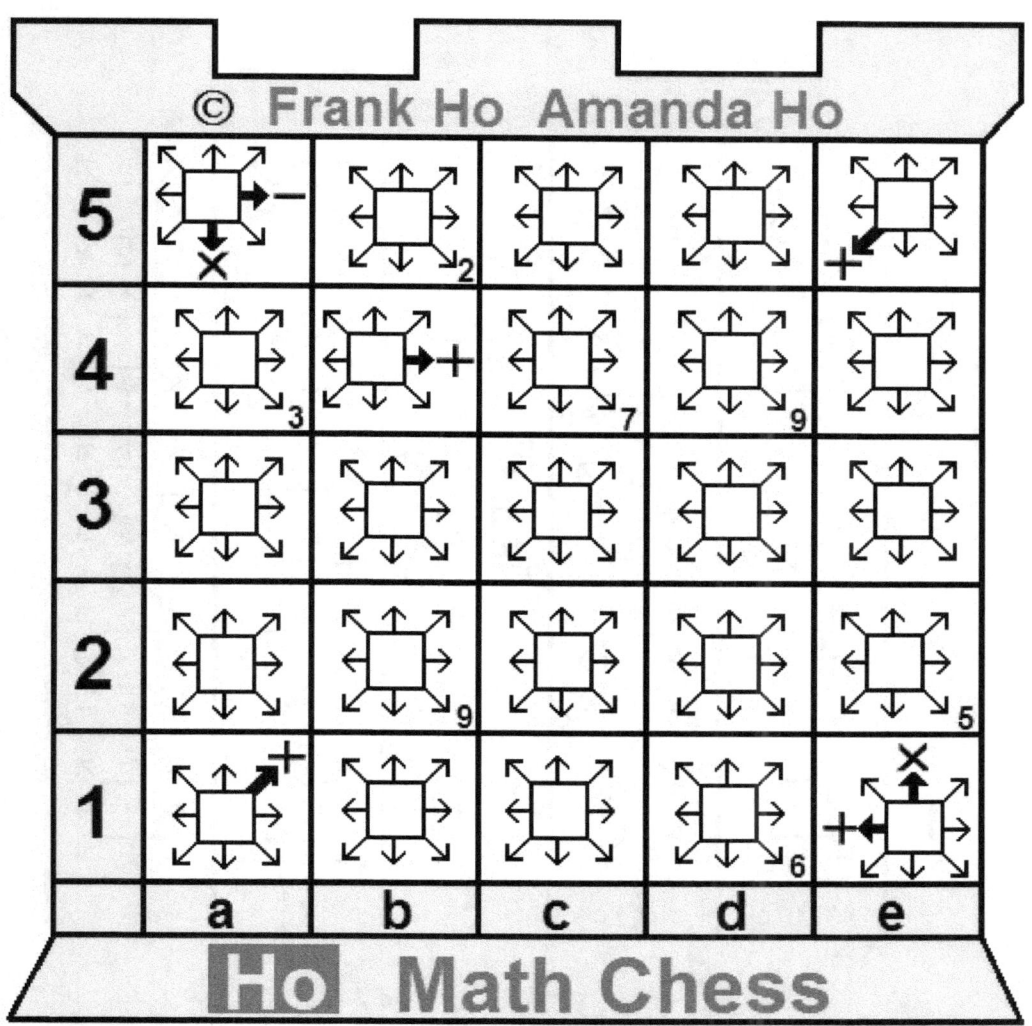

Frankho Puzzle™ # 198

Rule All the digits 1 to 5 must appear exactly once in every row and column. The number appears in the bottom right-hand corner is the end result calculated according to arithmetic operator(s) and chess move(s) as indicated by darker arrow(s).

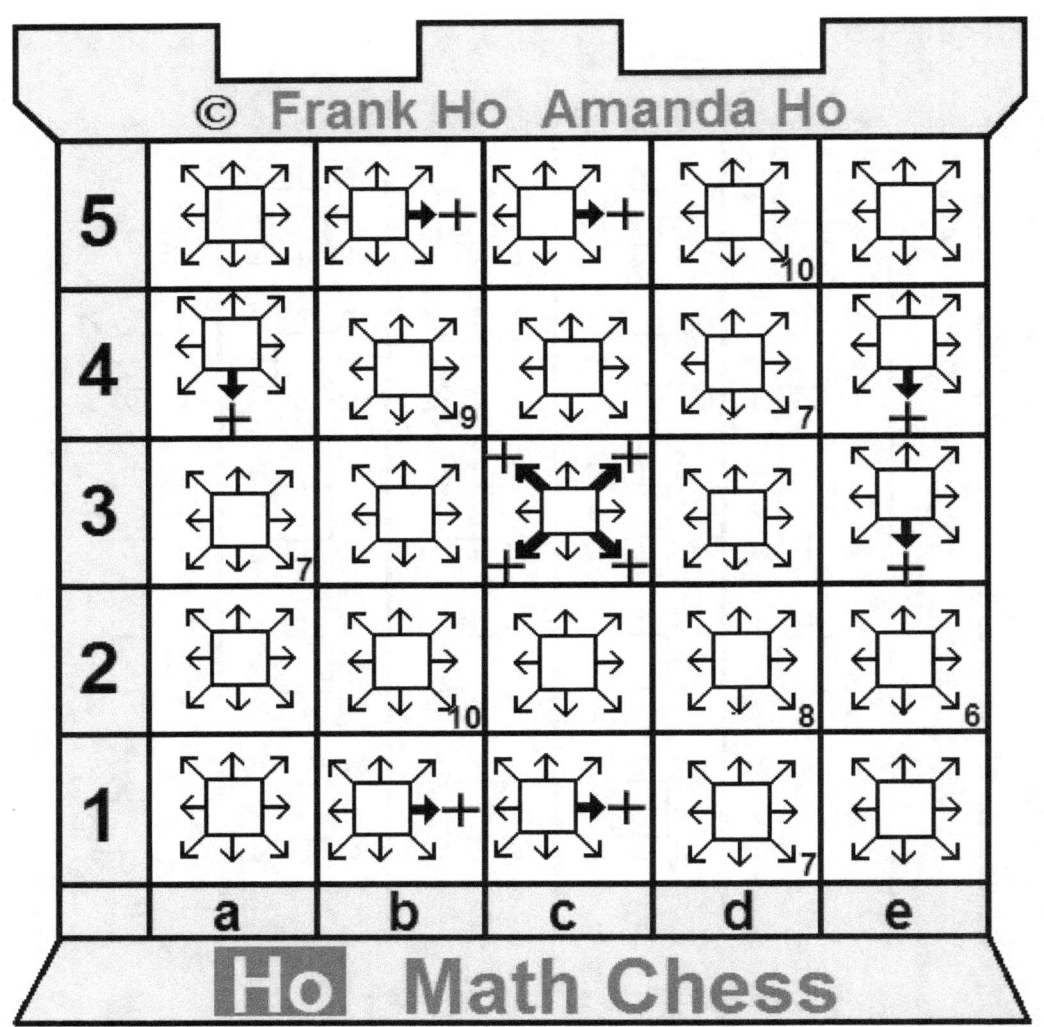

Ho Math Chess 何数棋谜 益智健脑非药物良方
Frankho Puzzle for KIDS – Brain Fitness Workbook
© 2007 — 2016 Frank Ho, Amanda Ho all rights reserved www.mathandchess.com

Frankho Puzzle™ # 199

Rule All the digits 1 to 5 must appear exactly once in every row and column. The number appears in the bottom right-hand corner is the end result calculated according to arithmetic operator(s) and chess move(s) as indicated by darker arrow(s).

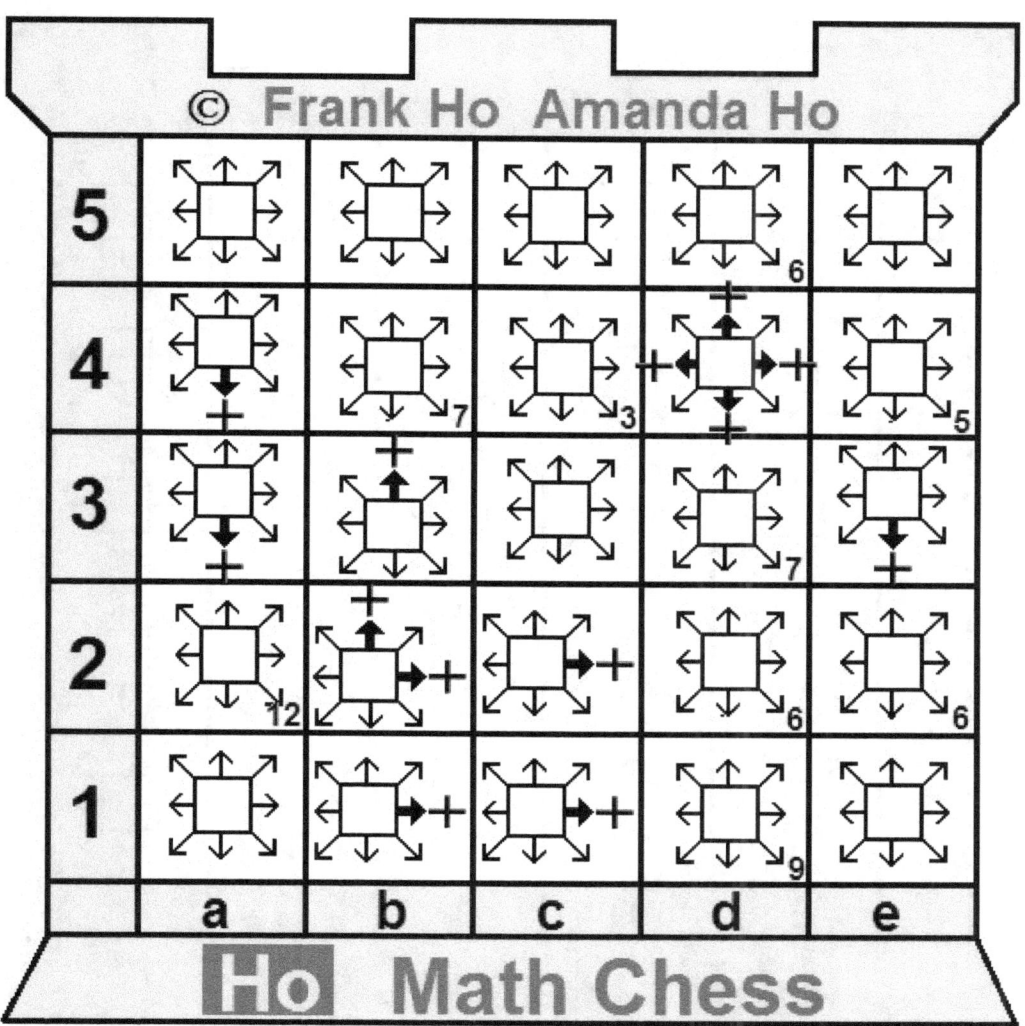

Ho Math Chess 何数棋谜 益智健脑非药物良方
Frankho Puzzle for KIDS – Brain Fitness Workbook
© 2007 — 2016 Frank Ho, Amanda Ho all rights reserved www.mathandchess.com

Frankho Puzzle™ # 200

Rule All the digits 1 to 5 must appear exactly once in every row and column. The number appears in the bottom right-hand corner is the end result calculated according to arithmetic operator(s) and chess move(s) as indicated by darker arrow(s).

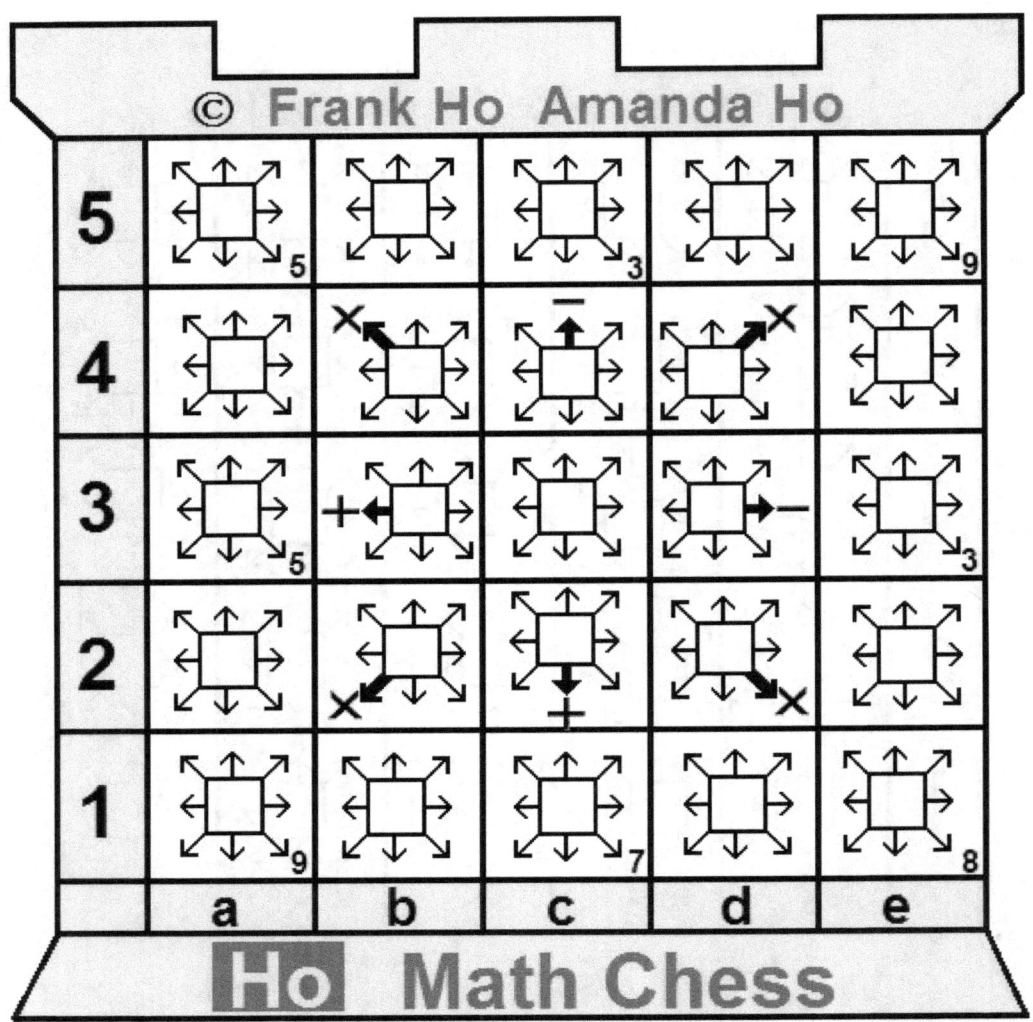

Ho Math Chess 何数棋谜 益智健脑非药物良方
Frankho Puzzle for KIDS – Brain Fitness Workbook
© 2007 — 2016 Frank Ho, Amanda Ho all rights reserved www.mathandchess.com

Frankho Puzzle™ # 201

Rule All the digits 1 to 5 must appear exactly once in every row and column. The number appears in the bottom right-hand corner is the end result calculated according to arithmetic operator(s) and chess move(s) as indicated by darker arrow(s).

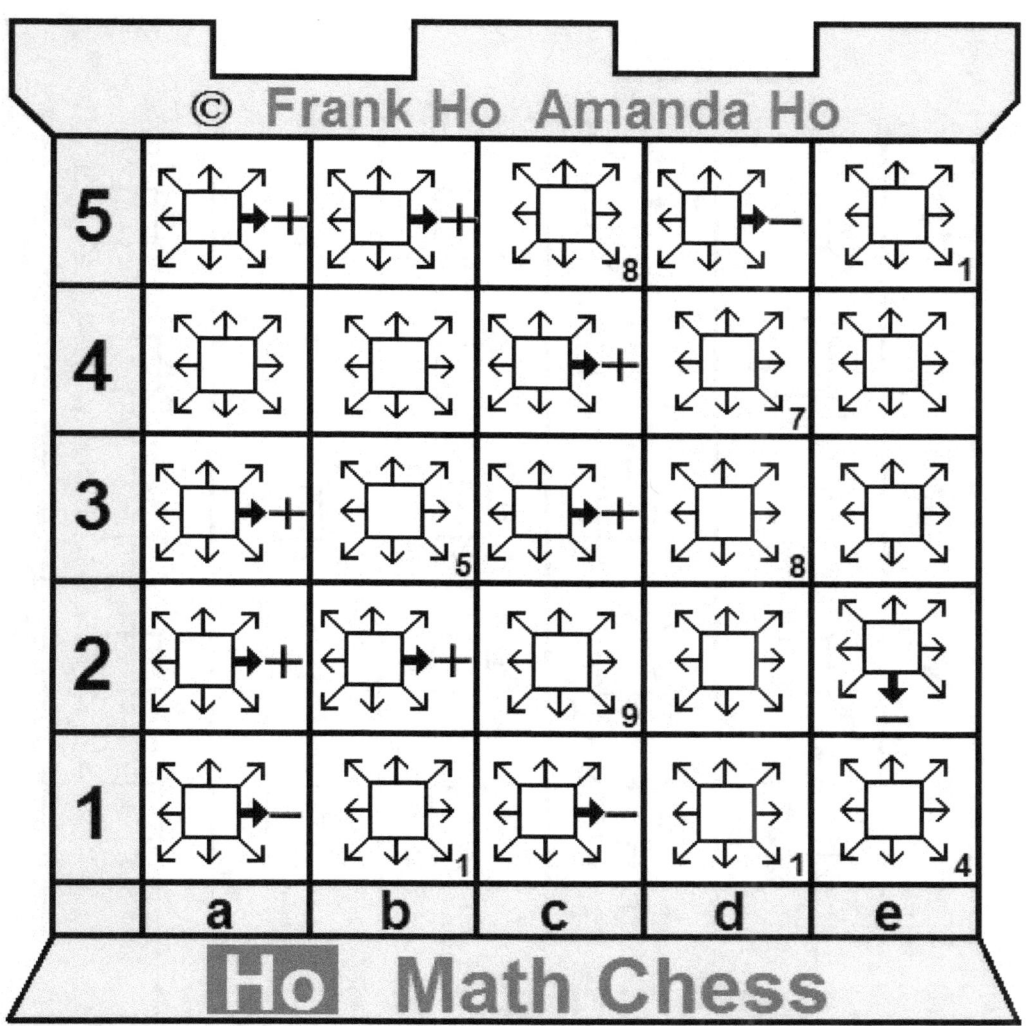

Frankho Puzzle™ # 202

Rule All the digits 1 to 5 must appear exactly once in every row and column. The number appears in the bottom right-hand corner is the end result calculated according to arithmetic operator(s) and chess move(s) as indicated by darker arrow(s).

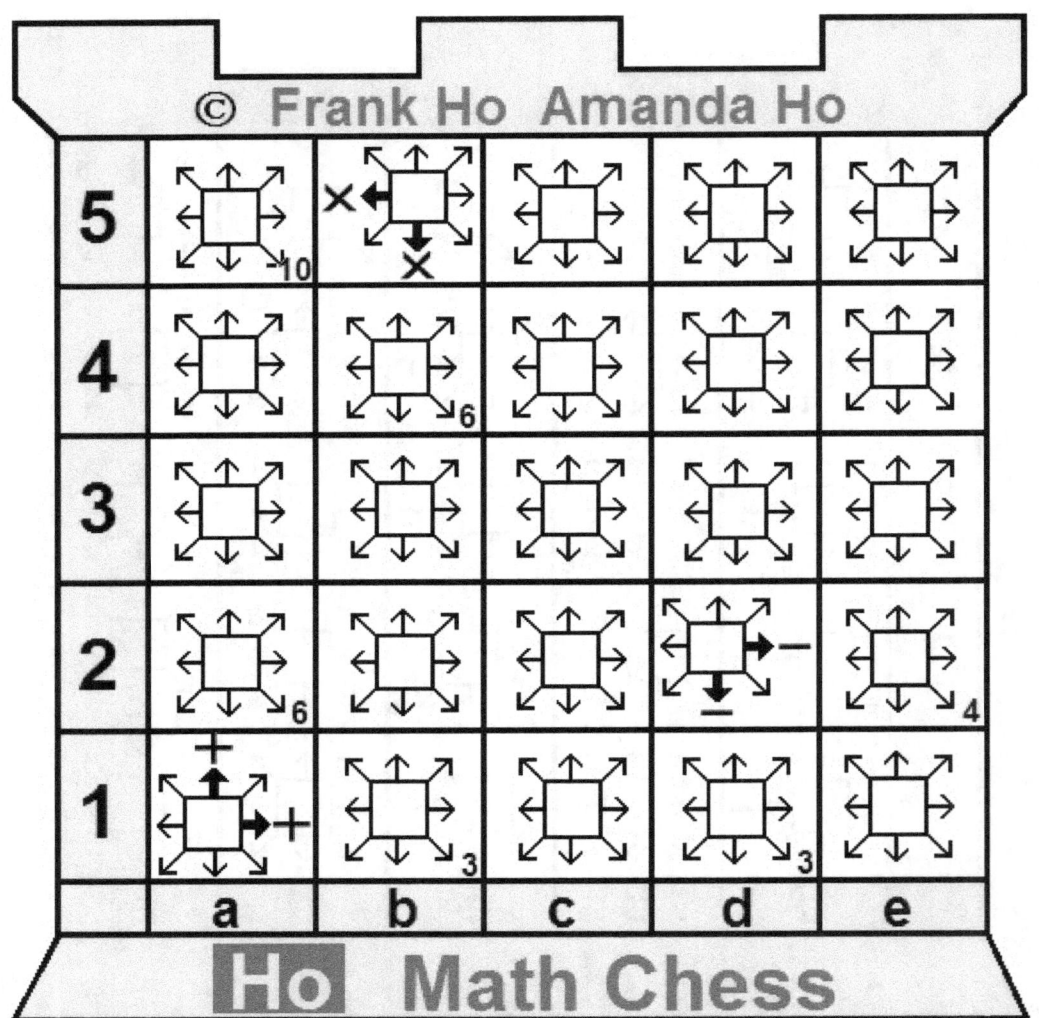

206

Ho Math Chess 何数棋谜 益智健脑非药物良方
Frankho Puzzle for KIDS – Brain Fitness Workbook
© 2007 — 2016 Frank Ho, Amanda Ho all rights reserved www.mathandchess.com

Frankho Puzzle™ # 203

Rule All the digits 1 to 5 must appear exactly once in every row and column. The number appears in the bottom right-hand corner is the end result calculated according to arithmetic operator(s) and chess move(s) as indicated by darker arrow(s).

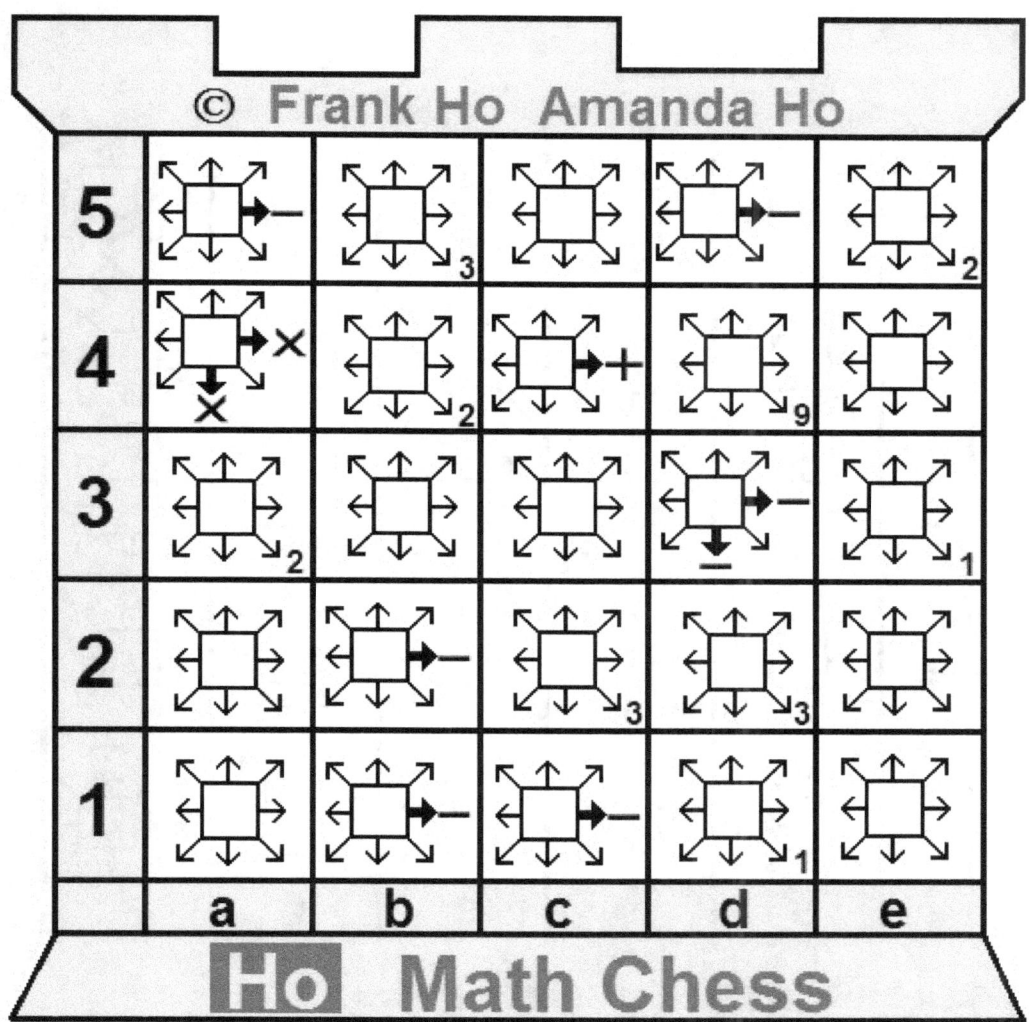

Ho Math Chess 何数棋谜 益智健脑非药物良方
Frankho Puzzle for KIDS – Brain Fitness Workbook
© 2007 – 2016 Frank Ho, Amanda Ho all rights reserved www.mathandchess.com

Frankho Puzzle™ # 204

Rule All the digits 1 to 5 must appear exactly once in every row and column. The number appears in the bottom right-hand corner is the end result calculated according to arithmetic operator(s) and chess move(s) as indicated by darker arrow(s).

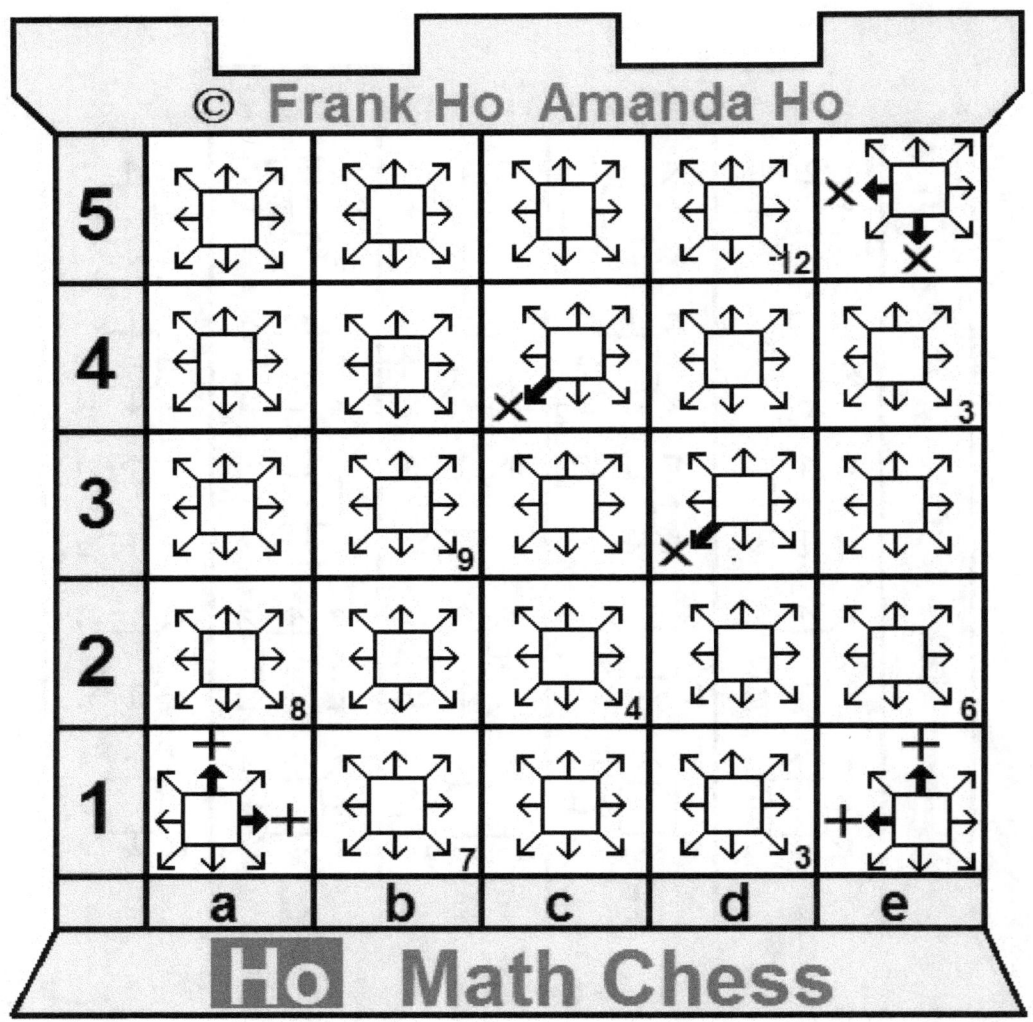

Ho Math Chess 何数棋谜 益智健脑非药物良方
Frankho Puzzle for KIDS – Brain Fitness Workbook
© 2007 — 2016 Frank Ho, Amanda Ho all rights reserved www.mathandchess.com

Frankho Puzzle™ # 205

Rule All the digits 1 to 5 must appear exactly once in every row and column. The number appears in the bottom right-hand corner is the end result calculated according to arithmetic operator(s) and chess move(s) as indicated by darker arrow(s).

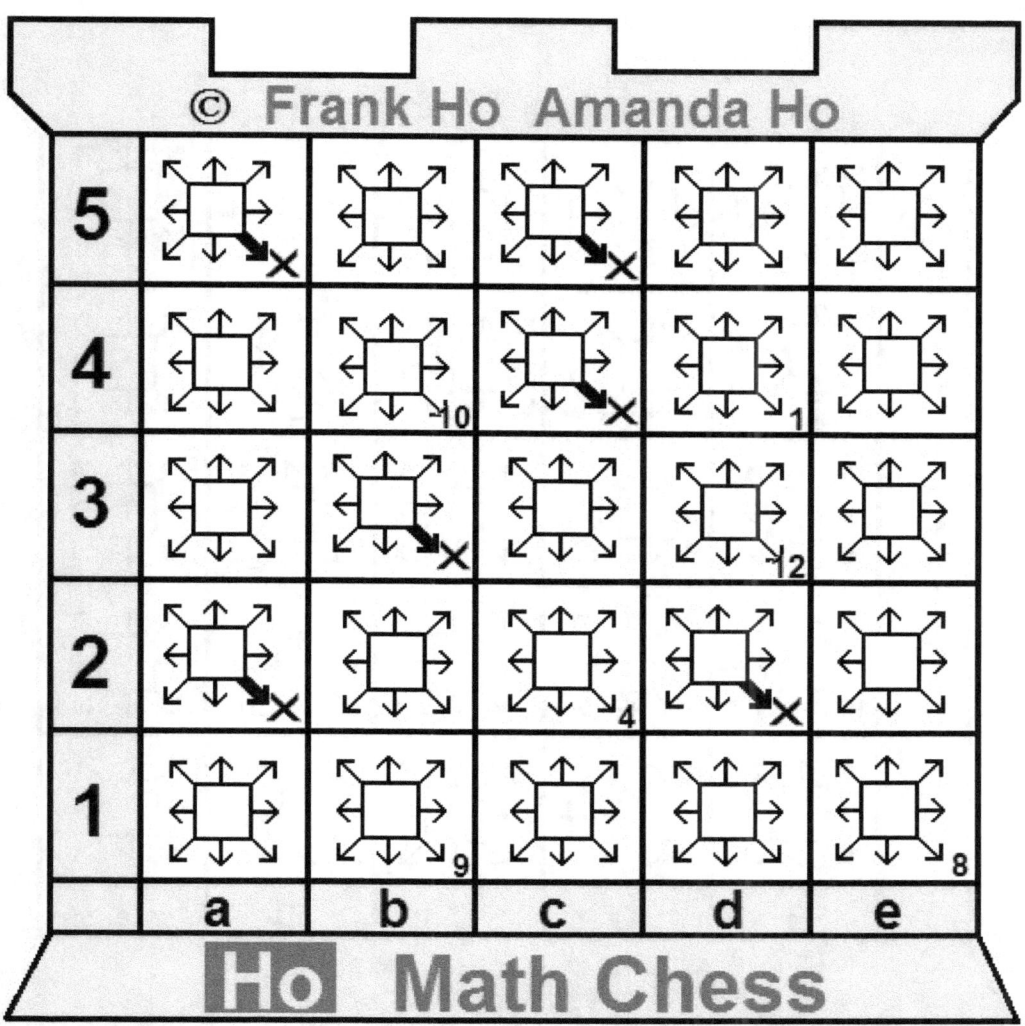

Ho Math Chess 何数棋谜 益智健脑非药物良方
Frankho Puzzle for KIDS – Brain Fitness Workbook
© 2007 – 2016 Frank Ho, Amanda Ho all rights reserved www.mathandchess.com

Frankho Puzzle™ # 206

Rule All the digits 1 to 5 must appear exactly once in every row and column. The number appears in the bottom right-hand corner is the end result calculated according to arithmetic operator(s) and chess move(s) as indicated by darker arrow(s).

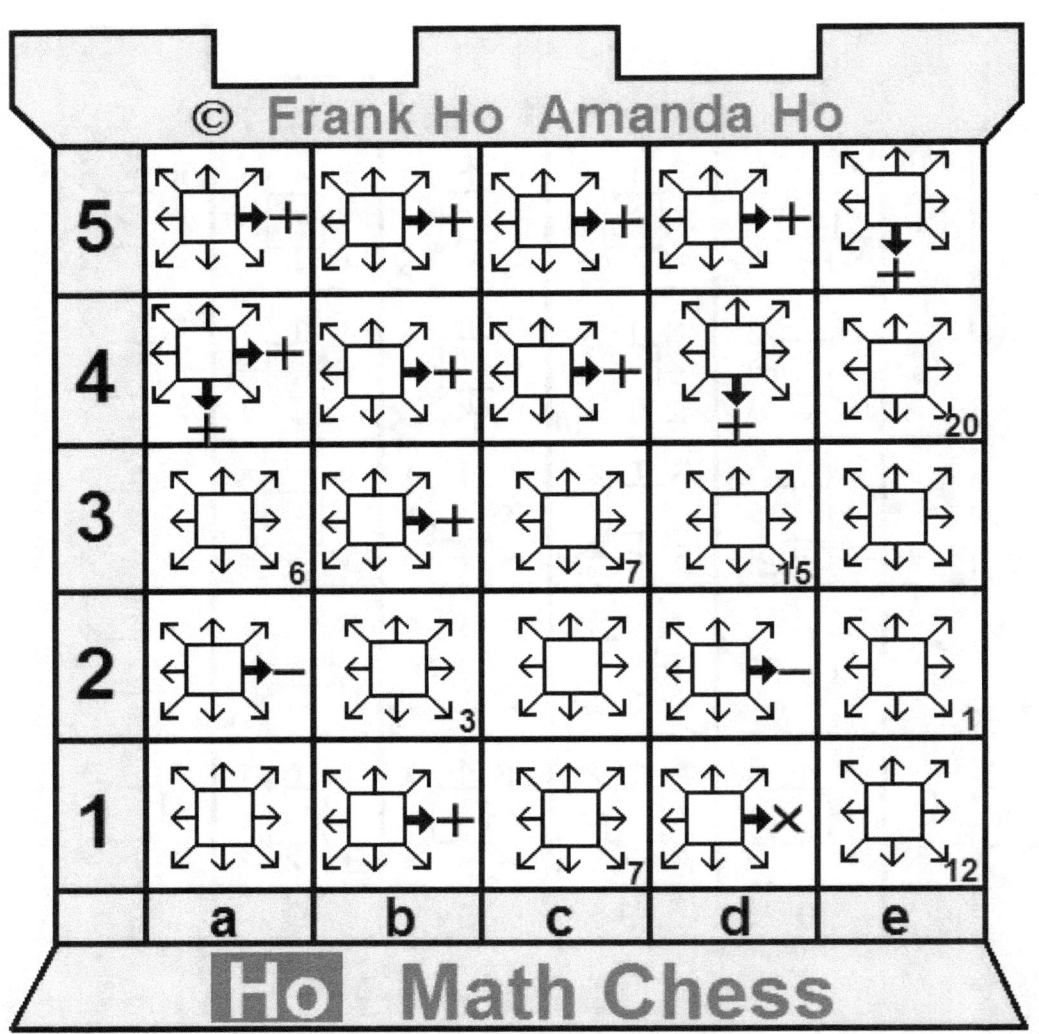

Ho Math Chess 何数棋谜 益智健脑非药物良方
Frankho Puzzle for KIDS – Brain Fitness Workbook
© 2007 — 2016 Frank Ho, Amanda Ho all rights reserved www.mathandchess.com

Frankho Puzzle™ # 207

Rule All the digits 1 to 5 must appear exactly once in every row and column. The number appears in the bottom right-hand corner is the end result calculated according to arithmetic operator(s) and chess move(s) as indicated by darker arrow(s).

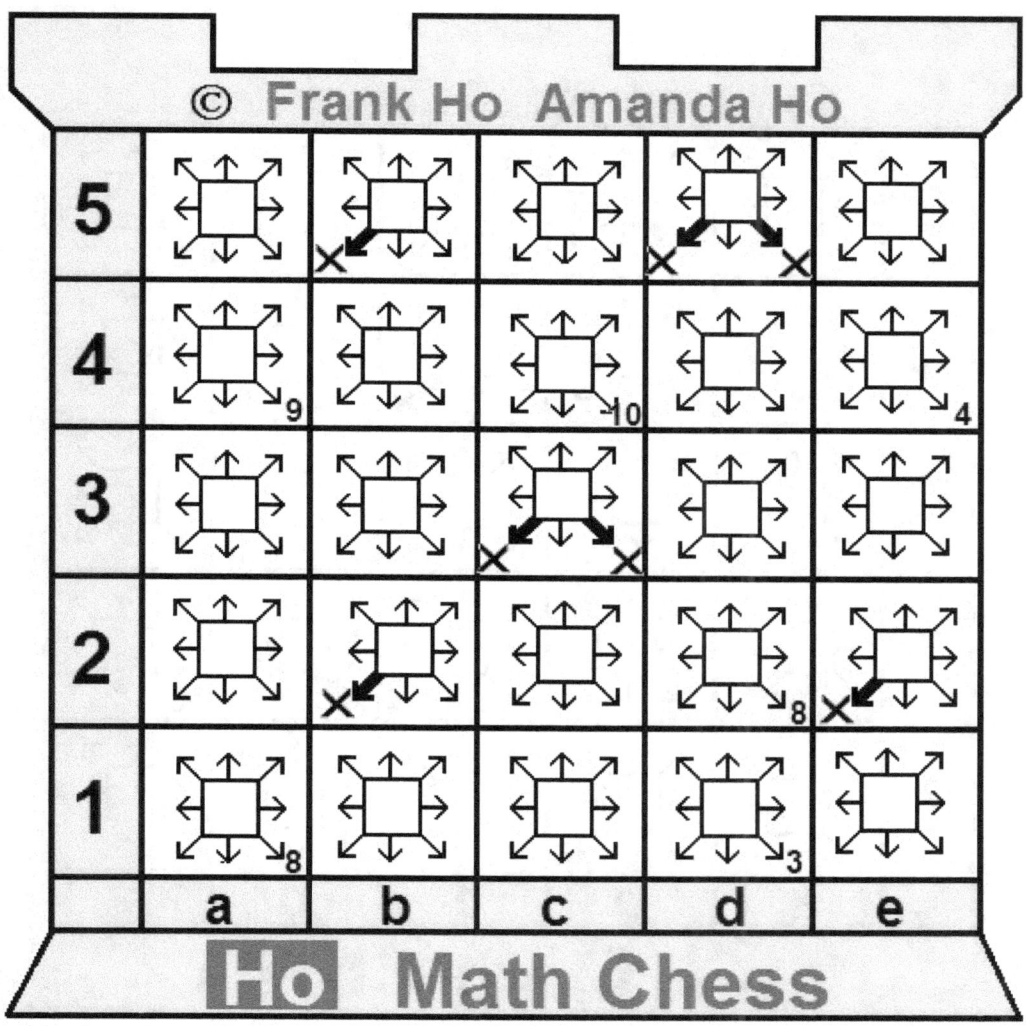

Ho Math Chess 何数棋谜 益智健脑非药物良方
Frankho Puzzle for KIDS – Brain Fitness Workbook
© 2007 — 2016 Frank Ho, Amanda Ho all rights reserved www.mathandchess.com

Frankho Puzzle™ # 208

Rule All the digits 1 to 5 must appear exactly once in every row and column. The number appears in the bottom right-hand corner is the end result calculated according to arithmetic operator(s) and chess move(s) as indicated by darker arrow(s).

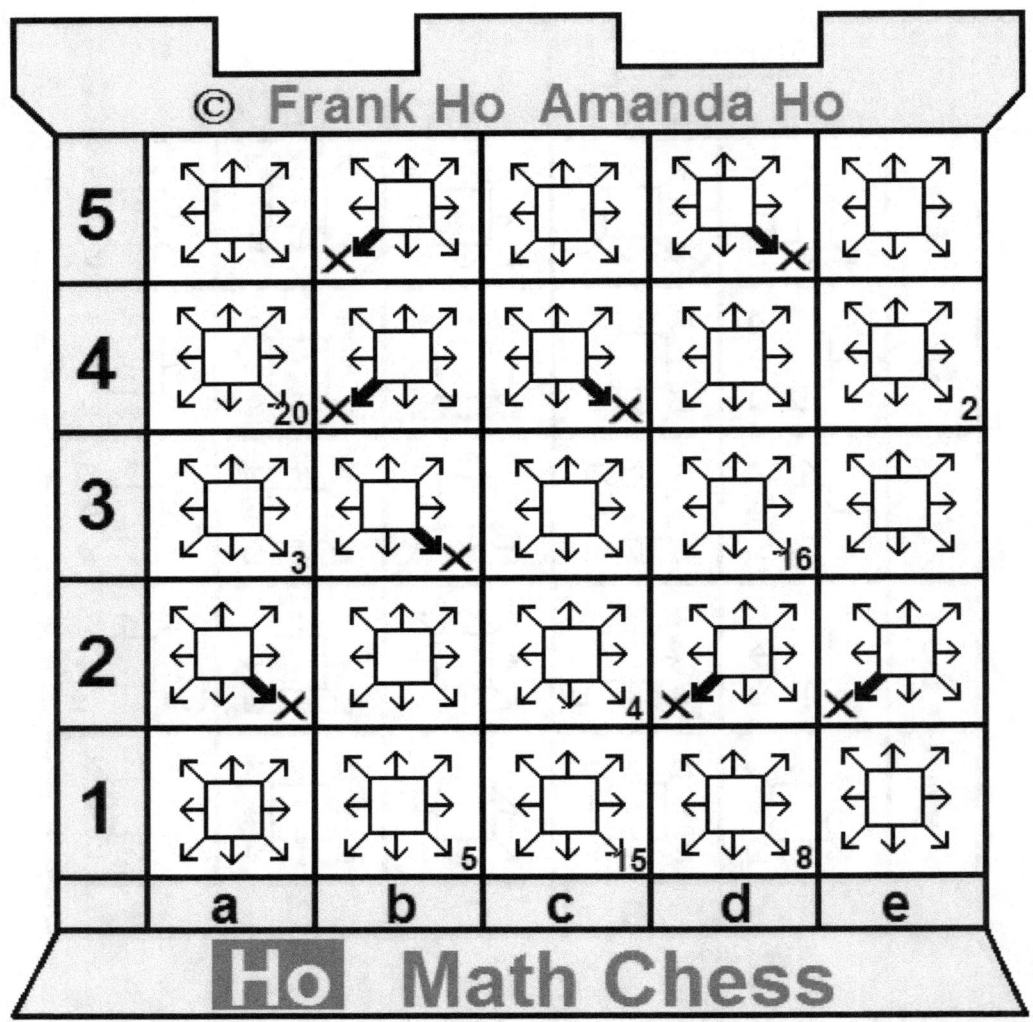

Ho Math Chess 何数棋谜 益智健脑非药物良方
Frankho Puzzle for KIDS – Brain Fitness Workbook
© 2007 — 2016 Frank Ho, Amanda Ho all rights reserved www.mathandchess.com

Frankho Puzzle™ # 209

Rule All the digits 1 to 5 must appear exactly once in every row and column. The number appears in the bottom right-hand corner is the end result calculated according to arithmetic operator(s) and chess move(s) as indicated by darker arrow(s).

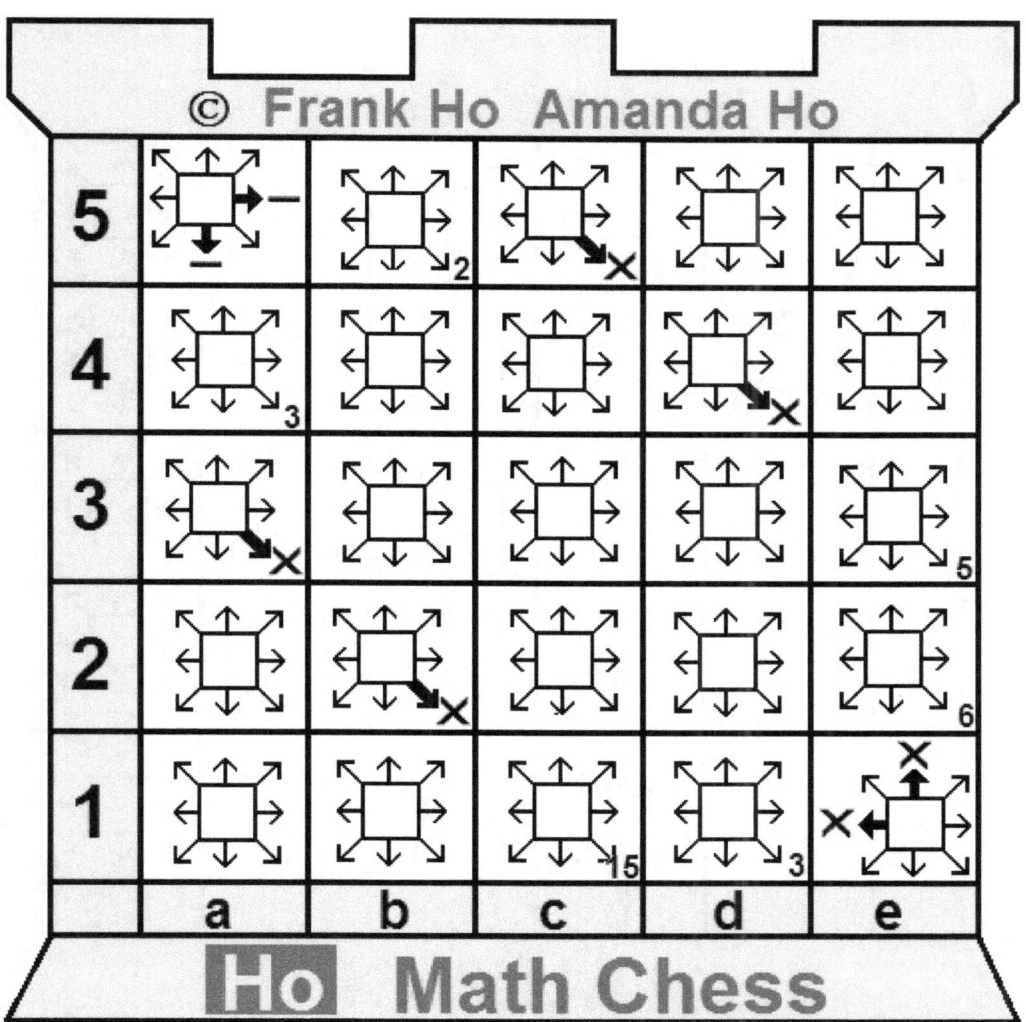

Ho Math Chess
Frankho Puzzle for KIDS − Brain Fitness Workbook
© 2007 — 2016 Frank Ho, Amanda Ho all rights reserved www.mathandchess.com

Frankho Puzzle™ # 210

Rule All the digits 1 to 5 must appear exactly once in every row and column. The number appears in the bottom right-hand corner is the end result calculated according to arithmetic operator(s) and chess move(s) as indicated by darker arrow(s).

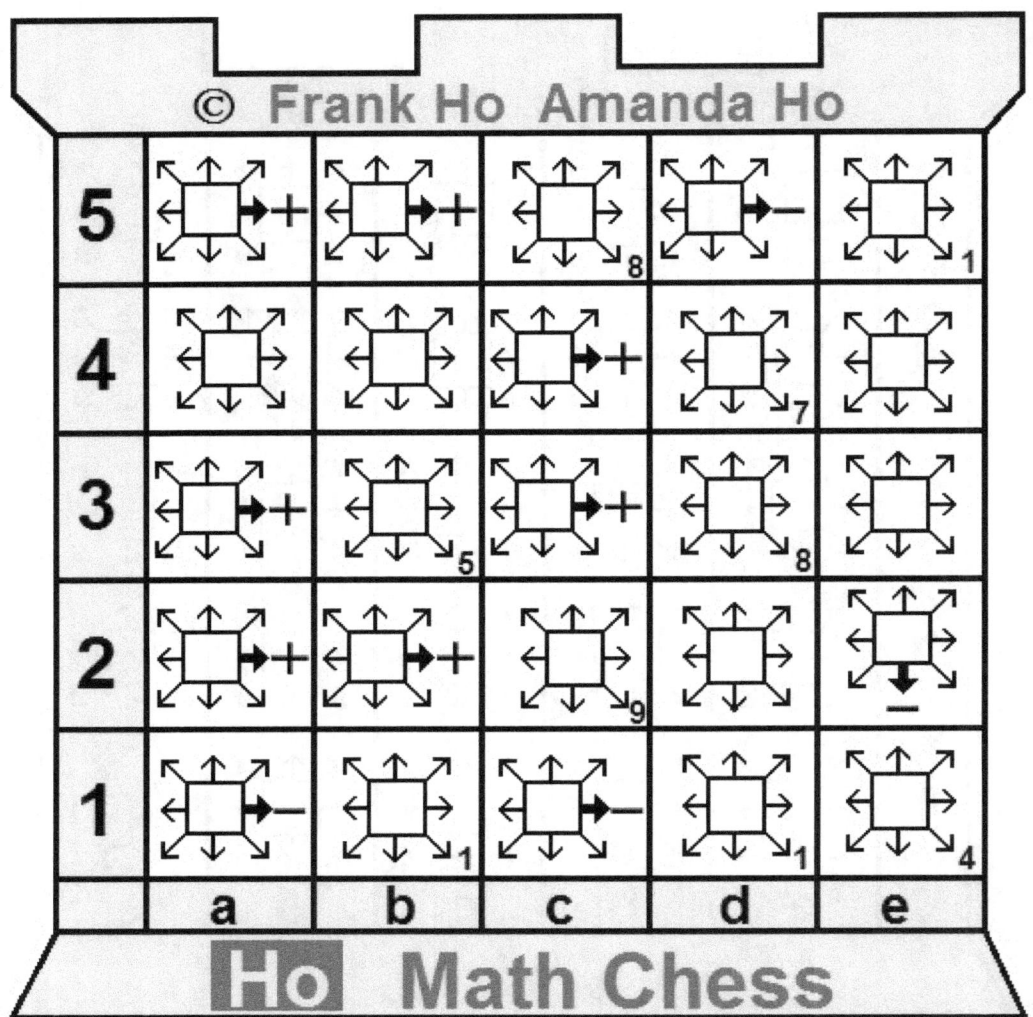

214

Ho Math Chess
何数棋谜 益智健脑非药物良方
Frankho Puzzle for KIDS – Brain Fitness Workbook

© 2007 — 2016 Frank Ho, Amanda Ho all rights reserved www.mathandchess.com

Frankho Puzzle™ # 211

Rule All the digits 1 to 5 must appear exactly once in every row and column. The number appears in the bottom right-hand corner is the end result calculated according to arithmetic operator(s) and chess move(s) as indicated by darker arrow(s).

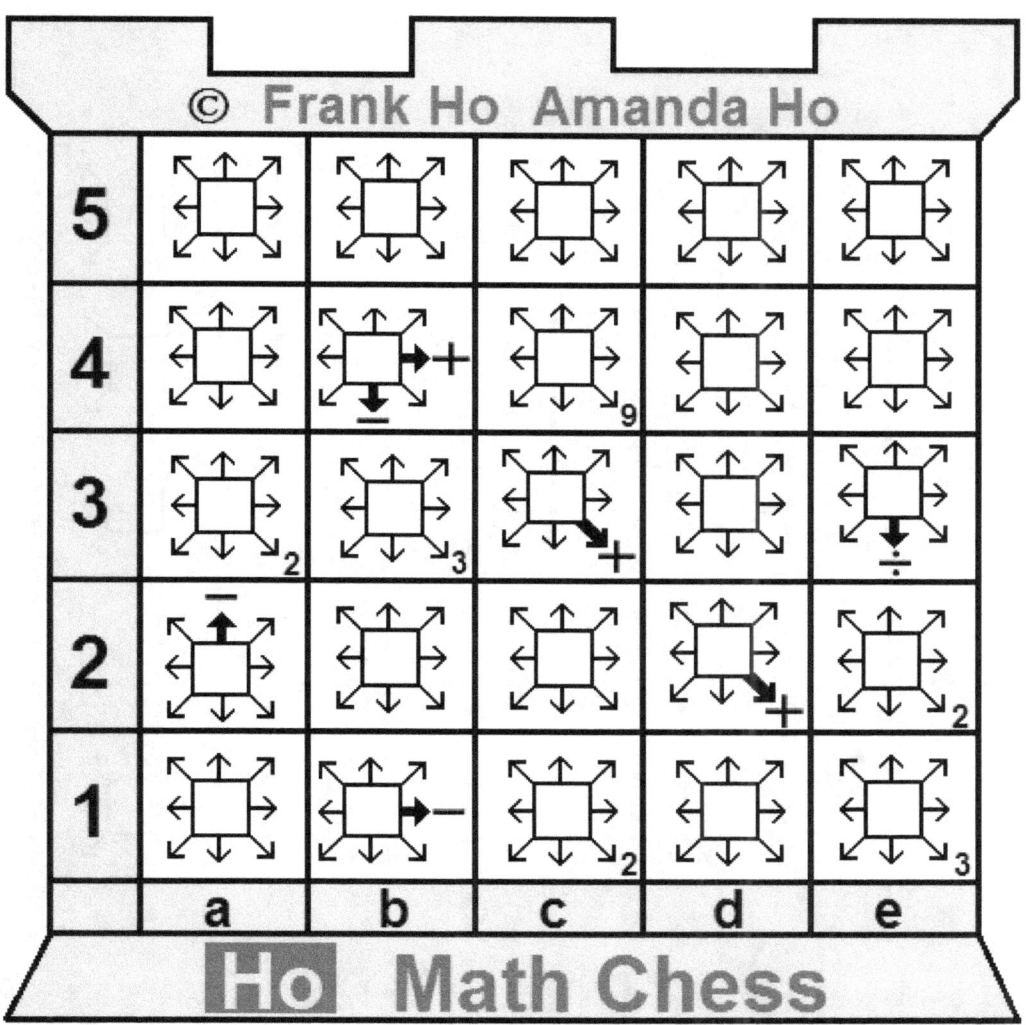

Ho Math Chess 何数棋谜 益智健脑非药物良方
Frankho Puzzle for KIDS – Brain Fitness Workbook

Frankho Puzzle™ # 212

Rule All the digits 1 to 5 must appear exactly once in every row and column. The number appears in the bottom right-hand corner is the end result calculated according to arithmetic operator(s) and chess move(s) as indicated by darker arrow(s).

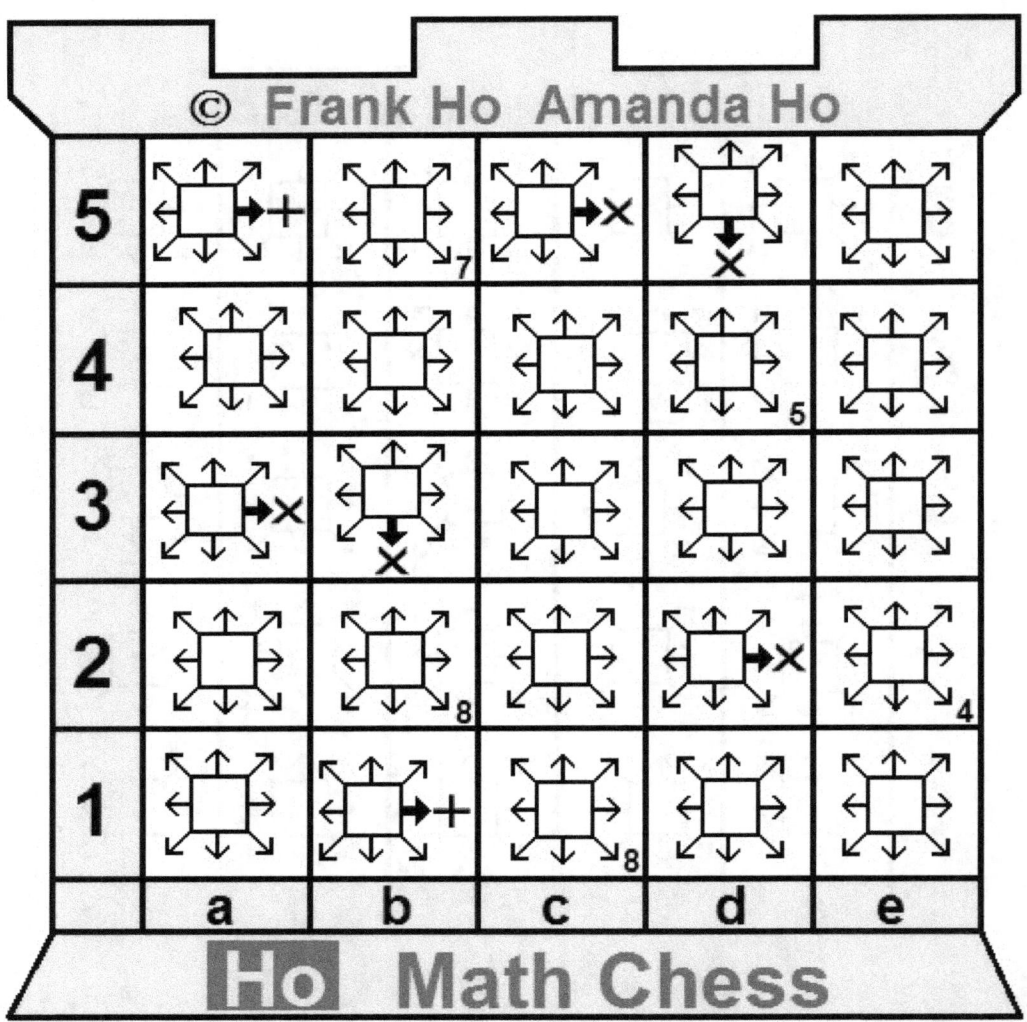

Ho Math Chess 何数棋谜 益智健脑非药物良方
Frankho Puzzle for KIDS – Brain Fitness Workbook
© 2007 — 2016 Frank Ho, Amanda Ho all rights reserved www.mathandchess.com

Frankho Puzzle™ # 213

Rule All the digits 1 to 5 must appear exactly once in every row and column. The number appears in the bottom right-hand corner is the end result calculated according to arithmetic operator(s) and chess move(s) as indicated by darker arrow(s).

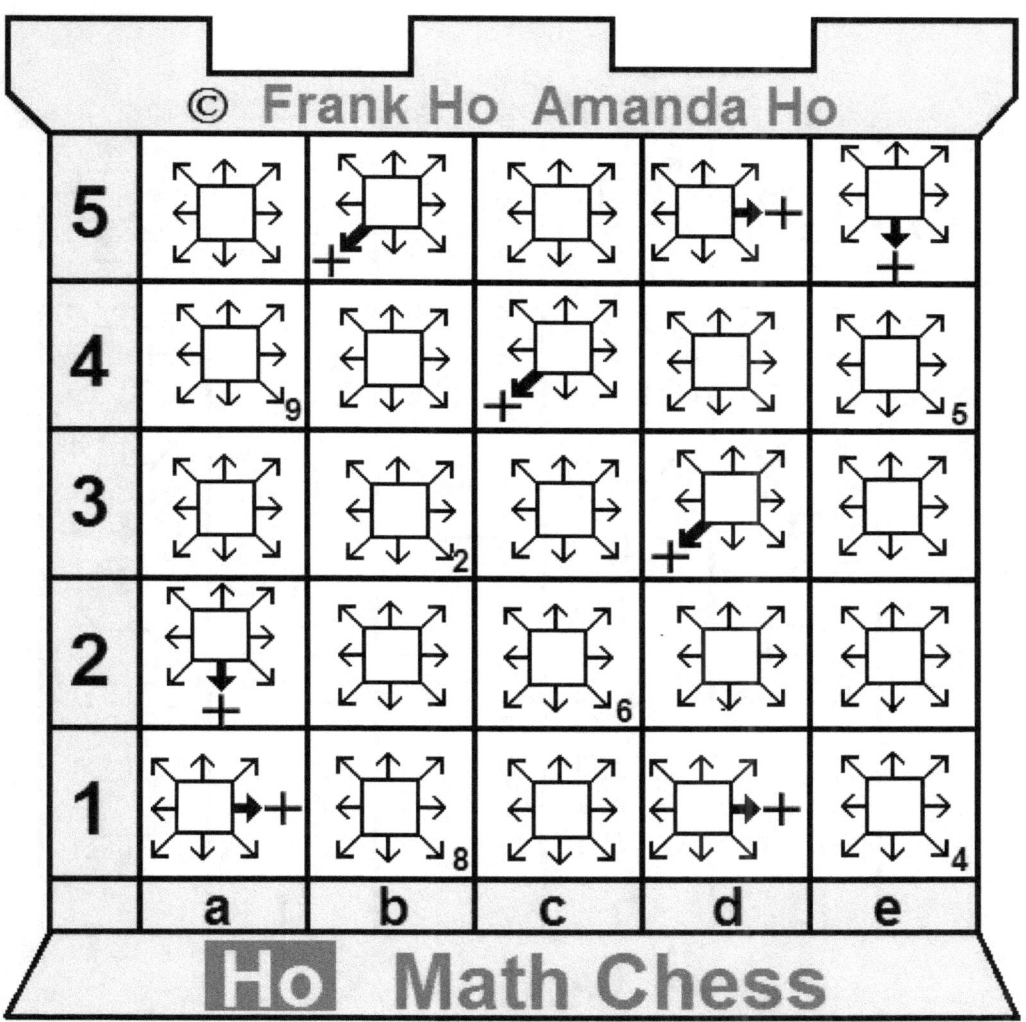

Frankho Puzzle™ # 214

Rule All the digits 1 to 5 must appear exactly once in every row and column. The number appears in the bottom right-hand corner is the end result calculated according to arithmetic operator(s) and chess move(s) as indicated by darker arrow(s).

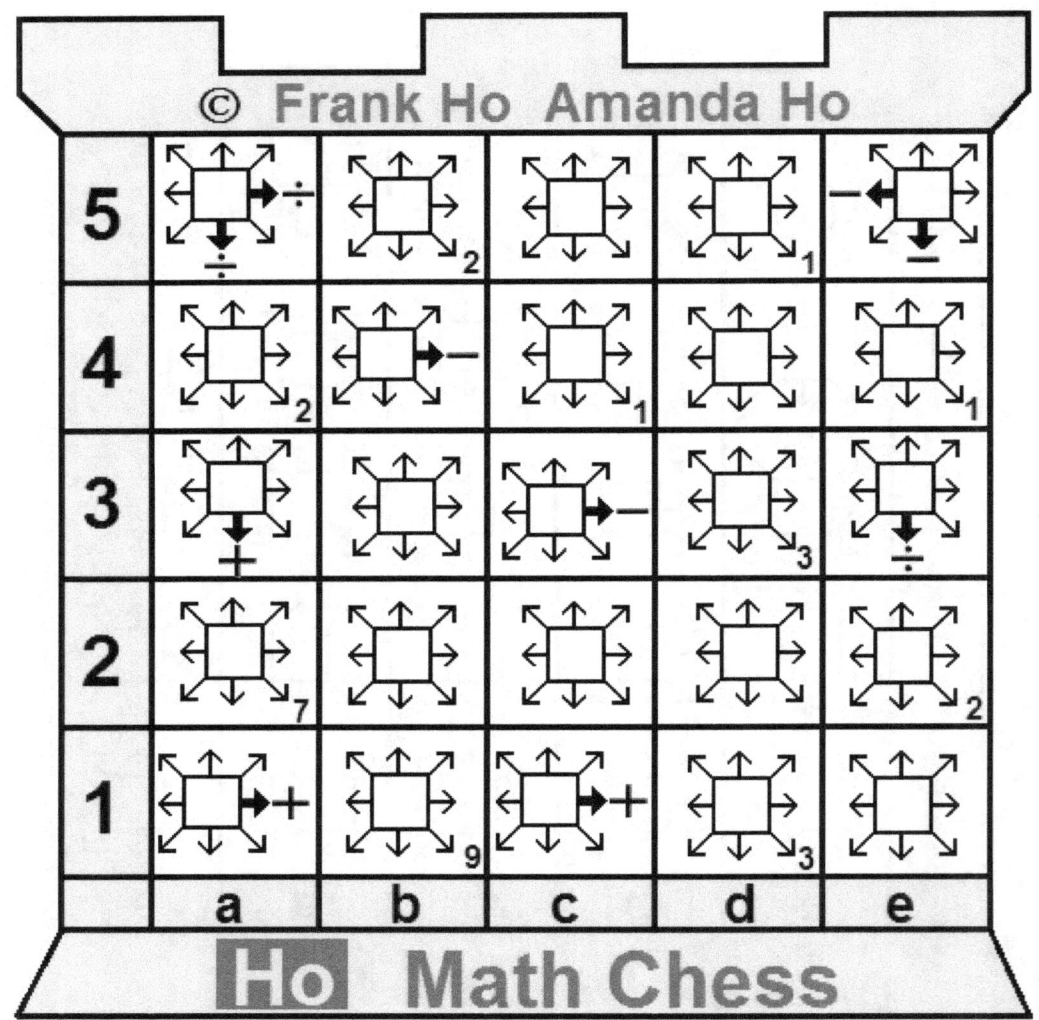

Frankho Puzzle™ # 215

Rule All the digits 1 to 5 must appear exactly once in every row and column. The number appears in the bottom right-hand corner is the end result calculated according to arithmetic operator(s) and chess move(s) as indicated by darker arrow(s).

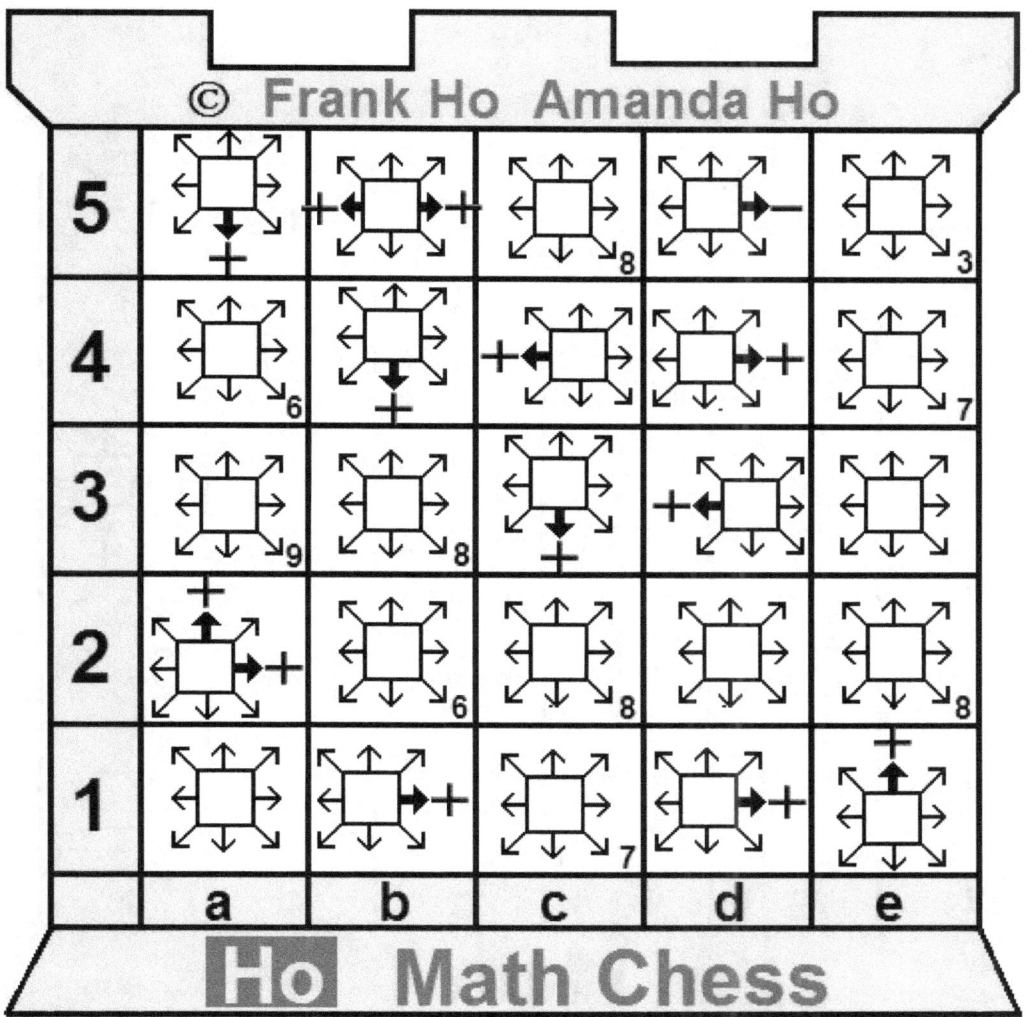

Ho Math Chess 何数棋谜 益智健脑非药物良方
Frankho Puzzle for KIDS – Brain Fitness Workbook
© 2007 — 2016 Frank Ho, Amanda Ho all rights reserved www.mathandchess.com

Frankho Puzzle™ # 216

Rule All the digits 1 to 5 must appear exactly once in every row and column. The number appears in the bottom right-hand corner is the end result calculated according to arithmetic operator(s) and chess move(s) as indicated by darker arrow(s).

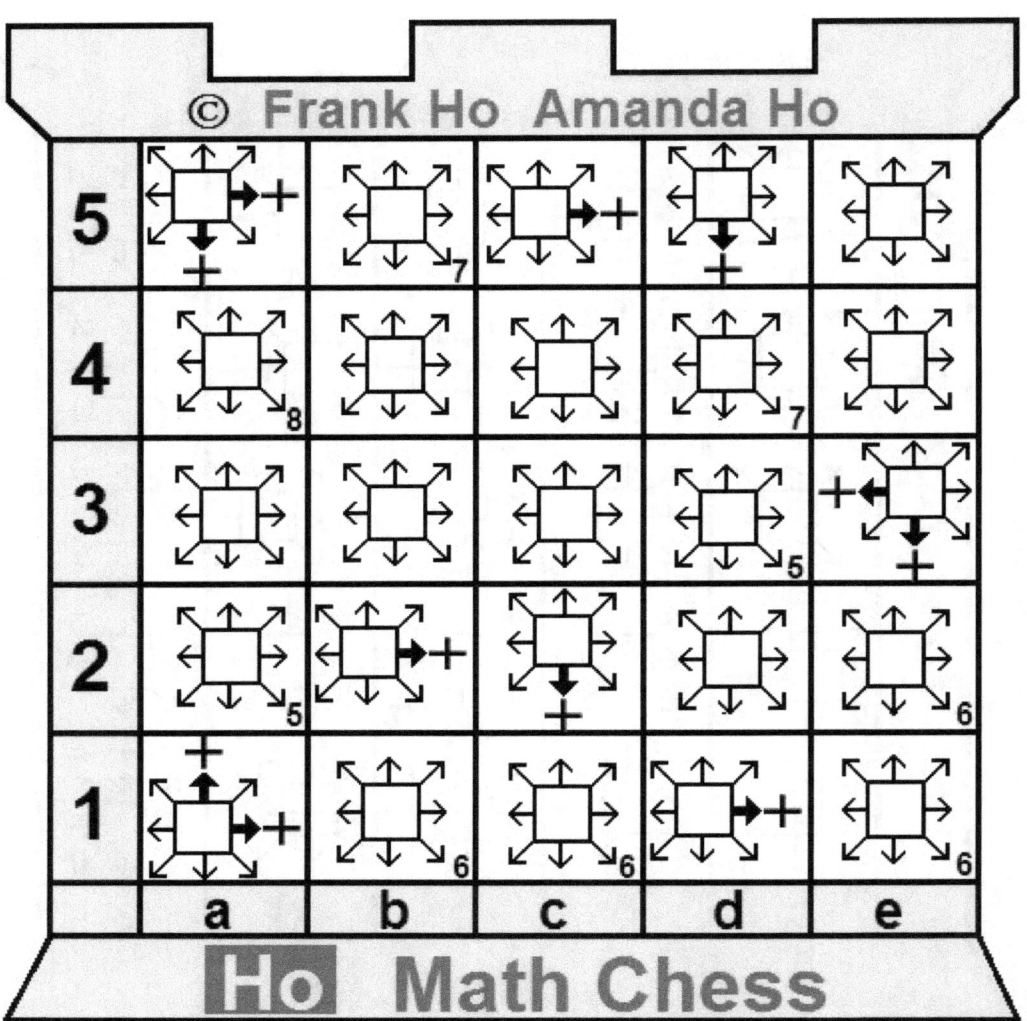

Frankho Puzzle™ # 217

Rule All the digits 1 to 5 must appear exactly once in every row and column. The number appears in the bottom right-hand corner is the end result calculated according to arithmetic operator(s) and chess move(s) as indicated by darker arrow(s).

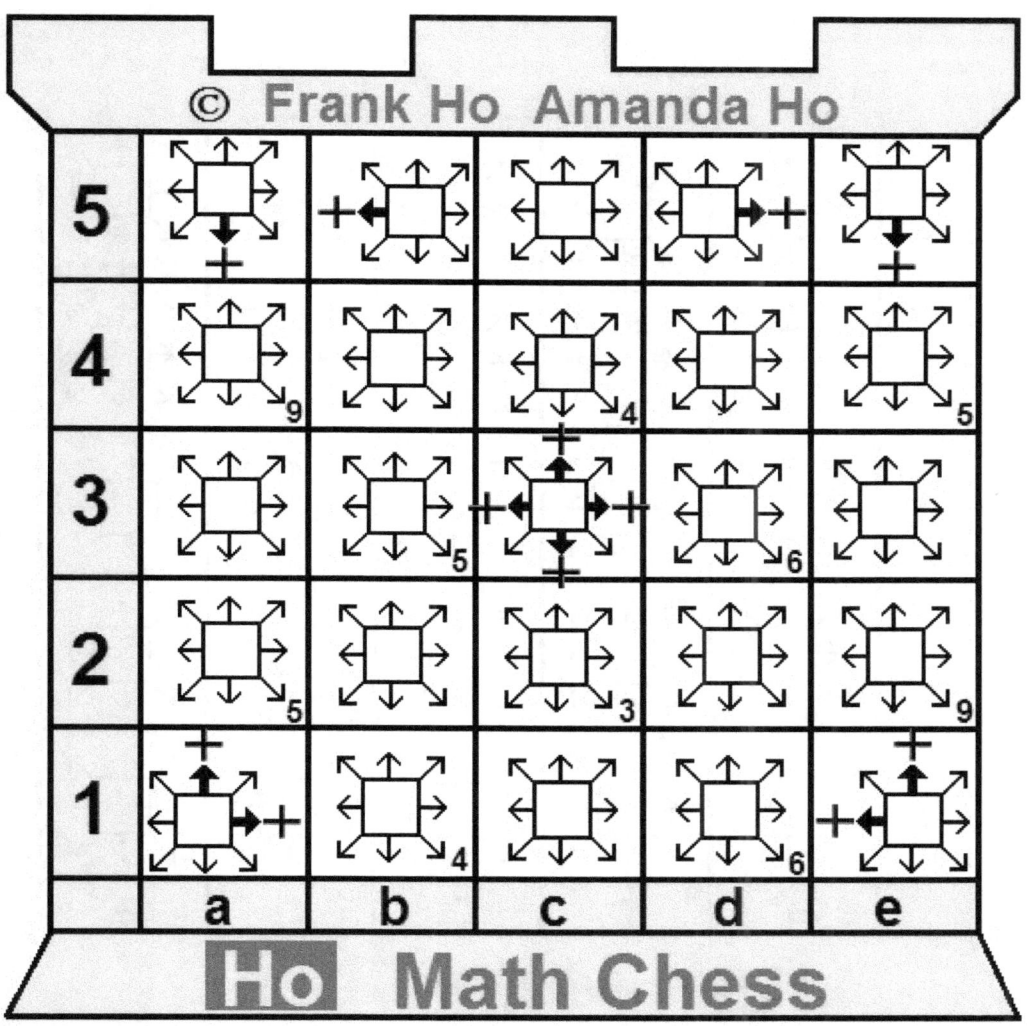

Frankho Puzzle™ # 218

Rule All the digits 1 to 5 must appear exactly once in every row and column. The number appears in the bottom right-hand corner is the end result calculated according to arithmetic operator(s) and chess move(s) as indicated by darker arrow(s).

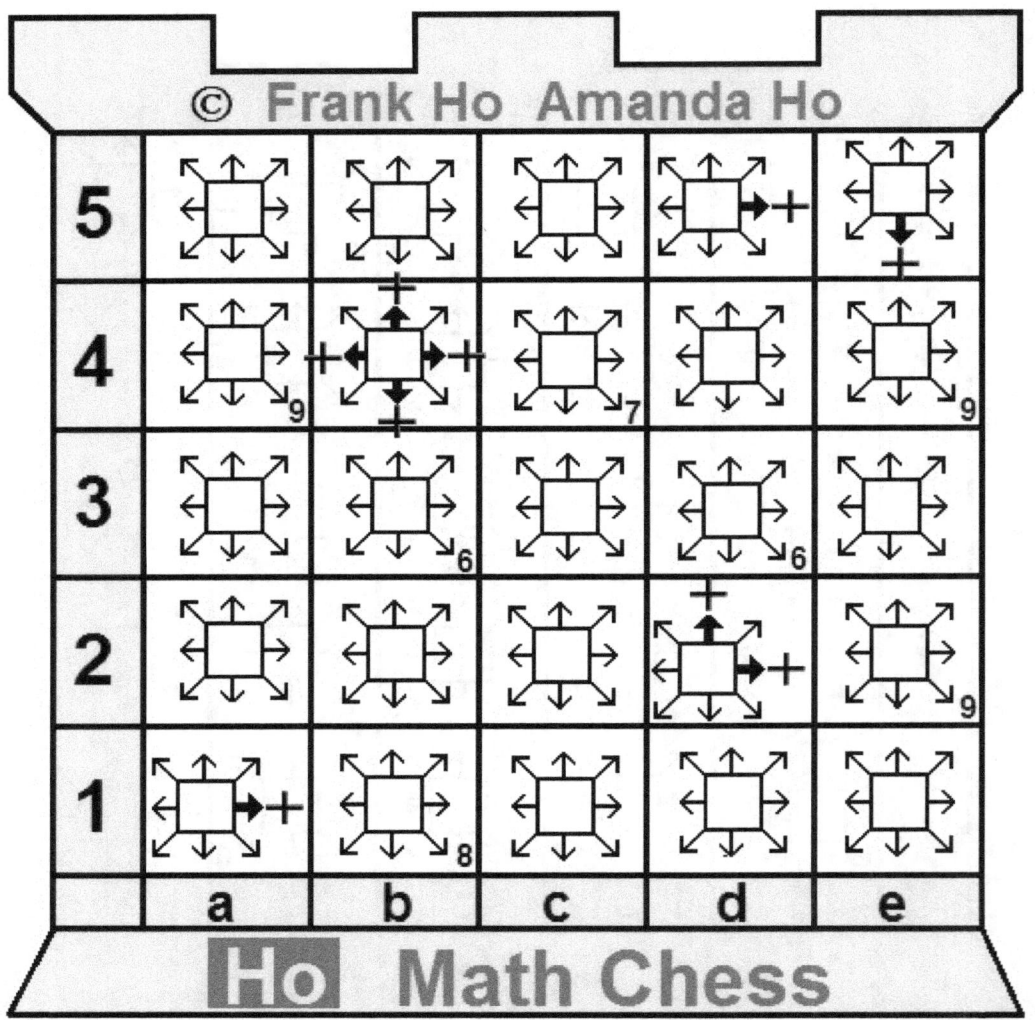

Ho Math Chess 何数棋谜 益智健脑非药物良方
Frankho Puzzle for KIDS – Brain Fitness Workbook

© 2007 – 2016 Frank Ho, Amanda Ho all rights reserved www.mathandchess.com

Frankho Puzzle™ # 219

Rule All the digits 1 to 5 must appear exactly once in every row and column. The number appears in the bottom right-hand corner is the end result calculated according to arithmetic operator(s) and chess move(s) as indicated by darker arrow(s).

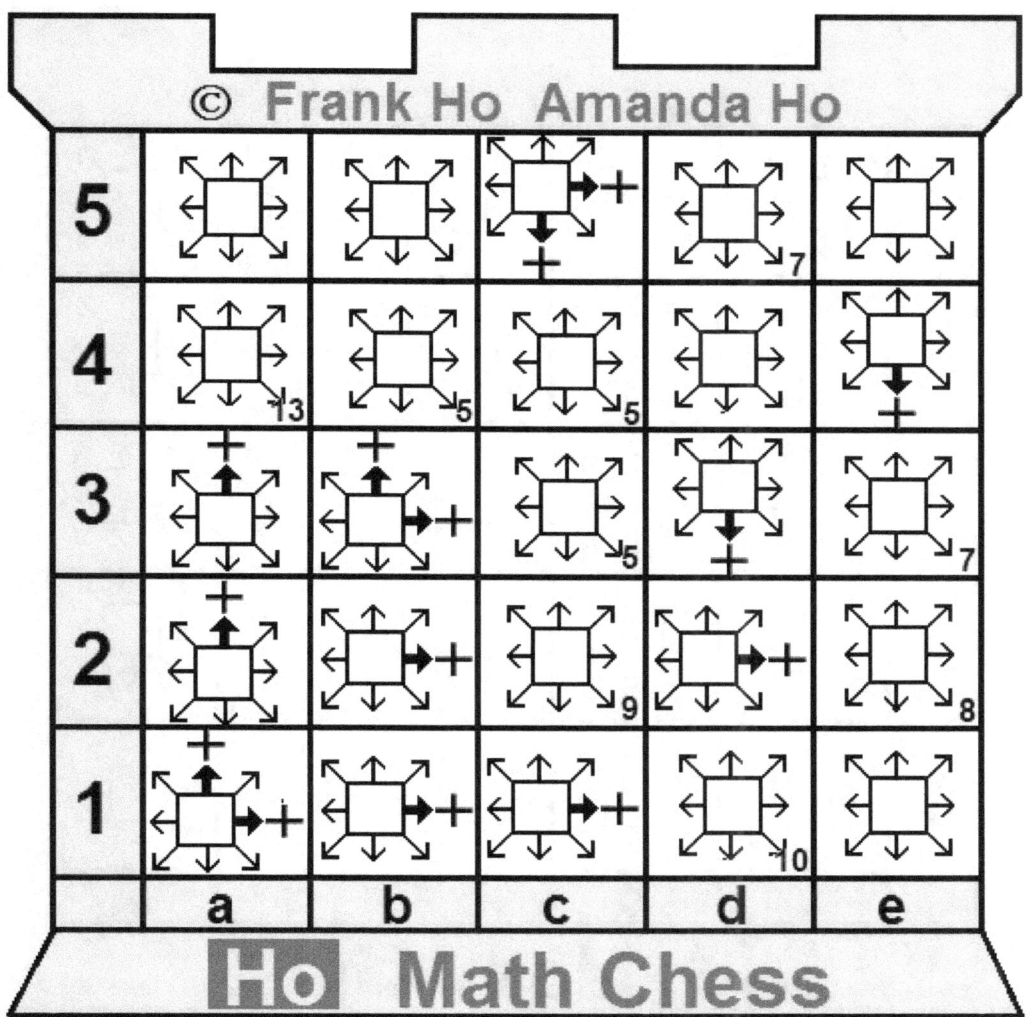

Ho Math Chess 何数棋谜 益智健脑非药物良方
Frankho Puzzle for KIDS – Brain Fitness Workbook
© 2007 — 2016 Frank Ho, Amanda Ho all rights reserved www.mathandchess.com

Frankho Puzzle™ # 220

Rule All the digits 1 to 5 must appear exactly once in every row and column. The number appears in the bottom right-hand corner is the end result calculated according to arithmetic operator(s) and chess move(s) as indicated by darker arrow(s).

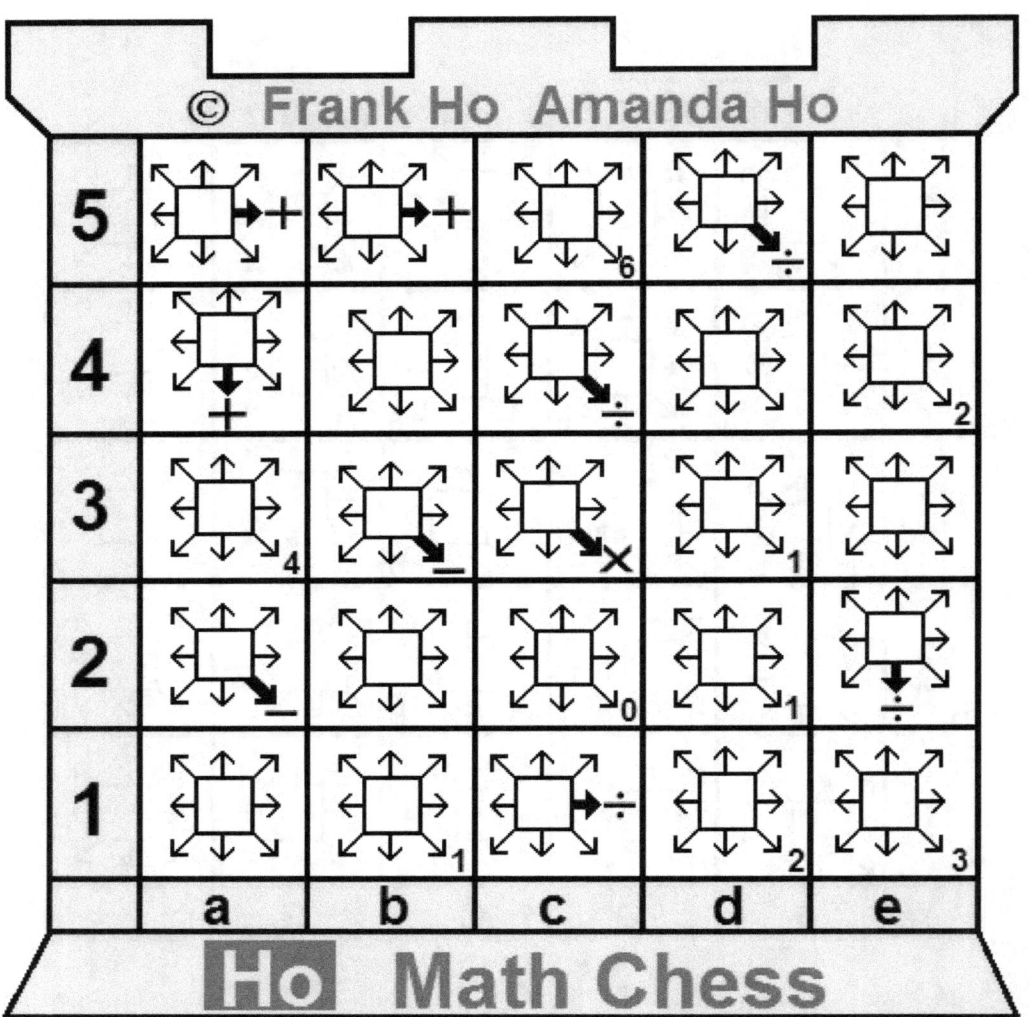

Frankho Puzzle™ # 221

Rule All the digits 1 to 5 must appear exactly once in every row and column. The number appears in the bottom right-hand corner is the end result calculated according to arithmetic operator(s) and chess move(s) as indicated by darker arrow(s).

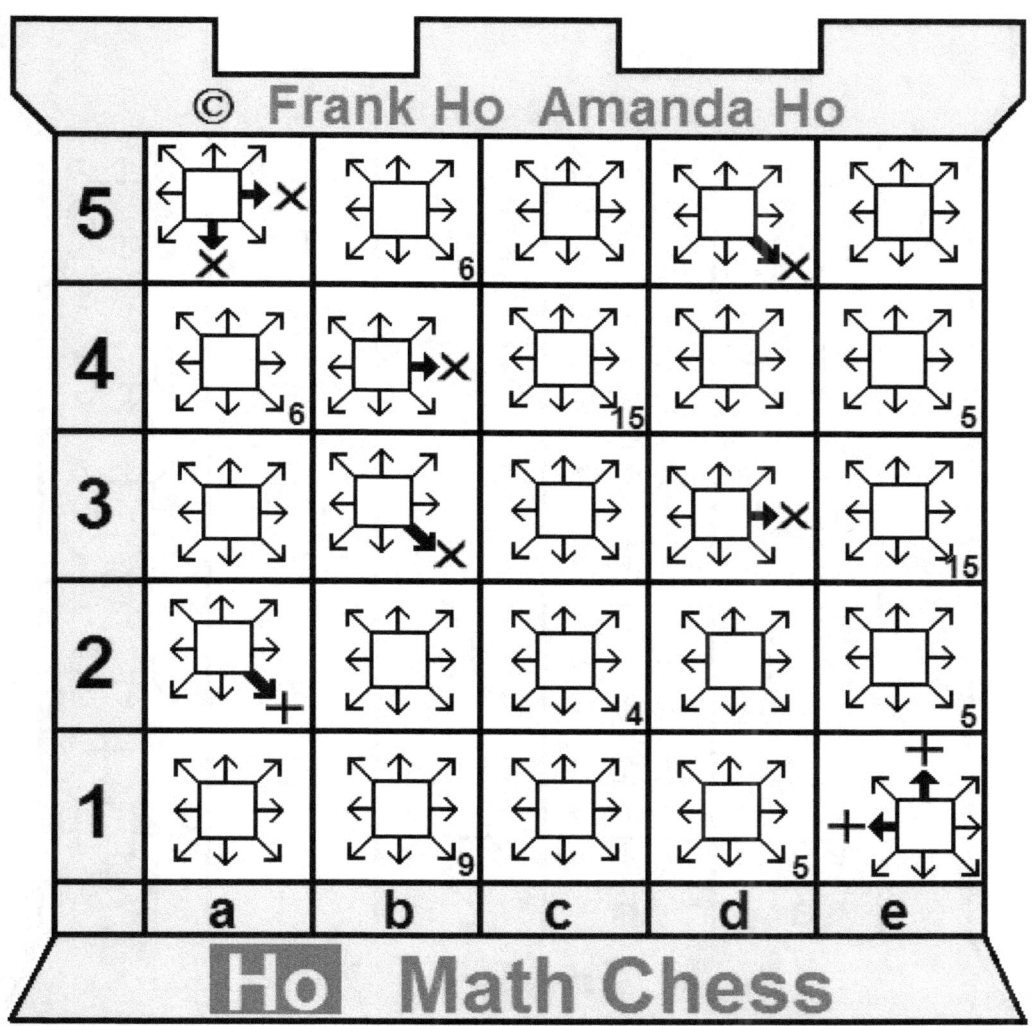

Ho Math Chess 何数棋谜 益智健脑非药物良方
Frankho Puzzle for KIDS – Brain Fitness Workbook
© 2007 — 2016 Frank Ho, Amanda Ho all rights reserved www.mathandchess.com

Frankho Puzzle™ # 222

Rule All the digits 1 to 5 must appear exactly once in every row and column. The number appears in the bottom right-hand corner is the end result calculated according to arithmetic operator(s) and chess move(s) as indicated by darker arrow(s).

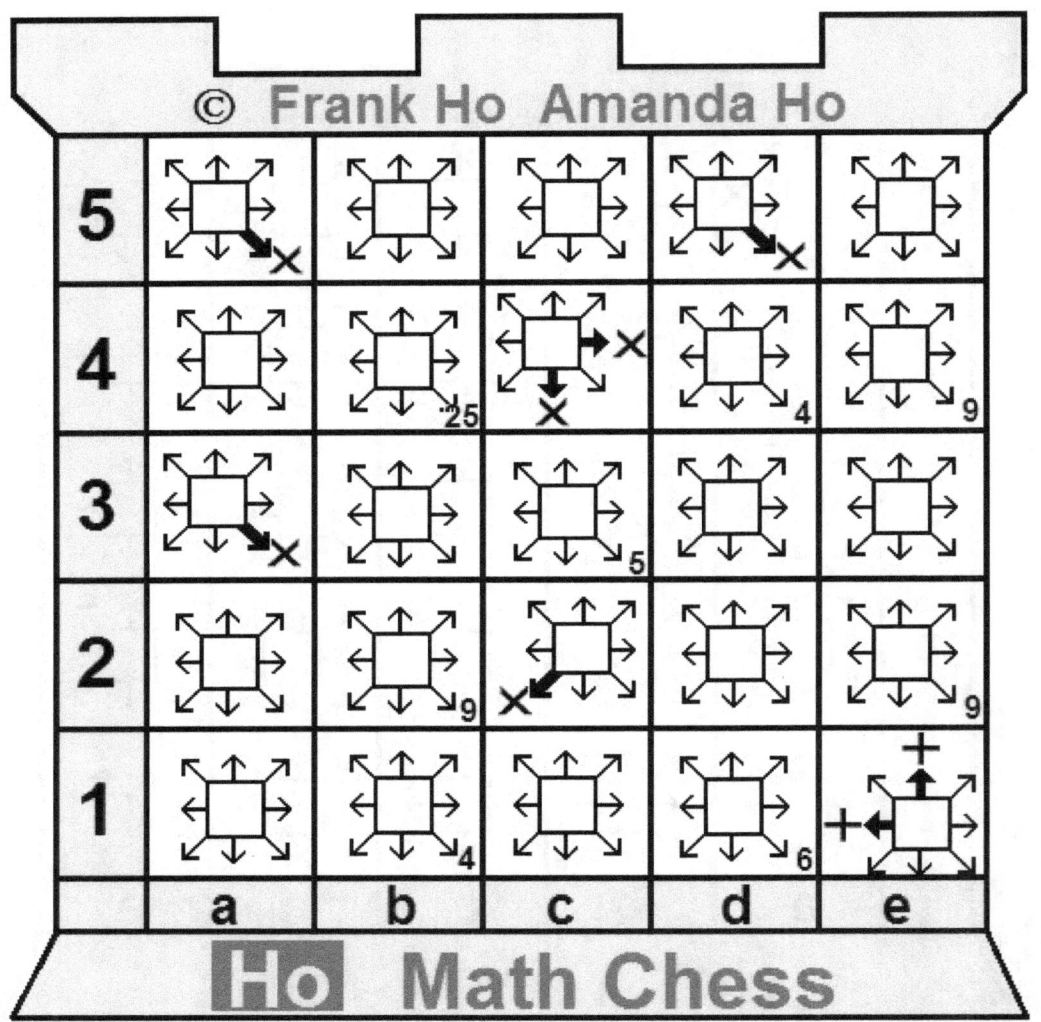

Ho Math Chess 何数棋谜 益智健脑非药物良方
Frankho Puzzle for KIDS – Brain Fitness Workbook
© 2007 — 2016 Frank Ho, Amanda Ho all rights reserved www.mathandchess.com

Frankho Puzzle™ # 223

Rule All the digits 1 to 5 must appear exactly once in every row and column. The number appears in the bottom right-hand corner is the end result calculated according to arithmetic operator(s) and chess move(s) as indicated by darker arrow(s).

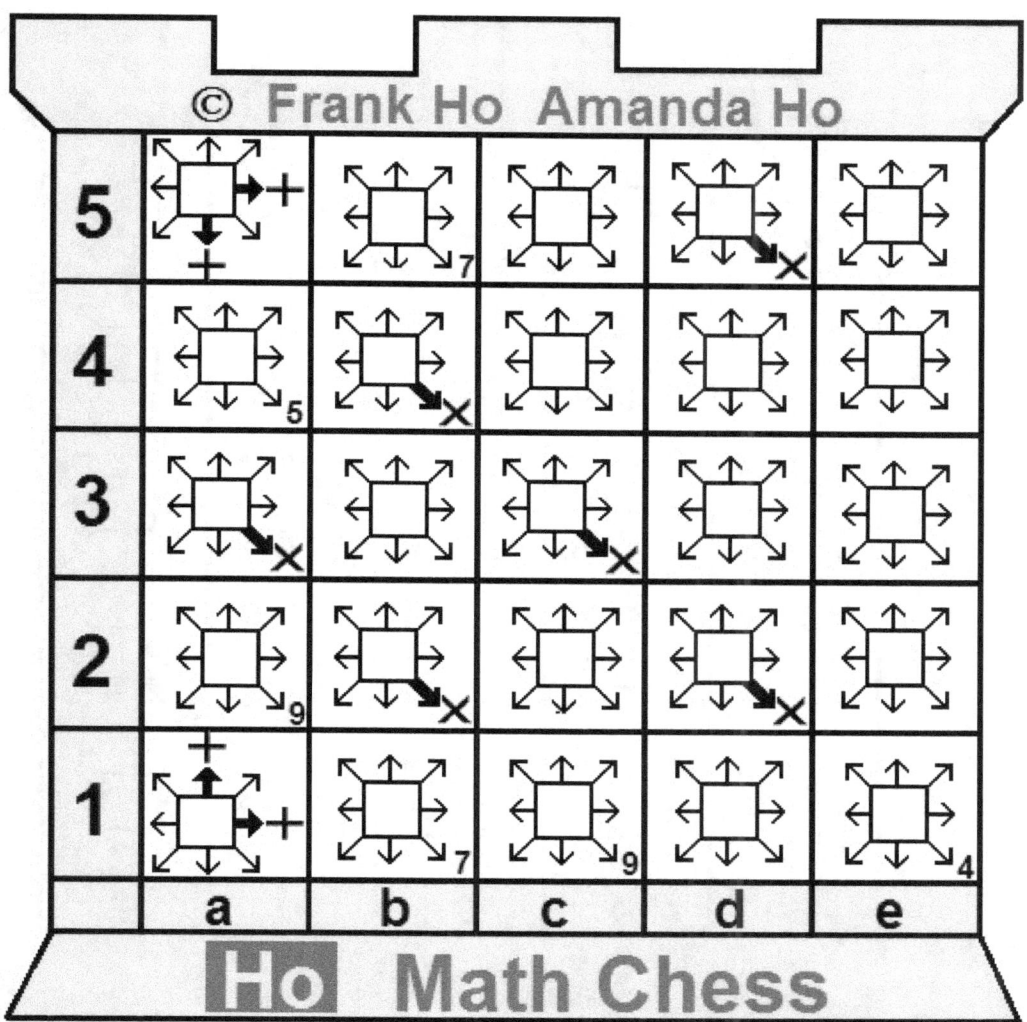

Ho Math Chess 何数棋谜 益智健脑非药物良方
Frankho Puzzle for KIDS – Brain Fitness Workbook
© 2007 — 2016 Frank Ho, Amanda Ho all rights reserved www.mathandchess.com

Frankho Puzzle™ # 224

Rule All the digits 1 to 5 must appear exactly once in every row and column. The number appears in the bottom right-hand corner is the end result calculated according to arithmetic operator(s) and chess move(s) as indicated by darker arrow(s).

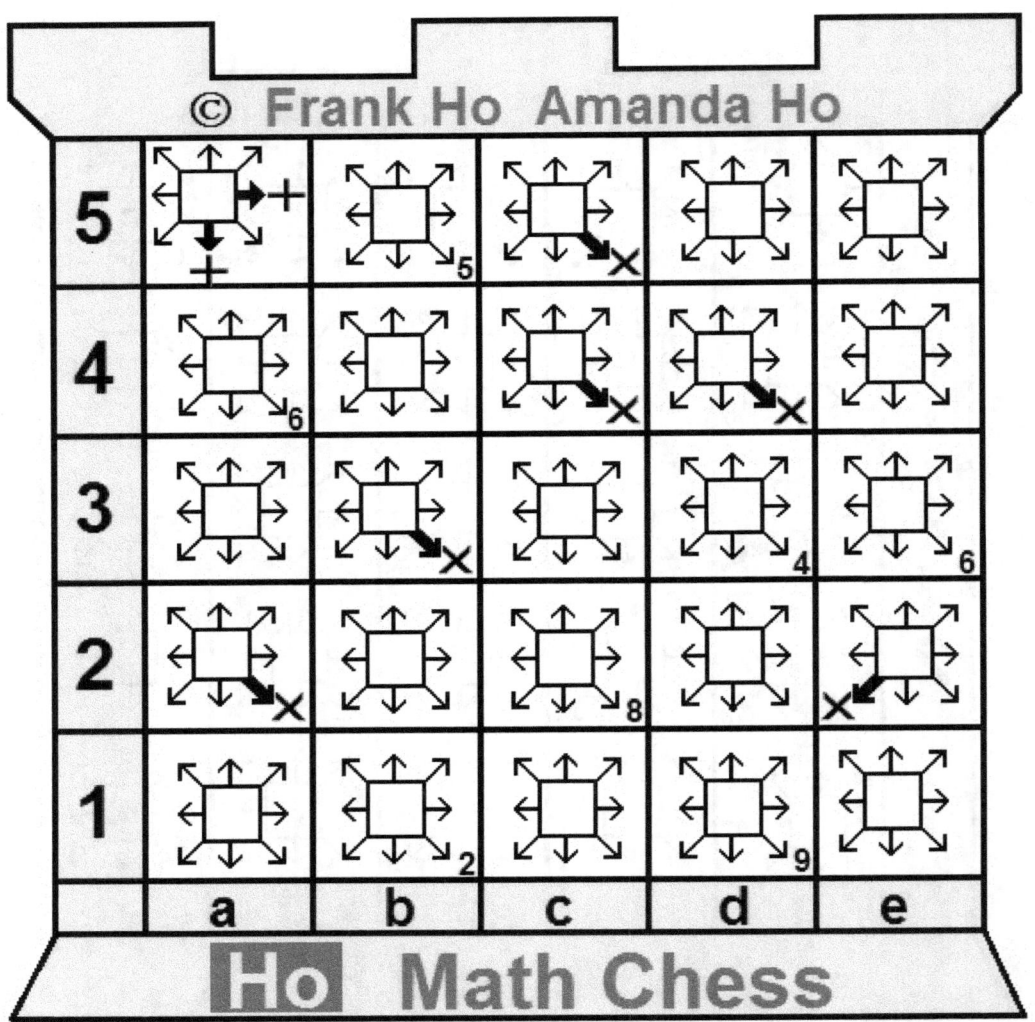

Ho Math Chess 何数棋谜 益智健脑非药物良方
Frankho Puzzle for KIDS – Brain Fitness Workbook
© 2007 — 2016 Frank Ho, Amanda Ho all rights reserved www.mathandchess.com

Frankho Puzzle™ # 225

Rule All the digits 1 to 5 must appear exactly once in every row and column. The number appears in the bottom right-hand corner is the end result calculated according to arithmetic operator(s) and chess move(s) as indicated by darker arrow(s).

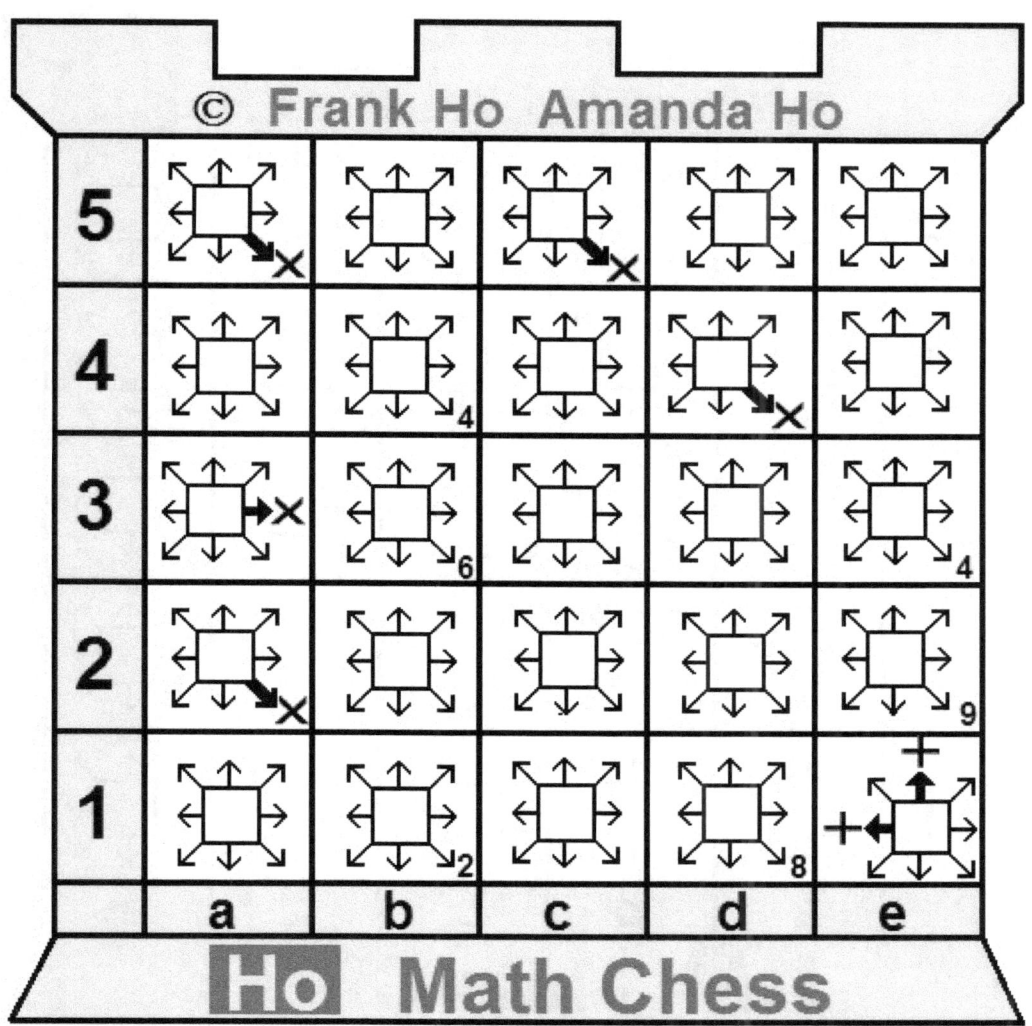

Frankho Puzzle™ # 226

Rule All the digits 1 to 5 must appear exactly once in every row and column. The number appears in the bottom right-hand corner is the end result calculated according to arithmetic operator(s) and chess move(s) as indicated by darker arrow(s).

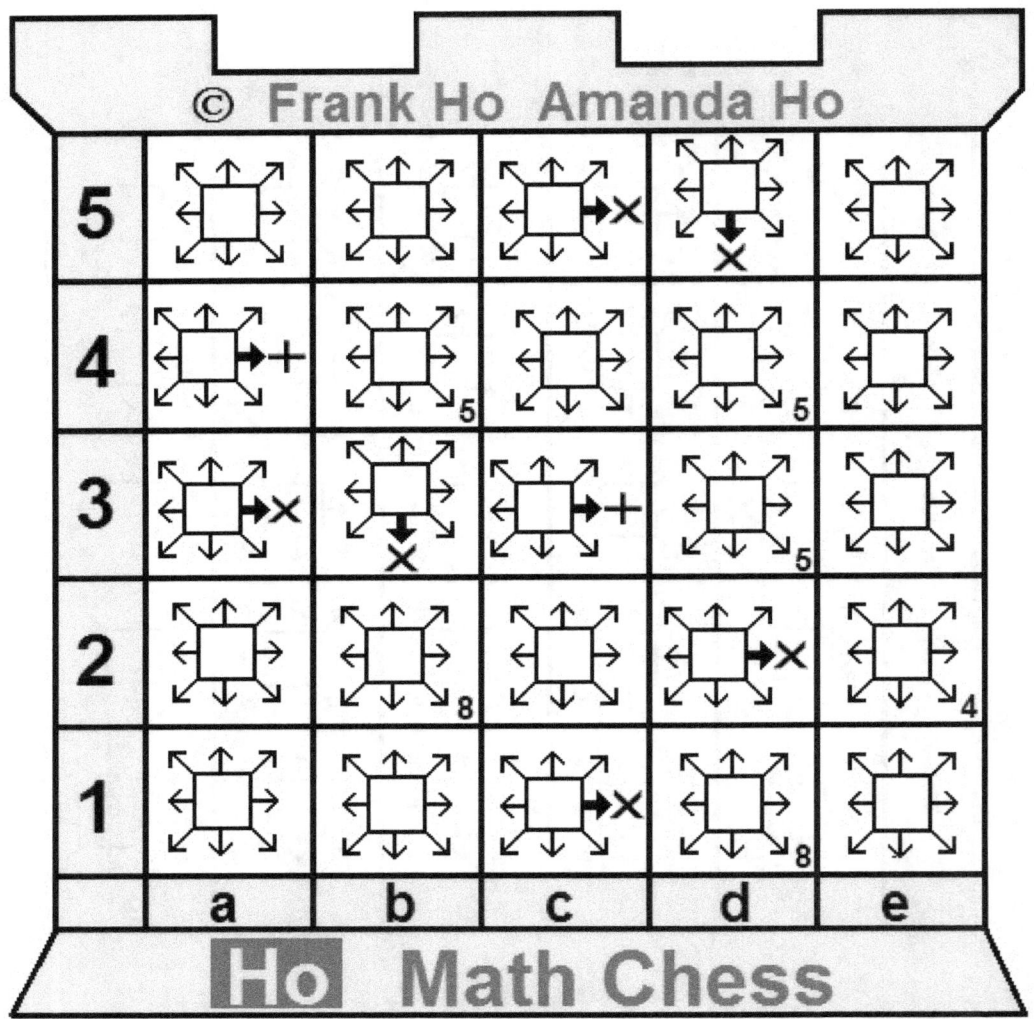

Ho Math Chess 何数棋谜 益智健脑非药物良方
Frankho Puzzle for KIDS – Brain Fitness Workbook
© 2007 – 2016 Frank Ho, Amanda Ho all rights reserved www.mathandchess.com

Frankho Puzzle™ # 227

Rule All the digits 1 to 5 must appear exactly once in every row and column. The number appears in the bottom right-hand corner is the end result calculated according to arithmetic operator(s) and chess move(s) as indicated by darker arrow(s).

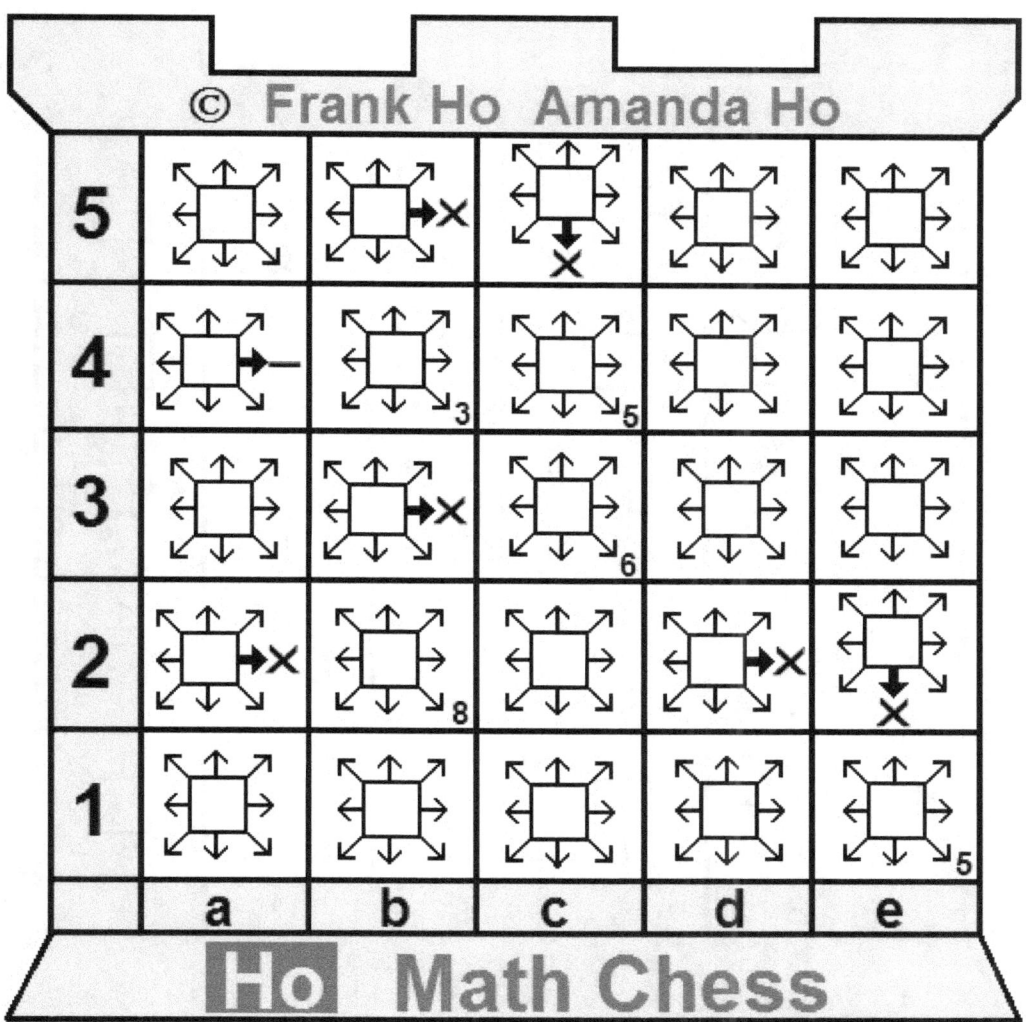

Ho Math Chess 何数棋谜 益智健脑非药物良方
Frankho Puzzle for KIDS – Brain Fitness Workbook

© 2007 — 2016 Frank Ho, Amanda Ho all rights reserved www.mathandchess.com

Frankho Puzzle™ # 228

Rule All the digits 1 to 5 must appear exactly once in every row and column. The number appears in the bottom right-hand corner is the end result calculated according to arithmetic operator(s) and chess move(s) as indicated by darker arrow(s).

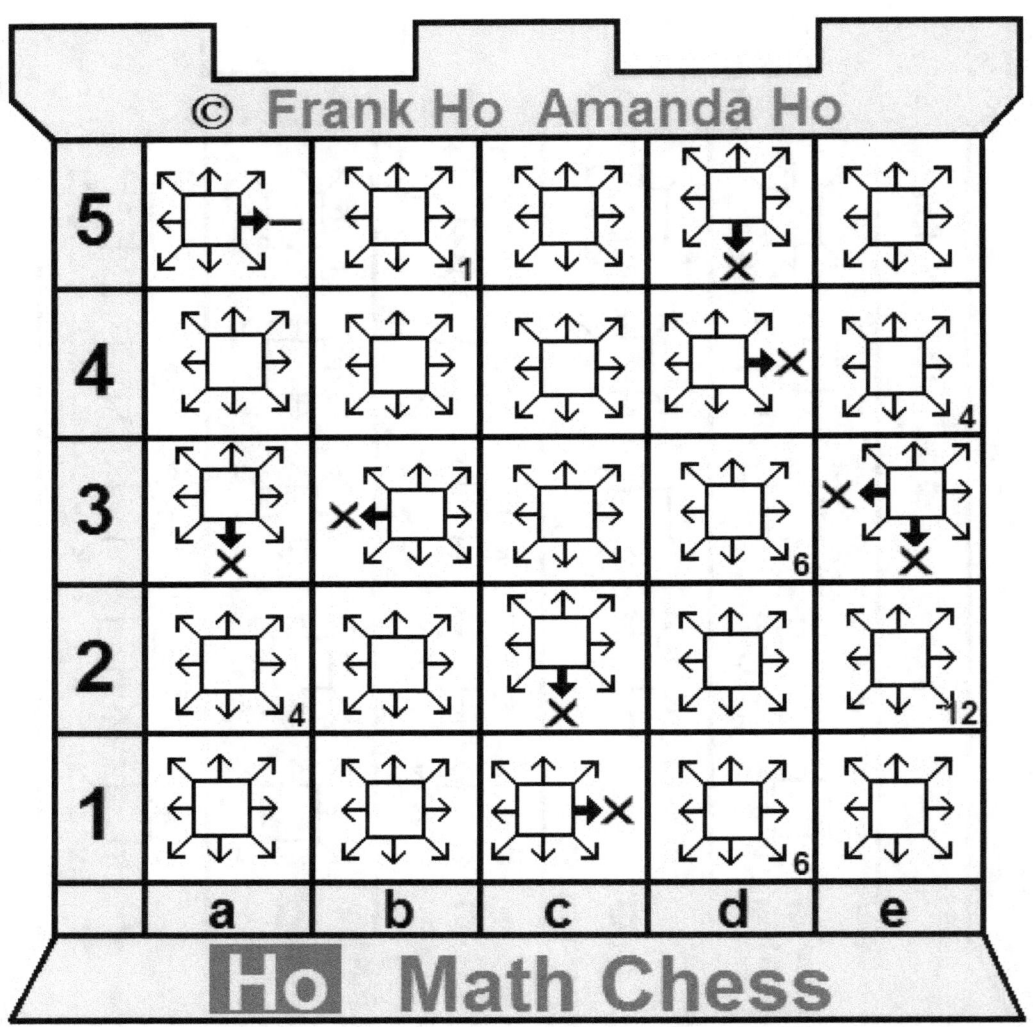

Ho Math Chess 何数棋谜 益智健脑非药物良方
Frankho Puzzle for KIDS − Brain Fitness Workbook
© 2007 — 2016 Frank Ho, Amanda Ho all rights reserved www.mathandchess.com

Frankho Puzzle™ # 229

Rule All the digits 1 to 5 must appear exactly once in every row and column. The number appears in the bottom right-hand corner is the end result calculated according to arithmetic operator(s) and chess move(s) as indicated by darker arrow(s).

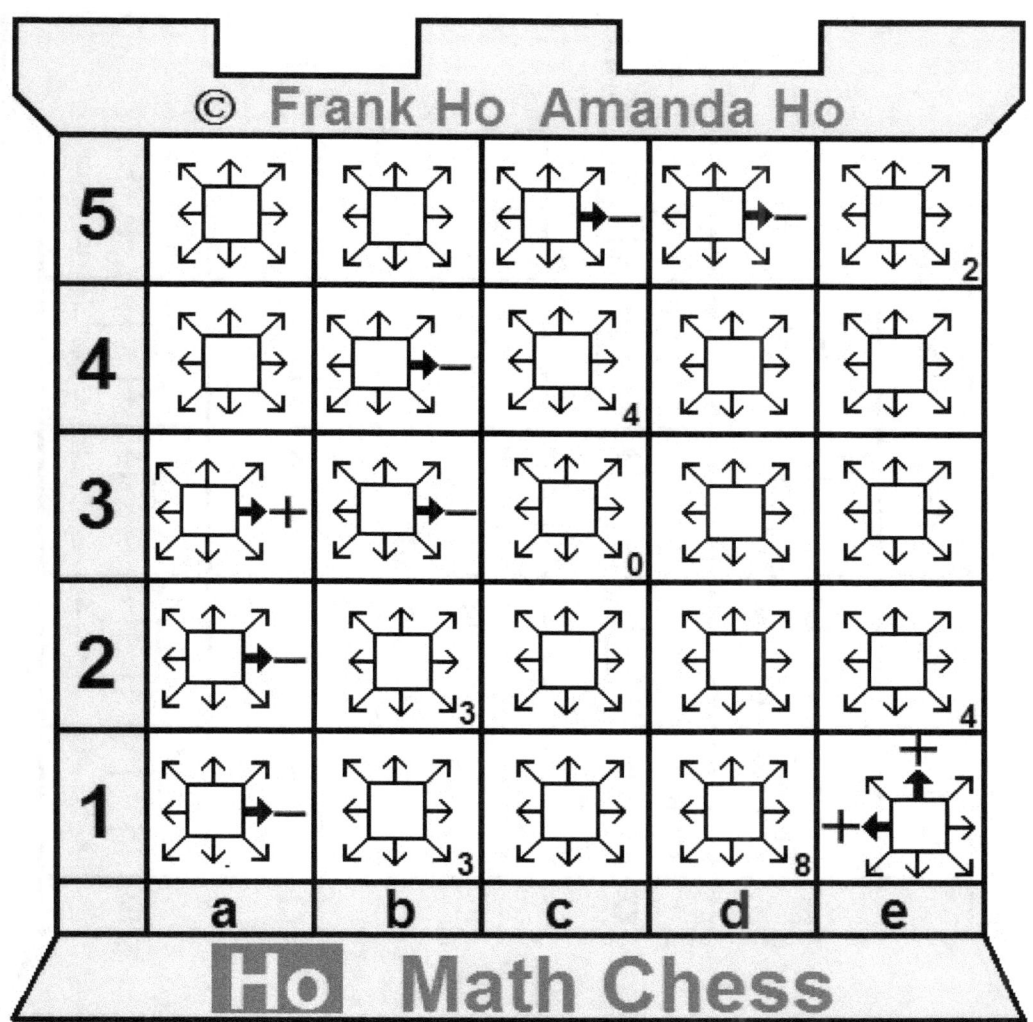

Ho Math Chess 何数棋谜 益智健脑非药物良方
Frankho Puzzle for KIDS – Brain Fitness Workbook
© 2007 — 2016 Frank Ho, Amanda Ho all rights reserved www.mathandchess.com

Frankho Puzzle™ # 230

Rule All the digits 1 to 5 must appear exactly once in every row and column. The number appears in the bottom right-hand corner is the end result calculated according to arithmetic operator(s) and chess move(s) as indicated by darker arrow(s).

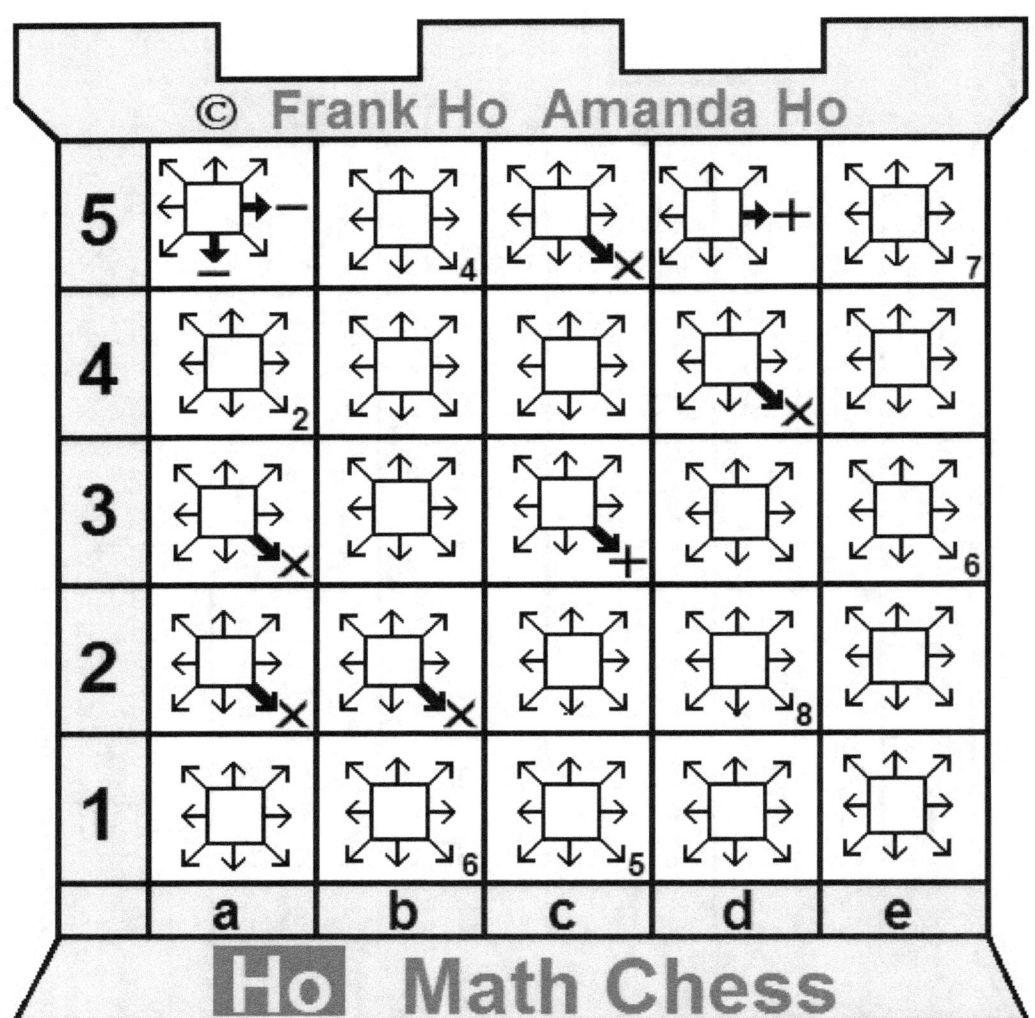

Ho Math Chess 何数棋谜 益智健脑非药物良方
Frankho Puzzle for KIDS – Brain Fitness Workbook
© 2007 — 2016 Frank Ho, Amanda Ho all rights reserved www.mathandchess.com

Frankho Puzzle™ # 231

Rule All the digits 1 to 5 must appear exactly once in every row and column. The number appears in the bottom right-hand corner is the end result calculated according to arithmetic operator(s) and chess move(s) as indicated by darker arrow(s).

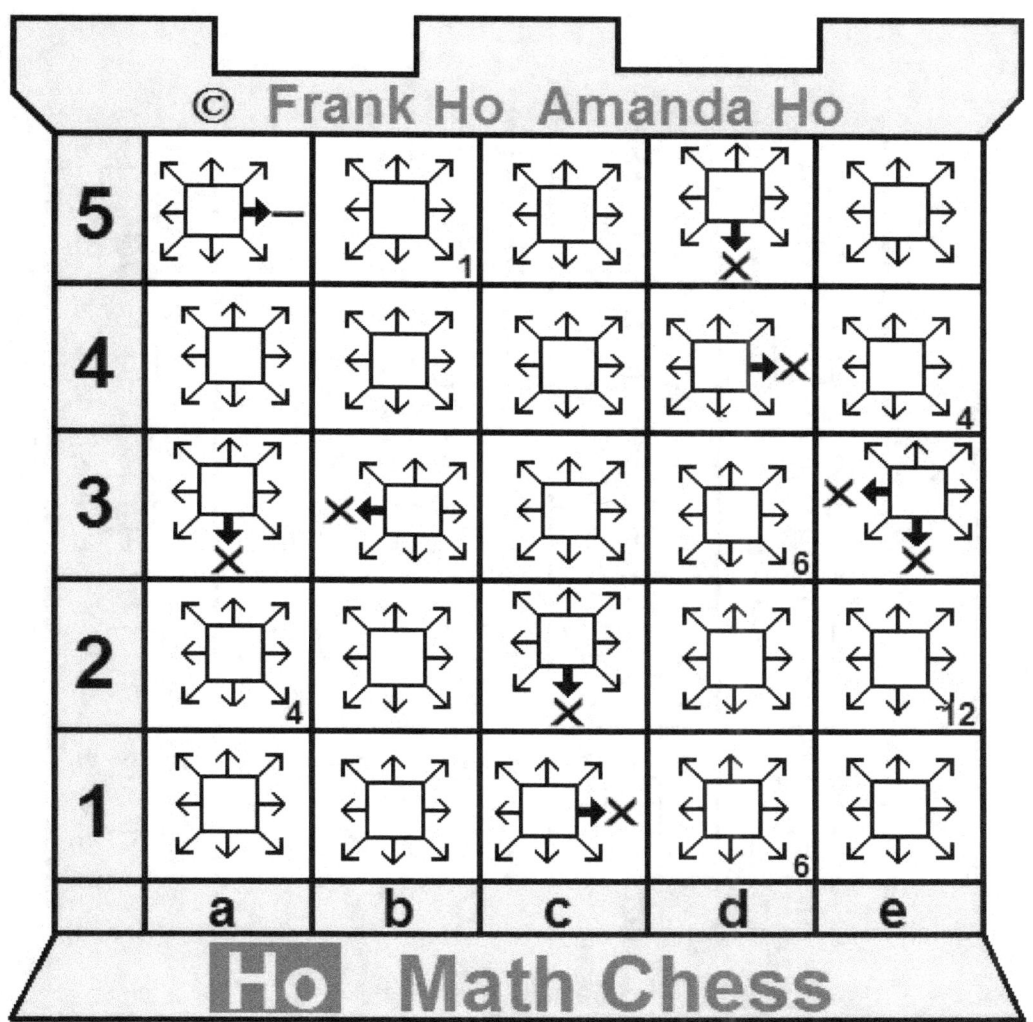

Ho Math Chess 何数棋谜 益智健脑非药物良方
Frankho Puzzle for KIDS – Brain Fitness Workbook
© 2007 — 2016 Frank Ho, Amanda Ho all rights reserved www.mathandchess.com

Frankho Puzzle™ # 232

Rule All the digits 1 to 5 must appear exactly once in every row and column. The number appears in the bottom right-hand corner is the end result calculated according to arithmetic operator(s) and chess move(s) as indicated by darker arrow(s).

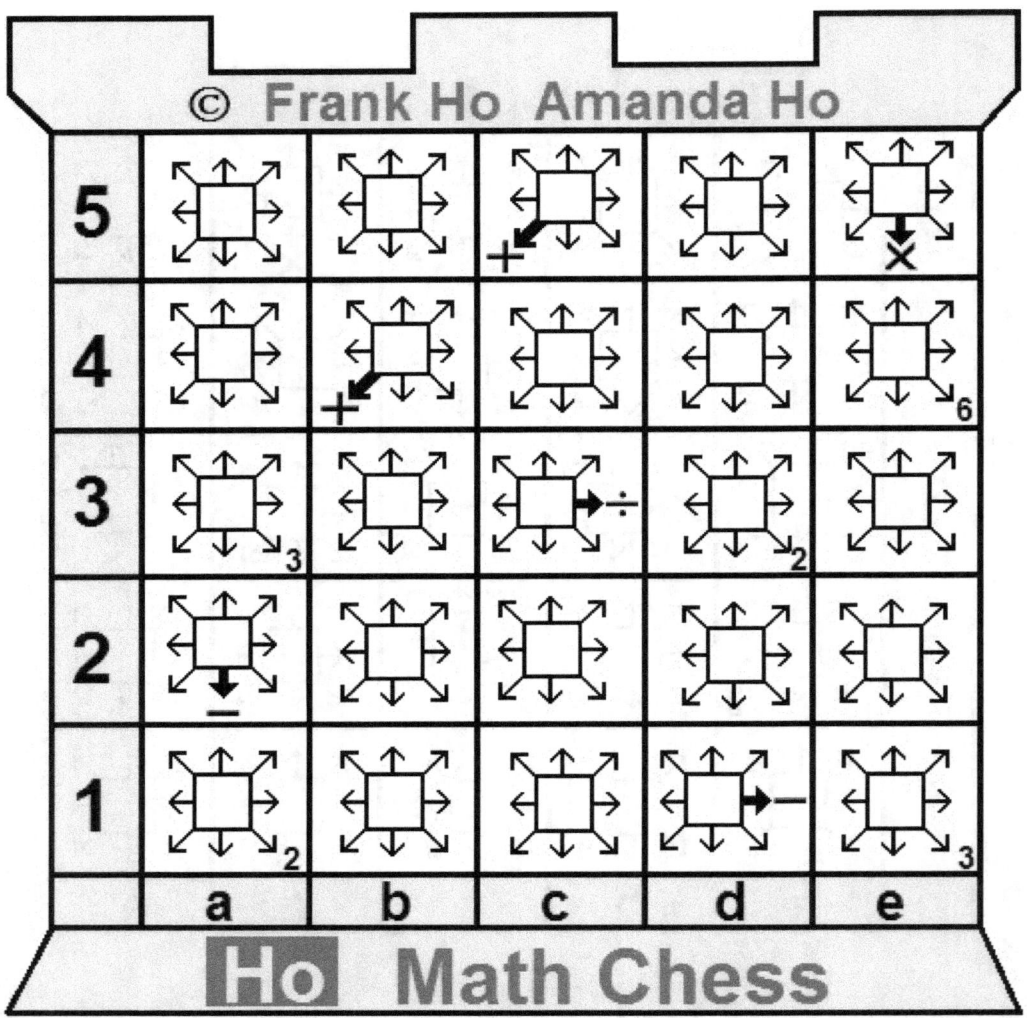

Ho Math Chess 何数棋谜 益智健脑非药物良方
Frankho Puzzle for KIDS – Brain Fitness Workbook
© 2007 — 2016 Frank Ho, Amanda Ho all rights reserved www.mathandchess.com

Frankho Puzzle™ # 233

Rule All the digits 1 to 5 must appear exactly once in every row and column. The number appears in the bottom right-hand corner is the end result calculated according to arithmetic operator(s) and chess move(s) as indicated by darker arrow(s).

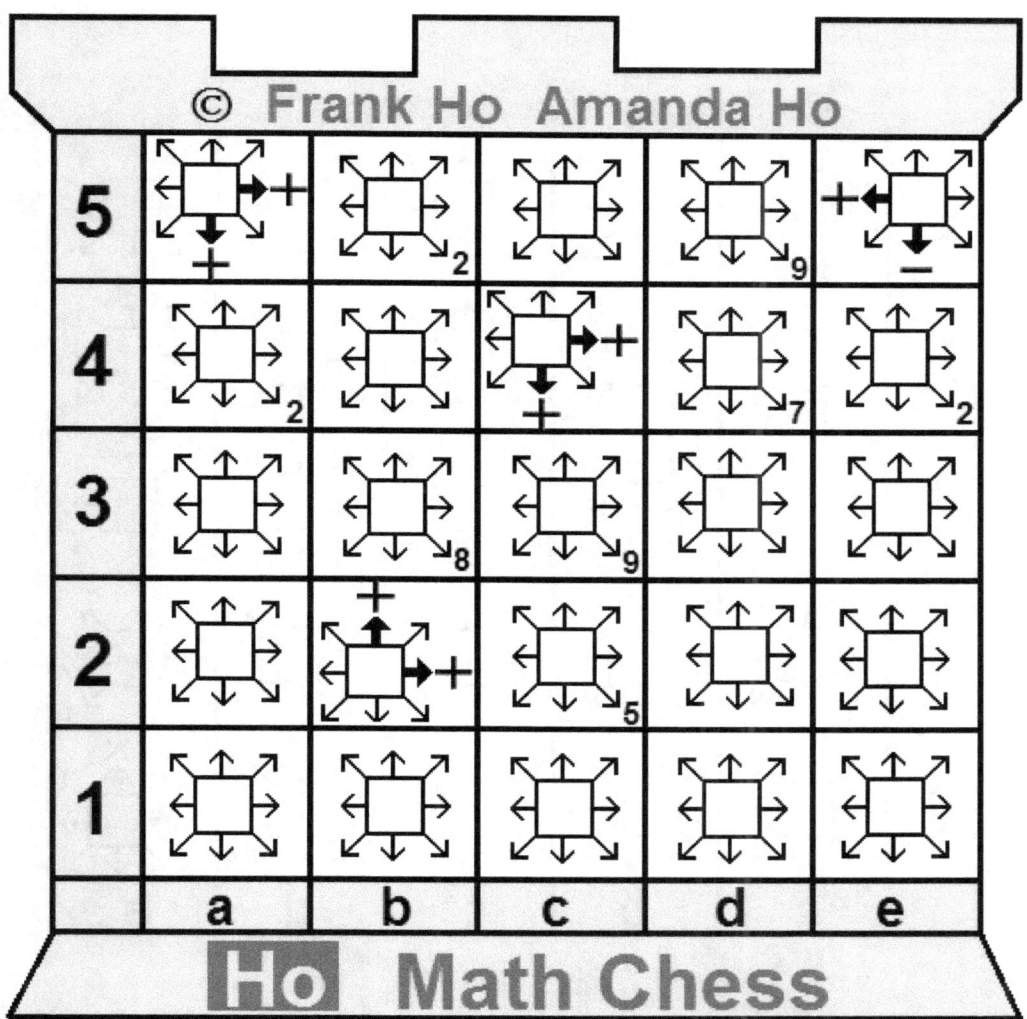

Ho Math Chess 何数棋谜 益智健脑非药物良方
Frankho Puzzle for KIDS – Brain Fitness Workbook
© 2007 – 2016 Frank Ho, Amanda Ho all rights reserved www.mathandchess.com

Frankho Puzzle™ # 234

Rule All the digits 1 to 5 must appear exactly once in every row and column. The number appears in the bottom right-hand corner is the end result calculated according to arithmetic operator(s) and chess move(s) as indicated by darker arrow(s).

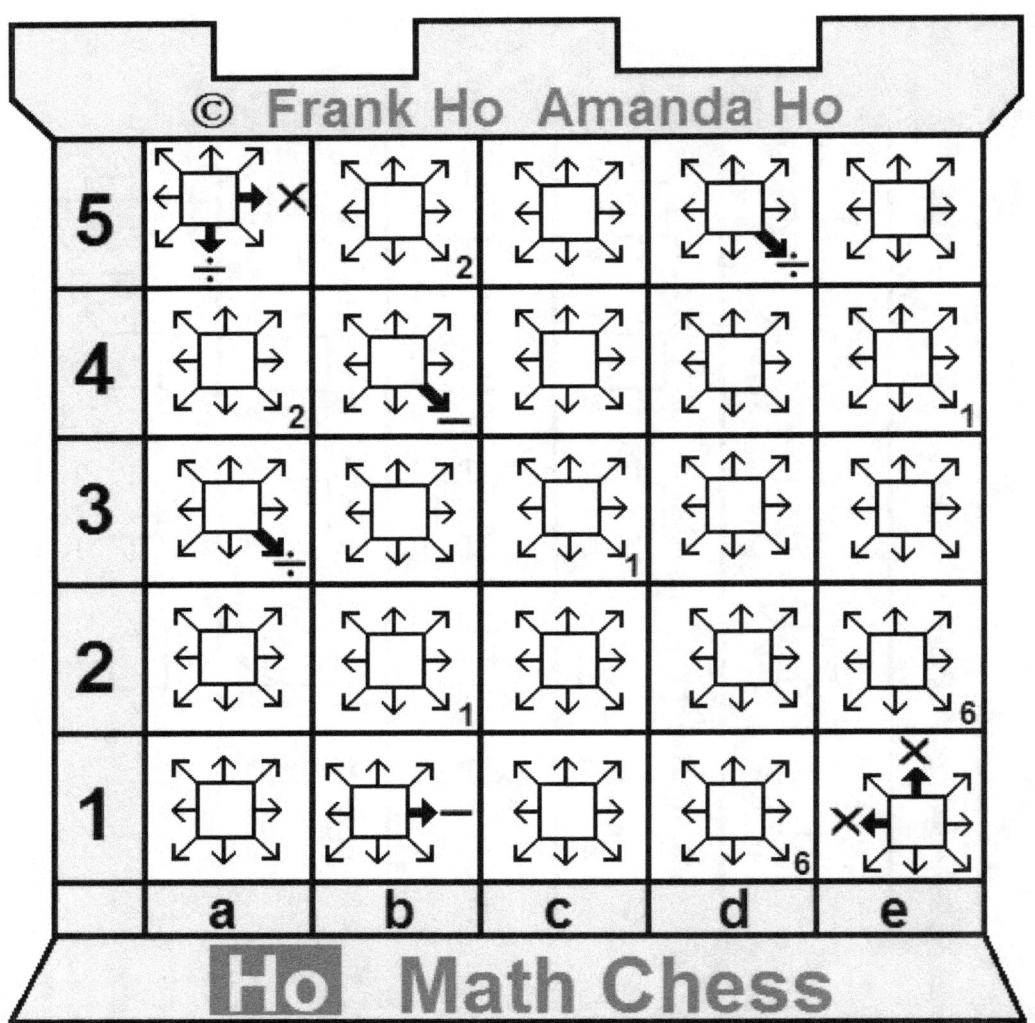

Ho Math Chess 何数棋谜 益智健脑非药物良方
Frankho Puzzle for KIDS – Brain Fitness Workbook

© 2007 – 2016 Frank Ho, Amanda Ho all rights reserved www.mathandchess.com

Frankho Puzzle™ # 235

Rule All the digits 1 to 5 must appear exactly once in every row and column. The number appears in the bottom right-hand corner is the end result calculated according to arithmetic operator(s) and chess move(s) as indicated by darker arrow(s).

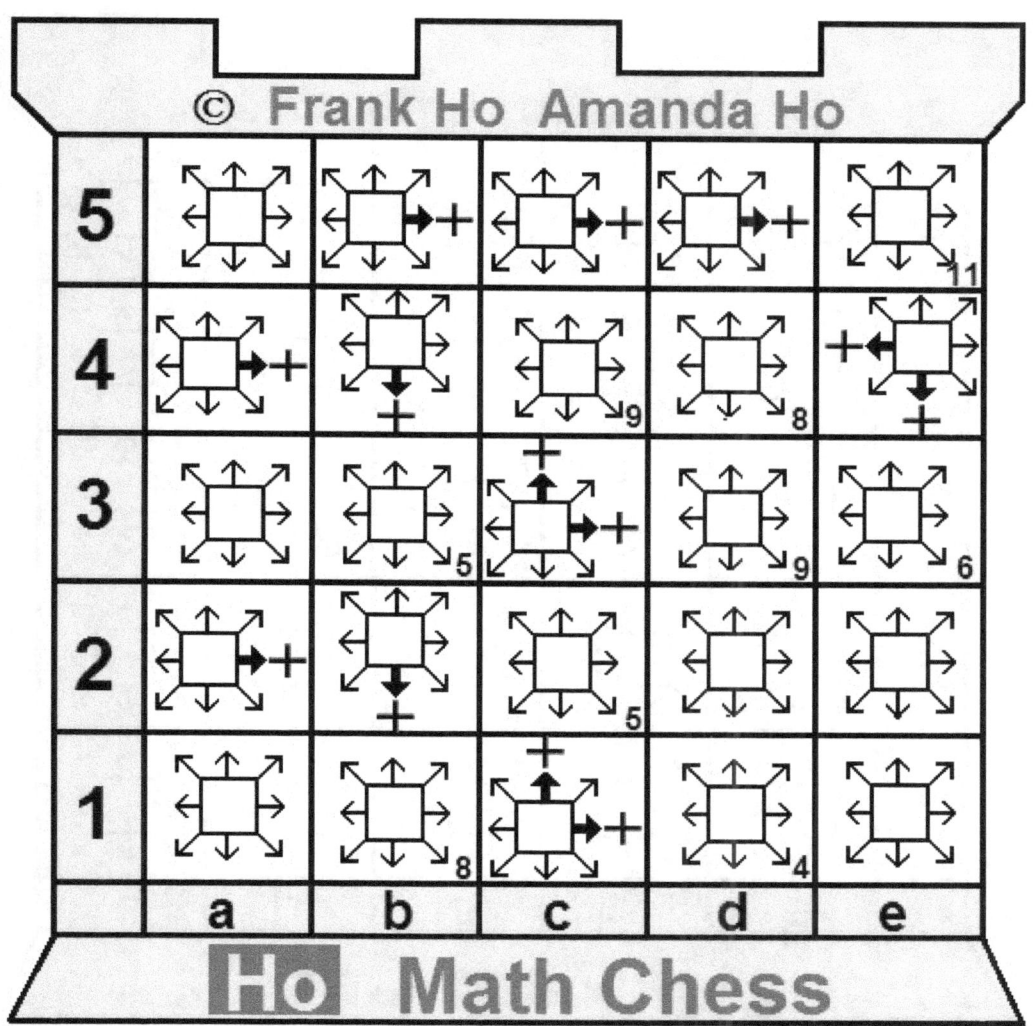

Ho Math Chess 何数棋谜 益智健脑非药物良方
Frankho Puzzle for KIDS – Brain Fitness Workbook
© 2007 — 2016 Frank Ho, Amanda Ho all rights reserved www.mathandchess.com

Frankho Puzzle™ # 236

Rule All the digits 1 to 5 must appear exactly once in every row and column. The number appears in the bottom right-hand corner is the end result calculated according to arithmetic operator(s) and chess move(s) as indicated by darker arrow(s).

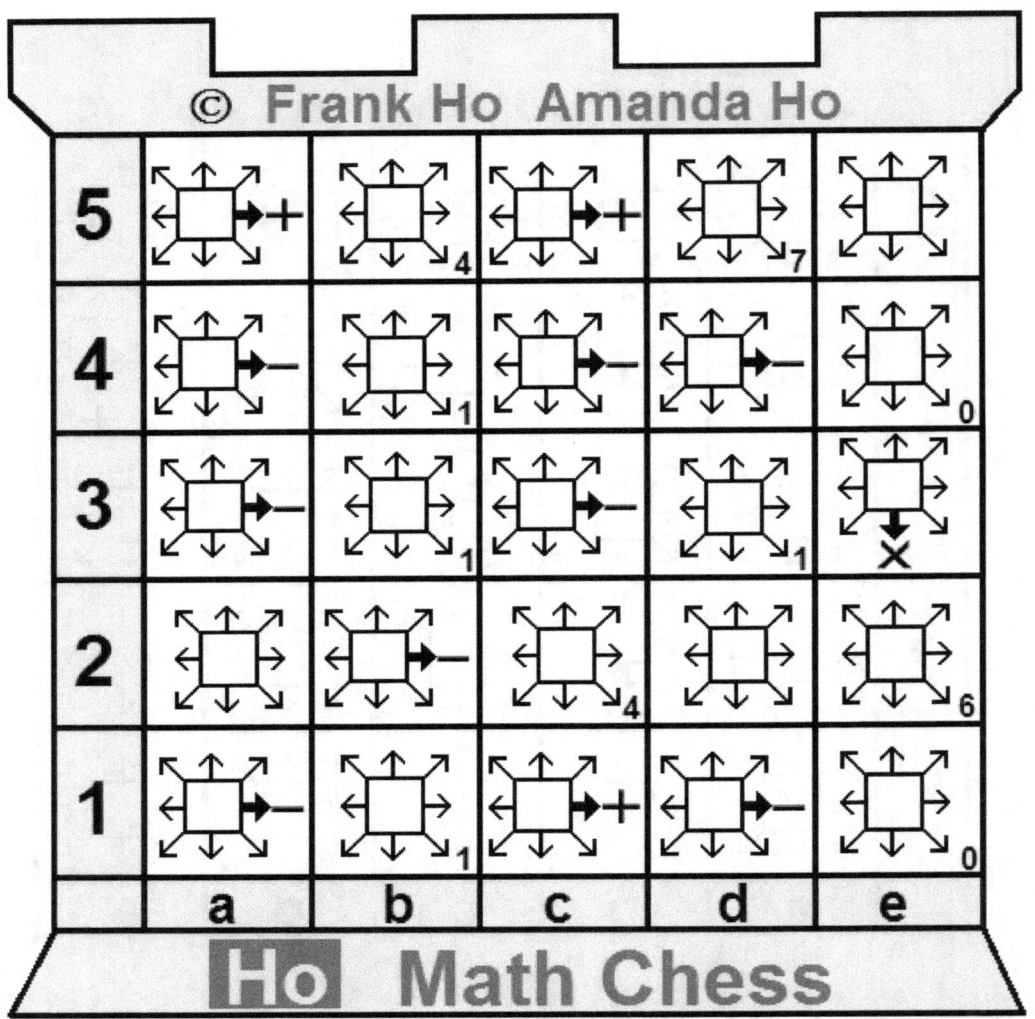

Ho Math Chess 何数棋谜 益智健脑非药物良方
Frankho Puzzle for KIDS – Brain Fitness Workbook
© 2007 — 2016 Frank Ho, Amanda Ho all rights reserved www.mathandchess.com

Frankho Puzzle™ # 237

Rule All the digits 1 to 5 must appear exactly once in every row and column. The number appears in the bottom right-hand corner is the end result calculated according to arithmetic operator(s) and chess move(s) as indicated by darker arrow(s).

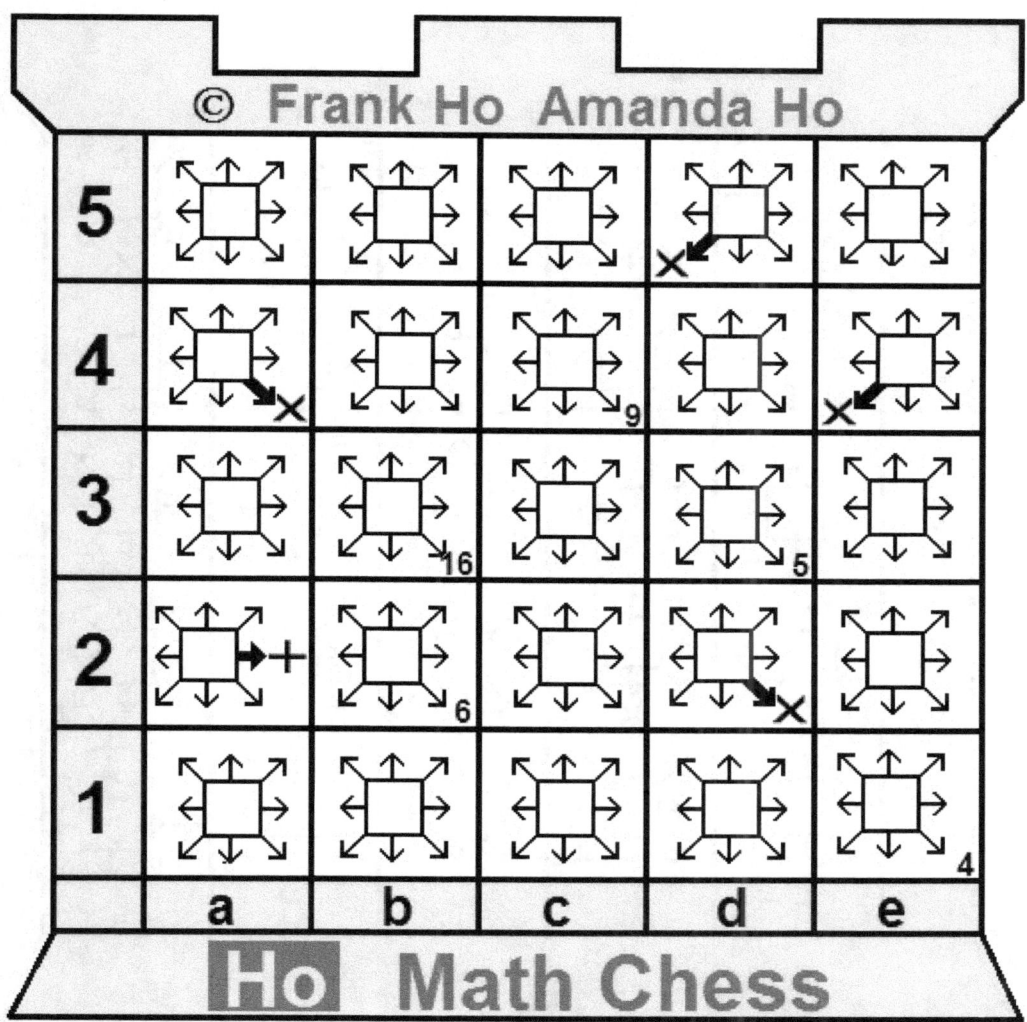

Frankho Puzzle™ # 238

Rule All the digits 1 to 5 must appear exactly once in every row and column. The number appears in the bottom right-hand corner is the end result calculated according to arithmetic operator(s) and chess move(s) as indicated by darker arrow(s).

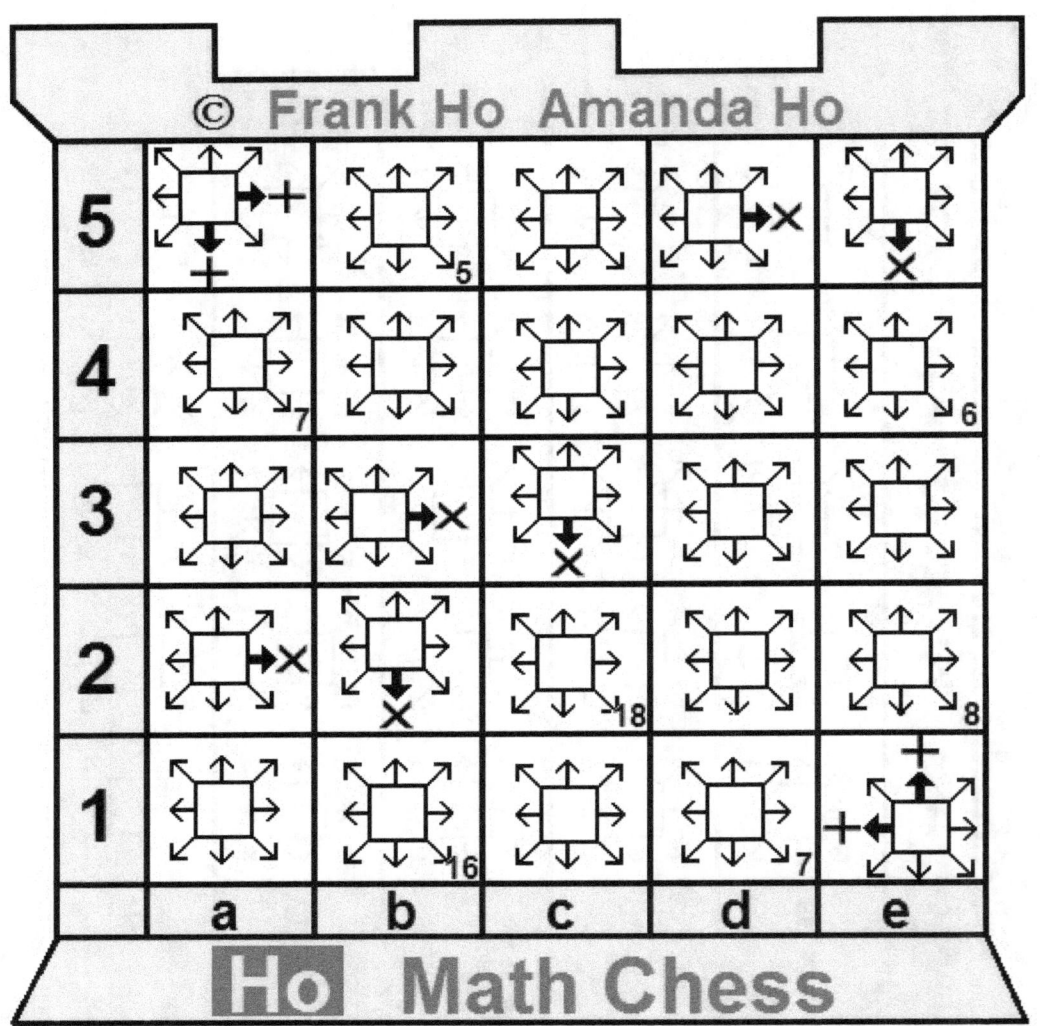

Ho Math Chess 何数棋谜 益智健脑非药物良方
Frankho Puzzle for KIDS – Brain Fitness Workbook
© 2007 — 2016 Frank Ho, Amanda Ho all rights reserved www.mathandchess.com

Frankho Puzzle™ # 239

Rule All the digits 1 to 5 must appear exactly once in every row and column. The number appears in the bottom right-hand corner is the end result calculated according to arithmetic operator(s) and chess move(s) as indicated by darker arrow(s).

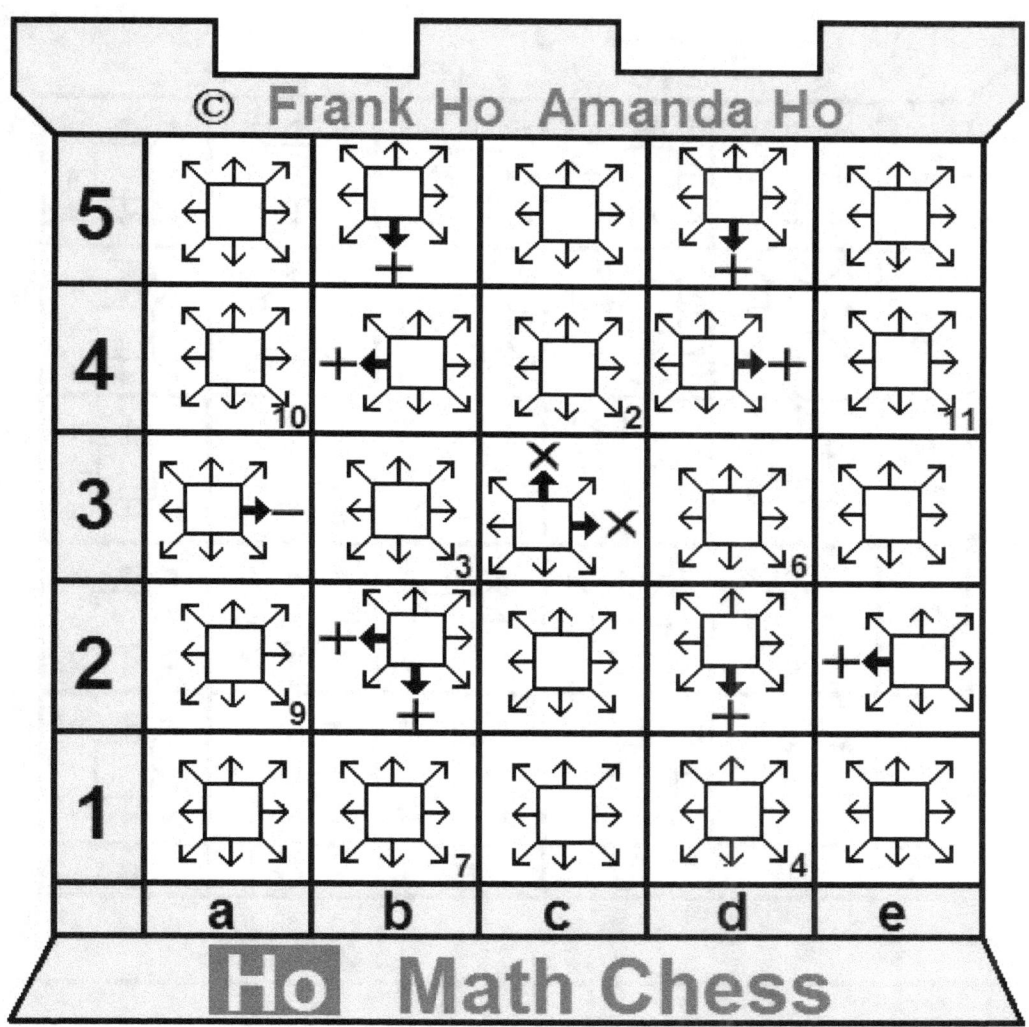

Frankho Puzzle™ # 240

Rule All the digits 1 to 5 must appear exactly once in every row and column. The number appears in the bottom right-hand corner is the end result calculated according to arithmetic operator(s) and chess move(s) as indicated by darker arrow(s).

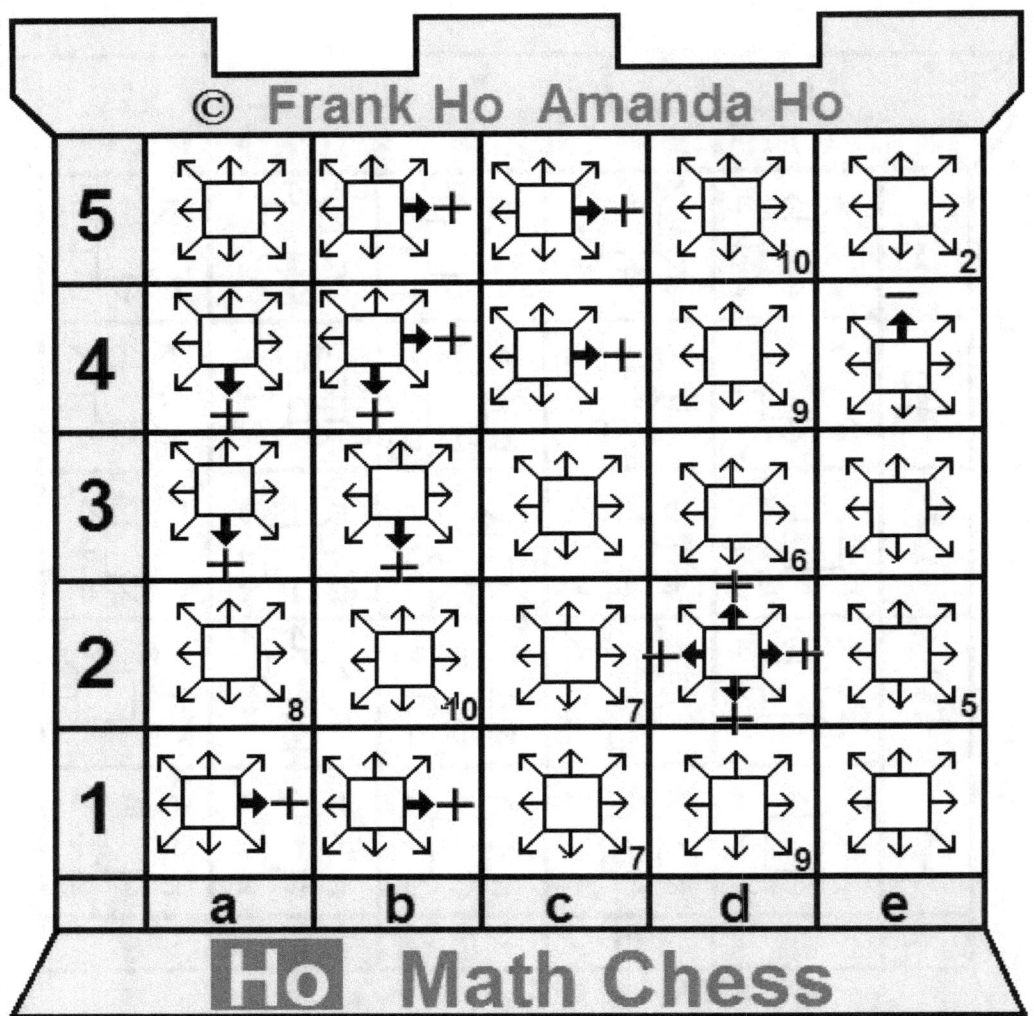

| Ho Math Chess 何数棋谜 益智健脑非药物良方 |
| Frankho Puzzle for KIDS – Brain Fitness Workbook |
| © 2007 — 2016 Frank Ho, Amanda Ho all rights reserved www.mathandchess.com |

Ho Math Chess™ Series Workbooks

Frank Ho, Amanda Ho
www.mathandchess.com

Chess Book:

    Chess for Kids

Puzzle Books:

    Frankho 3 by 3 ChessDoku

    Frankho 4 by 4 ChessDoku V1

    Frankho 4 by 4 ChessDoku V2

    Frankho 5 by 5 ChessDoku

Math Books:

    Kindergarten Math

    Addition

    Subtraction

    Addition and Subtraction – Carrying or Borrowing

    Multiplication

    Division

    Whole Number Operations

    Fundamental Math

    Math 8

    Math 9

    Pre-calculus 10

    Pre-calculus 11

    Pre-calculus 12

Publisher: Ho Math Chess™ Learning Centre Inc.

www.ingramcontent.com/pod-product-compliance
Lightning Source LLC
Chambersburg PA
CBHW080548230426
43663CB00015B/2749